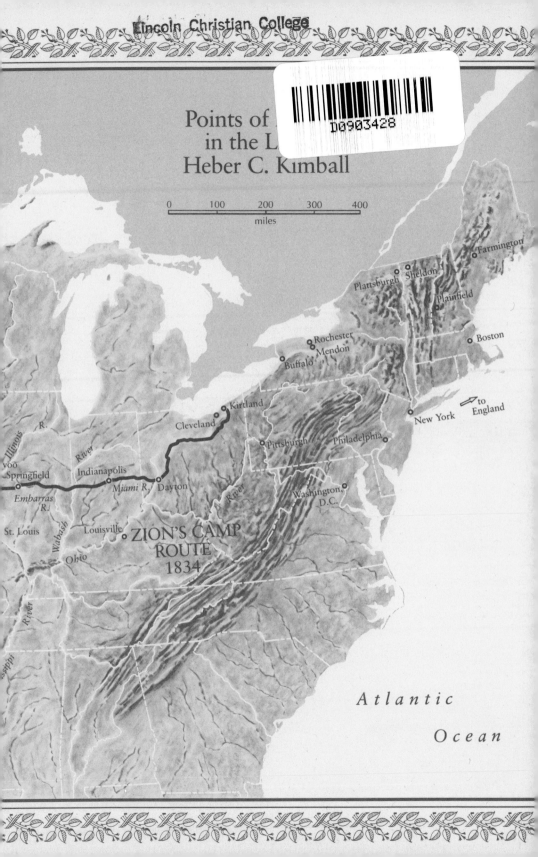

Points of
in the L
Heber C. Kimball

0   100   200   300   400
miles

Farmington

Plattsburgh   Sheldon
Plainfield

Rochester
Mendon   Boston
Buffalo

Kirtland
Cleveland   New York   to England

Illinois R.   River

Springfield   Indianapolis   Pittsburgh   Philadelphia
voo   Miami R.   Dayton
Embarras R.   Washington, D.C.

St. Louis   Louisville   ZION'S CAMP
ROUTE
Wabash   1834
Ohio

River

Atlantic

Ocean

HEBER C. KIMBALL

HEBER C. KIMBALL

MORMON PATRIARCH
AND PIONEER

STANLEY B. KIMBALL

UNIVERSITY OF ILLINOIS PRESS

Urbana   Chicago   London

LIBRARY OF CONGRESS CATALOGING IN PUBLICATION DATA

Kimball, Stanley Buchholz.
  Heber C. Kimball : Mormon patriarch and pioneer.

  Includes index.
  1. Kimball, Heber Chase, 1801–1868. 2. Mormons and
Mormonism in the United States—Biography.
BX8695.K5K55   289.3′3 [B]   80-21923
ISBN 0-252-00854-5

To Violet

CONTENTS

ILLUSTRATIONS

(following Part II)

Heber C. Kimball, from the original daguerreotype, c. 1850–60.
The Cock Pit, Preston, England.
Kirtland Temple, Kirtland, Ohio, dedicated 1836.
Heber C. Kimball home, Nauvoo, Illinois, c. 1910.
"Crossing the Mississippi on Ice, Leaving Nauvoo," by C. C. A. Christensen.
"Wagons Preparing to Leave Winter Quarters in 1847," by C. C. A. Christensen.
"Handcart Pioneers," by C. C. A. Christensen.
"The Mormon Battalion," by George Martin Ottinger.
Drawings from original Mormon pioneer journal kept for Heber C. Kimball by Peter O. Hansen across Iowa in 1846.
Drawings from Hansen journal.
Drawings from Hansen journal.
Vilate Murray Kimball, first wife of Heber C. Kimball.
Heber C. Kimball, from the original daguerreotype, c. 1850–60.
Six wives of Heber C. Kimball, Salt Lake City, Utah, 1888.
Twenty-five sons and daughters of Heber C. Kimball, Salt Lake City, 1887.
Salt Lake City as it appeared during Heber C. Kimball's lifetime.
Salt Lake City, c. 1871, from the hill on the north.
Southeast view of the Valley, from Arsenal Hill, c. 1877.
Old Kimball grist mill in Bountiful, Utah, c. 1907.
The old Kimball homestead on North Main, Salt Lake City.

Do your duty, and leave the rest to heaven.—Corneille

PREFACE

Heber C. Kimball was early Mormondom's most colorful leader, third in stature after Joseph Smith and Brigham Young, most dedicated though reluctant polygamist, and least inhibited preacher. No plaster saint, two-dimensional cardboard cutout, or religious ascetic, he was a masculine man, at home on the frontier, where he spent most of his adult life.[1]

For too long Heber has been known, if known at all, as Joseph Smith's missionary, Brigham Young's alter ego, or sire of the largest family in the Mormon Church, if not in the Western world.[2] But he was much more, as this work will show by presenting for the first time a full, affectionate, and candid portrait of this early leading Mormon Apostle, and an inside view of his unusual faith.

No other Mormon leader has exceeded his total devotion to Mormonism. For more than thirty-six years, in ten states and in England, he faithfully served his God and his people and strove to build both the spiritual and material Kingdom of God. From his acceptance of the new faith in 1832 until his death in 1868 he was in the forefront of the excitement, drama, and turbulence of Mormon history. His life exemplifies most of the strengths of Mormonism and some of its weaknesses.

The essence of Heber was his simplicity. Compared with the gothic nature of Joseph Smith or the baroque character of Brigham Young, Heber was rustic. As Douglas S. Freeman wrote of Heber's contemporary, Robert E. Lee, Heber was "humble, transparent, and believing." Surely the most uncomplicated of the early Mormon leaders, his doric nature produced strength and total integrity.

Heber's personal conviction manifested the essence of Mormonism to this day: that the heavens, allegedly sealed since biblical days, had been reopened, that the Church of Christ, which had changed over the centuries, had been restored (not just reformed) in 1830 by Joseph Smith, God's latter-day prophet, and that it was his, Heber's, duty to take this message to mankind whatever the cost.

His story and his life are uncomplicated. He wrestled little with mystic or psychological questions, or with the classical conflicts of man versus self, men, nature, or God. Not that his life was placid: he was frequently ill, was hounded from five different homes, and was criticized in and out of his church. Furthermore, as a husband to at least forty-three wives, father to at least sixty-five children, and a grandfather three hundred times over, his portion of domestic discord and disappointment was probably greater than that of any other modern Western man. In keeping with his character, however, he simply ignored most troubles. He took life as it came, acknowledging the Book of Mormon imperative that "opposition is necessary in all things."

An extension of his simplicity was his incurable optimism. He seldom complained or was discouraged. He was convinced that he was doing God's will—and that settled things in his mind. To him God's will was for him to do his duty, and his duty was simply to build the Kingdom with what talent and energy he had.

Although not a learned or even a very literate person, he had a highly developed sense of history and dutifully kept journals and wrote long letters. In some instances they are the best extant accounts of the events they chronicle, and have been cited many times. Without his writing our understanding of early Mormon history would be incomplete. He was the first diarist to be quoted extensively in early Mormon publications. Though his mastery of penmanship, spelling, and grammar was distinctly minimal, he did have a clear and artless prose style and an exceptional memory, and could dictate very well.

Voluble, visible, totally lacking in sophistication, this guileless Nathanael was an easy and ideal target for scoffers and detractors who delighted in pointing out his coarse language, his rambling style of speaking, his "arrogance," and his gauche references to women—something proper Victorians could neither ignore nor forgive. In spite of all this scrutiny, which he made no effort to avoid, no serious charges were ever sustained against him.

Heber C. Kimball lived fully, dramatically, and well—making his own way in the world, going abroad, fulfilling eight missions, fleeing persecution, crossing the plains, hunting buffalo, dealing with Indians, amassing wives, children, lands, cattle, and property, building the Kingdom, holding political office, damning his enemies, alternately praising and castigating his people, and suffering domestically and physically. His last years were saddened by what he took to be opposition from his closest friends, but he died confident that he had done his duty.

Most of what has been written about Heber to date is hagiographic. His only biography, published in 1888 and still in print, is a noninterpretive torso, covering mainly a sixteen-year period from 1832 to 1848, from his acceptance of Mormonism to his life in Utah, based on an account dictated by Heber in Nauvoo. Little has been written of his first thirty-one years, less about the last twenty. The real, three-dimensional Kimball is a much more important and interesting person, a far more inspiring churchman than the one usually presented in Mormon literature.

In this biography, Heber's many spiritual experiences are presented from his own viewpoint, allowing each reader to determine for himself their validity and meaning. His private family affairs are also tendered forthrightly and in detail, for it is here that he comes most to life.

More important, a detailed study of his family life provides a unique antidote to the past and present sensationalism written about the Mormon system of plural marriage. His bluntness and saltiness are not glossed over, for they were part of his personality and style, his way of causing people to think, to reform, to do good, and to build the Kingdom. He once said of himself, "I am just what I am, and cannot be anything else." I have tried to be as honest with my co-religionist and kinsman as Old Testament writers were with theirs. Heber has not been prettied up for contemporary tastes.

His life and development fall into four periods: his early life, work, and marriage in Vermont and New York up to his acceptance of Mormonism in 1832; the missionary and apostolic years through the Nauvoo period to 1846; a three-year pioneering interlude through 1848; and the First Presidency years in Utah to his death in 1868.

All known sources bearing on Heber have been examined. To acquire the feeling of locale, to experience the power of place, I have visited every important region connected with his life and followed the trails he used from Ohio to the Great Basin.

As a biographer, hedged round by the tyranny of fact, denied the omniscience and omnipotence of the novelist, and restricted to incomplete and haphazard literary remains, I could not have succeeded without the help of many others. Often I have reflected on Carlyle's dictum, "A well-written Life is almost as rare as a well-spent one," and hoped to say, along with Sainte-Beuve, "The portrait . . . speaks and lives; I have found the man!" In this respect I have been unusually favored. Thanks to Leonard J. Arrington, Mormon Church Historian, and Earl Olson, Assistant Managing Director of the Historical Department of the Mormon Church, the vast catalogued and uncatalogued resources of the Historical Department of the Church of Jesus Christ of Latter-day Saints were placed at my disposal. Many other members of the Historical Department, as well as employees of the Genealogical Society of the Mormon Church, went out of their way to ferret out obscure and revealing documents for me.

Arrington read various drafts of the manuscript and gave advice and help throughout the project. His two assistants Davis Bitton and James B. Allen, and Ronald K. Esplin, a research historian, read various drafts of the complete manuscript and graciously lent their expertise. Maureen Ursenbach Beecher made many helpful suggestions in form and content. Edward L. Kimball read the final draft and gave much help and advice.

Various specialists at the Utah State Historical Society and the University of Utah, especially Martha Stewart of the former and Everett Cooley of the latter, gave advice. I benefited much from the counsel of other Utah scholars such as K. Haybron Adams, D. Michael Quinn, Reed C. Durham, Lowell M. Durham, Jr., the late T. Edgar Lyon, and various specialists at Brigham Young University.

Special gratitude is extended to Spencer W. Kimball, President of the Church of Jesus Christ of Latter-day Saints and a grandson of Heber C. Kimball, who generously let me use and copy his hundreds of pages of little-known Kimball materials. J. LeRoy Kimball likewise let me use and copy his important collection of Kimball documents.

Two patient town clerks in Sheldon, Vermont, helped me solve the riddle of where Heber was born. J. Sheldon Fisher, George Hammell, and other specialists in the Rochester, New York, area provided me with much detail and insight regarding the Kimball family in the Bloomfield and Mendon, New York, area. One of the earliest thrills of discovery was thirty years ago in Preston, England, when an imaginative archivist helped me to unearth several Kimball documents from 1837 to 1838 which are, incidentally, the earliest records referring to the Mormons in the Old World. I have kept close to all sources but, at times, it was necessary to venture carefully beyond them.

Of the many scholars, clerks, librarians, archivists, and friends who aided me over the years, I would like to thank Lawrence Foster and Danel Bachman for comments regarding plural marriage, Harry Gibson for help regarding Mormon firearms and terms, Eldon J. Watson for suggestions on the Adam-God theory, La Gene Purcell for help with Heber's shorthand, and many members of the Kimball Family Association, particularly Miss Pat Geisler, Mrs. Kenneth Huffman, Mrs. Major P. Garff, Mrs. John Francis Watson, Mrs. Jesse K. Burrows, Mrs. Elwood G. Derrick, Mrs. Biard E. Anderson, and James L. Kimball, Jr. Special thanks must be extended to the late Paul Henderson, the great expert on the Oregon Trail in Nebraska and Wyoming, for his extensive help.

I would also like to thank the Graduate School of Southern Illinois University at Edwardsville for many research and travel grants, and my colleagues Patrick Riddleberger of the history department and William Tudor of the Southern Illinois University Press, who read earlier drafts and made valuable suggestions from the non-Mormon point of view. I wish also to express appreciation to Elizabeth Dulany and Nancy Krueger of the University of Illinois Press for their help and editorial skills. Portions of this text previously appeared in *Brigham Young University Studies*, the *Kimball Family Newsletter*, and in Joseph E. Brown and Dan Guravich, *The Mormon Trek West* (Doubleday, 1980). I wish to thank the various editors for permission to reprint this material.

As is always the case, however, the author is responsible for all errors of fact, interpretation, and judgment.

Stanley B. Kimball
Edwardsville, Illinois
Summer, 1980

NOTES

1. Early Mormon leaders were reassuringly human. "I saw Joseph Smith the Prophet," said one contemporary and future president of the church, "do things which I did not approve of; and yet . . . I thanked God that he would put upon a man who had these imperfections the power and authority which he placed upon him . . . for I knew I myself had weakness and I thought there was a chance for me. These same weaknesses . . . I knew were in Heber C. Kimball, but my knowing this did not impair them in my estimation. I thanked God I saw these imperfections." Lorenzo Snow, as quoted in George Q. Cannon Journal, Jan. 7, 1898, Church Archives, Historical Department of the Church of Jesus Christ of Latter-day Saints, Salt Lake City, Utah. Hereafter cited as Church Archives.

2. Technically Heber was a polygynist, a man having two or more wives at the same time. Polygamy means having two or more husbands or wives at the same time. Many Mormons try to avoid either term and prefer to use "plural marriage" or "plurality." This study uses the traditional term "polygamy" as well as "plural marriage."

Heber is usually credited with forty-five wives (it appears he had but forty-three) and sixty-five children. For simplicity's sake all pertinent statistical and marital data have been compiled in Appendix A.

PART I

THE MAN AND THE EARLY YEARS
1801–32

I am just what I am, and cannot be anything else.
Journal of Discourses, January 11, 1857

CHAPTER 1

New England Origins

Early in an October full of autumn color in 1832 a balding, powerfully built young blacksmith-potter turned his matched dapple-gray team and carriage off the dusty Chardon Road and headed up Temple Hill in Kirtland, Ohio. Asking directions and hardly stopping to freshen up, Heber C. Kimball hurried on to Four Corners to find the Mormon prophet he had driven 300 miles to meet. He soon found Joseph Smith, very un–prophetlike, cutting wood with two or three of his brothers. Seizing Joseph's hand, Heber eagerly introduced himself as a new convert from Mendon, New York, who, with his two companions, Brigham and Joseph Young, had come to Kirtland to learn more of the new religion. Then, impetuously and in a burst of good fellowship, Heber grabbed a double-bitted ax and began hacking away at oak logs. Weighing 200 pounds, standing six feet tall, and barrel-chested, Heber was proud of his strength and liked to boast that he had never seen the day he could not "whip out" twenty of the best men. For a few minutes the two young men, Joseph, twenty-seven, and Heber, thirty-one, chopped together in friendly contest. As Heber later recollected, it "was just nip and tuck between us."[1] Such was Heber's typically rough-and-ready introduction to Joseph Smith.

Joseph invited the trio to his nearby home that evening, where, after sharing a meal, Heber learned from the Prophet's own lips the startling story of the Restoration, commencing with a theophanic experience in 1820 generally known as the First Vision. In this vision, which came from petitioning God regarding which of the many contending faiths was correct, Joseph reported he saw "two personages. . . . One of them spake unto me . . . and said, pointing to the other—'This is My Beloved Son. Hear Him!'" Young Joseph was told to join no church for "they draw near to me with their lips, but their hearts are far from me." The Prophet went on to relate subsequent heavenly visitations through which he was prepared and called to become a latter-day prophet. He also told Heber and

3

Brigham the story of the "coming forth" of the Book of Mormon, about the early difficulties in New York, the Lord's commandment to move the small church to Kirtland, and Joseph's call to build the Kingdom of God on earth.

Heber tarried a week in Kirtland, being loath to leave the Prophet and the company of the Saints. Whatever reservations he had had about joining the new faith dissolved, and he decided to remove himself and his family to Kirtland. On the long return trip home via Erie, Pennsylvania, and Buffalo, New York, he may well have reflected on his life to that point and on what caused him to make such a trip and such a decision.

Heber was a seventh-generation descendant of a New England family which had been in the New World since Richard Kimball and his wife, Ursula Scott, left Ipswich, Suffolk County, England, in 1634 to avoid Charles I's persecution of Puritans and Separatists. Two hundred and twelve years later, religious persecution drove Richard's fourth great-grandson, Heber, westward beyond the Rocky Mountains of the American West.

Heber's grandparents, James and Meribah Kimball, seeking new lands and better opportunities, left their home in Hopkinton, New Hampshire, in 1796 and moved west to Vermont. They settled in the sparsely inhabited Sheldon town(ship), Franklin County, eleven miles east of Lake Champlain and nine miles south of the Canadian line.[2] This area, on the Missisquoi River, was known for its unsurpassed rich alluvial soil—so different from the rocky land of much of New England.

Shortly after James and Meribah moved to Sheldon they were joined by their six sons—Jesse, Moses, John, James, Stephen, and Solomon (Heber's father)—who bought up hundreds of acres of land. Solomon, born in Massachusetts in 1770, had been apprenticed out to a Mr. Chase, a commonsense country judge and blacksmith. He learned the trade and lived with the judge until he married Anna Spaulding of Plainfield, New Hampshire, in about 1794. Solomon "was baldheaded," Heber later remembered, "had blue eyes, sandy whiskers and sandy complexion, five feet eleven inches high, weighed 200 pounds and upwards—was captain of a company of militia in Sheldon, and wore a cocked-up hat, of the Old English style, and straight long stockings and Hessian boots with a pair of tassels."[3] Solomon also participated in Sheldon town government as a grand juror, a captain in the militia, and a hayward in charge of fences around public pastures.[4] Heber wrote or spoke little of his mother. She does not emerge from the shadows.

On April 1, 1799, Solomon and Anna bought 200 acres just north of

Sheldon Village near the confluence of Black Creek and the Missisquoi River.[5] There he farmed, grazed sheep, cleared land, did some black-smithing, and invested heavily in the manufacture of potash, the chief home industry and source of cash of northern and western Vermont. Potash, an alkali used in the manufacture of soap and glass, was essential to the cleaning and manufacturing of woolen and linen goods, two of the major industries of England.

Heber was born June 14, 1801, on the farm near the Missisquoi just three months after Jefferson's inauguration and two years before the Louisiana Purchase extended the borders of the young republic to the Rocky Mountains. He was named after his father's benefactor, (Heber?) Chase, who happened to visit Sheldon at that time, and was his parents' fourth child, after Charles, Eliza, and Abigail, and before Melvina, Solomon, and David, the son who died in infancy. His Vermont boyhood, his first ten years, was typical of his age, time, place, and station in life. He worked on his father's farm, herded sheep, cleared land, worked in the family smithy, and helped with the manufacture of potash, a tedious chore which he must have hated. The process consists of pouring water through the fine ashes of burnt hardwood trees to make lye, which in turn is boiled down in great iron kettles to a dense ashy deposit which must be chipped from the kettles or pots, hence its name. Economically the family was well off, and Heber's later memories of his early youth were mostly pleasant.

He liked to fish in the quiet Missisquoi, and the beautiful rolling foothills west of the Green Mountains offered an inviting place to roam and game to hunt. In Sheldon Village, a short walk distant, a boy with a little spending money could buy hard candy or could hang around the saw, grist, or carding mills.

The primitive village schools of those days provided scant formal education. Children normally attended school for only a few weeks each winter, acquiring what in those days was called a "plain English Education"—the ability to read, write, and reckon. As an adult Heber was keenly aware of his lack of formal education and at times signed up for what later generations would call adult education classes.

His religious education was even less formal than his schooling, taking place exclusively in the home, as there were no organized church activities in the area at that time. His parents, however, saw to it that their children had a moral upbringing. Heber's mother was a sober Presbyterian; his father was unchurched. This was not unusual: church membership was at that time probably lower in the United States than in any other Christian nation. In 1800, only about 7 percent of the American population were classified as active church members.

However promising Solomon's future seemed in Sheldon, it was ruined by some early conflicts with England—conflicts which led to the War of 1812. During the Napoleonic Wars (1796–1815) the British, to stop American trade with France, preyed on American commerce. In anger, Jefferson induced Congress to pass the Embargo Act of 1807, prohibiting all foreign trade, even with Canada. This embargo, lasting fourteen months, seriously hurt northwestern Vermont, for the foreign trade of beef, pork, grain, lumber, and especially potash was her economic lifeblood.

Among those ruined financially by the embargo was Heber's father. By 1809 Solomon had decided to do what many others were doing: go west and start over. Since the Revolution, western New York, the fastest-growing and most promising area in the country, had offered good, cheap land at attractive prices. Arranging for their uncles to help, Solomon turned the farm over to his older sons, Charles and Heber, then saddled up and left. At Scipio, New York, he fell in with another blacksmith and back-country judge, a Mr. Towsley. They worked their way west along the Seneca Turnpike and the Ontario and Genesee Turnpike (the superhighways of that day) and concluded to settle in the newly founded village of West Bloomfield (Bloomfield town), Ontario County, New York. West Bloomfield, a likely social and economic hub about twenty miles south of Rochester, was so named because of the beauty of the landscape and foliage. It soon became the most populated town in Ontario County. Solomon set up a blacksmithy, "took up" some land, built a home, and early in 1811 decided to move his family there.[6]

NOTES

1. From a speech excerpted in the *New York Tribune*, Nov. 10, 1865, reprinted in the *Daily Union Vedette*, Nov. 30, 1865.

2. A New England town (cf. townships in other parts of the United States) contained several villages or communities, one of which frequently bore the same name as the town. This fact has created much confusion in the early history of the Kimballs, Smiths, and Youngs. Heber was connected with four such towns, each of which contained a village by the same name—Sheldon, Bloomfield, Mendon, and Victor. To prevent confusion, this study distinguishes carefully between towns and villages.

3. "Synopsis of the History of Heber C. Kimball," *Deseret News* (Mar. 31–Apr. 28, 1858), Mar. 31, 1858. Hereafter cited as *Deseret News*, "Synopsis."

4. Information gleaned from Sheldon Townhall Records.

5. Solomon's land dealings are recorded in Sheldon Land Records, vol. 1, 98, 136, 159, 303, 188, 343, vol. 11, 101, 451, 452, Sheldon Townhall. Since there are several communities named Sheldon (Sheldon Village, Sheldon Springs, Sheldon Junction, and North Sheldon) in Sheldon town, we have never known just where he was born. A thorough study of the Sheldon Land Records, however, strongly suggests that Heber was born on the 200-acre farm his father had bought in 1799. Although Solomon sold or traded this farm for another just three days before Heber was born, it is hard to believe that he would have moved his wife prior to her delivery. But even if he did, the new farm which he bought or traded for was adjacent property. Heber would still have been born about one mile north of Sheldon Village near the Missisquoi River. Heber himself recorded, "I was born . . . between the Masisko [Missisquoi] and Black Rivers." Heber C. Kimball, Journal 94b, 6, Church Archives. A monument to his birth was erected by the Kimball Family Association in 1976 near the front entrance to the Sheldon Village Cemetery.

6. See Bloomfield Land Records in the Monroe County Records Office in Rochester, N.Y., Liber 14, 180, Liber 15, 543, 544, Liber 19, 278, Liber 20, 150, 410, Liber 23, 280, Liber 24, 455, Liber 29, 427, 428, Liber 49, 86, and Liber 58, 317. This homesite commenced 274 feet west of the main intersection in Bloomfield on the south side of present-day Highway 5 and 20. The farm was located 2.5 miles east of the south side of the same highway.

CHAPTER 2

On the Potter's Wheel in New York

To a nine-year-old boy who had probably never been out of the county of his birth, the trip to West Bloomfield was an adventure, especially since the first 110 miles were made in a sleigh on frozen Lake Champlain to the extreme southern headwaters of the lake at Whitehall, New York. Solomon may have left during the winter of 1811 because traveling on the frozen lake was much preferable to the primitive, rutted roads bordering the lake and also because before the frost came out of the ground, mud made the roads beyond Whitehall almost impassable.

Dashing down the lake between the Green Mountains of Vermont and the Adirondacks of New York, Heber would have passed frozen waterfalls, the Camel's Hump (the highest peak of the Green Mountains), and historic old Fort Ticonderoga. At Whitehall Solomon traded the sleigh for a wagon and proceeded west along the same turnpikes he had used previously, the family sleeping and eating at inns along the way.

Once settled in West Bloomfield, Heber attended school off and on to the age of fourteen, when he went to work full time for his father as an apprentice blacksmith. His older brother, Charles, set up a pottery on his father's property. As teenagers, the two brothers enrolled in an independent horse company of the New York Militia in which they trained for fourteen years. Their service, which would have commenced in 1817 or 1818, was probably not very demanding and may have been required only quarterly or even annually. These occasional military drills were frequently more like holidays than serious maneuvers. The idea was to inspect the equipment of the men and the state of combat readiness of the unit, and to drink many toasts. The uniform was specified as "citizen's dress"; that is, there was no uniform. Officers were distinguished by a sash, sword, epaulets, and hat plume. Heber was evidently well trained in

8

riding, for at the age of forty-six he was still a good enough horseman to bring down a buffalo at full gallop.

Ironically, the same Napoleonic War difficulties which drove Solomon from Vermont were the reasons for his initial economic success in West Bloomfield, near the U.S. military headquarters in the Lake Ontario region. The War of 1812 generated much business, and Solomon, busy making edge tools such as scythes, augers, axes, knives, and plowshares, kept eight forges going at once. He prospered, branched out into construction—building homes, schools, and taverns—and bought land.

Wartime booms, however, are frequently followed by postwar busts. Among those who declined financially after the war was Heber's father. In 1815 the family had to leave West Bloomfield and move to their farm two and a half miles east. Even then Solomon had to mortgage the farm for money to live on. At times all they had to eat was a little bread and boiled milkweeds. Solomon's financial reverses were so severe that during 1814 and 1815 he appeared as a plaintiff and as a defendant before the Ontario County Court of Common Pleas sixteen times.[1] Finally, it appears that he may have gone to jail for debts. On November 21, 1815, the *Ontario Messenger* reported, "By virtue of a writ . . . to me directed and delivered against the goods and chattels . . . together with the farm on which the said Solomon F. Kimball now resides, containing 156 acres, and one village lot . . . also, 8 acres of land on which stands a pottery . . . which I shall expose to sale at public auction . . . F. N. Allen, Sheriff." The same paper of January 2, 1816, ran the following: "NOTICE. All persons indebted to the subscriber . . . are informed, that Necessity, the mother of inventions, compels him to call upon those who are indebted to him, to make immediate payment. Those who wish to settle with him are informed, that it can be done by calling upon him, in the village of Canandaigua [location of the county seat and jail], where he has recently taken up his residence. Those who don't comply with this notice, will be called upon in the name of the People, whose imperious voice has placed him in this village. Solomon F. Kimball." In Solomon's time and place most persons in jail were debtors, many owing less than twenty dollars. This unwise and unjust practice was finally abolished by Congress in 1832.

Somehow he settled his debts and the family remained on the farm. Heber continued to work for his father as a blacksmith until 1820, when he turned nineteen. Then, as a result of the Panic of 1819, a severe post–War of 1812 depression, and his father's continued financial reversals, he found himself a slightly schooled and unemployed blacksmith. His past had been uneventful, his present was bleak, and the future promised nothing. As he later wrote, "My father, having lost his property and not taking the care for my welfare which he formerly did, I was left to seek a place of refuge or home of my own at this time. I saw some days of sorrow; my heart was troubled, and I suffered much in consequence of fear, bashfulness and timidity. I found my self cast abroad upon the world, without a friend to console my grief. In these heartaching hours, I suffered much for want of food and the comforts of life, and many times went two or three days without food to eat, being bashful and not daring to ask for it." [2]

In the meantime, Heber's older brother Charles had established himself as a potter in the town of nearby Mendon, close to the village of the same name. Organized in 1812, Mendon was another promising location along the Genesee Turnpike and a good place for a pottery. All of the necessary natural resources—clay beds of high silica content, water, and timber—were close at hand. The area also provided a growing market. At the invitation of Charles, Heber moved to Mendon in 1820 and became an apprentice potter, a decision which precipitated the three most important events in his life—his marriage to Vilate Murray, his meeting Brigham Young, and his acceptance of Mormonism.

One of Heber's tasks as his brother's helper was to haul clay to the pottery and to transport the finished wares to various markets, including the nearby village of Victor (in Victor Township), Ontario County. The most direct road from Mendon to Victor was east along what is still called Boughton Hill Road. One hot day, during the summer of 1822, about two miles from home Heber became thirsty and stopped at a farmhouse on the south side of this road. Jumping from his wagon he asked for a drink of water—a drink that changed his life.

The owner of the farm, Roswell Murray, with whom Heber may have had a nodding acquaintance, happened to be in his front yard. Exchanging pleasantries, Murray drew the requested water and called his sprightly sixteen-year-old daughter, Vilate,[3] to bring a glass and serve Heber. Standing under a shade tree, Heber, somewhat flustered by Vilate's appearance, mumbled some thanks and drove on. Up to this time in his life we can only guess what role romance had played. He had probably squired some young ladies to the Sulphur Springs resort, near Clifton, where there was dancing and, in the winter, sleigh riding.[4] In any event, as soon as decently possible, Heber arranged to become thirsty again in the same neighborhood and repeated his request. As Murray went to draw the water, Heber blurted out, "If you please, I'd rather Milatie [as he understood the daughter's name] would bring it to me."[5] Unoffended, and perhaps amused, Murray called for "Latie," as she was known in the family, and Heber and Vilate met for a second time. There, near the latticed wellhouse, with the father present and the eyes of the rest of the family on him, what did Heber, previously so bashful as to go hungry rather than ask for food, say to a sixteen-year-old young lady he had interrupted in her household duties just to hand him a glass of water? And how did Vilate respond? We will never know. Somehow, the awkward, unchurched, unschooled, unsophisticated Heber courted her. He was then twenty-one, clean-shaven, already balding, large and strong but shy and gentle. Vilate, though young and inexperienced, knew a good man when she saw one. They were married the following November 7, 1822, most likely in the bride's home.

At first the newlyweds lived with his brother or her parents. Soon, however, Heber bought out his brother's pottery, went into business for himself, and built a home. Land records suggest this first home was located about a quarter-mile east of "Tomlinson's Corners" on the north side of Boughton Hill Road, where Heber eventually owned property on both sides of the road.[6]

The marriage seems to have been happy. Vilate, as well educated as was considered necessary for females in Jacksonian America, reared to the four cardinal virtues of "True Womanhood"—purity, piety, submissiveness, and domesticity—and the belief that the home was her refuge from violence and harm, was a good complement to her sturdy consort. More important, they seem to have married for love, not for the social or economic considerations common at that time.

Vilate had grown up in a close-knit family in frequent contact with her farmer father, who was not away at a distant factory during most working hours. Heber, as a potter and blacksmith, likewise kept close to his wife and children. Ambitious and hard-working, he chopped wood, cleared land, did blacksmithing, planted an orchard, raised pigs, and built a barn and other outbuildings. His industry enabled him to make several additional land purchases. The Kimballs lived comfortably. As a potter Heber took pains to obtain good clay, even if it meant hauling it a great distance, and on a good day could turn out twenty dozen milk pans. Apparently he specialized in common brownware made from fine-textured clay burned to a very high degree and covered by a hard brown glaze. It was used mainly for simple kitchen and table items—jars, crocks, pitchers, bottles, mugs, pots, milk pans, cups, churns, and plates. Despite his great output, no completely authenticated piece of Heber's work has been found.

Heber and Vilate commenced their family immediately, for Judith Marvin was born July 2, 1823. Vilate's experience at childbearing was typical: four children rather evenly spaced (through nursing) over eight years, though two of these four died before their first birthdays. William Henry and Helen Mar lived to maturity; Judith Marvin and Roswell Heber did not. Extending the immediate family were other Kimballs who also moved to Mendon. Heber's brother Solomon came, as did Heber's father after his wife died in 1825.

Vilate did a lot of sewing and made many of the clothes for the family. From a local merchant she purchased for herself and her two children basics like calico, gingham, buttons, thread, indigo, and cloak clasps; for Heber plain shirting, green flannel, cambric, and mull. But once in a while she would splurge on pretty things, like blue satinette for William, and velvet, lace, and some silk twist for herself and Helen. Heber bought staples like iron, logwood, a scythe, as well as rifle powder, tobacco, and whiskey. The family also used nuts, pepper, tankey tea, and raisins and tried to ward off illness with the panacea of the day—sulphur and molasses.[7]

There is no evidence that Heber took much interest in three of the absorbing passions of his time and place: politics, religion, and education. About three years after his marriage, however, apparently in a desire for fraternal association with high-minded men (in a nonreligious atmosphere), for some benevolent activity, and perhaps for business connections, he joined the Milnor Masonic Lodge No. 303 in the village of Victor on September 14, 1825.[8] This lodge, founded in 1818 and named after the Reverend James Milnor, a Grand Master in Philadelphia, had about eighty members, who met in Felt's Hotel each Tuesday before a full moon. The Master was Asahel Moore.

In the young republic, Freemasonry was the most important fraternal and benevolent society, and, among many, almost a surrogate religion. Most of the early patriots and Founding Fathers had been Masons, and because of them Masonic imagery and symbols, such as the all-seeing eye, the clasped hands, the beehive, square, and compass, were everywhere present in the architecture and iconography of the new nation.

Heber took the first three degrees of the York Rite—Entered Apprentice, Fellowcraft, and Master—and petitioned the Excelsior Chapter at Canandaigua for the advanced degree of the Royal Arch. Before the degree could be granted, however, an outbreak of anti-Masonry in western New York led to the closing (not burning as Heber thought) of the Canandaigua lodge and ended his participation. Although Masonry had been very popular during and after the Revolution, with the growing democratization of

America its secrecy and elitism came under increasing attack, especially in western New York. By 1826 the first official third political party in U.S. history, the Anti-Masons, was headquartered in that state. Little more is known of Heber's Masonic activity until 1842 in Nauvoo, Illinois.

During this early period, on the evening of September 22, 1827, a celestial phenomenon of "aerial combat" took place at which Heber and his neighbors marveled. Gathered outdoors, they saw a great smoky bow along which a vast army marched to battle. Heber's vivid description of this reads like many others from Virgil, through John the Revelator, to Shakespeare and beyond, and is typical of real and imagined "signs" connected with Christian millennialism.

> It was one of the most beautiful starlight nights, so clear that we could see to pick up a pin. We looked to the eastern horizon, and beheld a white smoke arise toward the heavens; as it ascended it formed itself into a belt, and made a noise like the sound of a mighty wind, and continued southwest, forming a regular bow dipping in the western horizon. After the bow had formed, it began to widen out and grow clear and transparent, of a bluish cast; it grew wide enough to contain twelve men abreast.
>
> In this bow an army moved, commencing from the east and marching to the west; they continued marching until they reached the western horizon. They moved in platoons, and walked so close that the rear ranks trod in the steps of their file leaders, until the whole bow was literally crowded with soldiers. We could distinctly see the muskets, bayonets and knapsacks of the men, who wore caps and feathers like those used by the American soldiers in the last war with Britain; and also saw their officers with their swords and equipage, and the clashing and jingling of their implements of war, and could discover the forms and features of the men. The most profound order existed throughout the entire army; when the foremost man stepped, every man stepped at the same time; I could hear the steps. When the front rank reached the western horizon a battle ensued, as we could distinctly hear the report of arms and the rush.
>
> No man could judge of my feelings when I beheld that army of men, as plainly as ever I saw armies of men in the flesh; it seemed as though every hair of my head was alive. This scenery we gazed upon for hours, until it began to disappear.[9]

Some of Heber's neighbors thought the bow was one of the signs of the coming of the Son of Man.[10] We do not know what Heber thought, but seven years later, after he heard a Mormon missionary preach, he had reason to reflect back on it and wonder.

Death's pale horse was a frequent visitor to the Kimballs. By 1830 Heber had lost not only two infants, but also his parents, his brother Charles, Charles's wife and their two children, and Vilate's mother.[11] This series of deaths, so hard on Vilate that after her mother's death "she sank into a state bordering on despair,"[12] came at the time of the religious upheaval in western New York called the Great Revival. Nearby Rochester had been a center of religious revivalism and influenced the surrounding communities such as Mendon. It was a center of the Baptist General Tract Society. Furthermore, the famous Presbyterian and Congregational preacher, Charles G. Finney, the most powerful revivalist of his day, moved to Rochester from New York City during September, 1830, and mounted the sensational Rochester Revival.

Although belonging to no church, Heber and Vilate were caught up in this movement. "I received many pressing invitations to unite with different sects," Heber later recorded, "but did not see fit to comply with their desires until a revival took place in our neighborhood. I had passed through several of their protracted meetings, and had been many times upon the anxious bench to seek relief from the bonds of 'Sin and Death,' but no relief could I find until the meetings were passed by." Late in the fall of 1831 the Kimballs decided to accept baptism. "At this time," Heber added, "I concluded to put myself under the watch care of the Baptist church and unite myself to them; as soon as I had concluded to do this, the Lord administered peace to my mind, and accordingly the next day I went with my wife and we were baptized by Elder Elijah Weaver,[13] and we partook of the sacrament on that day for the first and also last time with them."[14]

The Kimballs hardly had time to become active in the Baptist congregation before they learned of a new religion. About three weeks later (most likely in November) a Mormon missionary came into the area, and the entire course of their lives was changed. Within two years they would leave not only the First Baptist Church of Mendon but everything else in the Bloomfield, Mendon, and Victor areas and move to Ohio.

In Mormonism the Kimballs would find their lives linked to two other families who had moved into western New York from Vermont at about the same time and for the same reasons. The Joseph Smith family settled in Palmyra; the Brigham Young family, after trying several other places, settled in Mendon. Although Palmyra, West Bloomfield, and Mendon lie within ten miles of each other, all three families were at first unknown to each other. The forming of the ties began in 1829, when Brigham Young moved from Oswego and joined the rest of his family in Mendon. Many years later in Salt Lake City, Heber told a New York writer:

> Came from there [New York] myself. Did't ye know that?
> Indeed! Is that so?
> *Cer*-tin! Joseph Smith, Brigham Young, 'n I, were all neighbors when we were boys. Lived right'n the same school-deestrick, Ontario County. Our parents came there'n settled when we weren't more'n so high (the apostle flattened his broad brown hand about three feet from the ground).[15]

It is not clear how Heber and Brigham met. Most likely it was through Brigham's widowed sister, Fanny, who was living with the Kimballs as early as 1827 to help Vilate, who was often sickly.[16] Further contacts between Heber and other members of the Young family were occasioned by compassion. The Youngs "were in lowly circumstances," Heber recorded, "and seemed to be an afflicted people and of course were looked down upon by the flourishing church where we lived . . . to them, my heart was united. . . ."[17] The resulting friendship between Heber and Brigham lasted until Heber's death more than thirty-nine years later.

It is unlikely that the presence of the Mormon missionary would have caused the stir it did among the Kimballs and Youngs had they not been acquainted previously with newspaper and word-of-mouth accounts of Joseph Smith and the Book of Mormon. Heber had heard and read rumors of "Old Joe Smith and a golden bible,"[18] and even before it appeared there were accounts in 1829 in the Rochester press about the "Blasphemy of the Book of Mormon." The *Rochester Daily Advertiser and Telegraph* of August 31, 1829, for example, reprinted a surprisingly accurate if unfriendly account from the *Palmyra Freeman*.

The following September 5 the Rochester *Gem* published a similar account, and after the Book of Mormon was published, the *Daily Advertiser and Telegraph* of April 2, 1830, printed an uncomplimentary review of the book. Several of the Youngs, and probably Heber, had also read the Book of Mormon. Joseph Smith's younger brother Samuel, the first missionary of the church, almost immediately after the March publication of the Book of Mormon had traveled through the surrounding area distributing it. By April, 1830, Samuel reached Mendon. He entered Tomlinson's Inn and proceeded to interrupt the lunch of the first person he saw, who, providentially or otherwise, was Phineas Young, an itinerant preacher for the Methodist Episcopal Reformed Church and brother to Brigham. Samuel talked him into buying a copy—perhaps the single most important copy of the Book of Mormon ever sold. Phineas read the book and in quick succession so did his father, his sister Fanny, his brother Brigham, and "many others," most of whom accepted it. According to tradition, Heber read the same copy.[19]

Just what role the book played in Heber's conversion is unknown. He never alluded to his introduction to or study of the Book of Mormon and he seldom quoted from it in his sermons. The book is a long, sprawling, complicated account of God's dealings through prophets with a chosen people in the Western Hemisphere generally for the period 600 B.C. to A.D. 400—in short, a New World Bible. Unique in many ways, it recounts the life of a group of Old Testament people led by God into geographical isolation and spiritual quarantine and given a form of pre-Christ Christianity, a New Testament.

Furthermore, this unusual record was intended mainly for future generations. Engraved on thin metal plates by various ancient religious leaders, Mormons believe that it was ultimately "sealed up, and hid up unto the Lord . . . to come forth [in the last days] by the gift and power of God . . . to the convincing of the Jew and the Gentile that Jesus is the Christ, the Eternal God, manifesting himself unto all nations . . ."[20] to become eventually a second witness for Christ. It also offers a fifth or "American" Gospel (see 3 Nephi).

Although the Book of Mormon has all the earmarks of an ancient, first-draft, religious record edited by a military man, and despite the fact that Mark Twain called it "chloroform in print," it is an exciting, readable adventure story. If, the first time through, it is read fast enough, its literary deficiencies and complexities are obscured by the grand sweep of the story line. The evolution of pre-Christ Christianity, wars, murders, burnings, beheadings, whoring, poisonings, storms, sunken cities, queens, kings, generals, robber bands, corrupt judges, villains, swordsmen, prophets, dreams, visions, miracles, and, above all, the visitation of the resurrected Christ—all can hold the reader's attention.

The missionary Alpheus Gifford, from Rutland, Tioga County, Pennsylvania, was traveling that November with his brother and four friends who were investigating the new faith. They were en route to Kirtland, Ohio, to visit with Joseph Smith. Gifford, who had previously been an independent preacher, was preaching along the way, and in the course of this "mission" came to the house of Phineas Young in Victor.[21] It is quite likely that Gifford learned from Samuel Smith that Phineas had a copy of the Book of Mormon and that the visit was a follow-up, or it may be that simply because Phineas had read the book, he invited Gifford and companions into his home to preach to his relatives and neighbors.

Learning of this and prompted by curiosity, Heber bundled up, hitched up his sleigh, picked up Brigham Young, and drove a mile through the snow to his friend's white clapboard home to hear the Mormon. There, in a lamp-lit parlor with pine knots blazing in the fireplace, he heard the characteristically simple, short, and direct message of early Mormon missionaries. Gifford rose and told with earnest, simple conviction of the new Prophet, the new faith. He related "that a holy angel had been commissioned from the heavens, who had committed the Everlasting Gospel and restored the Holy Priesthood unto men as at the beginning." Perhaps he quoted a Bible passage now popular among Mormons, "And I saw another angel fly in the midst of heaven, having the everlasting gospel to preach unto them that dwell on the earth, and to every kindred, and tongue, and people" (Revelation 14:6). Mormons generally believe that the visit of the Angel Moroni to Joseph Smith in connection with the Book of Mormon fulfilled this prophecy.

How much Gifford knew or told of Joseph Smith's 1820 vision in the numinous grove is not known, but he surely related how Joseph received, translated, and published the Book of Mormon in 1829 and organized the church in 1830.[22] Heber noted that he also "called upon all men everywhere to repent and be baptized for the remission of sins, and receive the gift of the Holy Ghost; and these things should follow those that believe, viz., they should cast out evils in the name of Jesus, they would speak in tongues, etc. and the reasons why the Lord had restored these things was because the people had transgressed the laws, changed the ordinances, and broken the Everlasting Covenant."[23] The accent was on the reopening of the heavens, the calling of a new prophet to dwell among the people to reveal anew the mind and will of God as in biblical days.

One sermon was enough for Heber. "As soon as I heard them," he said, "I was convinced that they taught the truth, and I was constrained to believe their testimony. I saw that I had only received a part of the ordinances under the Baptist Church. I also saw and heard the gifts of the spirit manifested in them, for I heard them speak and interpret and also sing in tongues which tended to strengthen my faith more and more. Brigham Young and myself were constrained, by the Spirit, to bear testimony of the truth, and when we did this, the power of God rested upon us."[24]

Up to that time, like his father before him, Heber had not been drawn to organized religion. Although he later claimed that at the age of nine he had lain on his bed and in a "vision saw those things that I have since passed through,"[25] and that from the age of twelve he "had had many serious thoughts and strong desires to obtain a knowledge of salvation,"[26] he does not appear to have done much serious searching. He had not been conventionally pious and had shown little interest in any of the standard recognized creeds such as the Presbyterian, Catholic, Methodist, or Baptist (even though he formally became one), nor does he appear to have been influenced by the Unitarians, Universalists, revivalists, restorationists, or communalist groups of his time and place, or by Christian Primitivism, which looked for the restoration of the original and simple church of the New Testament.

He does not fit the pattern of so many early converts to Mormonism in that he was neither seeking the principles of salvation from the Bible, nor some sort of restoration of a purer type of Christianity, nor the fellowship of the Saints. Furthermore he had not been moving from church to church, from faith to faith, as had many early Mormon converts. There is, in fact, no evidence that he had ever read the Bible. Had he been questioned on the matter of belief he probably would have admitted to a form of deism, believing in a God, an afterlife with rewards and punishments, and the necessity of leading a moral life.

In keeping with his simple nature, Heber's conversion was quick and uncomplicated. He accepted the message of the Restoration without anguished seeking or diligent study. The opportune and decisive moment came and he acted. His accounts of several spiritual experiences at that time read matter-of-factly with little mysticism or pentecostalism. His subsequent involvement with heavenly visitors, evil spirits, spiritual gifts, and prophecies he accepted as a matter of course. Once he embraced Mormonism his relaxed attitude toward religion and religious activity changed quickly to an intense, lifelong, and wholehearted devotion to the Restoration. Such devotion, typical of many Mormons then and now, is sometimes explained as "putting the church first," or, perhaps more accurately, as "being a Mormon first and whatever else second."

A partial explanation of Heber's change of attitude toward religion may be that the message of the Mormon missionary revived his memory of his childhood vision and intentions. When he learned from Gifford that Joseph Smith had received the records of the Book of Mormon from Moroni on the same day in 1827 that the "great smoky bow" appeared in the heavens, he may have considered it a "sign." The practicality of Mormonism, the accent on doing good and being "anxiously engaged in a good cause" rather than on ritual, contemplation, or sacrament, also may have appealed to Heber, who was by nature practical and active, not reflective. He may also have been favorably impressed with the practice of a lay priesthood in which he himself could participate.

Heber and Brigham soon had another spiritual experience. They were gathering some wood for Brigham's brother Phineas and "pondering upon those things which had been told us by the Elders" when "the glory of God shone upon us, and we saw the gathering of the Saints to Zion, and the glory that would rest upon them; and many more things connected with that great event, such as the sufferings and persecutions. . . ."[27]

Heber was so spiritually excited that during January, 1832, in spite of snow-choked roads and ice-filled rivers and streams, he took his horse and sleigh and, accompanied by Brigham and Phineas and their wives, traveled to the nearest branch of the church to learn more about it. This was at Columbia (now Columbia Crossroads), Bradford County, Pennsylvania, about 130 miles to the south, near where Gifford and his friends had come from. (Vilate, perhaps because of ill health or a lack of interest, did not go.) They stayed in Pennsylvania about six days, attended the Mormons' meetings, heard them speak in tongues, interpret, and prophesy. Heber was fully converted. For some reason, however, none of them was baptized in Columbia. Perhaps they wished to let Gifford perform the ordinance. Heber may have also wanted to wait until Vilate had sufficient faith to join him.

When Gifford and his newly baptized friends returned to Mendon the following April, he immediately sought out Heber, who was throwing at his wheel. At the mention of baptism, Gifford received a typical response from Heber. "I jumped up," Heber recalled, "pulled off my apron, washed my hands and started with him with my sleeves rolled up to my shoulders, and went the distance of one mile where he baptized me in a small stream in the woods. After I was baptized, I kneeled down and he laid his hands upon my head and confirmed me as a member of the Church of Jesus Christ. . . ."[28] Although Heber did not consider himself worthy, on April 16 Gifford ordained him an Elder on the spot. Vilate, somewhat more cautious, was not baptized immediately and Heber "mourned for her as one would mourn for the dead."[29] She had not enjoyed the spiritual experiences he had, and it was not until two weeks afterward that she was baptized.

Soon the Mendon branch numbered about thirty, including ten Youngs, two Kimballs, the John P. Greene family, and even the owner of Tomlinson's Inn, where Samuel Smith sold the first Book of Mormon in Mendon, and seems to have been led by Brigham Young's older brother Joseph.

Heber's spiritual experiences were heightened after baptism and the receipt of the Holy Ghost. He felt, as did the disciples of old, that he was on fire. "The people called me crazy," he claimed. "I continued in this way as though my flesh would consume away; at the same time the Scriptures were unfolded to my mind in such a wonderful manner it appeared to me, at times, as if I had formerly been familiar with them." [30]

A contemporary heard both Heber and Brigham preach, but seems to have confused their identities. "Brigham," he recorded, "was quite fervent, and spoke with much feeling and effect. He was regarded as stronger in heart than in head. His faith and piety were counted of more force than his intellect. Heber C. Kimball, on the other hand, was respected as a man of much more mental power, but not of the great devotion in comparison with this associate Young." This account would ring much more true if the names were reversed. [31]

Other members of the little Mendon branch appeared to have been enthusiastic. A Palmyra newspaper, the *Wayne Sentinel*, noted on April 18, 1832: "A Rochester paper mentions that Mormonism has 'taken root' in a certain church in the town of Mendon, Monroe County. The preacher says he shall never die, but be translated, after the manner of Enoch, and that in eighteen months Mormonism will be the prevailing religion; and that in five years, the wicked are to be swept from the earth." [32]

In some ways Heber fits the emerging profile of early Mormon converts. It appears that most of them were poor farmers or artisans, had little formal education, and were largely religiously alienated. As the owner of a successful pottery, however, Heber was moving up economically from artisan into the more affluent middle class.

Shortly after baptism, Heber was called as a missionary by Joseph Young. It was common in the early church to ordain new male converts as Elders and send them on short missions to preach what little they had learned. That summer of 1832 Heber and Brigham and Joseph Young labored in nearby Genesee, Avon, and Lyonstown, where they baptized several and built up small congregations. This first missionary experience set the pattern of his life for the next twelve years as he fulfilled a total of eight missions.

Heber also visited nearby Palmyra. It was too late, of course, to meet any of the Smiths or other church leaders, who had already left that community for Missouri and Ohio. He simply wanted to see the area, particularly Hill Cumorah, where the plates which formed the basis for the Book of Mormon were believed to have been found. Deeply regretting not having taken the occasion or trouble to visit Joseph Smith previously, Heber made his pilgrimage to Kirtland, Ohio.

As soon as Heber arrived back in Mendon, he began to arrange his affairs in order to move his family to Kirtland. The following spring, for example, he sold two lots for $475 and by the fall was ready to go. At that time, however, some of his neighbors issued attachments against his goods, although he was not indebted to any of them. The unseemly haste with which Heber and Vilate deserted the Baptist Church (after one service) and embraced Mormonism may have offended some and instigated the litigation.[33] It may also reflect the widespread religious intolerance of that time and place. Apparently these attachments were settled out of court, for no records of the case have been found.[34] Finally in October all was ready and Heber and family, accompanied by Brigham Young and his two daughters left. (After Young's wife Miriam Works died of tuberculosis September 8, 1832, he and his two young daughters, Elizabeth and Vilate [named after Heber's wife] had moved in with the Kimballs and lived with them part of the time.) Sending their belongings ahead by Erie Canal boats and Lake Erie steamers, the families went by wagon to join several other members of the Young family and Vilate's father and stepmother, who had already left for Kirtland.

Although neither Heber, Vilate, nor any of their children ever returned to the Mendon-Victor area to live and although Vilate's brother William and his family were the only members of either the Kimball or Murray families ever to follow them into the waters of baptism, fairly close family ties were maintained for decades. Letters were exchanged and Heber usually passed through Mendon and Victor to and from several missions in the East. Once or twice Vilate returned to Victor to visit her people. Later, when some of their sons went on missions in the 1840s and 1860s, they looked up uncles, aunts, and cousins.

As he drove westward, Heber stopped on a small rise and looked back at Mendon set in a frame of fall color. He was leaving behind his settled, comfortable, and obscure existence to throw in his lot with God's new Prophet. The first thirty-one years of his life had been formative. Had he not accepted Joseph Smith and the Restoration, he most likely would have stayed in Mendon, built up a major pottery business, become active once more in Masonry when it was safe to do so, and remained a nominal member of the local Baptist church. Part of the dedication he gave Mormonism he might have given Masonry, perhaps rising to a position of Grand Master. Outside of brief references in a history of New York Masonry and in a note on economic developments in some history of Ontario County, he would be totally unknown today.

NOTES

1. Court of Common Pleas Records, Ontario County Courthouse, Canandaigua, N.Y. These records do not state the nature of the litigation, although it appears that all concern debts—misdemeanors, not felonies.

2. *Deseret News*, "Synopsis," Mar. 31, 1858.

3. The name is pronounced Va-*late*. She was the daughter of Roswell and Susanna Fitch Murray, the youngest of five children. Her siblings were Roswell Gould, William Ellis, Brewster, and Lucretia. Her paternal grandparents, Ezra and Hanna Gould Murray, had moved from Connecticut to Florida, Montgomery County, New York, around 1770. From there Vilate's parents had moved to Victor town in 1810.

4. He suggested as much in Utah once to Fitz Hugh Ludlow. *In the Heart of the Continent . . . with an Examination of the Mormon Principle* (1870; reprinted New York: AMA Press, 1971), 343–44.

5. Helen Mar Whitney, "Life Incidents," *Woman's Exponent*, vol. 9 (Mar. 15, 1881), 154. Hereafter cited as H. M. Whitney, *Woman's Exponent*.

6. Monroe deeds, 27:144, 24:435, and 26:325. The quarter-acre lot was probably purchased from his brother Charles, for it was part of the tract bought by Charles in 1818.

7. Day Book of M. E. Sheldon, Mendon, New York, 1831, Wilford C. Wood Museum, Bountiful, Utah. I would like to thank LaMar Berrett for drawing this day book to my attention.

8. Milnor Lodge Records, vol. 66, Archives of the Grand Lodge F. & A. M., State of New York. It appears that none of the other thirty-nine members ever joined the Mendon Mormons. Heber recorded that he became a Mason in 1823, but this is apparently an error on his part or the printer's.

9. Daniel Peterson, "Heavenly Signs and Aerial Combat," *Sunstone*, vol. 4 (Mar.–Apr., 1979), 27–32. Heber's account is taken from O. F. Whitney, *The Life of Heber C. Kimball*, 15–17.

10. The Director of the Local History Division of the Rochester Public Library and the Monroe County Historian were unable to locate any contemporary account of this event.

11. Charles's wife, Judith, died June 20, 1824; Heber's mother died Feb. 25, 1825; his father died July 8, 1825; his brother Charles died June 16, 1830. The date of death of Vilate's mother is presently unknown. Heber's parents, Charles, Judith, and their two children are buried in the Tomlinson Corners Cemetery in Mendon, which still exists.

12. H. M. Whitney, *Woman's Exponent*, vol. 14 (Dec. 1, 1885), 98.

13. Orson F. Whitney, *The Life of Heber C. Kimball*, 2nd ed. (Salt Lake City: Stevens & Wallace, 1945), 18. First published in 1888. Weaver was the pastor of this church (organized in Dec., 1809) from Jan., 1823, through Apr., 1833. See "An Historical Sketch of the Baptist Church in Mendon, Monroe Co., N.Y.," *Minutes of the 37th Anniversary of the Monroe Baptist Association* (Rochester, 1864), 17–19. Since the Youngs were Methodists, it is surprising that the Kimballs did not join them. Apparently the Baptists were more active than others in proselytizing.

The *New York Baptist Register* of Utica was searched unsuccessfully for the period May, 1832–Dec., 1833, for further reference to Mormons in the Mendon area.

14. *Deseret News*, "Synopsis," Mar. 31, 1858.

15. Ludlow, *The Heart of the Continent*, 343–44.

16. It was Fanny who named Helen Mar after a heroine in a Scotch ballad. In 1832 Fanny became the second wife of Vilate's father, Roswell Murray. After the death of her husband, Fanny went to Utah with her brother, Brigham Young, and lived with his other wives in the Lion House.

17. H. C. Kimball, Journal 94b, 4, Church Archives. In the Church Archives are five items known as the Heber C. Kimball Journals. During the years I worked on this biography the numbering of these journals has changed. Following is a list of the old and new numbers with the time periods (sometimes overlapping) covered by each journal: Journal 90 (now 1), 1837–47; Journal 91 (now 2), 1840–45; Journal 92 (now 3), 1844–45; Journal 94 (now 4), Apr. 5–Oct. 30, 1847; Journal 93 (would now be 5, but it is restricted as it is largely a record of Nauvoo Temple work), Nov. 21, 1845–Jan. 7, 1846.

There are also two items which formerly were designated as Journal 94B and Journal 94C, which are now catalogued as the Heber C. Kimball Autobiography, 1838–48, n.d., two vols., dictated and in the handwriting of various church clerks. None of these last two items is in Heber's hand and much of the first five journals are also in other hands, including those of William Clayton, Peter O. Hansen, and Horace K. Whitney.

18. "Remarks by Heber C. Kimball," Aug. 1, 1859, recorded by George D. Watt, Winslow Whitney Smith Papers, Church Archives.

19. Some students consider that the critical copy is the one Samuel sold to Mrs. J. P. Greene of Mendon, sister to Brigham Young. Young left two conflicting accounts of which copy he read. In the *Millennial Star* (vol. 25, p. 124), he says it was Phineas's copy; in the *Utah Genealogical Magazine* (vol. 11, p. 109), he says it was the Greene copy.

20. From the original title page of the Book of Mormon.

21. The line separating the towns of Mendon and Victor ran between the homes of Phineas and Heber, so that although Phineas lived in Victor, he was still in the general area of the other Youngs and the Kimballs.

The chronology of this period is difficult and confused. Reading the manuscript versions of the Heber C. Kimball and Brigham Young biographical sketches which were printed in the *Deseret News* during 1858 in Salt Lake City suggests that there may have been an earlier visit by these same Elders to Mendon that spring. But it seems apparent that this was the first time Heber had heard the Elders. Gifford's son noted that his father, Alpheus, was baptized in 1830 and soon after went to Kirtland with his unbaptized brother and friends, returned home, and finally went to Jackson County, Missouri, in 1831. Samuel K. Gifford Journal, 1, Church Archives.

22. The official organization took place Apr. 6, 1830, in Fayette, Seneca County, New York. At first it was known simply as the Church of Jesus Christ. In 1838 the words "of Latter-day Saints" were added as a parallel to what might be called the "Early-day Saints" of the New Testament. "Mormons" is a nickname derived from the Book of Mormon. The term "Saints" is used in the New Testa-

ment sense of believers (1 Cor. 1:2) and not in the manner of beatified persons. Mormons consider the Restoration to have been literal, not some sort of "mystic union with the body of Christ."

23. H. C. Kimball, Journal 94, 3, Church Archives.

24. *Deseret News*, "Synopsis," Mar. 31, 1858.

25. Sermon by H. C. Kimball, *Journal of Discourses*, 26 vols. (London: Latter-day Saints' Book Depot, 1854–86; reprinted 1967), vol. 12 (Apr. 12, 1868), 190. The date in parentheses following each entry is the date on which the individual speech was given. This collection of discourses of early Mormon leaders is a sort of Mormon *Patrology*.

26. *Deseret News*, "Synopsis," Mar. 31, 1858.

27. *Ibid.*

28. *Ibid.*, Apr. 7, 1858. The stream, Trout Creek, ran through Brigham Young's property.

29. H. M. Whitney, *Woman's Exponent*, vol. 10 (Oct. 15, 1881), 74.

30. *Deseret News*, "Synopsis," Apr. 7, 1858.

31. Hyram K. Stimson, *From the Stagecoach to the Pulpit* (St. Louis, Mo.: R. A. Campbell, 1874), 92, as cited by Richard F. Palmer, "Brigham Young and the Mendon Branch," paper read at the Mormon History Association Annual Meeting, Canandaigua, N.Y., May, 1980.

32. As cited in *ibid.*

33. According to the "Historical Sketch of the Baptist Church in Mendon," in 1833, 1834, and 1835 the church experienced severe trials, and "they were under the painful necessity of excluding several of the members for imbibing the heresy Mormonism."

34. One writer has opined quite incorrectly that leaving Mendon was all that saved Heber from debtor's prison. Stanley B. Hirshson, *The Lion of the Lord: A Biography of Brigham Young* (New York: Alfred A. Knopf, 1969), 11.

PART II

THE MISSIONARY AND APOSTOLIC YEARS
1832–46

"Thou shalt be great in winning souls
for me, for this is thy gift and calling."
Revelation to Heber C. Kimball
Far West, Missouri
Apr. 6, 1839

CHAPTER 3

Ohio and the Call to Preach

It was bitter cold when Heber arrived in Kirtland, and his first concern was to acquire proper shelter. He first settled his family in a house belonging to Elijah Smith near the East Branch of the frozen Chagrin River.[1] As soon as possible, Brigham Young, out of gratitude for all Heber had done for him, as well as to provide a continued home for his own motherless children, built Heber a home (perhaps on the same section of land), and spent most of the winter with the Kimballs until he married Mary Ann Angell several months later.

In Ohio, Heber hoped to find a permanent home among those of his faith, but this was not to be. In 1833 Kirtland, nestled in gently rolling hills along the Chagrin River, near Lake Erie, and about twenty miles northeast of Cleveland, was a small trading and milling center with a population of perhaps 1,300. Mormon missionaries had been there as early as 1830 and had found it to be a fertile field for proselytizing. Consequently, as a result of an 1831 revelation, the Prophet advised his converts in New York and Pennsylvania to sell their properties and follow him to Ohio. (This is known as Section 39 of the Doctrine and Covenants, a published volume of Joseph Smith's revelations.)

Although the Mormons attracted the greatest attention in the area, they never did predominate numerically. When Heber arrived, there were probably less than 200 Saints in the Kirtland area. And the troubles which portended the eventual abandonment of Kirtland by the Mormons had already started. Early in 1832 in nearby Hiram, Joseph, for example, had been tarred, feathered, and nearly emasculated by a mob (at the last moment the doctor backed out). The sources of Mormon difficulties in Ohio were both internal and external. Too many inexperienced members developed strange spiritual ideas and claimed unusual manifestations leading to what Joseph himself decried as "false spirits." Some even claimed that they, not Joseph, were the real prophet. There was also fear and distrust of what some Ohio newspapers called a "vile imposture" and "Joe Smith's bible speculation." Some husbands were angered that their wives left them to join the Mormons, and many old settlers organized to prevent the conversion of their neighbors to the "Mormon delusion." To this end many false reports about the church were published, especially by apostates and disgruntled ministers who had lost their congregations.

According to Heber's daughter Helen, the Kirtland area devised a unique form of anti-Mormonism—grave-robbing. In nearby Willoughby was the Willoughby Medical College, newly founded in 1834. It was widely believed among the Kirtland Mormons that their graves were considered violable by medical students seeking cadavers. One family which suffered several deaths got into the habit at night of covering the graves with a wooden bier to which was secured the end of a heavy length of rope. The other end was tied to the father's arm to warn him of ghouls.[2] Later the medical school was forcibly closed in 1847 by the citizens of Willoughby, who suspected it of grave-robbing.

In spite of these difficulties, the Saints tried to live peaceably in the Kirtland area until the general exodus from there to western Missouri (where some Mormons were already settling in Jackson County) during the winter of 1837–38.

Heber was to have relatively little to do with either Ohio or Missouri developments, for he spent much of the time between 1833 and 1837 on various proselytizing missions. Of a total of fifty-six months in Kirtland, he was away for twenty-four—nearly half the time.

After his family was settled as comfortably as circumstances would permit, Heber threw himself wholeheartedly into the heady experience of Kingdom-building. While in Kirtland he participated in Zion's Camp (see pp. 29–33), worked on the temple, was chosen as one of the original Twelve Apostles, attended the Hebrew school, took part in the temple dedication, and invested in the ill-fated Kirtland Safety Society banking venture. In the center of things, in the direct force-field of Joseph Smith's personality, he donated freely to the building of the schoolhouse, the printing office, and especially the temple, to which he gave $200, a sizeable amount when the average day's wage was less than a dollar. It appears that, initially at least, Heber was economically well off in Kirtland.

It is not entirely clear, however, how Heber supported himself there; arriving in November, he could hardly have begun farming. Initially he probably lived off the money he brought from Mendon. He did some work as a potter and may have planted some crops the following spring, but

Mormon difficulties in Missouri, which caused him to go there in May, did not permit him to tend whatever he may have sown.

He also helped as a stonemason to build the temple—no ordinary task. Anti-Mormon feelings had created a situation much like that which faced Nehemiah when he tried to rebuilt the temple in Jerusalem. "We had to guard night after night," Heber remembered, "and for weeks we were not permitted to take off our clothes, and were obliged to lay with our firelocks in our arms to preserve brother Joseph's life"[3] and thus prevent the destruction of the temple.

The same missionaries who had visited Kirtland in 1830 also proselytized in western Missouri, where they organized a small branch in Independence, Jackson County. In June, 1831, despite the very recent establishment of the church in the Kirtland area, Joseph received what the Mormon faith holds to be a revelation, now recorded as Doctrine and Covenants, Section 52, that Missouri was a "consecrated" land. Joseph immediately left for Missouri, where during July he received still another revelation (Doctrine and Covenants, Section 57), that Missouri, not Ohio, was to be the New Zion, the gathering place. Since Joseph continued to live in Kirtland until January, 1838, however, there were two centers of the church for nearly seven years—closely connected administratively, but separated physically by nearly 900 miles.

For a variety of social, economic, and political reasons the Mormons were less popular in western Missouri than in Ohio. The rough, pro-slavery frontier elements—most of the original settlers in Missouri were southerners—did not care for the influx of a new, industrious, clannish, anti-slavery people, generally from New England, especially if they also espoused a strange religion, gave the impression that the surrounding land belonged to them as their Zion, and were numerous enough to dominate politics and form a powerful economic bloc. The old settlers were also greatly concerned over the Mormon interest in the Indians and suspected and feared some sort of an alliance. In short the old settlers feared that their "behavorial boundaries" were threatened. By spring of 1834 the Mormons in Missouri, driven from Jackson County by militia and mobs, were in exile across the Missouri River to the north in Clay County.

As a result of this expulsion Joseph Smith received a revelation on February 24, 1834 (Doctrine and Covenants, Section 103), commanding him to redeem his Missouri brethren and to reinstate them on their plundered land. Consequently Joseph, expecting some help from Missouri state officials, gathered as many of the faithful as he could to form what came to be known as Zion's Camp. The small army originally consisted of about 100 men, but by the time they reached Missouri it had swelled to 205, including eleven women and seven children. Heber signed up and gave into the general fund all the money he had, and took along a span of good horses and a wagon. Probably because of his previous military training, he was appointed captain of the third company of thirteen men.

That April as Heber started down the Chardon Road and watched the temple on the hill disappear behind trees just leafing out, he might have wondered if he would ever return, for, as he later recorded, the camp was "threatened both in that country and in Missouri by our enemies, that they would destroy us and exterminate us from the land."[4]

Their route lay generally westward, across more than 900 miles of the rolling, open prairie of the central lowlands covered with bluestem prairie grass, over deep-banked streams and rivers, and through oak, hickory, beech, and maple groves and forests. It was not a much shorter trek than the famous one to present-day Utah in 1847. From Kirtland they proceeded southwest through Wooster, Springfield, and Dayton, Ohio; straight west via Richmond, Indianapolis, and Clinton, Indiana; farther west by way of Paris, Springfield, and Atlas, Illinois; and finally through Louisiana, Keytesville, and Richmond, Missouri. They traveled generally on good roads. Across much of Indiana, for example, from the Ohio state line to near Greencastle, they were on the famous National Road (later U.S. 40)—the superhighway of its day—which extended from Cumberland, Maryland, to Vandalia, Illinois.

Various small groups rendezvoused on May 6 at New Portage (now Barberton, near Akron) about fifty miles from Kirtland, where there was a branch of the church. By that time the camp consisted of more than 130 men accompanied by twenty baggage wagons. The full camp started out from there May 8. Most of the twenty-five-day journey was over the flat, undifferentiated plains. Starting out each morning with prayer at 4:00 A.M., they averaged between thirty-five and forty miles a day.

The march was generally uneventful until they left Indiana. On June 3, while camped on the west bank of the Illinois River in Pike County, Illinois, Heber and a few others accompanied Joseph Smith to a mound on top of the high river bluffs. "On the top of this mount," Heber noted, "there was the appearance of three altars, which had been built of stone, one above another, according to the ancient order; and the ground was strewn over with human bones. This caused in us very peculiar feelings, to see the bones of our fellow creatures scattered in this manner, who had been slain in ages past." They felt prompted to dig into the mound, and "at about one foot deep we discovered the skeleton of a man, almost entire, and between two of his ribs we found an Indian arrow, which had evidently been the cause of his death." Heber inquired about the identity of the skeleton, and recorded Joseph's response: "It was made known to Joseph that he had been an officer who fell in battle, in the last destruction among the Lamanites, and his name was Zelph."[5] The location of this incident appears to have been what is now called the Naples-Russell Mound #8, about one mile south of present-day Valley City, Illinois, in a typical prehistoric Middle Woodland mortuary complex of the Hopewell culture.

A few days later Zion's camp crossed the Mississippi at Louisiana, Missouri, an established outfitting and jumping-off place for the West. Immediately east of Paris, Missouri, was a small Mormon community called the Salt River settlement. Here on June 8 Joseph's company met his brother Hyrum's company, which had come from Michigan. Combined, the small army now numbered 205 individuals and twenty-five baggage wagons.

They proceeded across the glacial plains and on through a wilderness area to just inside Clay County, where they camped between the two main branches of the Fishing River just west of present-day Excelsior Springs. The weather was fine and pleasant. There on the evening of June 19 occurred what was as close to a battle as Zion's Camp was to experience. "Just as we halted," Heber recorded, "and were making preparations for the night, five men rode into the camp, and told us we should see hell before morning, and such horrible oaths as came from their lips, I never heard before. They told us that sixty men were coming from Clay County, to assist in our destruction. These men were armed with guns, and the whole country was in a rage against us, and nothing but the power of God could save us."

These five men knew that Zion's Camp had inadvertently stopped in a natural trap, the breakdown of several wagons having prevented them from selecting a better and safer campsite. This choice of the first campsite in Clay County cannot otherwise be reconciled with the many facts and rumors Joseph had received concerning the intentions of Jackson County mobs to destroy them and the lack of will on the part of Missouri officials to render the Mormons justice. The two main branches of the Fishing River meander through a wide floodplain affording no cover and little elevation. The camp was caught in the open surrounded by steep-banked, deep-channeled rivers on three sides. A small band of Missouri "Pukes," let alone a projected force of over 300 men, easily could have pinned down the Mormons encumbered with women and children. The camp was trapped.

"Soon after these men left us," Heber continued,

we discovered a small black cloud rising in the west; and not more than twenty minutes passed away before it began to rain and hail, but we had very little of the hail in our camp. All around us the hail was heavy; some of the hailstones, or rather lumps of ice, were as large as hens' eggs. The thunders rolled with awful majesty, and the red light-ning flashed through the horizon, making it so light that I could see to pick a pin almost any time throughout the night; the earth quaked and trembled, and there being no cessation it seemed as though the Almighty had issued forth his mandate of vengeance. The wind was so terrible that many of our tents were blown over and we were not able to hold them; but there being an old [Baptist] meeting house close at hand, many of us fled there to secure ourselves from the storm. Many trees were blown down and others twisted and wrung like a withe.

The storm altered the situation. As the rain-swelled rivers rose, they changed from trenches trapping the Saints into protective moats barring the mob's attack. "The hail fell so heavy upon them [the mob]," Heber continued, "that it beat holes in their hats, and in some instances even broke the stocks off their guns; their horses being frightened fled leaving the riders on the ground, their powder was wet and it was evident the Al-mighty fought in our defense. This night the river raised forty feet."

Thus the camp was delivered. The men moved on and camped near the mouth of Rush Creek east of Liberty. There, on June 22, Joseph called his men together and reported he had received a revelation to "wait for a little season for the redemption of Zion. . . . For behold, I [God] do not require at their hands to fight the battles of Zion; even so will I fulfill, I will fight your battles." Joseph then discharged them. Before the Mormons moved on, however, thirteen men and a woman, Betsy Parrish, had died from cholera. Heber, who was stricken but recovered, considered this as God's punishment for the disobedience of some members of the camp. It was the Mormons' first encounter with this dread scourge, which had started in India in 1826, reached the New World in 1832, and followed waterways to the West. Many Mormon graves were dug along the western trails because of cholera.

By almost all criteria Zion's Camp was a total failure. Zion had not been redeemed, at least fourteen members had died, and a great amount of time and treasure had been expended. The venture does not seem quite so foolhardy, though, when it is noted that Joseph believed that the governor of Missouri would support their efforts and lend them the assistance of the state militia when they arrived. At the critical moment the governor failed to comply with his earlier assurances. But it was a constructive failure. Out of the 191 survivors of Zion's Camp came most of the men who later formed the original Quorum of the Twelve Apostles, and most of the subsequent leaders of the church for many years. And the march itself provided important field training for the great exodus to the West which lay ahead. Perhaps there were psychological benefits too. All concerned could feel unburdened of the task of rebuilding Zion in Jackson County; they could turn to the future. In any event, Heber and others must have been cheered when Joseph told them of a revelation (Doctrine and Covenants, Section 105) which explained, to some extent, the real meaning of the venture: "I [the Lord] have heard their prayers, and will accept their offering; and it is expedient in me that they should be brought thus far for a trial of their faith."

On June 30, Heber and several companions started the uneventful return trip to Kirtland, arriving on July 26, about three months after they left. Heber remained in Kirtland a year before being called away again on a mission. During this year he established a pottery and registered for a six-week term in a grammar school under the supervision of Sidney Rigdon and William E. McLellin to try to fill in the gaps in his formal education. He does not seem to have gained much from this experience, but it demonstrated his desire to improve his education. Of such efforts his grandson later wrote, "Heber's progress, however, was only moderate. Grammar, as a study, afforded him little delight. The mysteries of syntax seemed to elude his mental grasp . . . the technicalities of his mother tongue . . . seemed to baffle him."[6] Fortunately Heber's lack of knowledge of analytic grammar did not impair his native ability to speak and write effectively.

Early in 1835, shortly after the school term ended, two important events took place: the publishing of Joseph Smith's revelations and the organization of the Quorum of the Twelve Apostles. Early converts had had little opportunity to read about the church and its doctrines. Many had never seen the Book of Mormon, and most of Joseph's revelations had not been printed. (Only eighteen had appeared in full or in part in the Missouri-based Mormon monthly *The Evening and Morning Star*, of very limited circulation.) In 1833 the editors of this paper in Independence, Missouri, attempted to publish, as the Book of Commandments, the sixty-five revelations Joseph had received through 1831, but mob violence prevented them from doing so. The more peaceful atmosphere in Kirtland enabled

102 of these revelations to appear in 1835 in book form as the Doctrine and Covenants.[7]

Heber surely noticed that the book was basically a handbook of the Restoration, a collection of unconnected and disparate revelations to Joseph Smith, and, through Joseph, to other individuals and to the church at large, presented in no systematic way whatsoever, most coming as a result of Joseph's petitions to God for information. Certainly the revelations imparted a sense of urgency. Many were warnings that the Lord would come quickly; many were references to the importance of taking the Restoration to the whole world, which heightened Heber's missionary zeal.

Most of the information is practical, with theology tucked away here and there, almost as an afterthought. Perhaps that is why formal theology plays such a small role in Mormon thought and life. These bits and pieces of theology, however, are fascinating, "radical and fundamental," "Pelagianism in a Puritan religion," as one student has put it.[8] The most basic theological difference between Mormons and other Christians is the Mormon claim to continuous revelation directly from God through a living prophet who reveals the mind and will of God to mankind.

In these revelations Heber and subsequent Mormons read of the three degrees of glory in the next life, the purpose of mortal life, and the Word of Wisdom (a health principle). They learn that man cannot be saved in ignorance, that the glory of God is intelligence, that Satan cannot tempt children, that God's earth will become the heaven of the righteous after the resurrection, that all things are spiritual, that good works are necessary to salvation, that the Father, the Son, and the Holy Ghost are of one mind, spirit, and work, but not of body, that the Holy Ghost is a male personage of spirit, and many details about the millennium.

The revelations also made clear that evil is a positive good in human experience and advancement, that "it must needs be that the devil should tempt the children of men, or they could not be agents unto themselves," and that Jehovah (not Elohim or God the Father) and the pre-mortal Christ are one and the same being.

From the teaching that "Man was also in the beginning with God," that intelligence or the light of truth was not created or made, Heber might have come to the realization (as later and more sophisticated thinkers did) that man's essence is self-existent, that God is neither the totality of being nor the creator of all being, that man is not totally God's creature, that there was no creation *ex nihilo*, that nothing may compromise the freedom of will aided by the Light of Christ.[9]

At the same time the Doctrine and Covenants appeared, a major step in the evolution of the church organization was taken. The Quorum of the Twelve Apostles was finally formed. Instructions for such a quorum had been given to Joseph Smith by revelation, Doctrine and Covenants, Section 18, as early as June, 1829, even before the church was organized. The selection was to be made by the Three Witnesses to the Book of Mormon—Oliver Cowdery, David Whitmer, and Martin Harris—and the candidates were to be recognized by their desires and works.

By February, 1835, Joseph realized that it was time to effect the organization of the Quorum of the Twelve Apostles. Apparently the rigors of Zion's Camp had sufficiently tested and demonstrated the "desires and works" of the brethren. On Saturday, February 18, he called a general meeting especially for all who had been in Zion's Camp. Heber and Brigham, of course, were present. They heard Joseph explain the purpose of the meeting. Then they listened to Oliver Cowdery, Martin Harris, and David Whitmer pray for guidance and receive a blessing from the hands of the First Presidency. It was a most solemn meeting. (These three men are known collectively in Mormon history as "The Three Witnesses" for having testified that they had seen the original plates from which the Book of Mormon had been translated by Joseph Smith.) Following a hymn, a one-hour intermission, full of speculation, no doubt, was called.

Reassembling, another prayer was offered and Joseph instructed the Three Witnesses to proceed with the selection. It was so quiet Heber could hear his own heart beating. The first name called was that of Lyman E. Johnson. The second was that of Brigham Young. Heber saw Brigham start, but then he heard his own name. Only three were called that day. Rejoicing, they strode to the stand to receive their ordination blessings from the Three Witnesses.

Heber was promised he would "receive visions, the ministration of angels, and hear their voices, and even come into the presence of God," that many millions would be converted by his instrumentality, that angels would waft him from place to place, that he would stand unto the coming of our Lord and be made acquainted with the day when Christ shall come, that he would be made perfect in faith, that the deaf would hear, the lame walk, the blind see, and that he would have boldness of speech before the nations and great power.[10] After such promises, even if Heber had wondered how he could ever falter or betray the trust placed in him, his ordination insured enduring steadfastness.

On subsequent days, Orson Hyde, David W. Patten, Luke S. Johnson, William E. McLellin, John F. Boynton, William Smith, Parley P. Pratt, Orson Pratt, and Thomas B. Marsh were likewise chosen and ordained. All save four (Patten, McLellin, Boynton, and Marsh) had participated in Zion's Camp and had therefore proved themselves, at that point, strong in the faith. Not many years would pass, however, before most of these men would suffer complete or temporary relapse. Only Heber and Brigham never lifted their hands or voices against the Prophet.

After the Quorum had been organized, Oliver Cowdery instructed them in their duties in his "Charge to the Twelve," [11] which set the pattern for the rest of Heber's days. Cowdery warned them that they would need wisdom in a "ten-fold proportion to what you have ever had; you will have to combat all the prejudices of all nations." They were urged to let their ministry be first, to strive until they had "seen God face to face."

In respect to seniority, Cowdery said that the ancient apostles had sought to be great, "but brethren, lest the seeds of discord be sown in this matter, understand . . . God does not love you better or more than others . . . you are as one. You are equal in bearing the keys of the kingdom to all nations." This may be why Heber seldom deferred to anyone other than Joseph Smith until he became a counselor to Brigham Young in 1847.

After this signal honor of becoming an Apostle, a special witness for Christ, Heber changed little. He carried on much as before. The turning points in his life were his baptism and later when Young chose him as First Counselor in the First Presidency.

Since the main point of forming the Quorum of the Twelve was to send them as special witnesses, the Apostles departed, on May 4, 1835, for the eastern United States and upper Canada, traveling two by two "without purse or scrip" (baggage). For five months Heber preached in New York, Vermont, New Hampshire, and Maine. While at Sackett's Harbor, New York, he received word from Vilate of the birth of a new son, Heber Parley. His joy produced a characteristic burst of humor. To his companions he said, "I have three children and have not seen one of them." No one understood how this could be until he explained that the *one* he had not seen had just been born.

Later he went to Mendon, his former home where he was harshly treated by a Baptist minister named Fulton, possibly of Heber's former congregation. He called the new Apostle a false prophet and rejected his testimony. Heber responded by stating that if he did not repent and be baptized he would be damned. This only angered Fulton. Afterward, in biblical fashion, Heber cleansed his feet in testimony against him. More of his experience in Mendon has not been recorded. Apparently Heber was a prophet without honor in his own country; he had no success in Mendon.

He next went to his old home in Sheldon, Vermont, to preach to friends and relatives. Some believed, but would not submit to baptism. He was still a prophet without honor. From Sheldon he walked over fifty miles of lonely roads on blistered feet, crossing the Green Mountains to meet with others of the Twelve in St. Johnsbury, where several families accepted the message. Thence he traveled to the home of his mother in Plainfield, New Hampshire, where he found only opposition and reviling even among his own kin. After visiting the Saints in Boston, he participated in a conference on August 28 in Farmington, Maine. This conference was the formal end of the first mission of the Twelve, and at its conclusion the missionaries returned separately to Kirtland. Heber reached home safely on September 25.

The winter was much like the preceding one—Heber worked at his pottery and attended grammar school for five weeks. On March 27 and 31, 1836, possibly the most important single event of the Kirtland period took place—the dedication of the temple. Erected by the volunteer efforts of a few hundred persons between 1832 and 1836, the temple was one of the most impressive buildings in northern Ohio. Constructed of native stone along New England lines, it was three stories high and measured fifty-five by sixty-five feet. The exterior walls sparkled because the sisters had sacrificed their china, which was ground up in the plaster. The first floor was for divine worship; the second was designated as a place for general instructions of those holding the Priesthood; the attic contained five small classrooms and offices.

The consecration of the temple, considered by Mormons to have been the first House of the Lord since biblical days, brought to a head all the spiritual naiveté, zeal, and excitement characteristic of the church in Kirtland, and many spiritual experiences were reported. It was later affirmed by many who were present that a pillar of fire rested upon the steeple, that the sound of a great wind filled the building, that many spoke in tongues, prophesied, and had visions. Heavenly choirs were heard and angels appeared. Heber said he saw one: "He was a very tall personage, black eyes, white hair, and stoop shouldered; his garment was whole, extending to near his ankles; on his feet he had sandals. He was sent as a messenger to accept the dedication."[12] He also recorded seeing the resurrected apostle Peter, who "had on a neat woolen garment, nicely adjusted around the neck."[13]

Shortly after the dedication, Heber, along with other church leaders, received the ordinances of the washing of the feet and anointing with oil, and "witnessed many manifestations of the power of God." Thus was partially fulfilled the reference to endowments made during Cowdery's "Charge." Only partially, though, for the Kirtland temple was not a temple in the sense that the Nauvoo and subsequent temples were and are. Heber, for example, could not receive his endowments (special gifts and blessings) in the full sense there. These became available only in the Nauvoo temple. The Kirtland temple was more of a holy meeting place.

In May Heber inquired of Joseph Smith whether he should go on a mission to preach or go back to school. Told he could do either, and perhaps because he did not care much for school, he opted to go on yet another mission—alone.

This third mission, lasting from June 10 through October 21, took him back to Buffalo, Sackett's Harbor, and Plattsburgh, New York, and to friends in Vermont. He preached where doors were open, and baptized those who believed. This was the usual procedure in those days—one or two sermons, baptize, and move on.

In June, three miles from the village of Ogdensburg, New York, on the St. Lawrence River, he was driven by rain into the house of Heman Chapin. Learning of his mission, the Chapins called in their neighbors to hear him. Heber preached successfully and frequently for a week and baptized seven, some of whom spoke in tongues.

One day a troubled husband asked him to visit his wife, who had been confined to her bed for five years and had been given up to die. Heber went. Taking a chair by her bed, he held her wasted hand and told her of the Restoration. He asked her if she believed and would accept baptism from his hands. She affirmed she did and would. Forthwith Heber had her husband carry her to the pond or dammed-up stream where he did his baptizing. Afterwards Heber fixed her with the "dark, piercing eyes" so many people commented on and rebuked her disease. "In less than one week," he recorded, "she was performing her usual household duties . . . to the astonishment of the people." [14]

From Ogdensburg Heber crossed the Adirondacks and Lake Champlain to St. Albans, Vermont, thence to his place of birth, Sheldon, and elsewhere in Vermont. Apparently he again had no success with his friends or relatives, for his journals are silent on the subject.

At least one group appreciated his efforts. In St. Albans he visited the family of Priscilla Whitney Martin. She was impressed, and in a letter to her father she describes something of Heber's day-to-day activities and how he was received by some.

> The man you requested to call on us was here the 11th of July and I think he is a godly man. He appeared as such here. He went up to see

Phebe and preached in Fayettsville [probably today's Newfane, Wind-
ham, County] and was much liked by them all. Ben says it is the most
reasonable preaching he ever heard. On his return from there, he
came here again and I think he was penniless by his talk. I washed a
little for him and lent [him a] little change for he told me that God
would pay me four fold and left his blessing with me and prayed with
us and finally, I felt myself more than payed when he left the house.[15]

After a not very successful five weeks in Vermont, Heber returned for
a few days to the Chapins and those he had baptized in Ogdensburg and
organized a branch of twenty. He owed this success to a marvelous feat of
strength. One afternoon as Chapin was grinding his scythe and fixing his
cradle to cut a field of wheat, Heber offered to help and offhandedly declared that he could rake and bind as fast as Chapin could cut. The surprised Chapin replied that no living man could do that. "Never mind,
Brother Chapin, it's nearly as easy for me to do it as to say it," Heber announced. His account continues:

The next morning after the dew had passed off we went into the field,
commencing at a piece of wheat which he said had three acres in it.
Said I, "go ahead, Brother Heman, we'll cut down this piece before
dinner." About the time he took the last clip of the three acres I had it
bound in a bundle before he had hardly a chance to look around, and
about that time the horn blew to call us to dinner. We started back to
his house, he never spoke or said one word to me, appearing rather
confounded. The next Sabbath we had such a congregation of hearers
as I had never seen in the United States; for priests and people had
come for twenty-miles distance, to see and hear that Mormon who
had performed a thing that had never before been done in that country, for Brother Chapin had proclaimed this occurrence unknown to
me.[16]

Afterward Heber left for Victor, where, by previous arrangement, he
met Vilate. After visiting friends and relatives for a few days, they caught a
Lake Erie steamer at Buffalo for the overnight trip home to Kirtland.
Many of the passengers were Swiss going to their new homes in Cleveland,
then a popular place for Swiss and German immigrants. While sunning
himself on deck and hearing them talk for some time, the "Spirit of the
Lord" came upon Heber. He joined the immigrants, introduced himself,
and "was able to preach to them in their own tongue, they seemed much
pleased and treated us kindly," he laconically noted.[17] The purpose of this
incident is unclear. If anyone ever joined the Mormons because of this experience, it has not been recorded and Heber never again referred to it. He

was beginning to take such things for granted. Somewhat later Heber and Vilate caught sight of the lighthouse and pier of the Fairport Harbor and reached Kirtland on October 2.

During the eight months between this mission and another one to England the following June, we know little of Heber's activities, except for his involvement in the troubled Kirtland Safety Society banking venture. In 1836 Andrew Jackson abolished the National Bank, which he believed controlled the nation's money market too tightly. It then became both necessary and possible for state and private banks to provide money and credit. The Mormons understandably believed that if they had their own bank they could build up Kirtland faster, so they organized one that same year.

The bank had difficulties from the beginning. The State of Ohio refused the Mormons a charter, and the bank was poorly underwritten. Heber, for example, subscribed to $50,000 worth of shares for only $15 in cash. In all, 200 church members subscribed to 79,420 shares, worth at face value approximately $3,854,000 at $50 par value, which was backed up with only $20,725 cash.[18] The bank, furthermore, was weakened by speculation, mismanagement, and dishonesty. The insecurity of the venture was obvious. Joseph Smith warned all concerned, but his warnings went unheeded. The society slipped toward failure and was caught in the Panic of 1837—an inflationary spiral brought on by too much paper money and credit. Hundreds of banks across the country, including the Kirtland Safety Society, suspended payment.

The failure of the bank caused much bitterness in Kirtland. Joseph Smith received the blame and was called a fallen prophet by many, including five of the Twelve Apostles. According to Heber, scarcely twenty people still considered him a prophet of God. The strength of the six-year-old church was at nadir. It was facing dissolution.

For Joseph to have marked time would have been fatal. If ever the young Prophet needed providential guidance, it was then. In answer to prayer, Joseph received inspiration to send Heber to open a mission in England—more than 5,000 miles away. While this must have seemed a puzzling response to financial disaster, England was socially and economically ready for a new religion, especially one for the common people. Several days later, early in June, Joseph found Heber in the temple precincts and whispered to him, "Brother Heber, the Spirit of the Lord has whispered to me, 'Let my servant Heber go to England and proclaim my Gospel and open the door of salvation to that nation.'"[19]

Heber was overwhelmed. To him, England was a land "famed throughout Christendom for light, knowledge and piety, and as the nursery of religion" and the English a "people whose intelligence is proverbial,"[20] and he was well aware that others in the church were much more educated and cultured than he and consequently better suited to work in England. Although he was unaware of it then, his natural simplicity was to be far more effective in England than any amount of polish.

Heber's original account of his call to England at age thirty-six is important not only because we have the story in his own words, but because it is the beginning of his sporadic attempts to keep a journal. (See Appendix C for excerpts from this journal.) In his distinctive spelling he noted:

> June the 4-1837 Kirtland. The word of the Lord to me through Joseph the prophet that I should gow to England to open the dore of procklamation to that nation and to he[a]d the same; Likewise the same day Brother Joseph wanted we should meet at a confrance at Elder Rigdons. I met with them accordingly. . . . Joseph and Sidney [Rigdon] and Hiram [Smith] Lade there hans on my head and set me apart for this mission and dedicated me to the Lord. . . . The 2[nd] day we got together and I was mouth and we asked the Lord to carry us safely crost the great waters and to give us fare winds, and caus our journy to be spedy and to open the way before us when we should arrive on the chores [shores] of Europe.[21]

Heber wanted Brigham Young to be his companion. Joseph Smith, however, needed the dynamic Young to help with matters in troubled Kirtland and gave Heber six other companions: Orson Hyde, a member of the Quorum of the Twelve Apostles; Willard Richards, a church member for only six months; Joseph Fielding, a native of Bedfordshire, England, who had emigrated to Canada in 1832; and three other Canadians, John Goodson, Isaac Russell, and John Snyder. Fielding's brother, an Independent (formerly Methodist) minister in Preston, England, to whom they had written about Mormonism, had invited Joseph Fielding to come and preach this new religion in his chapel.

Heber made his preparations and in less than ten days was ready to go. He blessed his family, bade his friends farewell, and, in company with Hyde, Richards, and Fielding, started for New York City, where they arrived on June 22 and met Goodson, Russell, and Snyder.

A few days later on June 27, the night before they sailed, Heber wrote Vilate a long letter detailing his trip to New York, their activities in that city, and their preparations for leaving. (See Appendix C for a photocopy of this earliest extant Kimball letter.) Heber related how wicked New York City was, how he had to sleep in a warehouse belonging to a member, and how he and his companions had spent two days distributing Hyde's missionary broadside, *Prophetic Warnings* (the first definable Mormon tract). He asked Vilate to write to him often. "Tell me the Hole truth and nothing but the truth. Tell me how you guit [get] along how your health is and how you injoy your mind. Tell me how the children guit along . . . let me know all about your temprel and spiritual concerns."

In the letter he related his pleasure with the ship on which they booked passage: "We are going a bord of the Ship tomorrow; it is the largest packet ship that sales the Otion [ocean] . . . it is the noblest things that I ever see. The name of it is cald the Garrick. . . ."[22] The *Garrick* berthed 927 tons, about 100 tons larger than most packets and merchantmen, had the long, flat floor of the New Orleans packets, and was very fast. She was one of the famous ships of the E. K. Collins Line, noted for its excellent service. Her hold was crammed with typical New World exports to England: cotton for the Lancashire Mills and naval stores (wood, tar, and turpentine) for the Royal Dock Yards.

Heber and friends, dodging the gigs, hacks, coaches, and omnibuses which filled the streets, walked down to Packet Row on the East River between Martin's Lane and Wall Street, where they secured second cabin accommodations for $18 each. Although they provided all their own provisions and slept in buffalo robes on the floor, their quarters were superior to steerage. (First-class passage and board cost $150.) At 10:00 A.M. the *Garrick* weighed anchor and was towed down the East River by a steamer as far as Sandy Hook. There the captain from the quarterdeck gave orders to spread the great topsails, hoist the jibs, haul up the spanker and the staysails. Catching the wind, the *Garrick* loosed herself from the tug and sailed off into the Atlantic under her own power.

NOTES

1. This location is based on a study of the original Kirtland Platte Book, Church Archives, and several visits to Kirtland, Ohio. It is less than one mile northeast of the temple in the general area of today's Kirtland Ballpark, north of the Kirtland-Chardon Road.

2. H. M. Whitney, *Woman's Exponent*, vol. 10 (June 1, 1881), 6.

3. *Deseret News*, "Synopsis," Apr. 7, 1858.

4. Much of what follows is taken from Heber's account of Zion's Camp published in the *Times and Seasons*, Jan. 15, Feb. 1, Feb. 15, Mar. 15, and Apr. 15, 1845. No contemporary Kimball journal exists for this period. The *Times and Seasons*'s account appears to have come from his "Autobiography," which may have been dictated from no longer existing field notes.

5. The terms "Lamanite" (and "Nephite") are Book of Mormon names referring to some ancestors of the American Indians.

6. Orson F. Whitney, *The Life of Heber C. Kimball*, 70.

7. As the Book of Mormon reads like a first draft, so do many of these revelations. Certain infelicities of style (indefinite antecedents, tautologies, weak grammar, problems of person) strongly suggest that only ideas and not the actual wording of God's messages came to Joseph. We could say that Joseph received the *word* but not the *words* of God.

8. See Sterling McMurrin, *The Theological Foundations of the Mormon Religion* (Salt Lake City: University of Utah Press, 1965).

9. To Mormons God is a perfect man who attained Godhood by obedience to eternal laws and principles. Mormons believe that "as man is God once was, and as God is man may become." See below, p. 272.

10. B. H. Roberts, ed., *History of the Church of Jesus Christ of Latter-day Saints*, by Joseph Smith, Jr., 2nd ed. rev., 7 vols. (Salt Lake City: Deseret News Press, 1957), vol. 2, 180–89.

11. *Ibid.*, vol. 6, 317.

12. H. M. Whitney, *Woman's Exponent*, vol. 9 (Feb. 1, 1881), 130.

13. *Ibid.*

14. H. C. Kimball, Journal 94b, 36, Church Archives.

15. Priscilla Whitney Martin to Samuel Whitney, Aug. 15, 1836, Lake County Historical Society, Mentor, Ohio.

16. H. C. Kimball, Journal 94c, 45–46 of the section titled "History of Heber Chase Kimball by his own dictation," Church Archives.

17. *Deseret News*, "Synopsis," Apr. 14, 1858.

18. Stock Ledger, Kirtland Safety Society, Chicago Historical Society, microfilm copy at Southern Illinois University, Edwardsville.

19. H. C. Kimball, Journal 94b, 88, Church Archives.

20. R. B. Thompson, ed., *Journal of Heber C. Kimball* (Nauvoo, Ill.: Robinson and Smith, 1840), 10. Hereafter cited as *Journal of Heber C. Kimball*.

21. H. C. Kimball, Journal 90, 7–8, Church Archives. The only changes made in Kimball's holographs in this biography have been to end all sentences with a period, to begin all sentences with capitals, to capitalize all proper names, and to correct all obvious oversights. It should be noted, however, that most Kimball quotes taken from secondary sources have already been "modernized."

22. H. C. Kimball to Vilate Kimball, June 27, 1837, H. C. Kimball Papers, Church Archives.

CHAPTER 4

The First Mormon in the Old World

Out of sight of land for the first time in his life, Heber experienced the power and awful primordial majesty of the sea, the humbling and intimidating encounter with endless water and sky. But eighteen days of salt air, spray, and relaxation must have provided a good change of pace, a salutary break in Heber's normal routine, and a time to prepare for his appointed task in the Old World in that year of 1837.

The most interesting part of the crossing was the daily excitement of the race between the *Garrick* and the *South America*, a speedy packet of the competitive Black Ball Line. Earlier that year, E. K. Collins had lost the first trans-Atlantic Ocean race on record. His *Sheridan*, on its maiden voyage, was beaten by two days by the Black Ball's *Columbus*. With his new *Garrick* Collins hoped to recapture his reputation for having the fastest ships on the New York–Liverpool run.

For this second match with the Black Ball Line, Collins wagered $10,000. Day after day Heber and companions stood at the rail and observed the race; they were up at daybreak on July 20, when it ended. "We arrived in the river Mersey, opposite Liverpool," Heber remembered, "being eighteen days and eighteen hours from our departure from the anchorage at New York. The packet ship *South America*, which left New York at the same time we did, came in a few lengths behind. . . . She had been seen during the voyage, but never passed us. The sight was very interesting to see these two vessels enter port with every inch of canvas spread."[1] Eighteen days and eighteen hours was a remarkably short run. The average time from New York to Liverpool was thirty-eight days, and for Collins's fast ships, thirty-one days.

As they drew near Liverpool, Heber, braced by the sea, excited, and characteristically impatient to get to work, leaped ashore when the landing boat was still six or seven feet from the pier at Prince's Dock. The first Mormon had reached the Old World.[2]

44

For three days the impecunious missionaries lodged with a widow in Union Street, waiting for their trunks to clear customs. Then, "feeling led by the Spirit of the Lord," on Saturday, July 22, they took the noon coach from the Golden Lion Inn on Dale Street for the three-hour-and-ten-minute ride to Preston, Lancashire.

The borough of Preston, located on the River Ribble about thirty miles north of Liverpool, was a grimy, crowded manufacturing community of some 45,000 inhabitants and was already 650 years old when the missionaries first arrived. The location was well chosen for the introduction of a new faith. It had been a strong Protestant center since the days of Cromwell and was considered as tolerant as any place in England. There was also an important temperance movement centered there. In fact, Preston was the birthplace of "teetotalism," an extreme form of temperance. (The expression derived from the declarations of Preston's reformed drunkards that they were "t-totally" against all alcoholic drinks—brewed, vinted, or distilled.) Furthermore, as already noted, Joseph Fielding's minister-brother had invited and was expecting the missionaries. All of this helps to explain why Preston, out of all of Britain, first heard of the Restoration.

When the missionaries arrived that sunny afternoon, a general election to Parliament was in progress, for Victoria had just ascended to the throne three days earlier. There was much excitement—music playing, flags flying, and thousands of men, women, and children parading the streets, decked in ribbons representative of their politics. Just as the missionaries stepped from their coach, someone raised a banner proclaiming, "Truth will prevail." So propitious and appropriate did this seem to Heber that he exclaimed, "Amen. So let it be."[3]

They soon found lodging with a widow in St. Wilford Street. That same evening Joseph Fielding contacted his brother James, who invited the missionaries to his church, Vauxhall Chapel, on Vauxhall Road, the next day, which was Sunday. The Reverend Fielding and two other ministers had left the Methodist Church and were, to the best of their ability, trying to restore what they thought was primitive Christianity. Fielding, greatly excited by what his relatives had written from Canada, had led his congregation in prayer for this message to be brought to them.[4] At the close of morning services he suddenly announced that an "Elder of the Latter-day Saints" would preach there that afternoon. Heber was delighted, considering such an opportunity an answer to prayer and one reason why they had felt inspired to commence their work there.

At the appointed hour, Heber and his companions returned to the plain, two-storied brick chapel. Mounting the elevated pulpit, Heber saw pews full of people wondering what to expect from this Yankee. In flat New England tones he declared that an angel had visited the earth and recommitted the everlasting Gospel to man; called attention to the first principles of the Gospel—faith in the Lord Jesus Christ, repentance, baptism by immersion for the remission of sins, and the laying on of hands for the gift of the Holy Ghost—and gave a brief history of the Restoration. This earliest known Heber C. Kimball sermon was much like the one he had heard preached by the Pennsylvania Elder. He never did become a calamity howler. His was a simple, rational theology, with the accent on an angelic visitation, by which he meant the Restoration in general. What he said specifically is unknown. He may have told of the First Vision of 1820, or of the restoration of the Priesthood in 1829, but it is much more likely that, given the simple missionary presentation of that day, he referred only to the 1823–27 appearances to Joseph Smith of the resurrected Moroni, the last of the Book of Mormon prophets, regarding the Book of Mormon.

Heber's first opportunity to preach was followed quickly by two more—another one that same evening, and still another Wednesday night. The good fellowship of the Reverend Fielding melted, however, when some of his congregation left him and requested baptism at the hands of the missionaries. James Fielding closed his chapel to the missionaries and later complained, "Kimball bored the holes, Goodson drove the nails, and Hyde clinched them."[5]

The Elders lost a chapel but gained audiences in private houses, on street corners, especially before the obelisk in Market Square. Heber quickly discovered the basic ignorance, spiritual immaturity, subservience, and economic depression of most of his listeners. Only half the laboring class in England at that time were literate. "They are quite ignorant," he confided to Vilate; "many of them cannot read a word and it needs great care to teach them the gospel so that they can understand; the people here are bound down under priestcraft in a manner I never saw before . . . they are in the same situation as the children of Israel were in Egypt." He added, "It is as much as they can do to live, there is not more than one or two that could lodge us over night if they should try; and in fact, there are some that have not a bed to sleep on themselves; and this is the situation of most of the people in this place. . . ."[6]

Heber and his companions turned such circumstances to their advantage. Their own limited education was not noted. They spoke on the level of their audience, acted as common men, wore no distinguishing garb, and did not teach for hire. It was, furthermore, easy for the Mormons to extend the hand of fellowship and brotherhood, to make all feel equal before God. They could even offer their male converts the Priesthood itself (which to Mormons means the power to act for God on earth in matters pertaining to the church). No longer need their hearers defer to the lordly class of English clerics.

Heber capitalized on his natural talents. He was simple, sincere, and personal. Although he often preached publicly, he sought individuals in their private homes, and most of his converts were made in more intimate gatherings rather than in open meetings. While no copy of his early sermons survives, Brigham Young did record that he would say to someone, "Come my friend, sit down; do not be in a hurry." Then he would begin to preach the Gospel in a plain, familiar manner, and "make his hearers believe everything he said, and make them testify of its truth, whether they believed it or not, asking them 'Now you believe this? You see how plain the Gospel is? Come along, now,'" and he would lead them into the waters of baptism. He was popular. Sometimes people would stay with him all day and were often converted after one sermon. At the right moment, "he would put his arm around their necks, and say, 'Come let us go down to the water.'"[7] When his own sons became missionaries, he urged them to preach short and simple sermons, directed by the spirit, and told them, "I said but little, but what I did say went straight to the hearts of the honest."[8]

Their message spread quickly and within the week they were preparing to baptize nine converts on Sunday, July 30. Before conducting this first baptism, however, Heber experienced what he considered to be the hostility of Satan:

> One Saturday evening, I was appointed by the brethren to baptize a number the next morning in the River Ribble, which runs through that place. By this time, the adversary of souls began to rage, and he felt a determination to destroy us before we had fully established the gospel in that land; and the next morning I witnessed such a scene of satanic power and influence as I shall never forget while memory lasts. . . . I was struck with great force by some invisible power and fell senseless on the floor as if I had been shot, and the first thing that I recollected was, that I was supported by Brothers Hyde and Russell, who were beseeching the throne of grace in my behalf. They then laid me on the bed, but my agony was so great, that I could not endure, and I was obliged to get out, and fell on my knees and began to pray. I then sat on the bed and could distinctly see the evil spirits, who foamed and gnashed their teeth upon us. We gazed upon them about an hour and a half, and I shall never forget the horror and malignity

depicted on the countenance of these foul spirits, and any attempt to paint the scene which then presented itself, or portray the malice and enmity depicted in their countenances would be vain.[9]

In spite of the terrors of the night, the baptism occurred in the morning, at ebb tide, in the River Ribble, which at Preston is estuarial. Thousands watched the event, which took place on the south side of present-day Avenham Park—tradition says near the Old Tram Bridge. George D. Watt, racing to the river, had the honor of being the first into the water, where Heber baptized him by immersion. George's mother, Mary Ann, was the first female baptized a Mormon in England.

One of the three female converts hung back a little: Elizabeth Ann Walmsely, a consumptive and bedridden invalid who (like the invalid Heber had met in Ogdensburg, New York) had been given up to die by the doctors. Heber had previously promised her that if she would believe, repent, and be baptized, she would be healed. Heber called for her husband, Thomas, to carry her to him. Hesitant but believing, Elizabeth Ann came. A week later she was up and attending to her household duties. She lived to immigrate to Utah and died several decades later in Idaho. This first baptism opened a floodgate of converts. By 1851, in spite of heavy emigration (over 7,800), there were more than 42,000 Saints and 642 congregations in England.

Heber's two missions to England, in 1837–38 and 1839–41, were his greatest contributions to the growth of the early church. The success of the British mission counterbalanced the Ohio apostasy and the Missouri persecution. The 4,700 converts who immigrated from England to Nauvoo by 1846 strengthened the church during the Illinois period, and the more than 19,000 British converts who went to Utah between 1847 and 1856 proved a necessary force in taming the desert and establishing a viable Kingdom in the Great Basin. Ironically during its formative years, the church drew most of its converts not from its native soil but from England and Europe, where, initially at least, the missionaries met less opposition and were accorded more respect.

From Preston the missionaries spread to surrounding communities, where they preached in chapels, squares, inns, and tithe barns and baptized many. Soon Heber had organized branches of the church in Preston, Walker Fold, Longridge, and elsewhere in that area. The congregation in Preston was destined to become the oldest continuous unit of the Mormon faith worldwide.

Heber and the other missionaries were so successful in making converts, especially among the "Aitkenites," that the Reverend Robert Aitken, a popular and independent Scottish clergyman, came from London to Preston to "expose" Mormonism and the Book of Mormon. He was not successful in stemming the tide, and within a week of his denunciation, a large number of his followers in Preston were baptized.

Another Protestant denomination, Methodism, was also closely involved with Heber's British mission. The Reverend James Fielding of Preston had been a Methodist, the Aitkenites appear to have been essentially Methodist, and some Methodist ministers in Preston disturbed Heber and caused him to secure a ministerial license. J. Livesey, a Methodist minister in Preston, also published in April, 1838, what appears to have been the first anti-Mormon tract in England. This publication was a reprint of the Reverend Richard Livesey's *An Exposure of Mormonism, Being a Statement of Facts Relating to the Self-Styled "Latter Day Saints," and the Origin of the Book of Mormon*, which was originally published in Winchedon, Massachusetts; the two men may have been related.

At the time of Heber's two missions to England, a sect called the Primitive Methodists was strong. This group, founded in 1810, had seceded from mainstream Methodism and laid great emphasis on camp-meeting evangelism, open-air preaching, and lay participation in religion and government. Most members of this faith were of the ill-used, underprivileged British working class, who rejected strongly the idea that religion should not wrestle with the problems of the day. They wanted more from religion than instruction on how to prepare for the next life. Heber's simple message of good cheer, a Restoration, a new hope, a new beginning in a New World appealed to this group.

From Heber's written description of his early converts and from the fact that many of them were Aitkenites, we do know that, for the most part, they were of the poor, uneducated working class, who, for various reasons, had left mainstream English Protestantism—seekers looking for an expression of personal religion that would satisfy their needs.

The best study of the religious background of early Mormon converts in England concludes, "In the last analysis, it was the unsettled religious conditions in the 1840s that offer the key to understanding Mormon success. The strength of the movement lay in its ability to appeal to the disaffected from the sectarian congregations, and to inculcate within them the desire to build the kingdom in the last days. Conversely, the major limitation of the movement appears to have been its inability to appeal to those outside the perimeter of Christian fundamentalism." [10]

In Heber's first letter home from England, he wrote that he was quite sick, but continued to preach and baptize, for "the work of the Lord is rolling on in this Land in great power. . . ." The combination of Lancashire's excessively damp climate and repeated exposure to the water during baptisms was hard on his health. "I want your prayers day and night," he wrote, "that I may be supported and upheld from the powers of the devil for he is trying to destroy me sole and body. . . ."[11] A further problem, though he did not mention it in any of his letters, was the trouble he and his companions initially had in understanding the warm, blurred, and clipped "Lanky" dialect. Such statements as "Lad, wi' thi' sit doon" and "Coom in Lad, there's more light wi' thi' within than wi' thi' in t' 'ole i' t' wall" (there's more light with thee within than with thee in the hole [door] in the wall) required a bit of getting used to.[12]

His sympathetic account of the misery, poverty, and unemployment of many Englishmen, occasioned by the Industrial Revolution, the economic depression of 1836, and bad weather, reads like a page from Dickens's terrible indictments of the common man's misery in England. Of this world of *Oliver Twist* Heber wrote:

> This was very extraordinary weather for that country, as I was informed that some winters they had scarcely any frost or snow, and the oldest inhabitants told me that they never experienced such a winter before. In consequence of the inclemency of the weather, several manufacturing establishments were shut up, and several thousands of men, women and children were thrown out of employment, whose sufferings during that time were severe; and I was credibly informed, and verily believe, that many perished from starvation. Such sufferings I never witnessed before. The scenes which I daily beheld were enough to chill the blood in my veins. The streets were crowded by men, women, and children who begged from the passengers as they walked along. Numbers of those poor, wretched beings were without shoes or stockings, and scarcely any covering to screen them from the inclemency of the weather; and daily I could discover delicate females walking the street gathering up the animal refuse, and carrying it to places where they could sell it for a penny or half-penny. And thus they lived through the winter. At the same time, there were hundreds and thousands living in wealth and splendor. I felt to exclaim, O Lord, how long shall these things exist! How long shall the rich oppress the poor, and have no more care or interest for them than the brutes of the field, nor half so much! When the Lord Jesus shall descend in the clouds of heaven, then the rod of [the] oppressor shall be broken. Hasten the time, O Lord, was frequently the language of my heart when I contemplated the scenes of wretchedness and woe which I daily witnessed.[13]

The laissez-faire economic system of England at the time of Heber's first visit is sometimes described as predatory individualism. The government served as a passive policeman to protect life and property. It did not interfere with business, where the law of supply and demand ruled. Children of nine worked from fourteen to sixteen hours a day in the mills. Females of ten hauled carts weighing up to 500 pounds all day long in the low and narrow lateral shafts of the coal mines. There were no public schools. Workhouses were designed to be as uncomfortable as possible to discourage idlers.

Housing was often shocking. Whole families might live in one room; five might sleep in one bed. Many lived in fetid cellars reeking of intolerable stench. "Necessaries" frequently drained directly into wells used for water supplies. Streets were unpaved, badly drained open sewers. Living conditions at work were not much better, and many sought surcease in gin. Saloons guaranteed that patrons would get drunk for a penny. Immorality was rampant, ignorance and disease endemic, filth and squalor abounded.

These abject circumstances were one reason why so many listened to and accepted the Restoration—it imparted some hope. This was especially true after 1840, when the church not only encouraged immigration to the Land of Promise, but rendered financial aid to that end. Heber was not so naive as to misunderstand much of their interest. Years later in Utah he said, "Bless you, if you had not been poor and oppressed and in the depths of poverty, you would not have heard us at all when we went to proclaim the Gospel." [14]

The climax of the mission effort in 1837 was a special Christmas conference held in Preston. About 300 members from branches thirty miles around were present, registering the success of the missionaries. On that day they confirmed fourteen members and blessed about 100 children. Since his arrival in July, Heber himself had preached in Walker Fold, Longridge, "Barshe Lees" (Bashall Eaves), Ribchester, Wrightington, Hunter's Hill, Eccleston, Penwortham, Thornley, Leyland Moss, Askin, Dauber's Lane, Exton, Chorley, Stoney Gate Lane, and Downham—all in Lancashire. Only once during this first mission did Heber ever leave Lancashire or travel far from the valley of the River Ribble.

In some communities he healed those who believed, in others he felt led to certain homes. In Penwortham he met and converted William Clayton, who became a church leader in England and later a clerk and recorder to Joseph Smith and Brigham Young. In Preston he met and taught Alexander Neibaur, the first Jew to become a Mormon.

In Bashall Eaves two of Heber's converts, James and Nancy Knowles Smithies, had an infant daughter, Mary, their first child and also the first child born into the Mormon Church in Great Britain. The parents insisted on taking her to a church to be christened. In Mormon doctrine, infant baptism was contrary to the scriptures and the will of God, and Heber urged them against it. But they believed that if their daughter died she could not be buried in the churchyard. Their insistence caused Heber to utter the first of many prophecies for which he eventually became famous: "Brother and Sister Smithies, I say unto you in the name of Israel's God, she shall not die on this land, for she shall live until she becomes a mother in Israel." [15] Two weeks later Heber blessed the infant, who grew to womanhood, went to Utah, and in 1857 became the last plural wife of Heber himself, bearing him five children.

In Chatburn, where he converted twenty-five his first evening, Heber had perhaps the most moving experience of that mission. As he took leave of the Saints there, he was touched by their grief at his departure. "While contemplating this scene," he wrote, "I was constrained to take off my hat, for I felt that the place was holy ground. The Spirit of the Lord rested upon me and I was constrained to bless that whole region of country." [16]

After the Christmas conference, Heber's main efforts were to organize the branches so that they could carry on by themselves after he and his companions left. He arranged to lease the Cock Pit in Preston, a hall which, as its name suggests, had been built originally for gaming but had not been used for that purpose since 1830. Subsequently it had been utilized as a school and a lyceum, and in 1837 was the official meeting hall of the Preston Temperance Society. Throughout the early days of the church in England the elders benefited much from the organized temperance movement. Since Mormons then generally abstained not only from alcohol but even from tea and coffee, they were frequently welcomed to preach in temperance halls. Located in the heart of town and seating 800, the Cock Pit was an appropriate choice for the Mormons. (It no longer stands, although a plaque marks its site behind the parish church on Church Street.)

The Mormon request of January 4, 1838, to lease the Cock Pit is probably the earliest document in the Old World referring specifically to the "Latter day Saints." [17] The second general conference in England, held April 8, 1838, in the Cock Pit, was another confirmation of their success. From 600 to 700 attended, representing twenty-six branches with a total membership of about 1,300. [18] During this conference, twenty converts were baptized, 100 children were blessed, and much instruction was given, since Heber, along with Orson Hyde and Isaac Russell, was preparing to leave England. Joseph Fielding was sustained to preside in their absence, with Willard Richards and William Clayton as counselors.

On April 9 the three elders left Preston for Liverpool, whence they sailed for home on April 20, again on the *Garrick*. For several days they experienced seasickness and a storm so strong that the bowsprit was broken twice, the boom blown down, and the rigging much torn. For a few days the ship could spread only the jib sails. Thereafter the weather was calm. The missionaries again preached on the Sabbath, and Heber made himself much favored by assisting the ship's steward in treating a large but sick Durham cow—their only source of milk. Having been a farm boy, Heber quickly discovered that the cow could not raise her cud. He told the steward to cut a half-dozen slices of pork fat as large as his hand, which he gave to the cow. Heber knew that anything as foreign to a cow's stomach as pork fat would cause her to vomit and thereby resume her normal cud-chewing, but his real skill must have been in inducing Ol' Boss to swallow the meat in the first place. After the cow recovered, the steward sent the Elders turtle soup, wine, and other luxuries and presented them with many gifts.

Another company wager had been made at Liverpool regarding whether the Black Ball's *New England* or Collins's *Garrick* would arrive in port first. Although the *New England* kept four or five miles ahead of the *Garrick*, Heber assured his officers that their ship would go in first. And indeed, on May 12, near New York City, although neither of the ships was sailing at more than three knots, suddenly the wind left the sails of the *New England*, and the *Garrick* ran in one hour ahead.

The next day, Sunday, the missionaries met with the Saints in New York City and gave them an account of their work in England. On Monday they headed for Kirtland, arriving home on May 22, eleven months and nine days from the time they left. Heber's family was in good health and overjoyed to see him again.

By the time Heber reached Kirtland, few Saints were left in that city. Over half of the original membership had left the church, and many of those who remained were weak in the faith. During his absence the financial and spiritual trouble which had broken out in Kirtland before Heber had left on his mission had grown worse. The success of the dissidents, led by three former Apostles, John F. Boynton, Luke S. Johnson, and Lyman E. Johnson, can be gauged from the fact that during the winter of 1837–38 they had taken possession of the temple and caused both Joseph Smith and Brigham Young, together with many others, to flee to Missouri. The faithful Heber unhesitatingly made ready to join his brethren.

NOTES

1. *Journal of Heber C. Kimball*, 15.

2. Not only was Heber the first Mormon in Europe, he was the representative of "the first significant denomination indigenous to America which sent missionaries for systematic proselytizing work in Britain. . . ." Robert Lively, Jr., "Nineteenth Century British Saints in Context," paper read at the Mormon History Association Annual Meeting, Canandaigua, N.Y., May, 1980.

3. *Deseret News*, "Synopsis," Apr. 21, 1858.

4. O. F. Whitney, *Life of Heber C. Kimball*, 124.

5. H. C. Kimball, Journal 94c, 61, Church Archives.

6. H. C. Kimball to Vilate Kimball, Sept. 2, 1837, *Elder's Journal of the Church of Latter-day Saints*, vol. 1 (Oct., 1837), 5.

7. *Journal of Discourses*, vol. 4 (Apr. 6, 1857), 305.

8. H. C. Kimball to his sons David and Charles, Nov. 10, 1863, *Millennial Star*, vol. 26 (Feb. 6, 1864), 91–92; H. C. Kimball to his sons Brigham and Isaac, Dec. 7, 1866, *ibid.*, vol. 29 (Jan. 26, 1867), 59–60.

9. *Deseret News*, "Synopsis," Apr. 21, 1858. Years later in Utah he added some details to this experience. In 1856 he said, "I saw their hands, their eyes, and every feature of their faces, the hair on their heads, and their ears, in short they had fullformed bodies." *Journal of Discourses*, vol. 3 (Mar. 2, 1856), 229. A much disputed tradition places this house at today's 21 St. Wilford Street. This account, as related to Vilate, was originally featured and published in the first issue of the *Elders' Journal*, Oct., 1837, Kirtland, Ohio, and is the first of many subsequent Kimball letters and reports published in various church organs.

10. Malcolm R. Thorp, "The Religious Backgrounds of Mormon Converts in Britain, 1837–52," *Journal of Mormon History*, vol. 4 (1977), 51–65.

11. H. C. Kimball to Vilate Kimball, Nov. 12, 1837, H. C. Kimball Papers, Church Archives.

12. See Claire Noall, *Intimate Disciple: A Portrait of Willard Richards* (Salt Lake City: University of Utah Press, 1957).

13. O. F. Whitney, *Life of Heber C. Kimball*, 189–90.

14. *Journal of Discourses*, vol. 9 (Feb. 9, 1862), 374.

15. H. C. Kimball, Journal, Oct. 7, 1837, Church Archives.

16. *Ibid.* Joseph Smith later said that he had indeed been on "holy ground," that some of the ancient prophets had traveled in that region and dedicated the land, and that Heber had reaped the benefit of their blessing. O. F. Whitney, *Life of Heber C. Kimball*, 187–88.

17. Quarter Sessions Preston, Jan., 1838, no. 303, Lancashire Records Office, Preston, England.

18. Richard L. Evans, *A Century of Mormonism in Great Britain* (Salt Lake City: Deseret News Press, 1937), 244. There were 1,517 baptisms for the period 1837–39. Whitney credited Heber alone with 1,500 converts, but this is too generous a figure.

CHAPTER 5

<hr />

Unknown in Missouri

By late June or early July, 1838, Heber had left Kirtland for Missouri with his family and about forty of the faithful. They went by wagon about ninety miles south to Wellsville, where they took Ohio, Mississippi, and Missouri riverboats to Cairo, Illinois, and to St. Louis and Lexington, Missouri, making the last thirty miles by wagon to the town of Far West, which was located on a high, rather flat, and fertile prairie. En route they found some "western" (actually southern) ways strange—money called "bits," "toting" pails on the head, and, above all, the concept of slavery.

Much had happened in Missouri since Heber had been there in 1834 with Zion's Camp. Following their expulsion from Jackson County, Missouri, in 1833, the Mormons had resided for a while in Clay County. Eventually, however, the citizens of that county, hoping to avoid difficulties, peaceably and regretfully asked the Mormons to leave. During the summer of 1836, therefore, the Saints moved into the uninhabited northern part of adjacent Ray County, which was then organized into a new county named Caldwell. There, during two years of general peace, the Mormons built several settlements, the most important of which were Far West, the county seat and new church headquarters, and Haun's Mill on Shoal Creek. Elsewhere in northern Missouri, the Mormons laid out new towns: Adam-ondi-Ahman on the Grand River, Gallatin, and Millport in Daviess County, and De Witt on the Missouri in Carroll County. By the summer of 1838 there were at least 15,000 Mormons in northern Missouri.

The Kimballs were to find in Missouri, however, not only increased intolerance and frontier violence, brutality, and bigotry, but something worse—the dehumanizing practice of slavery. Slaves had been introduced into Missouri in the early eighteenth century by the French to work lead mines along the Mississippi, and after the Missouri Compromise of 1821, admitting Maine as a free state and Missouri as slave, slavery spread to all counties. By 1838 there were approximately 58,000 slaves in the state, concentrated along the Missouri River, where the large-scale growing of hemp was economical. (By 1860, Jackson and Clay counties, for example, were 21 and 36 percent black respectively.) Elsewhere in Missouri, most slaves were common fieldhands working small farms.

The slaveholding mentality of many western Missourians would affect the Mormons there in several ways. Their Yankee attitudes regarding slavery were unappreciated, and the Missouri men, accustomed to rigidly, if not mercilessly, enforcing the savage slave code, were not attuned to dealing gently with disliked Whites. By the time of Heber's arrival on the Missouri frontier, mobs had already destroyed a Mormon press, store, blacksmithy, and at least ten homes. They had whipped several men, tarred and feathered two, jailed some, crippled one, and killed one; they had harassed scores of women and children; and, finally, had driven about 1,200 Mormons from Jackson County. And worse lay ahead.

By the time Heber came to Far West that July, 1838, it had more than 5,000 inhabitants, 150 houses, 2 hotels, and at least 14 business establishments—and many must have been living in wagons and tents. Heber had a happy reunion with the Prophet Joseph Smith, Brigham Young, and others, and temporarily moved in with the David Patten family. The church gave him a building lot and timber for a home, and a friend gave him forty acres of land—presumably for a farm. How Heber supported himself and his family in Missouri is not recorded; his own efforts were probably supplemented from general church funds.

His first official act was to give the Saints an account of the British mission, which he did in the rude log church on the first Sunday after his arrival. Soon afterward, as a member of a small group which accompanied Joseph to the little settlement of Adam-ondi-Ahman, about twenty-five miles north of Far West, he was party to an unusual experience. On a hill overlooking the Grand River, Joseph showed his followers the ruins of three stone altars and revealed to them that according to Mormon belief this was the place where Adam had offered up sacrifice after he was cast from the Garden of Eden, and was the site to which Adam would someday return. Joseph even specified that the Garden of Eden had been in Jackson County. (According to Joseph, Adam-ondi-Ahman, from the primeval or "Adamic" tongue, means "the place of God where Adam dwelt.") Heber was impressed, but not amazed. He was getting used to such startling announcements by the new Prophet. Heber's account of this experience as recorded in his dictated "Autobiography" is unique and has been picked up by others many times.

After his re-entry into the Mormon community, Heber tried to arrange for his own housing. From the Pattens' the Kimballs moved to a storehouse on the main square and finally into a log cabin, which Heber intended to use as a cowshed after building a proper home. Caring for a family in an eight-by-eleven-foot cabin was probably trying, especially when the walls were only four feet high. It was possible to stand up straight only in the center of the room, and one of the roof poles ran directly over the Kimballs' bed. "One morning," Heber remembered, "Mrs. Kimball was making up the bed; she raised up her head suddenly and hit a sharp knot in the pole, she exclaimed 'dam it,' which was thought a very rough word; still we never think of it without a laugh, although it hurt severely."[1] One can only admire her remarkable restraint under such circumstances. And the long-suffering Vilate would have to live in more humble places than this before she would be comfortably housed again.

Whatever hopes Heber had of re-establishing a happy, normal home life were quickly marred by illness and mob activity. "I arrived there [Missouri]," he recorded, "in time to be sick three weeks and then the mob prevailed and [we] were driven out."[2] New troubles started over an election fracas in Gallatin, Daviess County, on August 6. When the Mormons tried to vote they were opposed and violence ensued. Mormons did not gladly suffer injustice or court martyrdom. They appealed, usually in vain, to whatever laws and law officials existed. Almost every time they fought fire with fire, however, they worsened the situation; Joseph and Joseph's God counseled forbearance. But this conflict signaled the end of the seven-year experience in Missouri. From August 6 until November 1 there was continued agitation, alarm, and permanent crisis. Although neither Heber nor his family were to suffer much personally in Missouri, he was to observe firsthand the results of mob arrests, murder, beatings, burnings, rape, and general destruction in Daviess, Ray, Carroll, and Caldwell counties.

Following the Gallatin affair, Missouri mobs and militia threatened other Mormon settlements in northern Missouri, including Adam-ondi-Ahman and Millport, where homes and haystacks were burned. The chief encounter between the Mormons and the Missourians, the Battle of Crooked River in Caldwell County, was fought October 25, 1838. The Mormons, under the command of an Apostle, Captain David W. Patten, set out to observe the movements of some Missouri troops and try to rescue some prisoners taken by the militia. When the Mormons were sighted they were fired upon and a battle ensued, during which several Mormons, including Patten, were mortally wounded.

When Heber, who was not in the battle, learned of Patten's condition, he rushed to his side and remained with him until he succumbed several hours later. Patten had received a ball in the bowels and died slowly, suffering excruciating pain. Heber recorded his death: "While the shades of time were lowering, and eternity with all its realities were opening to his view, he bore a strong testimony to the truth of the work of the Lord, and the religion he had espoused."[3]

The Battle of Crooked River precipitated Governor Lilburn W. Boggs's "extermination order" of October 27. "The Mormons must be treated as enemies," Boggs insisted, "and must be exterminated or driven from the state if necessary for the public peace—their outrages are beyond all description."[4] This order led directly to the October 30 massacre of seventeen Mormons at the Haun's Mill settlement on the banks of Shoal Creek, and the attack on Far West.

Anticipating the attack, Joseph Smith appointed Heber Kimball and Brigham Young captains of fifty men each. They immediately devised some temporary fortifications by pulling down some of their houses. Since the Kimball dwelling was on the outskirts, Heber sent Vilate and their children to the heart of the city to seek safety with the widow of David Patten. Vilate found Phoebe Ann Patten pushed beyond fear, outrage, shock, emotion itself. Instead of taking flight or dissolving into hysteria, she had marshaled her psychological strengths and achieved emotional insulation, almost detachment. Around her waist was a belt containing her dead husband's large bowie knife. On the fire was a kettle of boiling water and in her hand a tin dipper with which to throw it. "She did not seem in the least excited," Heber's daughter Helen later remembered. "Her countenance was perfectly calm and she shed no tears, the fountains seemed to have dried up and she only thought of avenging the blood of her husband."[5]

The community was soon surrounded, and further resistance appeared futile. Joseph Smith surrendered. Bloodshed was avoided, but the Prophet and a few other leaders were taken prisoner. As a leading Apostle, Heber expected to be included among the prisoners, but he discovered that he was so little known in Missouri that even some members of the church did not know he was at Far West. The same was true of Brigham Young. But the Mormons were disarmed and forced to sign over their property to pay the state for military costs, and there was some pillaging and rape. Vilate and Helen, however, were untouched—though Heber could have, and probably would have, torn asunder any man who tried.

At this terrible time, a former Apostle and a teacher of Heber's, William McLellin, who was with the anti-Mormon camp at Far West, unashamedly accosted Heber. "What do you think of Joseph the fallen Prophet now?" he said sarcastically. "Has he not led you blindfolded long enough; look and see yourself, poor, your family stripped and robbed and your brethren in the same fix, are you satisfied with Joseph?" Infuriated, Heber called McLellin a traitor. "I tell you Mormonism is true," he continued, "and Joseph is a true prophet of the living God, and you with all others who turn therefrom will be damned and go to hell and Judas will rule over you."[6] Surprisingly, after this rebuke McLellin made no effort to hurt or harass Heber or his family.

After the surrender of Far West, Joseph and the other prisoner-hostages were taken first to Richmond for a kangaroo court and then sent to jail at Liberty, and preparations for a general exodus from Missouri commenced. The fleeing Saints had little choice but to go east to Illinois, to put the Mississippi River between them and Missouri and to seek asylum. To the west was Indian territory—off limits to Whites. To the north was Iowa, a territory only since 1838, largely uninhabited, and possessed of no frontier to protect Mormons from Missourians, and wild Arkansas was far to the south. As many Saints as possible went by water from Lexington, via St. Louis, to Quincy, Illinois, the largest town on the upper Mississippi. Others went overland to the ferries at Quincy and Louisiana, Missouri. At Louisiana they crossed into Pike County, Illinois, settling temporarily in Atlas and just east of Pittsfield in a place still known as Mormon Town. A few fled to Lee County, Iowa.

Heber elected to remain in Far West as long as possible, visiting the prisoners as often as he was permitted, working for their freedom, assisting the Saints in leaving Missouri, and helping generally with church affairs. Before Emma Smith fled, she left a change of clothing with Heber for Joseph and asked him to keep her husband in clean clothing as best he could.[7]

From the Liberty jail on January 16, 1839, Joseph Smith addressed a letter to "Brothers H. C. Kimball and B. Young," saying that he did not want them to leave Missouri until he was out of jail, and that while he was in jail "the management of the affairs of the Church devolves on you, that is the twelve" (an important point that Brigham Young would refer to later when others claimed the mantle of the martyred prophet).[8] In a final postscript he wrote, "Appoint the oldest of those of the twelve who were first appointed to be the President of your Quorum."[9] Joseph may have put Heber's name first in this letter for alphabetical reasons, or because he may have thought the balding Heber was older than Brigham, or simply because Heber visited him in prison. In any event, Joseph did not name the president of the Quorum, remember who was the oldest member, or single out Young for special leadership. But because Brigham Young was thirteen days older than Heber, and because the senior Apostle Lyman E. Johnson had left the church, Young did become the president of the Quorum of the Twelve and the Prophet's successor as president of the church.

This simple act of re-establishing the line of authority (essential in Mormonism) appears to have enabled those church leaders out of prison to take some positive action. A few days later, on January 26, at a public meeting in Far West, several men, including Heber and Brigham, were appointed to draft a program for the safe removal of the Saints from Missouri. Three days later a seven-man Committee on Removal was selected to oversee the departure of the 12,000 to 15,000 Saints, especially the poor, from Missouri to Illinois. Although not members of the committee, Heber and Brigham appear to have been the principal leaders of the Saints at Far West. A little more than two weeks later, Brigham Young himself fled Missouri with his family to escape the excesses of the mob. Along with them went Heber's wife and three children. And thereafter, for a season, general leadership fell on Heber, who, because he was still relatively unknown, was left unmolested by the anti-Mormons.

The situation of the Mormons at this point was a sorry one. The Prophet, along with Sidney Rigdon, Lyman Wight, Parley Pratt, and Ebenezer Robinson, was in prison; David Patten was dead; Luke and Lyman Johnson, John Boynton, Thomas Marsh, and William McLellin had apostatized; Orson Hyde and William Smith "were suspended from exercising the functions of their office"; Orson Pratt was wavering; and Oliver Cowdery and Martin Harris, two of the Three Witnesses, had already left the church.

In the midst of all these troubles, on March 12 Heber was able to write an encouraging letter to Joseph Fielding and other church leaders in Preston, England.[10] He urged them to visit the branches of the church, exhorted them to be faithful, and assured them that he would be returning to England the following summer. He reported that most of the members, including his family, had left Missouri and that the leaders were in prison. And his incredible faith and optimism shone through, in spite of all he had experienced since returning from England, when he wrote: "I can truly say that I have never seen the Church in a better state since I have been a member of it. What there is left, they are firm and steadfast full of love and good works and have lost all that they have and now are ready to go out to preach the gospel to a dying world."

In his efforts to arrange release of the prisoners, Heber left on March 25 to present a petition to the supreme court at Jefferson City. The judges acknowledged that the imprisonment was illegal, but refused to interfere. Heber dejectedly returned to the ironically named Liberty jail to report to Joseph Smith. Climbing the outside stairs, passing through the iron-studded door set in four-foot-thick walls, Heber entered the upper level, a bare, dirty, dark, and cramped fourteen-foot-square cell. The dungeon, where the prisoners were sometimes confined, was much worse.

Here Joseph and four companions had been penned up for over four cold months. The Prophet was so discouraged he asked Heber to pray for them. They knelt. But Heber had barely started when the prison guard roughly forbade him to continue. Such pettiness reduced both Joseph and Heber to tears.[11]

On April 4, Heber visited Judge Austin A. King in Richmond, who was greatly enraged that his illegal papers had been presented to the supreme court. The prisoners remained in jail. Heber's efforts, however, may have indirectly freed Joseph, for about ten days later the prisoners received a change of venue to Boone County for trial. En route they were allowed to escape into Illinois, arriving in Quincy a week later. Since the Mormons were in full flight, these few prisoners were no longer important to Missouri officials. So intense was hatred of the Mormons that some anti-Mormons took a frightful revenge on William Bowman, the law officer who had Joseph Smith in custody at the time of his escape: he was ridden to death on a bar of iron, a lamentable fate for a man who had helped the Prophet.

Heber's work, however, was not quite done. There were still some impoverished Saints left in Missouri. Although unrecognized in October, 1838, by April, 1839, he had become well enough known so that to avoid mob harassment he was obliged to conceal himself during the day and operate at night. On April 18 he felt impelled to warn the Committee on Removal to settle their affairs and leave immediately. That same day, a mob tried to run him down in the streets of Far West and then sacked the town. Laughing like madmen, they broke clocks, chairs, windows, mirrors, and destroyed thousands of dollars worth of property. One member of the mob, finding no convenient place to fasten his horse, shot a cow and, to Heber's horror, "while the poor animal was struggling in death, he cut a strip of her hide from her nose to her tail to which he fastened his halter."[12]

For his continued and unquestioning fidelity during these terrible times, Heber was rewarded with a personal revelation on the ninth anniversary of the organization of the church. He told how the Spirit came and ordered him to write the words which came to his mind.[13] He sat down and, writing on a knee, recorded:

Far West, April 6, 1839

Verily, Verily, I say unto my servant Heber thou art my son in whom I am well pleased. . . . Thy name is written in heaven no more to be blotted out forever. . . . Thou shalt have many sons and daughters . . . for thy seed shall be a numerous as the sands upon the sea shore. . . . I will go with you and be your right hand. . . . Trouble not thyself about thy family for they are in my hands. . . . If thou wilt be faithful and go preach my gospel . . . thy tongue shall be unloosed to such a degree that has not entered into thy heart as yet and the children of men shall believe in thy words and flock to the water . . . thou shalt be great in winning souls for me for this is thy gift and calling. . . ."[14]

Heber's favor with God was confirmed; oratorical and proselytizing success was assured; and polygamy was presaged.

The Mormon experience in Missouri was ending. All that remained was for the Twelve to dedicate symbolically a temple site in Far West and then to depart for missions to the world. The specified date for this was April 26, 1839 (in accordance with Section 18 of the Doctrine and Covenants). Accordingly, Heber remained in Missouri until he was joined by members of the Council of Twelve and a few others who returned from Illinois for this purpose. On the pleasant moonlit night of April 25, Brigham Young, Orson Pratt, John E. Page, John Taylor, Wilford Woodruff, George A. Smith, and Alpheus Cutler rode into the public square shortly after midnight. They held a conference, proceeded to the temple site, sang a hymn, and laid the foundation stone of the temple on the southeast corner, where it remains to this day. They sang another hymn, prayed, and turned again toward Illinois.

NOTES

1. H. C. Kimball, Journal 94c, 84 of the section titled "History of Heber Chase Kimball by his own dictation," Church Archives.

2. *Journal of Discourses*, vol. 4 (Sept. 28, 1856), 108.

3. *Times and Seasons*, June 15, 1839.

4. *Document Containing the Correspondence, Order, &c, in Relation to the Disturbances with the Mormons* . . . (Fayette, Mo.: Published by order of the General Assembly, 1841), 61. Only during July, 1976, did Missouri officials remove this order from the books.

5. H. M. Whitney, *Woman's Exponent*, vol. 8 (May 5, 1880), 189.

6. H. C. Kimball, Journal 94b, Nov. 1, 1838, Church Archives.

7. Emma Smith to Joseph Smith, Mar. 7, 1839, Joseph Smith Collection, Church Archives.

8. See below, p. 113–14.

9. Joseph Smith to H. C. Kimball and B. Young, Jan. 16, 1839, Winslow Whitney Smith Papers, Church Archives.

10. H. C. Kimball to Joseph Fielding, Mar. 12, 1839. Original in possession of J. Leroy Kimball. Used by permission.

11. Minutes, Nov. 2, 1845, Thomas Bullock Collection, Church Archives.

12. H. C. Kimball, Journal 94c, 101, Church Archives.

13. *Ibid.*, 99.

14. There are two copies of this revelation. One is recorded in Journal 91 on (unnumbered) p. 50, following some Feb., 1841, entries in England, and is not in Kimball's hand. The other copy is Journal 94b in the back, and is in Kimball's own handwriting. He may have originally written the revelation in his own hand and later, for some reason, it may have been copied by one of his wives, children, or clerks.

CHAPTER 6

A Brief Sojourn in Nauvoo

In Illinois the Mormons reached social as well as doctrinal maturity and became a people—a complete social order, not just another faith. During the Illinois period Mormonism was more widely discussed in the public press than any other religion; certainly no other religious leader was as well known as Joseph Smith; and no city was more talked about than the Mormon headquarters, Nauvoo. During this period missionary work was enormously expanded and thousands were converted. Many of the Twelve Apostles went to England to enlarge that Old World beachhead which had been started by Heber in 1837, and nearly every state east of the Mississippi and parts of Canada was visited by other missionaries. Also, in Illinois the ever-expanding citadel of Mormon theology was enlarged. Several of its most esoteric doctrines, such as polygamy and temple ordinances, were here first enunciated and practiced, attracting both attention and condemnation.

The Illinois period of church history lasted nearly seven years, and for more than half of this time Heber was away. During this period he would go on four more missions, for a total of eight (including a second one to England), build three homes, receive a patriarchal blessing and a phrenological reading, help organize five Masonic lodges, enter into polygamy, help build and officiate in the Nauvoo Temple, contribute to the official history of the church, and aid in the preparation of the Saints for the exodus west.

On May 2, 1839, Heber found his family in Quincy in good health: they had been treated with kindness. For seven weeks after leaving Missouri, they had roomed with the wife of Colonel William Ross in Atlas,[1] a member of the Illinois General Assembly and a friend of Lincoln. (It is possible that Lincoln's later tolerance of the Mormons may have resulted, in part, from the stories of Missouri persecution he may have heard from the

Ross family.) Later, John P. Greene, Brigham Young's brother-in-law, moved Vilate and her children into a rented room in Quincy, where the refugees were generally made welcome by a people both sympathetic with their plight and sorely in need of settlers and tax dollars.

The next day the Apostles conferred with Joseph Smith about the condition of the church. On May 4 a general conference was held to discuss the future home of the Saints and to consider the proposition that the new gathering place be Commerce, Illinois, located about fifty miles north of Quincy on the Mississippi. This proposed gathering place was an extensive and fertile floodplain on a beautiful bend of the river surrounded by high bluffs. Its chief drawback was that it was marshy. Commerce, on part of a 3.5-million-acre military tract which had been originally set aside for land bounties to veterans of the War of 1812, was owned by an eastern land speculator, Isaac Galland, who made the exiled Mormons an attractive offer. After due consideration, the site was purchased, and on May 10 Joseph moved his family there.

On May 12, Heber and others of the Council of the Twelve joined Joseph in Commerce, later renamed Nauvoo, a unique place name which came out of the Hebrew class taught earlier in Kirtland during the winter of 1836. Joseph Smith had learned two Hebrew words—*nawaw* and *nawvaw* (or *nawveh*), both meaning attractive, pleasant, suitable, beautiful, a pasture, a place for rest and beauty, like the "green pastures" of the Twenty-third Psalm. Three years later in Illinois, standing on the bluffs above Commerce, Joseph was impressed with the charm of that particular bend in the Mississippi and was moved to give his future city a beautiful and unusual name.

Before Heber ever saw the new gathering place, however, he knew his first stay there would not be long, for he had been expecting to return to England for nearly a year. Unsettled conditions in Ohio and Missouri had prevented this return, but after spending four months resettling his family in peaceful Illinois, he would leave again for England.

Not only did he realize his first stay in Illinois would be of short duration, but he seemed to know that the whole Nauvoo period would not last long. On May 25, during deliberations with Galland, who also had quasi title to much land in Iowa, Heber accompanied Joseph Smith and others across the river to Montrose, Lee County, Iowa—just opposite Nauvoo. Standing by the boat's railing, enjoying an untroubled Illinois spring after a tragic Missouri winter and admiring Nauvoo's beautiful site, Heber remarked disconcertingly, "It is a very pretty place, but not a long abiding place for the Saints." Sidney Rigdon, stern, humorless, and possessed of a good stone home, was highly offended. He retorted, "I should suppose that Elder Kimball had passed through sufferings and privations and mobbings and drivings enough to learn to prophesy good concerning Israel."

Heber, who knew Rigdon's temperament and expected chastisement, then demonstrated another saving grace, one for which he became greatly loved in the church—a sense of humor. He quickly agreed with Rigdon, then slyly added, "President Rigdon, I'll prophesy good concerning you all the time if you can get it!"[2] Joseph laughed and Rigdon yielded the point.

Soon thereafter, Heber moved Vilate and their three children, William, Helen, and Heber Parley, from Quincy into a log shack which he had thrown together out of an old stable belonging to a "Brother Bozier" (possibly Bozarth, a pre-Mormon settler), who lived about a mile from Commerce.

It is difficult to imagine Heber's state of mind during his first few months in Nauvoo. The Ohio and Missouri trials had cost him his property and money, his wife was advanced in pregnancy, his family was living in a miserable hut, and he was supposed to be getting ready to leave on a second mission to England, over 6,000 miles away. Also, the swampy river bottoms were causing much sickness, including a form of cholera and "the ague," a debilitating disease of alternating chills and fever (probably typhoid or malaria) which could hang on for weeks or months and cause delirium. When Heber was not ill himself, he was often tending to the needs of his family and others who were. His *materia medica* would have been limited, however. He probably administered Sappington's pills (a compound of quinine), or perhaps the popular and all-purpose "cobweb" pill, and various brews made from the inside bark of fir balsam and yellow birch, from white ash bark, or from a mixture of sassafras and mullen roots.

As quickly as possible he tried to provide better housing for his family. Acquiring five acres of land about a mile from the river facing Munson Street between Fulmer and Cordon streets (just east of present-day Nauvoo State Park), he erected a fourteen-by-sixteen-foot log cabin. But he had not finished it by August 13, when in the Bozier shack Vilate gave birth to a new son named David Patten (spelled Patton by the Kimballs), after their great friend who had fallen in Missouri.

About two weeks later, Heber moved his family into their new home and prepared to leave for England. On September 14, Brigham Young, who was then living in the abandoned Fort Des Moines across the river in Montrose, left his sick wife with a ten-day-old infant to join Heber for England. But Young was so sick himself that he collapsed at the Kimballs. Heber, also ill, now had Brigham Young, in addition to his own sick wife and children, to care for. On September 17 Mary Ann Young came over to try to help. Four adults and several children, all sick in a small log cabin— that was the preface to Heber's second mission to England. On the next day, he and Brigham left in a wagon.

The circumstances of their departure were appalling and heartbreaking. With the exception of one child, no one was well enough even to see the missionaries to the door. Four-year-old Heber Parley could just manage to carry cups of water to the sick. Helen did not even have shoes, and all the money Heber could leave Vilate was nine dollars, which she had to spend the next day to pay a debt.[3]

As Heber drove off, he felt as though his "very inmost parts would melt" at the thought of leaving his family in such circumstances. He could not endure such a leave-taking. Asking the teamster to hold up, he said to Brigham, "This is pretty tough, but let's rise, and give them a cheer." They did so, swinging their hats three times over their heads and chanting, "Hurrah, hurrah, hurrah for Israel!" Vilate, hearing the noise, managed to get to the door and call out, "Good bye; God bless you!" Seeing her once more on her feet filled Heber with a spirit of joy and gratitude.[4]

The first part of the journey, from Nauvoo to New York, was an adventure in itself. Friends and relatives carried the missionaries in wagons by way of Lima, Quincy; and Pittsfield to Winchester, Illinois, to the home of Heber's father-in-law, Roswell Murray. Murray, who wished to visit his old home, joined them. Near Winchester they picked up the old Zion's Camp route and followed it generally back to Kirtland.

By the time they reached Terre Haute, Indiana, Heber was so sick it became necessary for him to seek medical help. Unfortunately the doctor he visited was drunk, and he carelessly gave him a tablespoon of morphine, which could have been lethal. Heber soon felt very strange and fell to the floor. When he came to, he found Brigham anxiously watching over him. "Don't be scared," Heber assured him, "I shan't die." Because he vomited frequently and was continuously in a cold sweat, his body eliminated the drug. Brigham attended him constantly, washing him and changing his underclothing five times that long night. Although he was better by morning, his father-in-law did not expect him to survive. Heber told the others to go on, that he and Brigham would still reach Kirtland before them.

This part of the trip was occasion for another minor miracle. At Pleasant Grove, Indiana, the two missionaries had noted they had only $13.50 between them. Arriving November 3 in Kirtland (before his companions, as predicted), Heber was amazed to reckon they had paid out over $87. "We had," he calculated, "traveled over four hundred miles by stage, for which we paid from eight to ten cents a mile, and had taken three meals a day, for each of which we were charged fifty cents, also fifty cents for our lodgings. Brother Brigham often suspected that I put the money in his trunk of clothes, thinking that I had a purse of money which I had not acquainted him with; but this was not so; the money could only have been put in his trunk by some heavenly messenger, who thus administered to our necessities daily as he knew we needed." [5]

Walking through the neglected and nearly deserted streets, Heber found Kirtland a desolate-looking place; about half the houses were empty and falling into ruin, and the town was still full of the same spirit of apostasy and dissension that had earlier driven the Saints to Missouri. "I am disappointed," he reported in one letter to Vilate, "in what I expected to find here. I anticipated meeting the Brethren united and enjoying the blessings of the people of God, but to my sorrow, I found them all broken up and divided into several different parties. . . ." [6]

Other letters reveal the surprising fact that Vilate wanted to leave frontier Nauvoo and return to more settled Kirtland or Victor. "As for going to Kirtland to live as things are now it is against my will," Heber responded, "for I had rather live in a cave or be driven with the Saints every other year while I live and be one than to have all the good things of the Earth and be at variance one with the other as they are there, for you can't find two that agree." [7] Again he emphasized, "I don't want to settle in the East now . . . I don't want to settle in the East without times change." [8]

As a counterproposal, he urged Vilate to come east for a visit, go to Victor the next summer, and stay with friends and relatives until he returned from England. Then, in a manner suggesting that there might have been some stigma attached to those leaving Nauvoo for personal reasons, he wrote, "I think no one will have any objections of your visiting your friends." [9] The actions of the Apostle's wife were obviously of public interest. Had Heber agreed to leave Nauvoo and return east he would have appeared disloyal and most likely would have forfeited his apostleship. That Vilate must have realized this but still wanted to leave is surely an indication of the degree of hardship she was facing.

Following three weeks in Kirtland, Heber spent the next six in western New York, visiting and preaching to relatives in Byron, Pike, Rochester, Mendon, and Victor. All were happy to see him, most were sympathetic to what he had suffered since he left Mendon, some offered to help if he would forsake Mormonism, but only Vilate's brother, William E. Murray, and his wife (and perhaps their two children, Carlos and Jenette) accepted baptism at his hands.

Heber left Mendon on January 10, 1840, arriving in New York City about a week later—nearly five months after leaving Nauvoo. There Heber and his fellows did some proselytizing, strengthened the branch of about 200, and gathered a supply of potatoes, dried codfish, apples, plums, pork, beef, butter, bread, pickles, horseradish, salt, sugar, crackers, and mustard for the voyage. On March 9, Heber, Brigham Young, Orson Pratt, Parley Pratt, George A. Smith, and Reuben Hedlock went again to Packet Row on the East River and boarded the *Patrick Henry* of the Black Ball Line, on which they had booked second cabin. They stored their provisions and bedding, hired a cook for a dollar a day to prepare meals for them, and made themselves as comfortable as possible for the twenty-eight-day crossing, which, though it included sixteen days of storms, was otherwise uneventful.

NOTES

1. The Ross home was located east of the road about 100 yards north of the intersection of roads 54 and 96 in Atlas. Brigham Young probably stayed in the storehouse still standing on the northwest corner of this same intersection.

2. H. C. Kimball, Journal 94c, 104, Church Archives.

3. Vilate's obituary, *Deseret News*, Dec. 25, 1867.

4. H. C. Kimball, Journal 94c, 111, Church Archives.

5. *Ibid.*, 114–15.

6. H. C. Kimball to Vilate Kimball, Nov. 16, 1839, H. C. Kimball Papers, Church Archives.

7. H. C. Kimball to Vilate Kimball, Dec. 27, 1839. Original in possession of J. Leroy Kimball. Used by permission.

8. H. C. Kimball to Vilate Kimball, Mar. 5, 1840, H. C. Kimball Papers, Church Archives.

9. *Ibid.*

CHAPTER 7

Second Mission to England

The missionaries landed at Liverpool on April 6, 1840, the tenth anniversary of the organization of the church. Three days later they were in Preston—two years to the day since Heber had left England. During the interim, between 800 and 900 new members had been baptized, Scotland had been opened up to missionary work, and Manchester had come to rival Preston as church headquarters.

A general conference was quickly convened in Preston for April 14–16. Back again in the familiar Cock Pit, Heber conducted, and eight of the Quorum of the Twelve were in attendance—Brigham Young, Heber Kimball, Parley P. Pratt, Orson Pratt, Wilford Woodruff, John Taylor, George A. Smith, and Willard Richards—the largest number ever, before or since, assembled outside the United States, a fact that suggests the importance Joseph Smith placed on the British mission. Over 500 members attended, representing thirty-four branches and a total of 1,850 members. At this conference the British mission, until then a loose organization of individuals and branches, was formally institutionalized. Brigham Young was sustained formally as the President of the Quorum of the Twelve, and new missionary assignments were made; Heber Kimball, Brigham Young, and Parley Pratt were appointed as a publishing committee, and another conference was set for July 6 in Manchester. Thereafter the leaders scattered to Scotland, Liverpool, Manchester, Staffordshire, and Herfordshire.

Heber's assignment was to visit all the branches he had previously organized on his first mission. He found to his satisfaction that many had remained faithful and welcomed his return. After this tour he went to Manchester, the new center of church activities. There he helped with the publication of the *Millennial Star* (the first Mormon periodical in the Old World), the Book of Mormon, and some hymnals.

By the time Heber reached Manchester, he was aware that economic conditions had not improved since his first mission; rather, the depression and the plight of the poor had worsened. So bad, in fact, was the economic situation that the government was recommending migration, and the laboring classes were demanding political and economic reforms through the Chartist movement. Heber wrote Joseph Smith:

> With regard to the state of the country we may say it is bad indeed: trade appears to be growing worse, in fact, many branches of it is almost at a stand, and not expected much to improve for some months. Thousands are out of employ, and we may safely say that there are thousands famishing for want of bread: we often see in the streets whole families begging for bread; and in many instances some respectable looking characters may be seen singing through the streets to obtain a little bread; it is truly heart rending to see so many small children nearly naked, going from house to house begging. This scene of things is passing before our eyes daily, and we look upon it with sorrow and regret.[1]

As in 1837, the want and dilemma of the English people did not preclude their interest in the missionaries' message of hope and dignity. The July conference in Carpenters Hall in Manchester recorded 2,513 members in eighty branches—an increase of 842 members since April. To help with the work, fifteen local Elders were called as missionaries, another conference was scheduled, and a decision was made to take the message of the Restoration to the capital of the Empire—London.

Accordingly, on August 4, Heber, with Wilford Woodruff and George A. Smith, slowly made his way there by rail, visiting branches along the way at Barslem, West Bromwich, Birmingham, Ledbury, Dymock, Surry, Hull, Leigh, and Chattenham, on August 18 arriving at the Great Western Railway Station (now Paddington). Heber viewed London as Paul had Rome—"The Metropolis of England, the pride and glory of Britain, the boast of the Gentiles and the largest commercial city in the world . . . ripening in iniquity and preparing for the wrath of God"[2]—and he felt he must "bear witness" there.

On that day the *Times* was full of news about the visit of the king and queen of the Belgians, Parliament, the Irish question, the opening of the grouse season, the opera and theatre, some sensational murders, and many bankruptcies. During Heber's stay in London this newspaper took no notice of the Mormons there, but did print four brief notices about this "new sect" in Lancashire, Yorkshire, and on the Isle of Man.

Heber and his companions took a coach for four miles through the city, passing Hyde Park, then along the great commercial thoroughfare of Oxford Street, through Oxford Circus, down High Holborn Street, and past the Bank of England and the Royal Exchange to London Bridge.

Looking east from the bridge, they could see the famous gray stone battlements of the Norman fortress known as the Tower of London. To the northwest was the vast panorama of the Caput Regni dominated by St. Paul's. Straight ahead to the south lay the borough of Southark, where they called on a Mrs. William Allgood at 19 King (now Newcomen) Street, not far from where the famous Globe Theatre of Shakespeare's day stood. Mrs. Allgood, sister-in-law of Theodore Turley, one of Heber's companions, suggested they take lodging across the street in the King's Arms Inn until she could find them accommodations with a family.

For a few days they did extensive sightseeing, which they felt was perfectly consistent with their calling, and necessary in the overall task of building the Kingdom. They visited various Christopher Wren monuments, the Tower of London, the Bank of England, St. Paul's, Westminster Abbey, the Houses of Parliament, the Guildhall, St. James Park, the British Museum, St. Catherine's Dock, and the London Dock. An enormous wine vault especially impressed Heber. It covered nine acres and contained 40,000 pipes of wine and 30,000 of port. "We traversed every part of it," he later related, "each one carried a lamp in their hand: we tasted the wine, having an order granting us that liberty."[3]

Afterward they attended services in a synagogue. Although he had essayed Hebrew, this was apparently Heber's first meaningful experience with the Jewish religion. At the door they were requested to put on their hats. Inside, Heber was so impressed with the "beauty and splendor thereof" that he reverently removed his hat, only to be asked to replace it.

During the service he was unusually solemn. "I looked upon those sons of illustrious sires," he recorded, "with mingled emotions of joy and sorrow for the unparalleled cruelties which had been inflicted on their Nation, and joy that the day of their redemption was near."[4] A cardinal belief in Mormonism is that the Jews will eventually be gathered and "redeemed." Mormons also consider themselves to be cousins to the Jews. According to Mormon doctrine, modern Jews are descended from the Tribe of Judah of the House of Israel, and most Mormons consider themselves to be of the Tribe of Ephraim, one of the "Lost Ten Tribes" of the same house.

Heber may have been more than ordinarily interested in the Jews and the "gathering," for Apostle Orson Hyde had already passed through London on his way to Palestine by order of Joseph Smith to dedicate that land, then under Turkish misrule, to the return of the Jews—an act which ever afterward caused most Mormons to be sympathetic with Zionism.

On a January 26 ramble through London, Heber and his companions were among the several hundred thousand who saw Queen Victoria and her retinue pass St. James Park en route to the House of Lords to open Parliament, but he was too much of an egalitarian Yankee to be much impressed. "We stood within eight or nine feet of her when she passed and returned. She made her obeisance to us, and we returned it. She is a pleasant little body," he grumped, "but what a fuss there is over one little girl."[5] What a "stur thare is made over a little queen; at the same time thousands are starving to death for a little bread."[6] He did see to it later, however, that Victoria and Albert received specially bound copies of the Book of Mormon.

The missionaries began to preach in open-air meetings, to call on ministers, and to visit chapels. Among those called upon were the followers of Joanna Southcott (who had declared she would be the mother of Shiloh, a second messiah), various temperance societies, and the Reverend Robert Aitken himself. Heber found the followers of Southcott divided, the temperance societies friendly, and Aitken still smarting over his loss to the Mormons in Preston and Liverpool. "His people Seam to be Ripe here," he noted in his journal, "but we have now [no] way to bare our testimony to them as yet. He is a Smart man and tells what is going to befall the nations, but he himself does not know what to do, but ses all the Sex [sects] of the day are going down to Hell." They preached with little success in Tabernacle Square in Old Street and held services in Barrett's Academy on King's Square off Goswell Road. In general, London was obdurate and uninterested. "Thare has been so menny fals things Risen in this city," Heber explained, "the peoples Eyes are blinded against the truth. The Sex [sects] Seam to bee in a dredful State at present here as we have tended thare meetings in the Evning to see if thare is no place for us to Brack [break] in. All does Seam to be closed at present."[7]

Typically, he was not disheartened: "You may think I feel discouraged my dear Vilate. I will Say unto you: I never have Seen the first moment as yet, fore I dow not see anything to discourage me . . . I know that I am built on the foundation of Jesus Christ. . . ."[8]

The missionaries finally baptized a convert on August 31, but by the October conference in Manchester they had raised up a branch of only eleven members—not much, but ten years later there would be more than 3,000 Mormons in London, not counting those who had emigrated. Elsewhere in England, Scotland, Ireland, Wales, and on the Isle of Man the work had been progressing much better. A total of 3,626 members, for an increase of 1,113 (or 70 percent) in the preceding three months, was reported at the conference.

Following the Manchester conference, Heber and Wilford Woodruff returned to London, arriving there November 30. Taking Lodgings at 40

Ironmongers Row, St. Luke's Parish, they recommenced their work. A typical entry from Heber's journal for this period reads: "December the 20, 1840 being the Sabbath Day Mr. [James] Alburn a preacher of the Independent order cald on Elder Woodruff and myself to go with him to his chappel. After the fore noon Service Mr. Alburn gave out for us to preach in his chappel next Sunday Evening. On the Evening of 21 tended a place called the Consert [conservatory] of Musick of all kinds of instruments composed of French [and] Germans mostly. . . ." [9]

In his last letter home of the year 1840 Heber told of sightseeing, difficulties, and activities, and then made the earliest known reference to his oft-repeated metaphor of the clay and the potter. "I have got so I feel perfectly easy about these things," he assured Vilate, "for they are the work of God and not the work of man. I know no other way than to be subject to the powers that be. I pray my Father will give me this disposition, for I wish to be in the hands of God as the clay in the hands of the potter." [10]

The well known successes of these early Elders, recounted extensively in Mormon history, should be supplemented with the story of the hardships of the wives and children left behind in Nauvoo. With their husbands away so long and so often on missions, some Mormon women were more like widows than wives. The letters of Vilate and Helen to Heber reveal something of the life back home. The family continued to suffer with the ague. "All I can ask of you," Vilate wrote, "is to pray that I may have patience to endure to the end whether it is long or short." [11] She still wanted to leave Illinois and return to the amenities of Kirtland, but Heber remained adamant. "Do not be disheartened," he wrote. "I think I could communicate better with you if you should stay there than I could in Kirtland, for there will be saints coming through most of the time." [12]

During the spring, Vilate chided her husband for not writing, and he answered with uncharacteristic sharpness: "You thought I had forgotten my family; you have been quite out of your head for I have remembered you in all of my prairs. I think it is the other way . . . you have tried to palm things on me that you are gu[i]lty of your Self." [13]

In June, Vilate expected to get a cow; she had a pig, and plenty of potatoes, turnips, and other garden produce. "I hope I shall not have to call on the Bishop again while you are gone. . . ," she wrote. "I am glad Brother Brigham has sent some assistance to his family for they were needy. Their house could hardly be called a shelter. They will soon have it fixed nice. Elizabeth and Vilate [Young] are both sick with the chills, however, the rest of the families of brethren are well as far as I know." In October she reported that his missionary journal of 1837 would soon be printed.[14]

In a letter of December 8, Vilate started out cheerfully and sympathetically enough. She had enjoyed visiting with some recent converts who had just arrived in Nauvoo, but was pained that Heber was still in a land of strangers, with no one to administer him comfort. She then shared a recent sorrow: her father, who had accompanied Heber back east, had just died in Victor. "The last news that I had from father before," she reported, "he was well, and calculated to set out on his journey for this place the first of October, and had for some time daily been anticipating his arrival here, but alas! how are my fond anticipations blasted? and my joy is turned to mourning." She then added a lament she had written to express her grief. Her effort at poetry relates her trials in the context of her underlying faith in God:

> My husband's gone, my Father's dead,
> But my ever living head;
> Always hears my souls complaint
> And ever comforts me when faint.
>
> If I could fly to you I would,
> But the Lord is very good;
> He will care for him that's dead
> And you who from your family's fled.
>
> I, here with four children dear,
> But I know I need not fear;
> For the Lord is always nigh,
> And will all my wants supply.
>
> O Lord it is my souls desire
> That thou would my heart inspire
> With a fore knowledge of thy will,
> That I may all thy law fulfill.

Vilate was also having financial difficulties. "It costs a great deal to support your family," she reminded him; "we are continually on expence, and not earning a cent. There was rising of thirty dollars due this fall on our land, but I pled off for the present by paying fifteen dollars; I told [Hiram] Kimball[15] I would pay him the rest in the spring, or before if I could." She hoped Heber would soon come home. "The children are all impatient to have you come; you are loosing all the most interesting part of David's life, a child is never so pretty as when they first begin to walk and talk. He goes prattleing about the house, and you may be assured that we think he is cunning. Elizabeth [Young] calls him Heber altogether, and every one that sees him says that ought to be his name, he looks so much like you." [16]

Years later, Helen Kimball offered a few more glimpses of life back home at that time. Since Nauvoo had no chapels, several families held Sabbath meetings in the Kimball home; the spinsters Laura and Abigail Pitkin came from Quincy to live with Vilate; and Helen and William attended school during the winter. Helen and William received gifts from their father, copies of the new British edition of the Book of Mormon with their names printed thereon in gold letters. Helen also got handkerchiefs, little china dishes, and dolls. Once when Joseph Smith called by her home (to read a letter from Heber) he accidentally broke one of these dolls. According to Helen all the Prophet said, by way of excusing himself, was "As that has fallen, so shall the heathen gods fall." She thought this a "rather weak apology for breaking her doll's head off." Helen also told of the dread cholera and remembered that to keep the Saints from drinking unboiled water, Joseph advised tea and coffee, giving the Saints an excuse to backslide and no longer keep the Word of Wisdom (the stringent Mormon standard of health) so strictly as before. [17]

The grim circumstances of sickness were lightened somewhat by the childish games Helen and her brothers played to cheat the "old gentleman," that is, the ague. Sometimes when they began to feel the chills come upon them, they would run toward the bed as if to get on it, but suddenly dart under the bed, "thus cheating the old gentleman, who would go as usual on to bed." Once Helen hit her head so hard on the bed that she felt neither chills nor fever for three weeks, "but whether it was due to the blow on my head or my faith in the trick" she could never quite decide. [18]

During this time Vilate was cheered by the report that one of the Three Nephites had told Joseph that the work in England would be "short and powerful." [19] Tales of the Three Nephites abound in Mormondom to the present day; their origin is a Book of Mormon story that during Christ's short ministry in the New World, three of his Nephite disciples requested and received permission to tarry on the earth and do good until the Second Coming. Almost every Mormon community cherishes at least one experience with one of the Three Nephites, who suddenly appears to help in some hour of need and then mysteriously disappears.

Back in London, Heber's mission was drawing to a close. On February 8, 1841, he secured the British copyright to the Book of Mormon.

Going to Stationer's Hall in the shadow of St. Paul's, he deposited five copies of the book and paid the clerk three shillings. In the old hall's vaults, the "Entry of Copyright Ledger" records briefly the application for the copyright of the "First European Edition from the Second American Edition."

A week later, on February 14, the missionaries held the first conference of the London District. Four branches in London, Bedford, Ipswich, and Woolrich reported only 106 members. The London mission had not been very successful, but it was time to leave. After a quick visit to the famous dissecting room at Barts (St. Bartholomew Hospital, which was made even more famous for Sir Arthur Conan Doyle having had Dr. John Watson first meet Sherlock Holmes there in 1881), Heber placed Lorenzo Snow in charge and with Wilford Woodruff left to attend the April conference in Manchester and then return to Nauvoo. The conference reported 5,814 members, besides about 800 who had emigrated to the United States.

One contemporary summary of this mission reports that the missionaries had "baptized between seven and eight thousand and established branches in almost every noted town and city, printed 5,000 copies of the Book of Mormon, 3,000 hymnals, 50,000 tracts, 2,500 copies of the *Millennial Star*, established a permanent shipping agency, and arranged for the emigration of about 1,000 saints to Zion."[20] The Old World beachhead had been made secure. For decades thousands of British converts would immigrate to Illinois and the Great Basin. Of his own missionary prowess Heber later modestly said, "The Elders now have to labor a great deal harder to bring people into the Church than they did in the rise of it. There is not now one man brought to the knowledge of the truth by receiving the Gospel to where there was a hundred thirty years ago."[21]

Many of these early converts of the period 1837 to 1841 remained humble and steadfast in the faith and immigrated to the United States. Of those that stayed in England some also remained faithful, but many left the church. Part of the explanation for the high recidivism was the fact that many of the early converts were baptized immediately after hearing one or two sermons and received very little follow-up instruction. Many also fell away after the public admission of plural marriage in 1852. Many years later in Utah, Heber mentioned publicly how few of his early converts had remained true to the faith. "I do not believe," he declared, "of all the Branches of this church that were raised up twenty-five years ago, that there is one man out of twenty who now stands firm and is living. Of the two thousand whom I and my brethren baptized, when we first went to old England, I do not believe there are five hundred now in the Church."[22]

Others remained steadfast but not very humble. Of them, a later missionary George Q. Cannon wrote to Heber from Liverpool in 1863:

> There are many Branches of the Church which contain members who have held standing there from the time the Gospel was first preached here until the present. They have seen and heard yourself and others of the first missionaries to this county preach and what they think they don't know would scarcely be worth learning. There are some who seem to act as though they thought it was sufficient glory for them for one lifetime to have seen and heard Brother Brigham and yourself preach. . . . In the Branches where there are numbers of these old members, the Elders are apt to have more or less difficulty; for such persons imagine that they ought to be treated as full grown men in the Gospel of Jesus when in reality they are but babes.[23]

The Manchester conference closed the mission of the Twelve in England. On April 29, Heber and six other of the Twelve left Liverpool with a company of 130 emigrants aboard the *Rochester*. This company was the eighth to leave England since forty-one converts sailed June 6, 1840, on the *Britannia*. By April, 1841, Mormon emigrant routine and discipline had evolved and it was common knowledge among seamen that the Mormon groups were the most orderly and sanitary of all. Aboard ship the Mormons kept together, selected their own leaders, made their own regulations, set their own night watches, and insisted on saintly conduct. Rising, prayer, meals, cleaning, worship services, and retiring were at set times. During the days and evenings cultural and educational activities such as singing, study classes, and lectures were also arranged.

This crossing—Heber's fourth and last—was rough. The sea ran high, sails were frequently reefed, and they often shipped water. Once he and some other Elders had to help secure forty tons of baggage which threatened to break loose. There was much sickness, and one child was buried at sea. Thirty days later they landed in New York City, and by July 1 were back in Nauvoo.

NOTES

1. *Times and Seasons*, July 7, 1840.
2. H. C. Kimball to E. Robinson and D. C. Smith, Oct. 12, 1840, *ibid.*, Dec. 15, 1840.
3. *Ibid.*, Aug. 16, 1841.
4. *Ibid.*

5. *President Heber C. Kimball's Journal* (Salt Lake City: Juvenile Instructor's Office, 1882), 103.

6. H. C. Kimball to Vilate Kimball, Sept. 19, 1840, H. C. Kimball Papers, Church Archives.

7. H. C. Kimball to "Brother Robinson," Aug. 21, 1840. Original in possession of J. Leroy Kimball. Used by permission.

8. H. C. Kimball to Vilate Kimball, Sept. 19, 1840, H. C. Kimball Papers, Church Archives.

9. H. C. Kimball, Journal 91, Dec. 20, 1840, Church Archives. Alburn (Albion) and some of his congregation later joined the Mormons.

10. O. F. Whitney, *Life of Heber C. Kimball*, 298–301.

11. Vilate Kimball to H. C. Kimball, Sept. 21, 1836, H. C. Kimball Papers, Church Archives.

12. H. C. Kimball to Vilate Kimball, Sept. 21, 1839, H. C. Kimball Papers, Church Archives.

13. H. C. Kimball to Vilate Kimball, May 27, 1840. Original in possession of J. Leroy Kimball. Used by permission.

14. Vilate Kimball to H. C. Kimball, June 6 and Oct. 11, 1840, H. C. Kimball Papers, Church Archives. This is a reference to what was published as *Journal of Heber C. Kimball* . . . (Nauvoo, 1840)—a 60-page booklet printed by R. B. Thompson. Of the origin of this booklet we know only the following: in what is known as Journal 94b (a dictated account of Kimball's life to about 1840), p. 79, we find, "I here insert a copy of a pamphlet published by Robert B. Thompson while I was on my second mission to England; he and I went into the woods near the city of Quincy on a high hill, where we sat down and I gave him a short schedule of my first mission to England from memory, not having my journal in my possession. I omitted many dates in the copy which I here insert. I fill up the dates more particularly and also make corrections and additions."
This revised version has never been published (although Whitney copied extensive sections of it), and when Kimball's *Journal* was reprinted in the Faith Promoting Series in 1880, this revised manuscript was ignored.
The original journal which Kimball did not have with him in Quincy is known as Journal 90, and the portion written on his first English mission is only 39 pages long.

15. Three brothers, Hiram, Ethan, and Phineas Kimball, were pre-Mormon land speculators from Vermont living in Nauvoo. They were cousins of Heber. Only Hiram joined the church and went west.

16. Vilate Kimball to H. C. Kimball, Dec. 8, 1840. Original in possession of J. Leroy Kimball. Used by permission. She also told Heber that his English missionary journal of 1837, the first book to issue from the Mormon press in Nauvoo, had just been printed (see n. 14 above).

17. H. M. Whitney, *Woman's Exponent*, vol. 10 (July 15, 1881), 26, vol. 10 (Aug. 1, 1881), 24. See n. 5, chap. 17.

18. *Ibid.*, 26.

19. *Ibid.*, vol. 10 (Feb. 15, 1882), 138.

20. Elden Jay Watson, ed., *Manuscript History of Brigham Young: 1801–1844* (Salt Lake City: Elden Jay Watson, 1968), 97.

21. *Journal of Discourses*, vol. 10 (July 19, 1863), 240.

22. *Ibid.*, vol. 5 (Sept. 27, 1857), 275. Heber never mentioned working as a missionary outside Lancashire and London. There is some evidence that he did some preaching in Wales too. In a letter to his wife, Mary Ann, on Nov. 12, 1840, Brigham Young wrote, "We have hered from Wales whare Br Kimball and I went, a grate meny of the people was sorry they did not obey the gospel when we ware there. . . ." Blair Collection, University of Utah. I would like to thank Ronald Esplin for drawing this to my attention.

23. George Q. Cannon to H. C. Kimball, Jan. 10, 1863. Original in possession of Spencer W. Kimball. Used by permission. (Copies of all the Kimball materials in possession of Spencer W. Kimball are as of 1980 in the Church Archives.)

CHAPTER 8

New Experiences at Nauvoo

Stepping off the riverboat at Nauvoo, Heber found his sixteen-year-old son, William, waiting for him and anxious to escort his father home. But Joseph Smith was also there with other plans for the returning missionaries. Strangely ignoring their desires to meet first with their families, he insisted on taking them to his home for a dinner in their honor. It was, understandably, a hurried affair, and as quickly as possible Heber, accompanied by a few others, headed for home. At the sight of a company of horsemen bearing down on her, Vilate hid behind the cabin door to hide her confusion. Moments later Heber found her there overwhelmed in tears, which he kissed away as he tried to obliterate their twenty-two-month separation.

Heber's first desire at home in 1841 was to provide his family with a more suitable home. At the suggestion of Joseph, who wanted Heber living closer to him, he exchanged his property on high ground for corner lot 3 in block 6 on the flats closer to the river. There he built a log house of three lower rooms and one upstairs. To this log portion he later added one brick room. Still later he removed the log portion and replaced it with the two-story brick structure which is still standing and which has been restored close to its original state.

Not only did Joseph want Heber living closer to him, he wanted him and other Apostles to take over a large share of day-to-day administration. This was the beginning, as Leonard J. Arrington and Ronald K. Esplin have somewhere noted, of the development in 1835 of the Quorum of the Twelve from a rather loosely organized group without specifically assigned roles to their grooming by the Prophet to assume administrative duties. For this purpose he kept the Twelve in council to such an extent that Helen noted, "Brother Joseph seemed unwilling to part with my father . . . and she [Vilate] felt nearly jealous of him. . . ."[1]

For a season now Heber had no further missionary assignments. His new callings included the settling of emigrants, especially those from England, and the distribution of church lands. (Nauvoo was growing fast. When Heber left on his second British mission there were not even thirty buildings in the community; when he returned he found 1,200 finished, many others under construction, and new converts coming in from various places.) Heber also became a chaplain with the rank of colonel of infantry in the Nauvoo Legion, a member of the city council, and a member of the board of regents of the nascent University of the City of Nauvoo.

Almost since his arrival in Kirtland in 1833, Heber had been working full time for the church. His brick home in Nauvoo was built for him by the church, or at least by church members, and he occasionally received money and provisions from the church and generous Saints. There is evidence that he did some work as a potter in Nauvoo, and it is clear that he also bought and sold building sites from which he may have derived additional income. Apparently he continued to support himself as well as he could, and the difference was made up out of general church funds.

The rest of the winter passed quietly away, with Heber tending to many of the temporal affairs of Kingdom-building, and the spring of 1842 was full of strange and wonderful events. On March 9 he received his patriarchial blessing from Joseph's brother Hyrum. Such blessings, derived from Jacob's blessing of his twelve sons (Genesis 49), are believed to be inspired statements regarding the life mission of the recipient and are given by specially appointed patriarchs. Hyrum, laying hands on Heber's head, promised him, "You shall be blessed with a fulness and shall not be one whit behind the chiefest; as an Apostle you shall stand in the presence of God to judge the people; and as a Prophet you shall attain to the honor of the three [i.e., the First Presidency]."[2] This promise, which Heber believed implicitly, gave him yet another glimpse of his future. It assured him of eventual success, steeled him against any crisis, and gave him complete confidence in himself, in his calling, and in the meaning and purpose of his existence. It goes far in explaining his total dedication to the Restoration.

In April Heber had his first experience with phrenology, a pseudoscience based on the belief that the mind consists of a group of separate, localized faculties seated in particular areas of the brain and that their separate development (or lack of it) can be determined by the shape of the skull (hence the reading of "bumps"). It was of Viennese origin and spread rapidly in the young Republic. This fad was only one of many reflecting the astonishing public interest of people of Heber's day in formulas for life, self-improvement, self-knowledge, and guidance—similar to the mid-twentieth-century interest in transcendental meditation, transactional analysis, psychocybernetics, self-fulfillment, moodswing, jogging, psychiatry, Freudian analysis, psychotherapy, chemotherapy, drugs, primal-scream therapy, and various types of group interaction.

It was customary at that time for phrenologists to seek out special individuals and give them readings, and by 1842 Mormon leaders in Nauvoo would have been fair game for any practitioner. Heber submitted to his first reading by A. Crane, M.S., "Professor of Phrenology,"[3] out of curiosity and politeness much as one might today allow some practitioner to read his palm.

Crane's reading has been preserved, and it is an interesting curiosity.[4] Phrenologists considered several character traits and rated people on a scale of one to ten. Heber scored tens in Amativeness (fondness for the other sex), Approbativeness (sensibility to reproach), Firmness, Imitation (the ability to imitate), Ideality (lively imagination), Mirthfulness, and Comparison (the ability to perceive and apply analogies). He scored nines in Secretiveness, Self-esteem, Benevolence, Conscientiousness, Constructiveness (mechanical ingenuity), Tune (musical taste and talent), Color (skill in comparing and arranging colors), Order, and Causality (the ability to think and reason clearly). He scored low (fours and fives), in Inhabitiveness (the ability to adjust to changes of place), Time (a sense of time), and Size (a sense of measurement).

While we may dismiss phrenology rather quickly as an interesting but insignificant vogue, the real and imagined connections between Mormonism and Masonry which have fascinated scholars for years require more careful consideration.[5]

Heber, as already noted, became a Mason in 1825. He was, however, not the only "pre-Mormon" Mason in the church. Joseph Smith's brother Hyrum became a member of the Mount Moriah Lodge No. 112 at Palmyra, New York, sometime in the 1820s. Of the thirty-three founding members of the Nauvoo Lodge, nearly all were Mormon.[6] Even though some of the bitterest anti-Mormons were Masons, Heber remained loyal to Masonry all his life and on occasion publicly praised the organization and its members. Of his original activities as a Mason he later wrote, "No man was admitted into a lodge in those days except he bore a good moral character, and was a man of steady habits; and a member would be suspended for getting drunk or any other immoral conduct. I wish that all men were Masons and would live up to their profession, then the world would be in a much better state than it is now."[7]

On another occasion, when he was trying to free Joseph Smith from prison in Liberty, Missouri, several Masons were friendly to the prisoners and treated Heber with civility: "Generals Doniphan and Atchison and the tavernkeeper where I put up, and several of the foremost men, who belonged to the Masonic fraternity."[8] As late as 1861 in the Great Basin he publicly announced that he was still true to his Masonic brethren.[9] He did not, however, join the Masonic lodge established in Utah by the federal troops at Camp Floyd (the Rocky Mountain Lodge, No. 205) or in Salt Lake City in the 1860s (the Mount Moriah and Wasatch lodges, for example). In fact Mormons were for years excluded by the Masons from joining these lodges, and they still are.

It seems likely that among the reasons for Joseph Smith's acceptance of Masonry was the influence of men like his brother and Heber, the desire for some protection, community acceptance, and the theological and philosophical compatibility between the two systems. Mervin Hogan has speculated convincingly about another reason for the Mormons' adoption of Masonry: that Mormons were encouraged to become Masons by non-Mormons interested in furthering their political ambitions in Illinois.[10]

On March 15 and 16, 1842, Abraham Jonas, a Jewish Grand Master of the Grand Lodge, Free and Accepted Masons of the State of Illinois, organized the Nauvoo Lodge. "The lodge was organized . . . with forty members," Heber noted. "Joseph was made a Mason on the same Eve. Abraham Jonas was present and Acted as Master. First nite took the 1 and 2 degree. The next night took the 3 degree."[11]

Heber served in the Nauvoo Lodge as a Junior Deacon, and by checking certain passwords and grips, was responsible for seeing that no "cowans and eavesdroppers," or non-Masons, were admitted to lodge meetings. He also carried messages from the Worshipful Master in the East to the Senior Warden in the West and elsewhere about the lodge as required.

Five Mormon, or largely Mormon, Masonic lodges were established in the area: the Nauvoo, the Nye (named after Jonathan Nye, past Grand Master of Vermont), and the Helm (named after another Grand Master) lodges in Nauvoo proper, as well as the Rising Sun Lodge, No. 12, in Montrose, Iowa, and the Eagle Lodge in Keokuk, Iowa.[12] The lodge hall in Nauvoo was considered to be the best in the West.

Eventually the Nauvoo and surrounding lodges had 1,492 members, including the First Presidency and most of the Twelve Apostles. Since at this time there were only 414 Masons in all the rest of the Illinois lodges combined, one may conclude two things: that Mormon Masonry was hardly elitist, and that non-Mormon Masons might have had reason to fear such a large preponderance of Mormons and to suspect that Mormons did not carefully choose and train their initiates. Hogan refers to Nauvoo Masonry as being "dazzlingly unorthodox," and the Nauvoo

Lodge as a "degree mill under the cooperatively conniving administration of the three Grandmasters," especially Abraham Jonas, who wished to be elected to the Illinois legislature.[13]

Heber thought he saw similarities between Masonic and Mormon ritual. In a letter to Parley Pratt, June 17, 1842, Heber revealed:

> We have received some pressious things through the Prophet on the preasthood that would cause your Soul to rejoice. I can not give them to you on paper fore they are not to be riten. So you must come and get them for your Self. We have organized a Lodge here of Masons since we obtained a Charter. That was in March. Since that thare was near two hundred been made masons. Br. Joseph and Sidny [Ridgon] was the first that was Received into the Lodg. All of the twelve apostles have become members Except Orson Pratt. He hangs back. He will wake up soon, thare is a similarity of preas Hood in Masonry. Bro. Joseph Ses Masonry was taken from preasthood but has become degenerated. But menny things are perfect.[14]

Later at a special conference in Salt Lake City on November 9, 1858, Heber explained further: "We have the true Masonry. The Masonry of to-day is received from the apostasy which took place in the days of Solomon and David. They have now and then a thing that is correct, but we have the real thing."[15] Heber seems to have felt that both Mormonism and Masonry derived separately from ancient ceremonies connected with Solomon's temple, Masonry having changed from a religious to a fraternal orientation, preserving only the shadow of form without the original substance. Both the ancient Solomonic form and substance were then revealed anew to Joseph Smith.

Two months after Masonry was introduced in Nauvoo the first temple ordinances were given to a selected few. Heber had participated fully in the limited preparatory ordinances of washings and anointings which had been administered in the Kirtland temple. In Nauvoo on May 4, 1842, however, Joseph introduced the full endowment ceremony. This has been described, in an official statement, as "a course of instruction during which covenants of devotion to the teachings and commandments of Jesus Christ are made. Those making these covenants are then expected to live exemplary lives and to teach the same sacred principles to their families."[16] In addition, the Mormon temple experience prepares initiates (contingent on their personal and sustained worthiness) for the highest possible spiritual attainments after death. In short, the Mormon temple endowment ceremony is designed to help mankind find the greatest happiness in this life and exaltation in the life to come.[17]

To Mormons, temples are houses of the Lord where (and only where) a variety of special religious exercises may take place—ceremonial washings, sealings, marriage for time and eternity, vicarious ordinances for the dead, and receipt of endowments. More sophisticated thinking about Mormon temples relates them not only to the temple at Jerusalem, but to many of the holy places of the ancient world, especially in Mesopotamia and Egypt, and to a host of other rituals which have been (and still are) practiced in many different times and places, rituals suggesting that there was at one time in antiquity a God-given *Urtext* which has come down to the present day in many more or less corrupt forms. To such thinkers the temple becomes a scale model of the universe, the one point on earth where men may establish contact with other worlds, a symbolic Holy Mountain where ritual drama regarding the creation of the world, the fall of man, and his redemption are didactically performed for initiates who thereby participate in the most holy of rites.[18]

To the Mormon, "going through the temple" is as close in this life as he can get to heaven. He goes through the first time for his own blessings, and thereafter, for the rest of his life, whether he goes through rarely, occasionally, or several times a day (and some do), he does so to secure these same blessings for those no longer in mortality, preferably for his dead kin. That is the reason why Mormons are such dedicated genealogists, why they have created the finest genealogical society in the world, and why they are systematically microfilming genealogical records all over the globe.

On that May 4, six church leaders, including Heber Kimball, Brigham Young, and Willard Richards, participated in the first temple ceremony, which was presented in the upper rooms of Joseph's brick store on Water Street. About two years later, both Heber and Vilate participated in other special ordinances.[19] It is clear that Masonry filled some basic needs for Heber in his pre-Mormon and Mormon years, that the temple ceremonies, once introduced, were incalculably more important to him, and that he himself gave no evidence of being disturbed by any similarities.

Though some other Saints in Nauvoo obtained their endowments before the top story of the temple was completed, most had to wait until the temple officially opened between December, 1845, and the beginning of the general exodus west in February, 1846. (See pp. 116–19 for Heber's involvement in the Nauvoo temple.)

At about this same time, during the summer of 1841, Heber was introduced to the doctrine of plural marriage, a doctrine which appears to have been revealed to Joseph Smith as early as 1831 in Kirtland, but which was kept secret and not practiced (save for one or two possible instances in

Ohio) until 1841, when Joseph, Heber, and a few others secretly married additional wives.

It has long been common for non-Mormons to consider Joseph's teaching on plural marriage as a mere extension of the many radical religious and social ideas of his time and place, which ranged from celibacy to free love. The young Republic seemed to produce a proliferation of those who found conventional marriage and sexual relationships unsatisfactory.

Some, especially the Shakers and the Rappites, advocated celibacy. Others, such as John Noyes's Oneida group, resurrected some ideas of Reformation radicals regarding "spiritual wifery," a form of free love which taught that a spiritual affinity existed between certain men and women who could therefore properly unite without benefit of formal marriage. The more extreme, best represented by the later Victoria Woodhull, advocated free love with no constraints of any kind. The Mormon concept of plural marriage differed profoundly from these teachings.

The 1831 revelation was set down in writing and read before the Nauvoo High Council in July, 1843, but was not openly taught until 1852 in Utah and not officially published until 1876. Prior to 1876 the Doctrine and Covenants contained in an appendix an 1835 statement on marriage specifying monogamy as the norm. The first part of this 1831 revelation, known today as Section 132 of the Doctrine and Covenants, explained that the Old Testament practice was ordained by God and gave Joseph "an appointment [to] restore all things. . . ." In Joseph's mind, the reinstitution of the Old Testament practice was necessary, a commandment, a part of his call to restore all things, in keeping with the "restitution of all things" referred to in Acts 3:21, and a vital part of the overall Restoration which he dared not omit regardless of how much it conflicted with nineteenth-century American life. According to Heber's daughter Helen, a wife of Joseph Smith, Joseph put off the introduction of plural marriage as long as possible. He shrank from it for years "until the angel of the Lord threatened to slay him if he did not reveal and establish this celestial principle."[20]

The wording of the revelation gave the reason for plural marriage:

> If any man espouse a virgin, and desire to espouse another, and the first give her consent, and if he espouse the second, and they are virgins, and have vowed to no other man, then he is justified. . . . And if he have ten virgins given unto him by this law . . . he is justified . . . for they are given unto him to multiply and replenish the earth, according to my commandment, and . . . for their exaltation in the eternal worlds, *that they may bear the souls of men; for herein is the work of my Father continued, that he may be glorified* [italics added].

Not only did this lengthy revelation command and explain plural marriage, it contained the closely related law of "celestial marriage" which Mormons consider to be one of the greatest blessings that can come from righteousness. A celestial marriage, or a "temple marriage" as it is more commonly called, means that a couple is married or "sealed" to each other for "time and eternity," that they will be man and wife forever in the fullest sense, and that all children born of that union in this life and the next are likewise sealed to the parents.

The traditional, neutered, winged, harp-playing-choir-singing-angel holds no place in Mormon thought. Mormons argue that love, as the most divine attribute of the human soul, will be as eternal as the soul itself. To the question "Whom shall we love?" the answer is "Everyone," and, as in life, some more than others—especially spouses and children. (One of Heber's saltier sons, Jonathan Golden, later remarked typically, when asked if he really loved his neighbor, "Hell yes, only I love some a damn sight more than others.") And to the question "How is it possible to properly love more than one wife?" Heber would have said that it was as possible as fully loving more than one child.

The revelation continued:

> And again, verily I say unto you, if a man marry a wife by my word, which is my law, and by the new and everlasting covenant, and it is sealed unto them by the Holy Spirit of Promise, by him who is anointed . . . Ye shall come forth in the first resurrection, and shall inherit thrones, kingdoms, principalities, and powers, dominions, all heights and depths . . . and they shall pass by the angels; and gods, which are set there, to their exaltation and glory in all things . . . and a continuation of the seeds forever and ever. Then shall they be gods . . . because they have all power, and the angels are subject unto them.

In their defense of plural marriage, Mormons were always able to make good use of the Bible. There is simply nothing in the Old or New Testament forbidding polygamy (except, as has been wryly noted, the divine affirmation that "man cannot serve two masters").[21] Furthermore it is difficult to argue that Abraham, Isaac, Jacob, Joseph, David, and Solomon did not practice it—to say nothing of the hero Gideon, the judges Ibzan, Jair, and Abdon, Samuel's father Elkanah, the kings Saul, Ahab, Ashur, Rehoboam (and all twenty-eight of his sons), and Abijah, the priest Jehoiada, and that poor fellow of whom Isaiah said, "In that day seven women shall take hold of [him] . . . saying . . . let us be called by thy name, to take away our reproach." Moreover, in biblical days men were expected to live a special law, the levirate, which obligated them to marry a dead brother's wife to "raise up seed" for the deceased. (Whether the living brother was married or not was unimportant; see Deuteronomy 25:5–10.) In one instance the Lord slew Onan because he refused to live this law (Genesis 38:19).

The Book of Mormon gives a more qualified sanction to polygamy than does the Bible. In it David and Solomon are held up as bad examples for having "had many wives and concubines, which thing was abominable before me, saith the Lord . . ."; monogamy is stressed as the norm, "For there shall not any man among you have save it be one wife; and concubines he shall have none. . . ." But then followed the approbation of polygamy under special circumstances: "For if I will, saith the Lord of Hosts, raise up seed unto me, I will command my people; otherwise they shall hearken unto these things" (Jacob 2:24–30).

Female defenders of plural marriage—and there were many outspoken ones including Heber's daughter Helen—sometimes went beyond a scriptural defense and invoked what they thought was a law of nature. The sixth wife of Parley Pratt wrote:

> The morality of nature would teach a mother that during nature's process in the formation and growth of embryo man, her heart should be pure, her thoughts and affections chaste, her mind calm, her passions without excitement; while her body should be invigorated with every exercise conducive to health and vigor; but by no means subjected to anything calculated to disturb, irritate, wear, or exhaust it of its functions. Not so with man. He has no such drawback upon his strength. It is his to move in wider sphere. If God shall count him worthy of an hundred fold in his life, of wives and children, and houses and lands and kindreds, he may even aspire to Patriarchal sovereignty to empire; to be like the prince or head of a tribe, or tribes . . . like Abraham. . . ."[22]

In her 1882 booklet *Plural Marriage as Taught by the Prophet Joseph*, considered to be the most thorough defense of polygamy from the viewpoint of a wife, Helen made another point in defense of plural marriage.

> I know that this system tends to promote and preserve social purity, and that this alone can remedy the great social evils of the present day. When lived up to as the Lord designed it should be, it will exalt the human family, and those who have entered into it with pure motives and continue to practice it in righteousness can testify to the truth of these statements.

She then added a purely practical vindication:

> There are real and tangible blessings enjoyed under this system which cannot be obtained in any other way. Not only can the cares and burdens be equally distributed among the members of the family, but they can assist one another in many ways, and if blessed with congenial natures and filled with the love of God, their souls will be expanded, and in the place of selfishness, patience and charity will find place in their hearts, driving therefrom all feelings of strife and discord.[23]

It is unwise to push Old Testament parallels with the Mormon practice of polygamy too far. While the overall purpose seems to have been the same—to raise up a large and righteous seed quickly—there were important differences. Jewish and non-Jewish society appeared to support and tolerate the practice. There is no biblical record of Jewish polygamists having been slandered or persecuted as were the Mormons. Old Testament polygamy appears to have been restricted generally to a few leaders, and there is no evidence that the common people were urged to practice it as was the case among the Mormons. Romantic love and female sexuality in polygamy seem to have been much more important to the ancient Jews than to nineteenth-century Mormons, for whom polygamy often seems to have been a religious chore with little romantic love. In the Old Testament each wife's conjugal rights were taken seriously, and we find many beautiful love stories about, for example, Jacob and Rachel, Shechem and Dinah, Sampson and the woman of Timnah, Rehoboam and Maacah, David and Bathsheba, and Adonijah and Abishag. Old Testament polygamy was more standardized and normalized than among the Mormons. There were long-standing rules and norms which were generally followed. Among the Mormons there was a condition of "normlessness."[24] Lacking rules and a supportive society in and out of the church, Mormon polygamy seems to have been played mainly by ear, a situation which brought great criticism to the whole church. In time, of course, the Mormons would have evolved their own rules and norms, but they were not given that opportunity.

NOTES

1. H. M. Whitney, *Woman's Exponent*, vol. 10 (Aug. 15, 1881), 42.
2. O. F. Whitney, *Life of Heber C. Kimball*, 385.
3. A second reading took place Sept. 20, 1843, at the famous Fowler Studio in Boston, run by Orson, Lorenzo, and Charlotte Fowler, leaders of the movement in the United States. A third occurred in 1853 in Utah.

4. This chart is reprinted in O. F. Whitney, *Life of Heber C. Kimball*, 318–20. The charts of Joseph Smith, Brigham Young, and Wilford Woodruff were printed in the Nauvoo *Wasp* during July, 1842. Joseph Smith is said to have considered phrenology a false science. William P. McIntire Daybook, Brigham Young University Library.

5. To date there is no satisfactory study of Mormonism and Masonry. Mervin Hogan has published a number of informative articles which are presently being compiled into a book. See, especially, Hogan, "Mormonism and Freemasonry: The Illinois Episode," in *Little Masonic Library, Book II* (Richmond, Va.: Macoy Publishing, 1977), 267–326. See also Reed Durham, "Is There No Help for the Widow's Son?," paper read at the Mormon History Association Annual Meeting, Nauvoo, Ill., Apr., 1974. Of the three older standard treatments, S. J. Goodwin, *Mormonism and Masonry* (Washington, D.C.: Masonic Service Association of the United States, 1924); Anthony W. Ivins, *The Relationship of "Mormonism" and Freemasonry* (Salt Lake City: Deseret News, 1934); and E. Cecil McGavin, *Mormonism and Masonry*, 4th enlarged ed. (Salt Lake City: Bookcraft, 1956), the latter is the least vacuous and discursive. Ivins and McGavin knew almost nothing about Masonry and Goodwin knew even less about Mormonism.

6. Mervin B. Hogan, "Utah's Memorial to Free Masonry," *Royal Arch Mason* (Missouri ed.), vol. 11 (Fall, 1974), 199–204; Mervin B. Hogan, ed., *Minutes of Nauvoo Lodge, U.D., December 29, 1841–May 6, 1842* (mimeographed, Salt Lake City, 1974); and Mervin B. Hogan, *The Vital Statistics of Nauvoo Lodge* (Des Moines, Iowa: Research Lodge No. 2, 1976), 5–7.

7. H. C. Kimball, Journal 94b, part 2, 5, Church Archives.

8. *Ibid.*, 67.

9. *Journal of Discourses*, vol. 9 (July 7, 1861), 128.

10. Hogan, *Vital Statistics*, 19–20.

11. H. C. Kimball, Journal 92, Apr. 10, 1845, Church Archives.

12. John C. Reynolds, *History of the M. W. Grand Lodge of Illinois . . .* (Springfield, Ill.: Masonic Trowel Office, 1869), 192–202.

13. Hogan, *Vital Statistics*, 2, 22.

14. Parley P. Pratt Papers, Church Archives. Joseph Smith allegedly told his private secretary, "Freemasonry was the apostate endowment as sectarian religion was the apostate religion." Benjamin F. Johnson, *My Life's Review* (Independence, Mo.: Zion's Press, 1947), 96. This argument is further strengthened by the fact that during the Nauvoo period neither apostates, like John C. Bennett and Increase Van Dusen (who were Mormons, Masons, and anti-Mormon writers), nor anti-Mormon Masonic officials ever accused Joseph Smith of stealing Masonic secrets and incorporating them into the endowment ceremony.

In reference to the highly debated question of the origins and antiquity of the Masonic order (which in its present form dates from 1717 in London), it is interesting to note that the date on the cornerstone of the Nauvoo Masonic Hall is A.L. 5843, which means Anno Lucis (in the year of light); reckoning the era from the creation of the world in 4000 B.C., A.L. 5843 then is the equivalent of A.D. 1843.

15. Manuscript History of Brigham Young, unpublished, Nov. 13, 1858, Church Archives.

16. *The Washington Temple*, a pamphlet published at the time of its dedication in 1974.

17. By way of explanation, Brigham Young once publicly defined the temple ordinances, or the receiving of one's endowments, as follows: "Your endowment is to receive all those ordinances in the House of the Lord, which are necessary for you, after you have departed this life, to enable you to walk back to the presence of the Father, passing the angels who stand as sentinels, being enabled to give them the key words, the signs and tokens, pertaining to the Holy Priesthood, and gain your eternal exaltation in spite of earth and hell." *Journal of Discourses*, vol. 2 (Apr. 6, 1853), 31.

18. See Hugh Nibley, *What Is a Temple? The Idea of the Temple in History* (Provo, Utah: Brigham Young University Extension Publications, 1963).

19. On Feb. 1, 1844, Heber and Vilate were anointed as a priest and priestess, and on Apr. 1 he received from Vilate the washing and anointing of his feet, head, and stomach "as Mary [sister of Lazarus] did Jesus that she might have a claim on him in the Resurrection." H. C. Kimball, Journal, Church Archives. (This idea comes from the fact that some Mormons once taught speculatively that Christ married Mary and Martha.) The author has discovered nothing else about this unusual practice although it may in some way be connected with a temple marriage or perhaps with the second anointing (see below, p. 105).

20. Helen Mar Whitney, *Why We Practice Plural Marriage* (Salt Lake City: Juvenile Instructor Office, 1884), 53.

21. More seriously, some nineteenth-century ministers argued, rather unsuccessfully, that the marginal reading of Leviticus 18:18, "Neither shalt thou take one wife to another . . . beside the other in his lifetime," and Paul's statement in I Timothy 3:2, "A bishop then must be . . . the husband of one wife . . ." precluded polygamy.

22. Belinda Marden Pratt, "Defence of Polygamy by a Lady of Utah, in a Letter to Her Sister in New Hampshire," Jan. 12, 1854 (n.p.: Martin Mormon Pamphlet Reprint Service, 1973).

23. Helen Mar Whitney, *Plural Marriage as Taught by the Prophet Joseph* (Salt Lake City: Juvenile Instructor Office, 1882), 27.

24. Eugene E. Campbell and Bruce L. Campbell, "Divorce Among Mormon Polygamists: Extent and Explanation," *Utah Historical Quarterly*, vol. 46 (Winter, 1978), 4–23.

CHAPTER 9

A Time of Testing

During the summer of 1841, shortly after Heber's return from England, he was introduced to the doctrine of plural marriage directly through a startling test—a sacrifice that shook his very being and challenged his faith to the ultimate. He had already sacrificed homes, possessions, friends, relatives, all worldly rewards, peace, and tranquility for the Restoration. Nothing was left to place on the altar save his life, his children, and his wife. Then came the Abrahamic test. Joseph demanded for himself what to Heber was the unthinkable, his Vilate. Totally crushed spiritually and emotionally, Heber touched neither food nor water for three days and three nights and continually sought confirmation and comfort from God. On the evening of the third day, some kind of assurance came, and Heber took Vilate to the upper room of Joseph's store on Water Street. The Prophet wept at this act of faith, devotion, and obedience. Joseph had never intended to take Vilate. It was all a test. Heber had passed the ordeal, as had Vilate. How much she knew, however, of what was going on is not known. No reference of hers to the matter has been found. Then and there Joseph sealed their marriage for time and eternity,[1] perhaps the first sealing of this kind among the Mormons.

During Heber's lifetime there were four types of marriage in the church. The first was a standard civil marriage for life. The second was a temple marriage for life, which differed from a civil marriage only in solemnity. The third was a temple marriage for eternity, sometimes referred to as "a sealing," a spiritual or "celestial" union or marriage. It could be performed between two living persons, two deceased persons, or between one living and one dead person. It could even be performed between two living persons one or both of whom had living spouses. Such a marriage, however, had no binding effect during their lifetimes on the two people who entered into it. It simply meant that they would be united in the world to come. The fourth type, the most important and today considered the ideal, was the temple (or celestial) marriage during mortality and in eternity. This marriage could be entered into only by two living persons and meant that their union was not "until death do ye part" but rather forever, in the fullest sense, both in this life and the next. (In wedding announcements modern Mormons look for some variant of the words "sealed for time and eternity in the . . . temple" much as Catholics watch for the phrase "fortified with Sacraments of Holy Mother Church" in obituaries —both expressions suggesting a happier afterlife to their adherents). Such a belief, even in conjugality in the next world, makes marriage a total commitment for most Mormons. Divorce is relatively rare, and Mormon men are constantly reminded to be good husbands and fathers. "No success in life can compensate for failure in the home" is a twentieth-century Mormon saying.

Following the sealing, Joseph turned to Heber and said, "Brother Heber, take her and the Lord will give you a hundred fold." [2] The last part of this statement foreshadowed a further test. Sometime later it came— Heber was commanded to take another wife, and not merely to do it but to do it secretly—to betray his wife's confidence. Secrecy was the great problem in plural marriage. In Nauvoo plural marriage was never openly practiced, taught, or admitted. In fact, to prevent wholesale apostasy over such a radical doctrine, the teaching was not only kept secret but was officially denied. A few knew about it and accepted it, a few opposed it, and most knew nothing about it. This, of course, led to many tales and rumors of seduction and adultery, which stirred up anti-Mormon sentiments, disturbed many faithful Mormons who had not been taught the doctrine, and embittered many in and out of the church against Joseph Smith.

These tales, rumors, misrepresentations, charges, countercharges, denunciations, unauthorized acts by some Mormons, and denials became and have remained the stock-in-trade of many sensation-seeking writers. Had the doctrine been made public the reaction could hardly have been worse than it was. Joseph was placed in the position of being damned if he did and damned if he didn't admit to it.

Heber appears to have been involved in only one such rumor, that of the Martha Brotherton affair. During July, 1842, Martha accused Heber of having been party to a "locked room" attempt to persuade her to become the plural wife of Brigham Young, and the charge spread far and wide. While Heber might well have interceded with her in Brigham's behalf, he vigorously denied having done anything improper. His statement is easy to believe, for he was very open in his affairs. He was in fact so guileless that a study of his family life (see also chapters 20 and 21) offers a unique example of what plural marriage was really like and is a good anti-dote to the sensational and negative accounts of the practice.

It is impossible to say how extensively plural marriage was practiced in Nauvoo, but in addition to Joseph Smith, Heber Kimball, and Brigham Young, at least nineteen others are known to have entered into it there. They were Ezra T. Benson, Gladden Bishop, William Clayton, Howard Egan, Thomas Grover, Orson Hyde, Benjamin F. Johnson, Joseph Bates Noble, Parley P. Pratt, Willard Richards, Hyrum Smith, John Smith, William Smith, Erastus Snow, Charles C. Rich, James J. Strang, John Taylor, and Lyman Wight as well as Edwin D. Woolley and Alpheus Cutler.[3]

When Helen's friend Sarah Ann Whitney became a plural wife of Joseph Smith, it was kept secret. Sarah Ann was not even permitted to tell her brother Horace, to whom she was very close and devoted. Horace soon thereafter took a trip east, and according to Helen (who later married Horace), "He had some slight suspicion that the stories about Joseph were not all without foundations, but had never told them, nor did he know the facts till after his return to Nauvoo, when Sarah hastened to tell him all. It was no small stumbling-block to him. . . ."[4]

There is no evidence that Mormon males ever welcomed the practice of plural marriage. Even the faithful Heber resisted. (He had, after all, read the 1835 statement in the Doctrine and Covenants stressing monogamy.) In spite of his 1839 revelation that he would have "many sons and daughters" and that his posterity would "be as numerous as the sands upon the sea shore,"[5] Joseph had to warn him that he could lose his apostleship and to command him three times to obey.

Finally, in an effort to spare Vilate's feelings, Heber agreed early in 1842 to marry one or perhaps two spinster sisters, Laura Pitkin (fifty-two years old) and Abigail Pitkin (forty-five), who were friends of Vilate.[6] Joseph, however, commanded him to marry the thirty-one-year-old Sarah Peak (Noon),[7] an English convert with two young daughters, abandoned in Nauvoo by her husband when he returned to England. Heber complied. The date of the marriage is unknown, but it was early in 1842. Sarah and her daughters, of course, did not live with the Kimballs, but elsewhere in Nauvoo. The question about whether Sarah was legally divorced seems to have been of small importance. Some church leaders at that time considered civil marriage by non-Mormon clergymen to be as unbinding as their baptisms. Some previous marriages, as was surely the case with Sarah, were annulled simply by ignoring them. There is no evidence that Sarah's husband ever knew or cared what happened to her.

After the marriage, the awful secret weighed on Heber and, according to his daughter,

> My mother had noticed a change in his looks and appearance, and when she enquired the cause, he tried to evade her question, saying it was only her imagination, or that he was not feeling well, etc. But it so worked upon his mind that his anxious and haggard looks betrayed him daily and hourly, and finally his misery became so unbearable that it was impossible to control his feelings. He became sick in body, but his mental wretchedness was too great to allow of his retiring at night, and instead of going to bed he would walk the floor; and the agony of his mind was so terrible that he would wring his hands and weep, beseeching the Lord with his whole soul to be merciful and reveal to his wife the cause of his great sorrow, for he himself could not break his vow of secrecy. His anguish and my mother's, were indescribable and when unable to endure it longer, she retired to her room, where with a broken and contrite heart, she poured out her grief to [God]. . . .
>
> Her mind was opened, and she saw the principle of Celestial marriage illustrated in all its beauty and glory, together with the great exaltation and honor it would confer upon her in that immortal and celestial sphere if she would but accept it and stand in her place by her husband's side. She was also shown the woman he had taken to wife, and contemplated with joy the vast and boundless love and union which this order would bring about, as well as the increase of kingdoms, power, and glory extending throughout the eternities, worlds without end. . . . She returned to my father, saying, Heber, what you have kept from me the Lord has shown me.
>
> She related the scene to me and to many others, and told me she never saw so happy a man as father was, when she described the vision and told him she was satisfied and knew that it was from God.[8]

However strange such an experience seems to twentieth-century minds, the record of Vilate's life to her death twenty-five years later in 1867 adequately demonstrates that she firmly believed that she indeed had had such a revelation. Vilate knew of all Heber's plural marriages from then on, and she became and remained a staunch supporter of her husband and several of her children who also entered into the practice.

Although such a vision of the celestial order was unusual if not unique, other women claimed to have received divine sanction of "the Principle." On June 27, 1843, Vilate wrote to Heber, who was on a mission in Philadelphia at the time:

> I have had a visit from brother Parley [Pratt] and his wife, they are truly converted it appears that J[oseph] has taught him some princi-

ples and told him his privilege, and even appointed one for him. I dare not tell you who it is, you would be astonished and I guess some tried. She has been to me for council. I told her I did not wish to advise in such matters. Sister [Mary Ann] Pratt has been rageing against these things. She told me herself that the devil had been in her until within a few days past. She said the Lord had shown her it was all right. She wants Parley to go ahead, says she will do all in her power to help him; they are so ingagued I fear they will run to[o] fast. They ask me many questions on principle. I told them I did not know much and I rather they would go to those that had authority to teach.[9]

The woman about whom Vilate felt Heber "would be astonished" was Elizabeth Brotherton, the sister of Martha Brotherton, who, as noted above, had spread her unfavorable views of plural marriage.

Lucy Walker, who first married Joseph Smith and, then after his death, became one of Heber's plural wives, felt she too had some sort of divine sanction. After she first refused Joseph Smith's proposal of marriage, he promised her a "manifestation of the will of God. . . . 'It shall be that joy and peace that you never knew.'"[10] This manifestation came, and Lucy married Joseph on May 1, 1843.

Not all to whom Joseph Smith confided the doctrine of plural marriage accepted it and passed this test of obedience as did Heber. Some men thought Joseph was trying to seduce their wives. One of Joseph's counselors, William Law, for example, apostatized and became a bitter enemy of Joseph, and Apostle Orson Pratt was rebellious for a season. Such tests gave rise to widespread rumors of seduction in Nauvoo and brought much antagonism.

Helen Kimball was only thirteen in 1842 when her father took a second wife. She suspected nothing, even when Sarah Peak had a child in December, 1842, or January, 1843. "I had no knowledge then of the plural order," she later wrote, "and therefore remained ignorant of our relationship to each other until after his [the infant's] death, as he only lived a few months. It's true I had noticed the great interest taken by my parents in behalf of Sister Noon [Peak] but . . . I thought nothing strange of this."[11]

During the summer of 1843 Heber decided to explain plural marriage to Helen, who was then nearly fifteen. Perhaps he was at that time thinking of joining his house to the Prophet's through Helen. Helen later explained that her father offered her to Joseph because of his "great desire to be connected with the Prophet."[12] In the early years of the church a loose form of "Mormon dynasticism" did evolve through such intermarriages among leading families.[13] One afternoon Heber called Helen to him privately. He explained the principle to her and asked if she would accept it. Disturbed and indignant, she answered that she wouldn't. Heber wisely did not push the issue. Later, after Joseph came to the Kimball home and explained the principle more fully, Helen accepted it and was sealed to Joseph.[14]

Many years later in Utah she wrote a retrospective poem about this marriage from which we learn that it was "for eternity alone," that is, unconsummated. Whatever such a marriage promised for the next world, it brought her no immediate earthly happiness. She saw herself as a "fetter'd bird" without youthful friends and a subject of slander.[15] This poem also reveals that Joseph Smith's several pro forma marriages to the daughters of his friends were anything but sexual romps. Furthermore, the poem reinforces the idea that, despite the trials of plurality in mortality, a "glorious crown" awaited the faithful and obedient in heaven.

That same summer Heber went on another mission. In a effort to ease Helen's mind, he wrote from Pittsburgh, "My Dear Helen . . . You have been on my mind much since I left home, and also your dear mother, who has the first place in my heart. . . . My dear daughter, what shall I say to you? I will tell you, learn to be meek and gentle, and let your heart seek after wisdom. . . ."[16]

Helen did find wisdom, or at least she remained obedient. After the death of Joseph, her second husband also practiced plural marriage. Although she published two booklets, *Plural Marriage as Taught by the Prophet Joseph* (1882) and *Why We Practice Plural Marriage* (1884), a 108-part series of "Life Incidents" in the *Woman's Exponent* (1880–86), and came to be regarded as a staunch advocate of plural marriage, she never alluded to her marriage to Joseph and made but two slight references to ever having lived "the principle" herself. Her personal affairs were not for the public. Once she said, "I have encouraged and sustained my husband in the celestial order of marriage because I knew it was right." On another occasion she wrote, "I have been a spectator and a participant in this order of matrimony for over thirty years . . . being a first wife. . . ."[17]

Helen did, however, feel free to record some pertinent information about the much-debated question of Emma Smith's knowledge of and reaction to plural marriage: "He [Joseph] taught the principle to his wife, Emma, who humbly received it and gave to him three young women to wife, who had been living with her in her family, and had been like adopted daughters. Until she lost the spirit and her heart became hardened, they lived happily together. . . . Emma deceived her children and denied to everyone that the Prophet had ever received a revelation on Celestial marriage, or had ever practiced it; although she had heard the revelation and was eye witness to the marriage of the three wives above mentioned." [18]

Although Heber was sealed to at least forty-three women before he died in 1868, he had children by only seventeen. There is little indication that he ever considered plural marriage as more than a chore, a religious responsibility for raising up a large family and providing for widows. The principle certainly did not contribute to domestic tranquility. Heber was not able to give his various wives equal attention and he appears to have been much less emotionally involved with his other plural wives than with Vilate. Many years later in 1893 one of his wives, by whom he had nine children, admitted that there was "not any love in the union between myself and Kimball, and it is my business entirely whether there was any courtship or not." [19]

He did not act hastily or out of romantic inclination and did not take any other wives for two years after marrying his first plural wife. In his letters, journals, and discourses there are frequent references to Vilate and her children, but seldom a mention of others in his family, which eventually totaled at least 108 persons. It was always Vilate who remained the center of his emotional life. He frequently felt the necessity of trying to comfort her, to assure her that she was the first in his life, the love of his youth, and that no one could or would ever take her place.

Shortly after entering his first plural marriage, Heber was on a mission in Illinois. From Apple Creek [20] on October 16 he wrote Vilate. This letter is the earliest known record of how polygamy affected their relationship, and, surprisingly, it appears that the practice of plural and temple marriage brought them closer together. He had never before written anything so tender and romantic as "I dream about you most every night, but always feel disappointed for when I awake, behold it is a dream and I could cry if it would do me any good. I am quite a child some of the time." Or "You was speaking about if I had sent a kiss to you. I will send you several on the top of this page where those round marks are, no less than one dozen. [These tender symbols are still clearly discernible.] I had the pleasure of receiving those that you sent. I can tell you it is a pleasure in some degree, but when I come home I will try the lump itself." [21]

Nine days later, from Springfield, he wrote how he regretted the sorrow he had caused her: "I never suffered more in all my life," he affirmed, "than since this thing came to pass." [22] At the time of this letter he had been gone from home less than five weeks and had never been more than 100 miles from Nauvoo. Compared with previous separations, this 1842 parting was nothing. The strain of the ordeal of obedience through which they had just passed offers an explanation for the tenderness of these and subsequent letters compared with the business-like travelogues written on his earlier missions.

We learn further of their early adjustment to plurality from Vilate's letter, written that same October. "Our good friend S[arah Peak] is as ever," she wrote, and "we are one. You said I must tell you all my feelings; but if I were to tell you that I sometimes felt tempted and tried and feel as though my burden was greater than I could bear, it would only be a source of sorrow to you, and the Lord knows that I do not wish to add one sorrow to your heart, for be assured, my dear Heber, that I do not love you any the less for what has transpired neither do I believe that you do me. . . ."[23]

Sarah added a postscript to this letter, one of the few extant notes or letters from any of his other wives:

> My very dear friend: inasmuch as I have listened to your counsel hitherto I have been prospered, therefore, I hope that I shall ever adhere to it strictly in the future.
>
> Your kind letter was joyfully received. I never read it but I received some comfort and feel strengthened and I thank you for it. You may depend upon my moving as soon as the house is ready. I feel anxious as I perceive my infirmities increasing daily. Your request with regard to Sister Kimball I will attend to. Nothing gives me more pleasure than to add to the happiness of my friends; I only wish that I had more ability to do so. I am very glad we are likely to see you so soon, and pray that nothing may occur to disappoint us. When you request Vilate to meet you, perhaps you forget that I shall then stand in jeopardy every hour, and would not have her absent for worlds. My mind is fixed and I am rather particular, but still, for your comfort, I will submit. I am as ever.

Some of her comments are more meaningful when it is known that both Sarah and Vilate were then about seven months pregnant. Heber had hardly adjusted to the realities of multiple pregnancies or he certainly would not have asked Vilate to join him. Sarah shows spunk in her honesty to Heber, and for whatever reason, Vilate did not leave her to join him. The letter also suggests considerable harmony between Sarah and Vilate.

In 1843, while her husband was on another mission, Vilate rather anxiously wrote, "Let your heart be comforted and if you never more behold my face in time let this be my last covenant and testimony unto you that I am yours in time and throughout all eternity. This blessing has been sealed upon us by the Holy Spirit of promise, and cannot be broken only through transgression. . . ."[24] In response Heber, instinctively knowing what Vilate wanted to read, reaffirmed that she was the love of his youth, and his first and best love for time and eternity—exactly what a first wife in plurality would need to be told.[25]

Sometimes Vilate wrote poems to her husband. In the midst of the harsh winter of 1846–47 at Winter Quarters, when living among at least twenty of Heber's other wives—several under her own roof—she could write:

> No being round the spacious earth
> Beneath the vaulted arch of heaven
> Divides my love, or draws it thence
> From him to whom my heart is given,
>
> Like the frail ivy to the oak
> Drawn closer by the tempest riven
> Through sorrows flood he'll bear me up
> And light with smiles my way to heaven.
>
> The gift was on the altar laid
> The plighted vow on earth was given
> The seal eternal has been made
> And by his side I'll reign in heaven.[26]

Although plural marriage is not mentioned here, several ideas that were part of the developing Mormon theology are poetically expressed: the eternal duration of marriage, the necessity of trials and sacrifice during the earthly existence, and the promise of a future "reign" in heaven.

The last known written affirmation of Heber's special love for Vilate dates from 1849 in Utah, when he explained plaintively and candidly what, to him at least, plural marriage was all about: "No one can supercede you . . . every son and daughter that is brought forth by the wives that are given to me will add to your glory as much as it will to them. They are given to me for this purpose and for no other. . . . What I have done has been done by stolen moments for the purpose to save your feelings and that alone on the account of the love I have for You. I beg you to consider my case as you cannot do the work that God has required of me. . . ."[27] Whether Heber likewise reassured his plural wives of his love for them or their place in the grand scheme of things we do not know. Secrecy, if nothing else, dictated extreme caution. Heber may have said or written many kind and comforting things to his other wives, but he does seem to have considered them as "friends." In one of his rare letters to other wives (written in 1855 from Fillmore when he was attending the territorial legislature) he wrote to Ann and Amanda Gheen, Lucy Walker, and Sarah Ann Whitney, wives with whom he had already had eleven children and would have fourteen more, "Now my dear friend Ann . . . I can say God bless Ann, Lucy, Amanda, Sarah Ann. . . . I do feel verry kind and tender in my heart toards you all. I have not but good in my heart toards you all. . . . I shall give my heart and feelings to my friends for thare reflections, for I do love my friends. I do consider you all of that cast."

He closed this letter in an equally friendly manner. "Now this letter is for Ann, Amanda, Lucy, Sarah Ann and fore my fine little men and Ladies that Live with you. God bless you all in the name of Jesus Christ, amen. From your servant H. C. Kimball." [28]

These early letters and many documents of the Utah period clearly indicate the emotional stress, strain, and challenge that this Old Testament social order caused in nineteenth-century America. It is remarkable that it worked as well as it did. From the beginning Heber remained not only a puritanical but also a reluctant polygamist. The sophisticated world, of course, does not allow for such a thing as a "puritanical" or "reluctant" polygamist; to them it appears to be a hypocritical *contradictio in adjecto*. Even so Heber was one. His devotion to Vilate and her total support of him were even noted by travelers in Utah. A later traveler to Utah commented that Heber was very sociable, had a "harem of twenty-five to thirty," but, "strange to say, has continued to treat his real wife (so the story goes) as superior to the rest." [29] Another visitor reported that Heber acknowledged that Vilate was his counselor and right-hand helper. "Indeed," the visitor declared, "I am half inclined to think that she embraced Mormonism more than her husband . . . she was unmistakenly his favorite." [30] Still another traveler noted that Vilate was "the wife to whom he most deferred, and in whose wisdom he had the most implicit confidence." This same traveler found that easy enough to believe but he was "nearly staggered" when he heard "that in plain terms, *he* was *her* convert to the . . . dogma of polygamy. . . . Paradoxical as this assertion may be, I have repeatedly heard it made among Mormons, never with the faintest hint at a denial." [31]

"Dutiful" best describes his relationships with his other wives. Certainly the circumstances of his marriages hardly suggest romance. He was pressed into his first plural union and procrastinated over all subsequent ones—marrying most of his wives either immediately prior to the enforced exodus from Nauvoo or during the intense Mormon Reformation of 1856–57.

Polygamy certainly never brought Heber domestic bliss; rather it created many familial problems. Few Mormons had anywhere near the number of wives he did; only his fervent dedication caused him to take so many. More than four-fifths of married Mormon males were monogamists, and most polygamists had but two wives.[32] Heber was no more a typical polygamist in Utah than David and Solomon were in Judea.

Rumors concerning the practice of plural marriage continued to circulate in Nauvoo. Among those who sought to make both trouble and money out of the question of polygamy was John C. Bennett, one-time counselor to Joseph Smith and mayor of Nauvoo, who had been excommunicated in May, 1842, for immorality. That same year he gave some anti-Mormon lectures and published a series of anti-Mormon articles in the Springfield, Illinois, *Sangamon Journal* which were enlarged and published that same year in Boston in book form as *The History of the Saints: or, An Exposé of Joe Smith and Mormonism*—a 344-page mélange of every kind of charge against the Mormons.

To offset Bennett's writings and lectures, scores of Elders were called during the fall of 1842 to travel throughout the country refuting Bennett's charges. Heber Kimball and Brigham Young made a three-month preaching tour to "southern" Illinois, to Lima, Quincy, Payson, Atlas, Pittsfield, Glasgow, Apple Creek, Jacksonville, Springfield, and Morgan City. How Heber answered Bennett's charges of polygamy is not known, but with two pregnant wives in Nauvoo it would have been awkward for him to deny it or argue that it existed only in a spiritual sense. He felt good about their missionary efforts. Most of their meetings were well attended. They baptized twelve in Lima, and Governor Thomas Carlin of Illinois attended the meeting in Quincy. In Atlas, Mrs. William Ross, who had cared for Vilate after the Missouri expulsion, permitted them to preach in her home. They arrived back safely on November 4, 1842.

Heber remained at home in Nauvoo for the next seven months, during which time Vilate had a new son, Charles Spaulding, born January 2, 1843; as was noted earlier, near that same time Sarah also had a son, who lived only about nine months.

Later that same winter Heber was instrumental in organizing the Young Gentlemen and Ladies Relief Society of Nauvoo. One evening in January, 1843, a group of young people visited the Kimball home. "The company," reported the *Times and Seasons*, "were lamenting the loose

style of the morals, the frivolous manner in which they spent their time."
Heber, realizing a golden opportunity, offered to give them some instruction. At subsequent meetings he addressed them "upon the duties of children to their parents, to society and to their God," and encouraged them
to apply "their minds with determined perseverance to all the studies commonly deemed necessary to fit them for active life and polish them for society," and to acquit themselves like men and women of God.[33] Eventually
on March 21 the society was formed with a constitution and officers. Why
Heber should have played such a central role in this first instance of a
Mormon youth organization is not immediately apparent. Probably his
open, animated personality and obvious commitment to the cause appealed to the Nauvoo teenagers.

At the April, 1843, conference he was appointed to go on a mission to
the eastern states, to preach the Gospel and to collect tithing. He left Nauvoo June 10, 1843, on this seventh mission, and returned four months
later. Apparently the first part of this trip was turned into a small family
vacation, for he noted in his journal, "This day I left my home at Nauvoo
in company with my wife and fore of my children, [and] Sister [Sarah
Peak] Noon. . . . On the 11th preached at Lima. On the 12th reached
Quincy. I had a preshus time with my dear wife."[34] Going on alone he visited St. Louis, Pittsburgh, Philadelphia, New York City, and Boston. On
this mission he and his companion, George Smith, had occasion to travel
on the Mainline Canal between Pittsburgh and Philadelphia. While Heber
was atop the boat observing the scenery, about a dozen Baptist ministers,
returning from a conference, cornered George in the main cabin and were
very abusive of him and his faith. After a while Heber went back to the
cabin in time to come to his companion's aid. He began by announcing
that he had been a Baptist himself once for three weeks, but at that time,
he recalled, Baptist ministers had been gentlemen. After putting the tor-
mentors in their place he then proceeded to bait them by quoting as scripture things he knew were not in the Bible. When the Baptists challenged
him he gravely turned to George and said, "Will you find that passage?"
As George pretended to search, the ministers, to save face, suddenly remembered the passages."[35]

During this absence he and Vilate exchanged seven letters. Two (already noted) are very tender and reinforce their mutual love. In other letters he told of a healing in Cincinnati, of his suffering with the "cholera
morbus" (gastroenteritis), influenza, and a bowel complaint, of how kind
people in general had been, how he missed his family, that he needed their
prayers, and that he had not been very successful in raising funds. He also
had bought some clothes for the family. One member of the church, he

told Vilate, wanted to know if she was "very dressy," to which Heber replied "quite so." He also told Vilate that he was getting her something out of black silk, and then prudently added that she should keep this to herself—it would be just as well that Sarah, his other wife, didn't know about the new gowns.[36]

He arrived back in Nauvoo safely four months later, on October 22, and turned over what moneys he had to Joseph Smith. Heber now had another seven months at home before being called on his eighth and last mission. "I remained in Nauvoo all winter," he related, "enjoying the teachings of the Prophet, attending councils, prayer meetings . . . preaching in Nauvoo and Branches round about, and doing all I could to strengthen the hands of the First Presidency."[37]

That December Joseph permitted a few of his most faithful followers, those who had proven themselves in many ways, to receive their second anointing or endowment in the temple. Among those so honored were Heber Kimball, Brigham Young, Orson Hyde, Orson Pratt, Willard Richards, Wilford Woodruff, and their first wives.[38] When Heber and Vilate had originally received their temple endowments during May, 1842, all of their blessings were conditional. Through the second anointing their blessings were no longer conditional, but actual (although they were not to be effected, for the most part, until the next life). This unusual doctrine appears to be connected with Peter's admonition "to make your calling and election sure" (2 Peter 1:10).

That same winter there were also plenty of parties, balls, and concerts. Plays, in which members of the Kimball family participated, were presented in the Masonic Hall. The first drama, in fact the inauguration of theatre among the Mormons, presented April 24, 1844, as a project to raise money to help Joseph Smith pay off his Missouri debts, was *Pizarro or the Death of Rolla*. Written by the German playwright Augustus von Kotzebue, and titled *Die Spanier in Peru oder Rollas Tod*, the play had been popular in Europe, England, and America for nearly fifty years before it was produced in Nauvoo.[39]

Brigham Young played the High Priest, a nonspeaking but important part. A "Mr. Kimball" was one of the nine Spaniards (spear carriers) in the play.[40] It is most unlikely that this was Heber, but possibly it was his son William, then nineteen years old. Even Heber's sixteen-year-old daughter, Helen, despite the generally low opinion of females in the theatre at that time, played one of the chorus of virgins in the production. Since Joseph Smith considered the theatre to be good and useful, all Mormons have felt free to enjoy it and practice its art. The same amateur company produced several other dramas that season, one of which was the *Orphan of Ge-*

neva, in which Helen was called upon at the last moment to substitute as the Countess. And thus passed a relatively peaceful winter.

Politics were also much discussed in Nauvoo in 1844, an election year. The Mormons debated about whether to support the Democrat, ex-president Martin Van Buren, or the Whig, Henry Clay, the "Great Compromiser," for president. Both candidates had refused to do anything to help the Mormons secure redress for Missouri's wrongs. Out of this dilemma came a proposal to establish an independent electoral ticket and nominate Joseph Smith as a candidate for the presidency. This was done at the annual April conference, and on May 17, a convention was held in Nauvoo at which Heber and 343 Elders were appointed to go through the states and present the name of Joseph Smith and his views on the powers and policies of government in the United States. Naturally, Heber was in the middle of these discussions and, as one of the church's seasoned preachers, participated in the electioneering campaign.

In May he left to stump for Joseph and to petition in Washington, D.C., for help in securing justice from Missouri. Helen, William, and Vilate accompanied him to the steamer *Osprey* for his overnight trip to St. Louis. It was understood that Vilate should later meet him in Philadelphia and that Helen would come too if possible. "Come with your ma if you can," he told Helen at the wharf, "but I beg you not to stand in the way of her coming, but do all you can to help her off."[41]

During his layover between vessels in St. Louis, Heber sent some supplies to his family, recording the following purchases in his journal:[42]

24 P[ounds] of Chugar	2.00
15 P Coffee	1.50
4 Pounds of rasons	.60
½ half bushel of aples	.60
8 Pounds of lump chugar	1.00
15 Pounds of chugar	1.00
4 P of solaratus [saleratus, baking soda]	.40
½ Pound of Tea	.31
One Quarter [pound] nutmeg	.37
One Pound of nuts	.25
One dozen of Lemmons	.18
2 Packs nives fore boys	.25

On June 3 under some potted palms in the foyer of the National Hotel in Washington, D.C., Congressman Stephen A. Douglas of Illinois called on Heber. "Ses he will do anny thing fore us that we wish," Heber wrote home. "He ses he will give me an introduction to sevrel of the Congress-men. To day he ses thare is no prjudis of anny acount toards us in this place. He ses all thare is is among the ignerant class."[43] Douglas, however, was merely being polite. Nothing came of Heber's visit and petition.

Heber's last letters home are full of indignation at Washington's indifference. "We will," he wrote portentously to Helen, "go where we can find a home and worship God in his own way and enjoy our rights as free citizens, and it will not be long. Now my daughter I have spoken plain to you . . . you must not show this letter to anny but our family."[44] Little good came from this mission. At the same time much more important personal and political events were taking place back home in Nauvoo. Vilate's letters enable us to relive some of that excitement and tragedy.

She wrote that Sarah was sick with a "nervous headache," and that she herself had an upset stomach and could not eat much, and that "I am so sick and faint that I cannot set up a good deal of the time. . . . There is cause for this," she added, "which cause you will no doubt rejoice in. A hint to you is sufficient."[45] Seven months later, January 29, 1845, her sixth son, Brigham Willard, was born.

Of vaster significance to the community, and thus to the Kimballs, was the explosive *Expositor* affair. Several disaffected Mormons set up an opposition newspaper, the *Nauvoo Expositor*, and succeeded in printing one issue, that of June 7, 1844. The editors declared "many items of [Mormon] doctrine . . . heretical and damnable" and sought "to explode the vicious principles of Joseph Smith." Joseph and most church leaders were outraged and the marshal was ordered to destroy the printing press, scatter the type, and burn all the copies of the *Expositor* he could find. Such interference with the freedom of the press created a sensation and was the beginning of the end of Nauvoo.

Vilate reported this to Heber and said that Joseph had written letters to all the Twelve advising them to return to Nauvoo as quickly as possible, and guessed she would have to give up her trip to the East. (That was her last chance: she never did return to her people in Victor.) Vilate reported that troops looking for Joseph had been sent by Governor Thomas Ford to Nauvoo, and that Joseph had fled across the river to Montrose, Iowa, leaving word for the brethren to hang on to their arms and take care of themselves as best they could. "Some were tried, almost to death," she added, "to think Joseph should leave them in the hour of danger. . . . I have not felt frightened . . . neither has my heart sunk within me, until yesterday, when I heard Joseph had sent word back for his family to follow him."[46] Vilate's fears were shared by many Latter-day Saints.

The traditional account of why Joseph Smith gave up freedom in
Iowa and took instead the road to Carthage and martyrdom is that he
gave in to taunts of cowardice and the requests of his family to return. His
utterance "If my life is of no value to my friends, it is of none to myself" is
famous.[47] This may all be true, but a letter of Vilate's suggests a much
more important reason, and expresses the feelings of the Saints for their
Prophet as well as their fears for the future: "Joseph went over the river
out of the United States, and there stopped and composed his mind, and
got the will of the Lord concerning him, and that was, that he should return and give himself up for trial. . . . They have just passed by here. . . .
My heart said Lord bless those dear men, and preserve them from those
that thirst for their blood. Their giving themselves up, is all that will save
our city from destruction. . . ."[48]

At about twenty-one minutes past four on the afternoon of June 27,
Joseph and Hyrum Smith, in the Carthage jail awaiting trial, were murdered by an anti-Mormon mob. Three days later Vilate wrote to Heber:

> Never before did I take up my pen to address you under so trying
> circumstances as we are now placed, but as Mr. Adams the bearer of
> this can tell you more than I can write, I shall not attempt to describe
> the scene that we have passed through. God forbid that I should ever
> witness another like unto it. I saw the lifeless corpse[s] of our beloved
> brethren when they were brought to their almost distracted families.
> Yes, I witnessed their tears, and groans, which was enough to rend the
> heart of an adamant. Every brother and sister that witnessed the scene
> felt deeply to sympathize with them. Yea, every heart is filled with
> sorrow, and the very streets of Nauvoo seem to mourn. Where it will
> end the Lord only knows. We are kept awake night after night by the
> alarm of mobs. Those apostates say, their damnation is sealed, their
> die is cast, their doom is fixed and they are determined to do all in
> their power to have revenge. [William] Law says he wants nine more,
> that was in his quorum. Some times I am afraid he will get them. I
> have no doubt but you are one. . . .
>
> I have felt opposed to their sending for you to come home at pres-
> ent. . . . I have no doubt but your life will be sought, but may the
> Lord give you wisdom to escape their hands.[49]

On the day of the assassination, Heber was traveling from Philadelphia to New York and unaccountably felt very sorrowful and depressed
in spirit. It was not until July 9, however, while in Salem, Massachusetts,
that he first learned of the murders. "The papers were full of News of the
death of our Prophet," he confided in his journal. "I was not willen to believe it. Fore it was to[o] much to bare. . . . It struck me at the heart."[50]

From Salem, along with Brigham Young, Parley P. Pratt, Wilford Wood-ruff, and Lyman Wight, Heber started the sad return to Nauvoo.

NOTES

1. This information comes from James Lawson, a son-in-law of Heber, who told the story to O. F. Whitney. See O. F. Whitney, *Life of Heber C. Kimball*, 439–40.

2. *Ibid.*, 440.

3. See Danel W. Bachman, "A Study of the Mormon Practice of Plural Marriage before the Death of Joseph Smith" (unpublished M.A. thesis, Purdue University, 1975).

4. H. M. Whitney, *Woman's Exponent*, vol. 11 (Mar. 1, 1883), 146.

5. See above, p. 62.

6. H. M. Whitney, *Woman's Exponent*, vol. 10 (Oct. 15, 1881), 74.

7. For consistency and simplicity throughout this study Heber's wives are always referred to by their maiden names. Where necessary their married names will be added in parentheses.

8. H. M. Whitney, *Woman's Exponent*, vol. 10 (Oct. 15, 1881), 74.

9. Original letter in possession of Spencer W. Kimball. Used by permission.

10. "Statement of Mrs. L. W. Kimball," typescript, 5, Lucy Walker Kimball Papers, Church Archives.

11. H. M. Whitney, *Woman's Exponent*, vol. 11 (July 11, 1882), 26.

12. Helen Mar Kimball Smith Whitney [to her children], Mar. 30, 1881, Helen Mar Whitney Papers, Church Archives.

13. Dennis Michael Quinn, "Organizational Development and Social Origins of the Mormon Hierarchy, 1832–1932: A Prosopographical Study" (unpublished M.A. thesis, University of Utah, 1973).

14. H. M. Whitney, *Woman's Exponent*, vol. 11 (Aug. 1, 1882), 39.

15. Helen Mar Kimball Smith Whitney [to her children], Mar. 30, 1881, Helen Mar Whitney Papers, Church Archives. The full poem reads as follows:

> I thought through this life my time will be my own
> The step I now am taking's for eternity alone,
> No one need be the wiser, through time I shall be free,
> And as the past hath been the future still will be.
>
> To my guileless heart all free from worldly care
> And full of blissful hopes—and youthful visions rare
> The world seemed bright the thret'ning clouds were kept
> From sight and all looked fair but pitying angels wept.
>
> Then saw my youthful friends grow shy and cold,
> And poisonous darts from sland'rous tongues were hurled,

Untutor'd heart in thy gen'rous sacrifice,
Thou did'st not weigh the cost nor know the bitter price;

Thy happy dreems all o'er thou' it doom'd alas to be
Barr'd out from social scenes by this thy destiny,
And o're thy sad'nd mem'ries of sweet departed joys
Thy sicken'd heart will brood and imagine future woes,

And like a fetter'd bird with wild and longing heart,
Thou'lt dayly pine for freedom and murmur at thy lot;
But could'st thou see the future & view that glorious crown,
Awaiting you in Heaven you would not weep nor mourn.

Pure and exalted was thy father's aim, he saw
A glory in obeying This high celestial law,
For to thousands who've died without the light
T'will bring eternal joy & make thy crown more bright.

I'd been taught to revere the Prophet of God
And receive every word as the word of the Lord,
But had this not come through my dear fathers' mouth,
I should ne'r have received it as Gods' sacred truth.

16. H. M. Whitney, *Woman's Exponent*, vol. 11 (Aug. 1, 1882), 39.

17. See Augusta Joyce Crocheron, *Representative Women of Deseret* (Salt Lake City: J. C. Graham, 1884), 114, and H. M. Whitney, *Plural Marriage as Taught by the Prophet Joseph*, 27.

18. H. M. Whitney, *Woman's Exponent*, vol. 11 (Aug. 1, 1882), 39.

19. Testimony of Lucy W. Kimball as cited in the *Abstract of Evidence, [Independence] Temple Lot Case, Circuit Court of the United States* (Lamoni, Iowa: Herald Publishing House, 1893), vol. 2, 375.

20. A now-defunct community in Green County. It may have been on the Illinois River.

21. H. C. Kimball to Vilate Kimball, Oct. 16, 1842, H. C. Kimball Papers, Church Archives.

22. H. M. Whitney, *Woman's Exponent*, vol. 11 (July 15, 1882), 26.

23. *Ibid.*, vol. 11 (June 1, 1882), 1–2.

24. Vilate Kimball to H. C. Kimball, June 8, 1843, in H. C. Kimball, Journal 91, Church Archives.

25. H. C. Kimball to Vilate Kimball, Sept. 3, 1843. Original in possession of J. Leroy Kimball. Used by permission.

26. H. C. Kimball, Journal 91, following Jan. 17, 1847, Church Archives.

27. H. C. Kimball to Vilate Kimball, Feb. 12, 1849. Original in possession of Spencer W. Kimball. Used by permission.

28. H. C. Kimball to Ann, Lucy, Amanda, and Sarah Ann, Dec. 31, 1855. Original in possession of Mrs. Kenneth Huffman. Used by permission. In this same

letter, he wrote, "Some say they do not want anny more children that is all rite as far as I am concerned." Were these wives tired of him, the children, or both?

29. Mrs. B. G. Ferris, *The Mormons at Home with Some Incidents of Travel from Missouri to California, 1852–53* (1856; reprinted New York: AMS Press, 1971), 157.

30. Fitz Hugh Ludlow, "Among the Mormons," *Sharpe's London Magazine*, vol. 33 (1869), 32–33.

31. Ludlow, *The Heart of the Continent*, 311–12.

32. See Stanley S. Ivins, "Notes on Mormon Polygamy," *Western Humanities Review*, vol. 10 (Summer, 1956), 229–39.

33. *Times and Seasons*, Apr. 1, 1843.

34. H. C. Kimball, Journal 91, June 10, 1843, Church Archives.

35. Watson, ed., *Manuscript History of Brigham Young, 1801–1844*, 153.

36. H. C. Kimball to Vilate Kimball, Sept. 3, 1843. Original in possession of J. Leroy Kimball. Used by permission.

37. *Deseret News*, "Synopsis," Apr. 28, 1858.

38. Watson, ed., *Manuscript History of Brigham Young: 1801–1844*, 158–59.

39. The first English adaptation was made in 1800 by the great English dramatist Richard Sheridan. (Later William Dunlap, the "father of American theatre," made an American adaptation.) It is a sentimental, bombastic, pretentious, and turgid piece regarding the tragic fate of the Incas (led by Rolla) in defending their king, country, religion, and lives against the rapacious Spanish Conquistador, Pizarro. Despite its shortcomings as literature, it was good theatre and often produced throughout the nineteenth century.

40. See Stanley B. Kimball, "Pizarro: A Lost Play Bill," *The Ensign* (Oct., 1975), 51–52.

41. H. M. Whitney, *Woman's Exponent*, vol. 11 (Dec. 1, 1882), 98.

42. H. C. Kimball, Journal, May 22, 1844, Church Archives.

43. H. C. Kimball to William Kimball, June 3, 1844. Original in possession of J. Leroy Kimball. Used by permission.

44. H. C. Kimball to Helen Kimball, June 9, 1844. Original in possession of Spencer W. Kimball. Used by permission.

45. Vilate Kimball to H. C. Kimball, June 9, 1844. Original in possession of Spencer W. Kimball. Used by permission.

46. *Ibid.*

47. Roberts, ed., *History of the Church*, vol. 6, 549. Another of Kimball's wives commented on Joseph's return. According to Lucy Walker (who was married to Joseph at the time), he said, "I have the promise of life for five years, if I listen to the voice of the spirit." But when Emma and some of the brethren besought him to return, he said, "If my life is worth nothing to you it is worth nothing to me." She then added, I have often heard him say he expected to seal his testimony with his blood." "Statement of Mrs. L. W. Kimball," p. 4, Church Archives.

48. Vilate Kimball to H. C. Kimball, June 9, 1844, from that part of the letter written June 24. Original in possession of Spencer W. Kimball. Used by permission.

49. Vilate Kimball to H. C. Kimball, June 30, 1844. Original in possession of J. Leroy Kimball. Used by permission.

50. H. C. Kimball, Journal, July 9, 1844, Church Archives.

CHAPTER 10

Preparations for the Exodus

Back in Nauvoo on August 6, 1844, Heber and his fellow Apostles found Sidney Rigdon, the only surviving member of the First Presidency, claiming leadership. Rigdon, after a falling-out with Joseph, had been living in Pittsburgh for the past several years. As soon as he learned of Joseph's and Hyrum's deaths he hurried to Nauvoo and presented himself as the "guardian" of the church. Wanting to act immediately, before the Quorum of the Twelve could be assembled, he prevailed upon William Marks, President of the Nauvoo Stake, to call a meeting. This was opposed by the four Apostles who were in Nauvoo—John Taylor, George A. Smith, Parley P. Pratt, and Willard Richards—who delayed action until the other Apostles in the East arrived. It was not until August 7, in a special meeting in the Seventies' Hall, that Rigdon was able to present his claims before the Quorum of the Twelve, the Nauvoo Stake High Council, the President of the Stake, and the High Priests. No action was taken that day. On the following morning a general conference was convened in the grove near the temple (there never was a chapel in Nauvoo) to give Rigdon the opportunity of laying his claim before the whole church. Rigdon argued that he was the only living member of the First Presidency and that in 1833 he had been appointed and ordained as a spokesman for Joseph Smith.

That afternoon Brigham Young addressed the gathering. Rigdon's spokesmanship ended with the death of Joseph, Brigham said, and, citing Joseph's letter of January, 1839, to Heber and himself, insisted that all of Joseph's keys and powers had devolved upon the Quorum of the Twelve. While he was speaking, many later claimed that the voice and appearance of Brigham changed to such an extent that he looked and sounded like Joseph Smith. The startled congregation strained to see and hear and to comprehend this manifestation. "If Joseph had risen from the dead and stood before them," Helen Kimball wrote, "it could hardly have made a deeper or more lasting impression. It was the very voice of Joseph himself." [1] This settled the debate. To those present, it was clear that the mantle of Joseph had fallen on Brigham Young. The congregation sustained the Twelve as the acting First Presidency, with Brigham Young, as senior member of the Twelve, their leader. Although Rigdon was treated with kindness and invited to remain in Nauvoo, he continued to work against the Twelve (secretly ordaining men to be prophets, priests, and kings, for example). He was excommunicated in September, and afterward returned to Pittsburgh.

Heber, partly because he was next in seniority and partly because of his closeness to Brigham Young, became and remained until his death twenty-four years later de facto and de jure first counselor to Young and the second-ranking leader in the church. Although he did not know it, he had been on his last mission. Thereafter he became an administrator, and a new phase of his life commenced. Up to Joseph's death all of the Apostles had been generally equal, and since nothing had occurred to reveal the importance of seniority, it had not been of much significance. Later it became increasingly meaningful.

Throughout the life of Joseph Smith, Heber had been a mild, independent, easygoing missionary-apostle with little flair for leadership or feel for authority. After the death of Joseph, he voluntarily subordinated himself to Brigham Young and became a dynamic, authoritarian lieutenant. His sermons of this period show how quickly he began to assume the role of authority, how soon he commenced to change from a follower to a strong leader. These early sermons were as commanding, hortatory, vigorous, and straightforward (though not quite so salty) as any from the Utah period.

With the all-important question of succession settled, Nauvoo turned from its grief to effecting the plans of its martyred prophet—completing the temple, building a better Nauvoo, and expanding the proselytizing program. To accomplish this, Wilford Woodruff was sent to England to preside over European affairs, and a special committee of three—Brigham Young, Heber Kimball, and Willard Richards—was organized to preside in North America. Endless council meetings were held among church leaders, frequently with the Council of Fifty, a partially secret group of leading church members and citizens of Nauvoo which Joseph had organized during the spring of 1844. Its purpose was to function as a sort of symbolic government or political arm of the church and to concern itself with temporal matters of building the Kingdom. Its existence reflected the beliefs of early Mormons that a literal, physical Kingdom of God was soon to be established on the earth. After the death of Joseph Smith and until the 1880s the Council of Fifty sometimes aided in the civil and temporal affairs of the church.

At the October, 1844, conference, the first since the death of Joseph, missionary work was furthered by dividing the United States and Canada into ecclesiastical districts and urging converts to gather and build Nauvoo. The minutes of the conference report that Heber moved that "we as a church endeavor to carry out the principles and measures heretofore adopted and laid down by Joseph Smith as far as in us lies, praying almighty God to help us to do it." The motion carried unanimously and the people rallied around their leaders and strove mightily to fulfill it.

Heber was especially busy preaching, administering, building a home, reading and writing history, tending to family affairs, looking after the sick, building the temple, negotiating with anti-Mormon forces, preparing for an uncertain future, and hiding occasionally to avoid writs and summonses on various charges against him—in short, building up Nauvoo and at the same time preparing to leave it.

Symbolically, Nauvoo was renamed the "City of Joseph," and the "History of the Church," which had been appearing in leisurely fashion in the *Times and Seasons*, was changed to the "History of Joseph Smith" and was henceforth written and published more rapidly. Heber had a direct hand in this compilation. He contributed to it and was often consulted as an authority.

Joseph took the writing of his own history seriously. For years he kept one or more clerks busy collecting and compiling records, but as a result of unsettled conditions, little history had been produced. After Willard Richards was appointed Church Historian in July, 1843, he found many records lost or stolen and tried to bring order out of ten years of neglect and chaos. It was his work that was published in the *Times and Seasons*. Richards, to fill in the lacunae in the record, would compile an account of a certain period as well as he could from the records he inherited and then read it aloud to Heber, Brigham Young, and others, who would correct errors and add information. Unfortunately for later students, much of what Richards learned from others was added to the official record in the first person, giving the impression that Joseph himself had said or written it. (In an effort to keep a better record of his own life, Heber began to study "phonography" [phonetic or shorthand writing] with George D. Watt, Heber's first convert in England, but other than two attempts to write the Lord's Prayer in Pitman in his journal of that period, there is no evidence that Heber ever mastered or used the method.)

To fully understand Heber's actions after January, 1845, it is necessary to know that by then the Quorum of the Twelve had decided to abandon Nauvoo and move west. This decision, however, was not made public until the following September, when anti-Mormon activities resumed in earnest. Brigham and Heber therefore, were for most of 1845 in the awkward position of encouraging the people to labor mightily to build a city that was soon to be abandoned.

In January, 1845, the Quorum of the Twelve issued a General Epistle exhorting the Saints to do all in their power to build the temple and assuring the people that "our city is progressing, and the work of the Lord is rolling forth with unprecedented rapidity." At the same time the *Nauvoo Neighbor*, and later the *Times and Seasons*, commenced a series of articles about Indians and Oregon which were most likely designed to prepare the Saints, psychologically at least, for a westward move.

Early in 1845, to improve Nauvoo's cultural and economic life, the Seventies' Library, the Nauvoo Trades Committee, the Nauvoo Manufacturing Association, and the Mercantile and Mechanical Association were organized. And during the April conference, in an effort to make the church independent, Heber advised the Saints to cultivate "corn, peas, and beans . . . and every other thing we need for our own comfort . . . we want to see every lot in the city of Joseph fenced up and cultivated, and let every street that is not used, be fenced up, and planted. . . ."

He urged the people to make their own cloth, stockings, shoes, bonnets, and caps, in order to be independent of the Gentiles (non-Mormons). Fathers were urged to keep their daughters at home—not to let them work in Gentile homes. The brethren were asked not to reap, plow, or dig for the Gentiles, and their grogshops were not to be patronized. To show his contempt for Gentiles, Heber announced, "I will bet you a dollar, I can go and buy, and drink a gallon of their liquor every day and I will not get drunk, because it is mostly water." In response to his motion the conference withdrew all fellowship from the Gentiles and agreed to "deliver them up to the buffetings of Satan."[2] Thus did Heber teach economic independence, self-sufficiency, and a boycott of non-Mormon goods—exactly as he would teach it later in the Great Basin.

Above all, however, special attention was devoted to completing the temple. The site and the cornerstone had been dedicated April 6, 1841. At the time of Joseph's assassination the temple was only one story high. Eleven months later, on May 24, 1845, the capstone was laid. Thereafter interior work continued feverishly. The temple consisted of a basement floor for baptismal work, a first-floor assembly for worship services, an unfinished second floor, and an attic for several endowment rooms and offices.

On October 5, 1845, the first general meeting was held in the finished lower assembly room; on November 21, the painters finished painting the upper rooms in the attic, which were dedicated November 22; on December 2, Heber and his son William drove around Nauvoo picking up potted evergreens for the attic garden room. Two of Heber's wives, Clarissa and Emily Cutler, made a cotton veil for the main endowment room, which was hung December 5, and endowment work began on December 10.

Thereafter through at least February 7 more than 5,600 persons received their endowments, with as many as 295 going through in a single day. So great were the desires of the people to secure their temple blessings before the exodus that during this sixty-day period Heber sometimes worked in the temple all night. He seems to have slowly assumed general charge of temple work. One of his journals became an official temple record, his room in the temple became an office "for the convenience of transacting business with persons from without," and he himself often officiated at the veil and took various parts in the ritual.[3]

Throughout the winter of 1845–46, dancing and recreation were permitted in the unfinished second floor of the temple. After the endowment work of December 30, for example, there was some dancing and singing in the temple during which time "Mother" Elizabeth Ann Whitney sang in tongues. The spirit of glossolalia affected Heber as well, for he also spoke in tongues on that evening. Unfortunately we know nothing of what he said, whether anyone "translated" for him, or what the response of the people was. Later in Utah he adroitly evaded the question of his ability to speak in tongues. "As for the gift of tongues," he said, "I do not speak in tongues often. Can I speak in tongues? Yes, I can speak in a good, beautiful language to this people at any time."[4]

The gift of tongues can be understood in two senses—the power to speak in a foreign tongue previously unknown to the speaker (as in Acts 2:4–11 on the day of Pentecost) or to speak some totally unidentifiable language such as the "tongues of angels" (see 1 Corinthians 13:1) or the so-called "Adamic" tongue. When Mormon missionaries learn foreign languages quickly they like to think they are enjoying the gift of tongues in some sense, but it is otherwise rare among twentieth-century Mormons. Seldom will someone have the immediate but short-term ability to speak (or understand) a foreign tongue as Heber did among the Swiss immigrants in 1856 (see p. 39). Even less frequently will Mormons speak in some completely unidentifiable language, as Heber did in the Nauvoo temple.

As would be expected, there were those who questioned the propriety of dancing in the temple. To them Brigham Young said in his usual forceful manner, "Now as to dancing in this house—there are thousands of brethren and sisters that have labored hard to build these walls and put on this roof, and they are shut-out from any opportunity of enjoying any amusement among the wicked—or in the world—and shall they have any recreation? Yes! Where? Why in the Temple of the Lord. That is the very place where they can have liberty—and we will enjoy it this winter and then leave it." [5]

As is frequently the case, however, some people went too far and became too casual while inside the temple. The total sacredness which today surrounds everything about temple work had not then evolved. The Kirtland and Nauvoo temples resembled churches and were perceived, like cathedrals in medieval Europe, more as community centers than as buildings enclosing holy space. This concept developed in Utah, where the very architecture of temples, with turrets, towers, and crenelated crests, suggested fortresses defining and protecting this holy space from a sinful world.

Work in the temple sometimes went on night and day, and it was not uncommon for some people to cook, eat, tend babies, even sleep in the side rooms at times. When Heber discovered this and other more serious irregularities, he was angry and warned all, "You can't sin so cheap now as you could before you came to this order [i.e., received their endowments in the temple]." [6] At his insistence, thereafter no one was allowed into the temple without an official invitation (the origin of today's temple "recommend"), and strict order and decorum were maintained within the holy precincts.

Work continued on the temple even after the city was partly deserted. "The Million-Dollar Sacrifice" was not dedicated until April 30 and May 1, long after Heber Kimball and Brigham Young and their first group of exiles had disappeared into Iowa. Practical, conservative, businesslike Mormons sometimes do strange things. Untold wealth and energy, for example, have always been expended in proselytizing, even in unfruitful areas and among uninterested peoples, but encouraged by both the New Testament admonition "to teach all nations, baptizing them" and by Joseph Smith's injunction that "the greatest and most important duty is to preach the Gospel," missionary work has always gone forward regardless of cost. Likewise no expense has ever been spared in building temples. Non-Mormons, puzzled by why Mormons do some of the things they do, often consider them quixotic. Surely the push, at all costs, to complete the Nauvoo temple after the death of Joseph, throughout the later preparation for quitting Nauvoo, and even after the exodus had begun must seem to many as strange. Wallace Stegner has correctly appraised the reason for such behavior: "Without the completion of the endowments, the Mormons' departure from Nauvoo would have been only flight, but with the endowments completed, they could go as saved and as convenanted people. . . ."[7] It could also be pointed out, from a more practical point of view, that Brigham Young, Heber Kimball, and others probably realized that a completed building would be easier to rent or sell after the Mormons left.

Heber constantly harangued the people to work on the temple. "Roll out your rusty dollars, and your rusty coppers," he urged, "and let us rush on this house as fast as possible. When you gent [get] it done you will have joy and gladness, and greater shouting, than we had when the cap stone was laid. We will make this city ring with hosannas to the Most High God." Then he added encouragingly, "You can see how fast that house is going up. You will see an addition to it all the time until the last shingle goes on. We will have our next conference in it . . . I do not go out of doors, and look at that house, but the prayer of my heart is, 'O, Lord save this people, and help them to build thy house.'"[8]

What Heber saw when he looked at the temple was a modified New England church high on the bluffs. Made of finished light gray limestone blocks, it measured 128 feet long by 88 feet wide and was three stories tall, lighted by rows of traditional painted gothic windows and by an unusual use of round windows. The walls at the eaves were 60 feet high and the tower eventually soared to 158 feet. Set into the walls were thirty pilasters with sun-stone capitals and moon-stone bases; star-stones were on the frieze—all symbolizing the three degrees of heavenly glory mentioned by Paul. ("There is one glory of the sun, and another glory of the moon, and another glory of the stars . . . so also is the resurrection," I Corinthians 15:40–42). Early Mormons had a predilection for symbols; they felt a need to express their shared values, to express the uniqueness of their faith and the distinction of their community.[9]

Heber was so intent on finishing the temple that he even practiced a bit of deception. "I went to work and built that large house (his Nauvoo home]," he admitted years later in Utah, "when I knew we should leave in a short time, to excite your feelings with the belief we were going to stay there, that you might build and complete that Temple. This course was for your own salvation."[10]

So successful were the Mormon people in carrying out the ideas of their dead Prophet that by September, 1845, it was obvious that the church was not going to wither away, as many had expected. Anti-Mormon activities then resumed in earnest. Heber's journal records many mob activities, as well as Mormon attempts to negotiate. That fall, over 200 Mormon homes and farm buildings located outside Nauvoo were burned. Eventually the anti-Mormon convention headquartered in Carthage decreed that the Mormons could remain in Illinois until the spring of 1846, and until then peace would be maintained on both sides. Compelled to accept these terms, the Mormons made every effort to meet this deadline. Every home, including Heber's, became a workshop in preparation for the exodus.

Anti-Mormon fanatics, however, did not keep the peace, and harassment continued, occasionally forcing Heber and other leaders into hiding.[11] Among the anti-Mormon charges were aiding and abetting Joseph Smith in the treasonous designs against the state, building an arsenal, keeping cannons in peacetime, and counterfeiting. On one occasion, Brigham Young, John Taylor, Parley P. Pratt, Orson Hyde, and others, including the colorful non-Mormon, Edward Bonney, were indicted for counterfeiting.[12] Later all charges were dropped except those against Bonney, who was sentenced to be hanged. Heber noted: "Amos Bonny [sic] came to my house in the Eve and Said his brother Edwin [sic] Bonny was sentenced to be hung. If so, it is in answer to praying."[13] Heber, at least, was tired of his people being blamed for the wrongs of others. There is some evidence, however, that a few Mormons may very well have been involved in "making bogus." We learn from Heber that during the summer of 1845, two Mormons (or would-be Mormons) had been in jail in Quincy for counterfeiting and that "Bishop Haywood [Joseph L. Heywood of Quincy] said they were guilty."[14]

The theme of the October, 1845, conference was optimistic. "I am glad," Heber said from the pulpit of the first floor of the temple: "the time of our Exodus is come . . . and although we leave all our fine houses and farms here, how long do you think it will be before we shall be better off than we are now?" He then did something which he was to do with increasing frequency and confidence—prophesy. "I will prophesy in the name of Heber C. Kimball, that in five years, we will be as well again off as we are now."[15]

The year 1845 ended with Heber Kimball and Brigham Young examining maps and reading various travel accounts of the Far West in preparation for an exodus. Among the works they read were John C. Frémont, *Report of the Exploring Expedition to the Rocky Mountains in the Year 1842, and to Oregon and California in the Years 1842–43.* (In September, 1843, Frémont had actually camped on the site which became Salt Lake City.) They also consulted Lansford W. Hastings's *Emigrants' Guide to*

Oregon and California. Since for fifteen years the Mormons had lived on the frontier, they were basically well informed about the Far West. From 1832 articles had appeared in the Mormon press regarding the West, and between 1843 and 1845 more than fifty articles on this subject had been published in the *Times and Seasons* and *Nauvoo Neighbor.*

The year 1846 began badly. The charters of the Nauvoo Legion and of the City of Nauvoo were revoked in January, thus eliminating what legal and military protection the Mormons had. Rumors were spreading that the U.S. government would prevent the Mormons from leaving because they were suspected of counterfeiting and of secretly planning to go to Oregon to strengthen England's control over that disputed area. Apparently these rumors led church leaders to decide to quit Nauvoo as soon as possible rather than to await the agreed-upon spring departure time. But the fact that Heber and others would leave pregnant wives and young children behind in Nauvoo after they started west suggests that there was little fear of mob violence at that time.

On top of all this public activity Heber still had many private concerns. In 1843 he had added a brick addition to his log home on the flats. During the summer and fall of 1845 the old log portion was razed and replaced by a two-story brick structure. The house was built in the severe Federal style of the period, with stepped fire gables on the ends. (The gingerbread widow's walk and porch of today were added years later and alter the original design. When Heber lived there it would have looked more like the restored homes of Brigham Young and Wilford Woodruff.) When the house was finished November 12, 1845, it was the first adequate dwelling the Kimballs had had in the twelve years since they had left Mendon. They were to enjoy its comforts for only four months and five days, however. Then it would be another six years of tents, wagon boxes, and log cabins before Vilate had another comfortable home.

During the short time Vilate was in her new home she did a little socializing. One evening in October, 1845, she invited some friends to their home, and Helen's piano teacher, Ann Pitchforth, entertained. The family also sat for a portrait by a "Brother Major" from England. "It was upon a large canvas," Helen noted, "tastefully arranged, my father and mother sitting with baby in the center, myself at her side and my brother William and his wife and little daughter on the left, and four younger brothers made up the family group. . . ."[16]

In spite of the pressures and responsibilities placed on Heber and Brigham Young, they took time to worry over piano lessons for their daughters. Helen had no piano at home to practice on, but she later wrote,

"President Brigham Young had a small piano and invited me to come to his house and practice with his daughter Vilate, who though younger than myself, had previous advantages, but was rather indifferent, and he thought if I practiced with her, she would take a greater interest. Their piano stood in Sister Young's room, and her health being very poor, he proposed to have it brought to our house when the upper part was done. This pleased us both immensely."

Helen practiced diligently until "it was decided that we were to be broken up and move to the Rocky Mountains. Though the piano remained there throughout the winter I felt no encouragement to continue taking lessons, though father tried to stimulate me to and said, to encourage me, that they should have the necessary materials taken to manufacture pianos and I should have one, but I knew that I would forget it all."[17]

Heber's family continued to grow. During September, October, and November, 1844, when great consideration was being given to the future welfare of the widows of church leaders, especially of Joseph's, Heber married one of the latter—Sarah Lawrence.[18] He also married Rebecca Swain, widow of Frederick G. Williams, a former counselor to Joseph who had died in 1842, and six other women: Frances Jessie Swan, Charlotte Chase, Mary Ellen Harris, Ellen Sanders, Ann Alice Gheen, as well as Nancy Maria Winchester (who was later sealed to Joseph). During 1845 he married two more of Joseph's widows, Sarah Ann Whitney and Lucy Walker, and three other women—Amanda Gheen (sister of Ann Alice), and the sisters Clarissa and Emily Cutler.

By January, 1846, Heber had sixteen wives (of whom Frances Swan, Sarah Ann Whitney, Clarissa and Emily Cutler were pregnant), at least eight living children, and partial responsibility for some of the fourteen other children three of his wives had had by previous husbands. Then, just prior to the February exodus from Nauvoo, he married at least twenty-two more women, including two more real widows of Joseph, Presendia (also spelled "Prescindia") Huntington and Martha McBride, four more posthumous "widows" (that is, women sealed to Joseph after his death), Sarah Scott, Sarah Stiles, Sylvia Porter Sessions, and Mary Houston, and a widow of Hyrum Smith, Mary Fielding—giving Heber a total of at least thirty-eight wives.[19] Although Heber eventually was sealed to forty-three women, not all these were connubial marriages: his sixty-five children were by only seventeen wives. Heber married the widows of Joseph Smith not only to care for them, but because he believed it was necessary to raise up children to the martyred Prophet. This doctrine was based on Deuteronomy 25:5–10, which stipulated that if a man died without posterity his brother should marry his wife and produce it for him. One of Joseph's widows, Lucy Walker, later testified, "The contract when I married Mr. Kimball was that I should be his wife for time, and time only, and the contract on the part of Mr. Kimball was that he would take care of me during my lifetime, and in the resurrection would surrender me, with my children, to Joseph Smith." [20]

Rumor and fantasy to the contrary, there was apparently little romance in Mormon plurality. Heber's sealing to so many wives just prior to leaving Nauvoo was not only unromantic (still less sybaritic), it was foolhardy. The last thing Heber needed at that time was more responsibility. By doing so, however, he indicated his willingness to assume full liability for these women (and their children) while heading into the unknown. It was also the last chance to have such marriages solemnized in the temple. Further, it appears that some single women were very much concerned over the prospect of going into the unknown without some kind of husband to protect them. But Heber, despite all his marrying, was not sympathetic. "Some single women think they can't go into the wild without being married—what a pity—they are foolish stories. . . ." [21] The unusual and pragmatic nature of many of these marriages goes far in explaining why ten wives left him and six are unaccounted for after the move to the West, and why he had children by only seventeen.

The advance party was ready to leave Nauvoo, and the first crossing of the Mississippi took place on February 4, 1846. Heber, turning his home over to part of his large family, started transporting another part of his family across the river on flatboats on February 16, and joined others huddling together at the temporary camp and staging ground being established west of Montrose on Sugar Creek about seven miles from the river. Thereafter, until the camp moved out on March 1, there was continual crossing of the river in both directions. During the last few days in February, it was so cold that wagons crossed on the ice. Many dared not let the leaders out of their sight and crossed in near panic for fear of being left behind.

The initial crossing and camping were neither orderly nor disciplined, and few people had followed advice and had adequate food supplies with them. Those leaving Nauvoo had been previously admonished to have (for every family of five) a good wagon, three yoke of oxen, two cows, two beef cattle, three sheep, 1,000 pounds of flour, 20 pounds of sugar, two pounds of tea, five pounds of coffee, one rifle, ammunition, and a tent. In addition to this "fit-out," costing about $250, they needed all the clothing, bedding, and other foodstuffs they could acquire. Although Heber entered the Sugar Creek camp with a two-year supply of food, the mismanagement and unpreparedness of others caused it to be consumed within two weeks.

In spite of this and other difficulties attending the evacuation, months of planning and preparation made the exodus, even though several months ahead of schedule, much more orderly and successful than is generally believed, and far from the fiery and bloody route of folklore. (The real horrors would take place the following September, when those who had not yet left were literally driven to the water's edge by mobs.)

And so Heber's home and the partially abandoned Nauvoo were behind him across the nickel-colored Mississippi. His future lay in the West. He and the part of his family who were with him were commencing a new phase in their lives.

NOTES

1. H. M. Whitney, *Woman's Exponent*, vol. 11 (Feb. 1, 1883), 130.

2. *Times and Seasons*, July 15, 1845. Years later in Utah he once said that he had never been "so drunk, but once, but what I could whip any man I ever saw except Brother Brigham." *Journal of Discourses*, vol. 5 (July 12, 1857), 30–31.

3. This journal, no. 93, gives great detail about all aspects of the temple—construction, decoration, sessions, etc.

4. *Journal of Discourses*, vol. 4 (Jan. 11, 1957), 170.

5. H. C. Kimball, Journal 93, Jan. 26, 1846, Church Archives.

6. *Ibid.*, Dec. 21, 1845.

7. Wallace Stegner, *The Gathering of Zion* (New York: McGraw-Hill, 1964), 37.

8. *Times and Seasons*, Aug. 1, 1845.

9. See Allen D. Roberts, "The Origin, Use, and Decline of Early Mormon Symbolism," *Sunstone*, vol. 4 (May–June, 1979), 22–37.

10. "Discourse in the Tabernacle," Mar. 23, 1853, H. C. Kimball Papers, Church Archives.

11. During Oct., 1844, Heber and Brigham Young visited the Norwegian Branch of Ottawa, Illinois, where Heber may have first met two of his future wives—Ellen and Harriet Sanders.

12. The documents pertaining to the indictment and proceedings are in the National Archives, Records of the Solicitor of the Treasurer, RG 206, Part II, microfilm copy at Southern Illinois University, Edwardsville. Edwin Bonney came to Nauvoo in 1844 from New York and Indiana with his wife and three daughters. He never became a Mormon and generally associated with Mississippi River counterfeiters and thieves. In 1845 he moved across the river to Montrose, Iowa, and was eventually acquitted of the 1846 charges of counterfeiting. His book, *The Banditti of the Prairies* (1850), became a best-seller and made him famous. He died in Chicago in 1864.

13. H. C. Kimball, Journal 91, Nov. 12, 1845, Church Archives.

14. *Ibid.*, June 4, 1845.

15. *Times and Seasons*, Nov. 1, 1845.

16. H. M. Whitney, *Woman's Exponent*, vol. 12 (Oct. 15, 1883), 74. A similar painting by William M. Majors of the Brigham Young family has survived. It shows the parents and six children in an English country mansion setting.

17. *Ibid.*, vol. 11 (Mar. 15, 1883), 154. She got the piano.

18. Little is known about the financial support of Joseph's widows. One, Lucy Walker, recorded that they all had to fend for themselves, to learn a trade. Maria (Nancy Maria Winchester?) and Sarah Lawrence, for example, went to work in a millinery shop in Quincy. "A Brief Biographical Sketch of the Life and Labors of Lucy Walker Kimball Smith," Lucy Walker Kimball Papers, Church Archives.

19. For the record, Heber married five actual widows of Joseph and five who had been married to Joseph posthumously, and he had nineteen children by four—Huntington, McBride, Walker, and Whitney. Eleven of these children survived Kimball and at his death ranged in age from six to eighteen. Walker was the mother of five, Whitney of five, and Huntington of one. This practice raises a question: whom did these children consider to be their real father—Heber or Joseph? To date I have found no document with reference to this question. There is no evidence that these children were treated in any way differently from Kimball's other children. Their relation to Joseph probably was explained to them as they matured.

20. Testimony of Lucy W. Kimball as cited in the *Abstract of Evidence, [Independence] Temple Lot Case*, vol. 2, 379.

21. Minutes, Nov. 16, 1845, Thomas Bullock Collection, Church Archives.

Heber C. Kimball, from the original daguerrotype,
c. 1850–60. Courtesy of Historical Department, Church
of Jesus Christ of Latter-day Saints.

The Cock Pit, Preston, England. Leased by Heber C. Kimball in 1838 as Mormon meeting hall. Courtesy of Historical Department, Church of Jesus Christ of Latter-day Saints.

Kirtland Temple, Kirtland, Ohio, dedicated 1836. Courtesy of Historical Department, Church of Jesus Christ of Latter-day Saints.

Heber C. Kimball home, Nauvoo, Illinois, c. 1910. The ornate woodwork is not original. Courtesy of Historical Department, Church of Jesus Christ of Latter-day Saints.

"Crossing the Mississippi on Ice, Leaving Nauvoo," by C. C. A. Christensen. Courtesy of Brigham Young University Art Museum Collection.

"Wagons Preparing to Leave Winter Quarters in 1847," by C. C. A. Christensen. Courtesy of Brigham Young University Art Museum Collection.

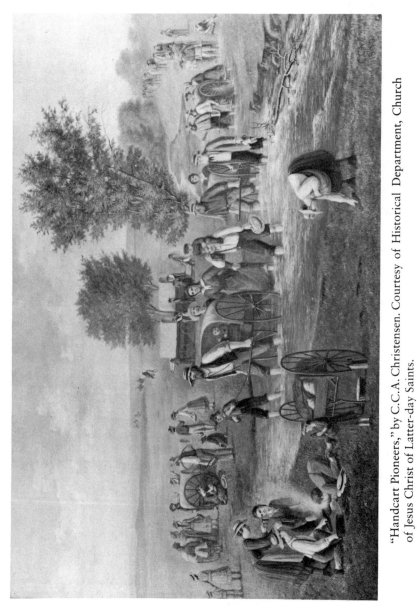

"Handcart Pioneers," by C.C.A. Christensen. Courtesy of Historical Department, Church of Jesus Christ of Latter-day Saints.

"The Mormon Battalion," by George Martin Ottinger. Courtesy of Historical Department, Church of Jesus Christ of Latter-day Saints.

Drawings from original Mormon pioneer journal kept for Heber C. Kim
ball by Peter O. Hansen across Iowa in 1846. Mountain men, Indians, an

U.S. soldiers, Council Bluffs, Iowa, 1846–47. Courtesy of Historical Department, Church of Jesus Christ of Latter-day Saints.

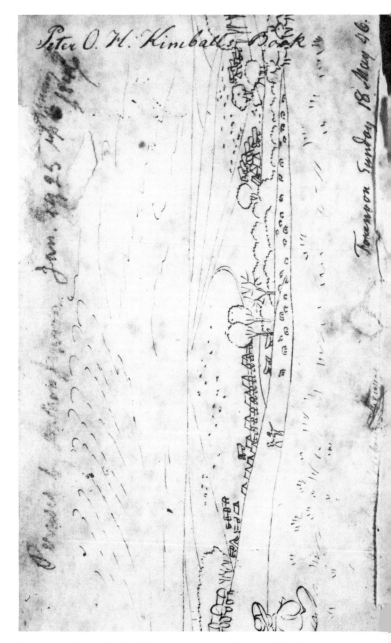

Drawings from Kimball-Hansen journal. Views of Mt. Pisgah, permanen[t]
Mormon camp in Iowa, May 18, 1846. Courtesy of Historical Depart[ment]

ment, Church of Jesus Christ of Latter-day Saints.

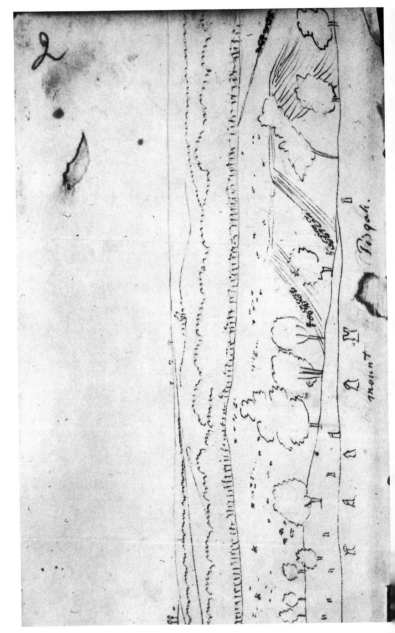

Drawings from Kimball-Hansen journal. *Left*, another view of Mt. Pisgah. *Right*, north end of the City of the Saints at Cutler's Park, Nebraska (near

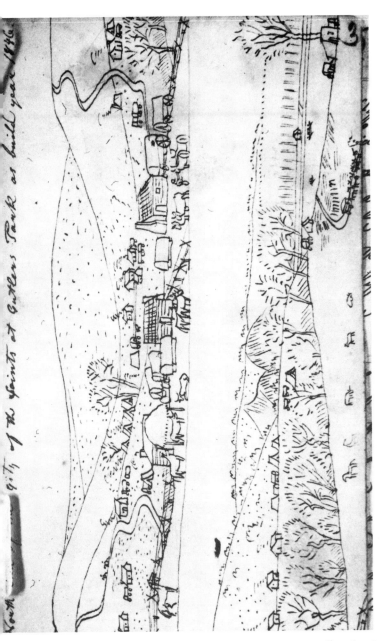

(Winter Quarters), 1846. Courtesy of Historical Department, Church of Jesus Christ of Latter-day Saints.

Vilate Murray Kimball, first wife of Heber C. Kimball. Courtesy of Historical Department, Church of Jesus Christ of Latter-day Saints.

Heber C. Kimball, from the original daguerrotype, c. 1850–60. Courtesy of Historical Department, Church of Jesus Christ of Latter-day Saints.

Six wives of Heber C. Kimball, Salt Lake City, Utah, 1888. Courtesy of Daughters of Utah Pioneers.

Twenty-five sons and daughters of Heber C. Kimball, Salt Lake City, 1887. Courtesy of Historical Department, Church of Jesus Christ of Latter-day Saints.

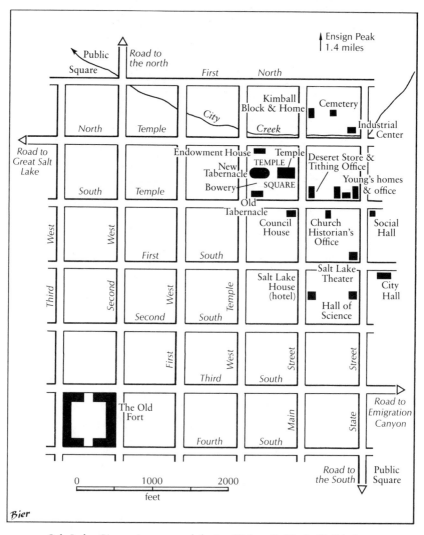

Salt Lake City as it appeared during Heber C. Kimball's lifetime.

Salt Lake City, c. 1871, from the hill on the north, looking south. Heber C. Kimball homes in immediate foreground. Courtesy of Utah State Historical Society.

Southeast view of the Valley from Arsenal Hill, c. 1877. C. R. Savage photo. Courtesy of Historical Department, Church of Jesus Christ of Latter-day Saints.

Old Kimball grist mill in Bountiful, Utah, c. 1907. Erected by Heber C. Kimball in 1852–53. Courtesy of Utah State Historical Society.

The old Kimball homestead on North Main, Salt Lake City, c. 1897. Courtesy of Historical Department, Church of Jesus Christ of Latter-day Saints.

PART III

THE PIONEERING INTERLUDE
1846–48

It was pretty hard and laborious, I admit;
but it was one of the pleasantest journeys I ever performed.
Journal of Discourses, Aug. 2, 1857

The Trek across Iowa

By the time the exodus began, Heber's family consisted of at least thirty-eight wives (four of whom were pregnant), six small children, and two married children and their families. He was also responsible for several foster children his wives had borne before marrying him, and seven adopted sons, some of whom had families of their own.[1] The fact that polygamy was still semi-secret, neither publicly admitted nor generally known throughout the church, makes it very difficult to account for the number and whereabouts of members of Heber's family, since information on them is very scanty.

Sometime in February 1846 he gathered at Sugar Creek the thirty or so of his family going west with him. This group, living in wagons and tents, probably consisted of twelve to fourteen wives, including Vilate, Ellen Sanders, Harriet Sanders, Sarah Lawrence, Sarah Peak, Christeen Golden, and the pregnant Sarah Ann Whitney; Vilate's four small sons; Helen and her husband, Horace Whitney; William and his wife Mary Davenport and their daughter; and Heber's adopted sons.

Among the wives Heber temporarily left behind were Sarah Peak with an eight-month-old infant, Lucy Walker with a one-month-old infant, the sisters Clarissa and Emily Cutler, and Frances Swan, all three of whom were pregnant.

Camp life at Sugar Creek, where several thousand people were gathered, was grim, with the temperature often below freezing—the wind was not tempered to these shorn lambs. Heber's family lived in their wagons and tents. In spite of the harsh conditions, however, there was some merriment in camp and along the trail. Almost every night William Pitt's Brass Band played the grand marches, quick-steps, and gallops popular at the time. The people also frequently danced—reels, jigs, polkas, quadrilles, and other square and line dances—to the music of fiddles. (Round dances, especially the new waltz, were suspect). Around the campfires they sang such favorites as "Home Sweet Home," "The Old Arm Chair," and "Dandy Jim from Caroline." Later on they made up some of their own songs, such as "The Way We Crossed the Plains":

> In a shaky wagon we ride, for to cross the prairie wide.
> As slowly the oxen moved along,
> We walloped them well with a good leather thong.
> The way we crossed the plains.

or "The Upper California":

> The upper California, Oh that's the land for me!
> It lies between the mountains and the great Pacific Sea;
> The Saints can be supported there,
> And taste the sweets of liberty.
> In the Upper California, that's the land for me!

Sunday, March 1, 1846, dawned crisp and clear, and the camp was ready to move out. In an effort to further prepare the Saints for the exodus and to chastise them for "running to Brother Brigham" so much, Heber had an area cleared of snow and gave notice that the entire camp was to assemble at 10:00 A.M. Climbing on a wagon wheel and pulling his greatcoat tightly around him, he warned them they would be tried, and made it clear that there was to be none of the disobedience which had earlier brought a plague upon Zion's Camp. "I want no man to touch any of my things," he insisted, "without my leave. If any man will come to me and say that he wants to steal I will give him the amount." Finally he warned, "Cease all your loud laughter and light speeches, for the Lord is displeased with such things, and call upon the Lord with all your might." Promising them that they should "see the kingdom of God established and all the kingdoms of the world become kingdoms of Our God and His Christ," he dismissed the congregation and urged them to prepare to leave.[2]

No accurate record was kept of how many wagons and people were at Sugar Creek that March 1—estimates vary from 400 to 500 wagons and from 3,000 to 5,000 individuals—but 500 wagons and 3,000 people is probably close to the truth.

The ubiquitous white-tops or covered wagons of the era were the favored vehicle for such travel. Families en route could live in and under these animal-drawn mobile homes, and at the end of the trail they could become temporary dwellings until permanent houses were erected. But the Saints used all kinds of wagons and carriages and a variety of draft animals—horses, mules, oxen, and even cattle. Oxen were preferred when available, for they had great strength and patience and were easy to keep;

they did not fight mud or quicksand, required no expensive and complicated harness, could forage on almost anything, were less likely to stray, and were more valuable at the end of the trail. The science of "ox-teamology" consisted of little more than walking along the left side and behind the lead oxen with a whip, prod, or goad urging them on and guiding them, and was considerably simpler than handling the reins of horses or mules. The oxen responded to the cry of "gee" for a right turn and "haw" for a left, and experienced teamsters might also lay their whip over the oxen's back when geeing and over the neck when hawing. With gentle oxen, widows with children could and did (with a little help, especially during the morning yoking up) transport themselves and possessions successfully all the way to the Valley of the Great Salt Lake.

What from the start was known as the "Camp of Israel" began to lumber out about noon to the gees and haws of teamsters and the yells of herdsmen and children and begin a nearly four-month journey of almost 300 miles across Iowa, that Mormon Mesopotamia between the Mississippi and Missouri rivers. As the Great Trek progressed, the Saints noted and cherished Old Testament parallels to a Zion, a Chosen People, an Exodus, a Mt. Pisgah, and later to a Jordan River, Dead Sea, being "in the tops of the mountains," and making the desert blossom as the rose. In this the Mormons were unique only in that they pushed the parallels further than the much earlier Puritans and the first Oregonians, who had only recently preceded them west.

The Mormons resembled the peoples of ancient Israel in other ways: they were divided into groups of fifties and tens, and they were at times fractious and whiny. To keep the camp together, or at least to keep in touch with the various leaders, Brigham and Heber appointed mounted couriers to ride back and forth, and also arranged for different colored signal flags to communicate messages and to call meetings.

Heber had several wagons, and one large family carriage for Vilate and the young children. Most of the others in his family had to walk or ride horses when they could. Since Helen was her father's pet and since she had just married Horace Whitney and was really on her honeymoon, they were permitted the luxury of a wagon to themselves, sort of a thirty-four-square-foot bridal chamber on wheels. Lamps, rugs, pillows, and a little furniture made this wagon rather comfortable. Their bed was made upon boxes and bags of grain in the rear of the wagon, a provision chest in front served as a table, and in the middle was a chair in which Helen read or knitted while Horace reclined and read or played epithalamia on his flute.

A few journals give a romantic cast to the exodus, but as most other journals make clear, the worst part of the entire journey from Nauvoo to the Valley of the Great Salt Lake was the beginning. No part of the long trek surpasses the tragedy and triumph of this hegira across the flat, open prairie of Iowa, which consisted then of little more than bluestem prairie grass and stands of oak and hickory forests along the numerous rivers and streams and dangerous swamps and bogs. Often, when roads did exist, they were more bridges than roads: logs lashed together with tough willows and thrown across the rolling swells. Wagon wheels easily cut through the foot-thick sod into muddy water. Heber may have reflected often on the frontier sarcasm that it was a middling good road when the mud did not quite reach one's boot tops while astride a horse.

Across Iowa they followed territorial roads as far west as possible. Thereafter, because few travelers had preceded them west of the settlements, they used vague paths and Potawatomi Indian trails. Although the Mormons made some improvements along the roads and trails they followed across Iowa, they did little, if any, trailblazing.

Injury, sickness, and death were commonplace: black scurvy, black canker (probably diphtheria), cholera morbus, typhoid fever, quick consumption (tuberculosis), and infection accompanying childbirth—in reference to the latter the journal of midwife Patty Bartlett Sessions makes melancholy reading. To these trials one must add the weaknesses of human beings under stress and faced with constant rain and mud.

The problem of privacy in elimination was solved by following the common rule of the day: men to one side, women to the other. If the women went in a group, several sisters standing with skirts spread wide could provide a privacy screen for each other.[3]

Across Iowa in 1846 and on the 1847 and 1848 treks to the Great Basin, the Mormons averaged, under normal conditions, two miles an hour, the usual speed of an ox pulling a heavy wagon all day long. For comparison, stagecoaches with frequent changes of horses averaged sixteen miles an hour. In the 1846 trek, it took a month to cover the first 100 miles—an average of only three miles a day.

The triumph of the Mormon exodus derived from the successful emigration of thousands of men, women, children, and livestock under such difficult conditions. By contrast, the original pioneer company that later went from Winter Quarters to the Valley of the Great Salt Lake, April–July, 1847, did not suffer the death of one person or animal.[4]

Along the Iowa trail the basic skills of emigrating and colonizing were practiced, and several permanent camps were established. This part of the westward march influenced Mormon history long afterward. The Saints had learned only the rudimentary lessons of emigration during the Zion's Camp march from Ohio to Missouri in 1834; the advanced training had to be acquired in Iowa. The skills gained there not only made the trek from Winter Quarters to the Valley of the Great Salt Lake easier, but also set the pattern for building and colonizing the Great Basin.

Although it was generally well known among the Saints that the Camp of Israel was headed beyond the Rocky Mountains and into the Great Basin, little was said about where the camp would cross the Missouri and pick up the Oregon Trail. They had little intention of returning to Missouri and crossing at Independence, Weston, or St. Joseph, and the only other well-established point of crossing to the north was Council Bluffs, Iowa, which was closer to Nauvoo anyway. In August, 1845, the Quorum of the Twelve had sent several men on a reconnaissance mission to find the best route across Iowa, and having seen Council Bluffs they reported favorably on that crossing. In any case, whatever doubt may still have lingered in anyone's mind regarding the Missouri crossing was settled on April 12 at Mt. Pisgah, a permanent camp, when a definite and public decision was made to proceed directly thence to Council Bluffs.

Eight days out of Sugar Creek, on March 8, near present-day Lebanon, one of Heber's wives, Sarah Ann Whitney, gave birth to a son, David, in a valley which Heber called, in Book of Mormon fashion, the Valley of David. This was the first of a series of place names which Heber would designate between Nauvoo and the Valley. (Few of his names, if any, survive, however.)

As the camp moved west some changes and improvements in organization became necessary. Only the fundamental arrangement of the trek had been effected at Nauvoo and Sugar Creek. Many of the original families for various reasons had returned to Nauvoo, and bad roads and weather had scattered others.

On March 22 on the Chariton River, near present-day Sedan, Brigham and Heber called the remaining emigrants together and insisted that they maintain better order. To this end they regrouped into three companies, each with a hundred families. All three were then subdivided into fifties and then tens, each unit led by a captain, the most important leaders of which were those of the six groups of fifty—Brigham Young, Heber Kimball, Parley Pratt, Peter Haws, John Taylor, and George Miller. William Clayton and Willard Richards were appointed camp clerk and historian respectively.

Thereafter the line of march continued somewhat to the southwest until the companies found themselves on Locust Creek, either close to or in Missouri, where they decided to bear more to the north. At that time, since the Missouri boundary was about ten miles north of where it is today, some of them actually dipped into what was then Putnam County. To prevent trouble with the feared Missourians for themselves and those who would follow, on April 14 Heber warned the camp never to be involved in any quarrels, strifes, or contentions with the inhabitants, but to court their favor by every possible means.[5]

That same day, while the camp was still in this disputed border area, a courier arrived with a letter from Nauvoo for Ellen Kimball; it told her of the safe birth of a son to William Clayton. She rushed this joyous news to him, and in celebration he had a little party in his tent that evening.[6] The next morning, walking off by himself, he wrote in joy and gratitude the words of the now-famous hymn "Come, Come, Ye Saints," often called, with some justification, the "Mormon Marseillaise" or the "Hymn heard round the world." The verses epitomize the Mormon motivation for going west and their experience on a dozen trails, some well known, some totally forgotten, between New York and California from 1831 to the completion of the transcontinental railroad in 1869.

> Come, come ye saints, no toil nor labor fear,
> But with joy wend your way;
> Though hard to you this journey may appear
> Grace shall be as your day.
> 'Tis better far for us to strive
> Our useless cares from us to drive;
> Do this, and joy your hearts will swell—
> All is well! All is well!
>
> Why should we mourn or think our lot is hard?
> 'Tis not so; all is right.
> Why should we think to earn a great reward,
> If we now shun the fight?
> Gird up your loins, fresh courage take;
> Our God will never us forsake;
> And soon we'll have this tale to tell—
> All is well! All is well!
>
> We'll find a place which God for us prepared,
> Far away in the West,
> Where none shall come to hurt or make afraid;
> There the Saints will be blessed.
> We'll make the air with music ring,
> Shout praises to our God and King;
> Above the rest these words we'll tell—
> All is well! All is well!

And should we die before our journey's through,
Happy day! All is well!
We then are free from toil and sorrow, too:
With the just we shall dwell!
But if our lives are spared again
To see the Saints their rest obtain,
O how we'll make this chorus swell—
All is well! All is well!

Later that month while the party was camped on Medicine Creek, a rattlesnake bit one of Heber's horses. Without hesitation he quieted the animal, handed its reins to someone, and laid his hands on the animal's head, blessed it, and rebuked the poison; the horse recovered. To those who wondered at the propriety of this, Heber answered simply, "It is just as proper to lay hands on a horse or an ox and administer to them in the name of the Lord, and of such utility, as it is to a human being, both being creatures of His creation, both consequently having a claim to his attention." [7]

By April 24 the Pioneers had reached a place which they named Garden Grove. It was located about halfway across Iowa, 155 miles west of Nauvoo and 130 miles east of Council Bluffs. Here, on the east bank of the Weldon Fork of the Grand River, they established the first of several permanent camps between Nauvoo and Winter Quarters. In three weeks they had broken 715 acres of tough prairie sod, built cabins, and established a community. A town by the name of Garden Grove still exists on this old campsite.

While at Garden Grove Heber requested his adopted son, Peter Hansen, to keep a journal for him, which Hansen began on May 12, 1846, and kept through February 7, 1847. This journal, which ought to be known as the Kimball-Hansen journal, is mainly a day-by-day account of small events—eating, sleeping, sickness, troubles, fun, the weather, the terrain, flowers, incidental visits from the Indians, and the strawberry feasts which Heber loved. It reveals little of Heber's feelings or thoughts, just some of his activities. In one way, however, the journal is unusual, unique perhaps in Mormon history. Peter Hansen was raised in Denmark and had originally learned to write in Danish script, similar to the old German *Handschrift*. Since this hand is difficult to read by English-speaking people, Hansen felt safe in recording in the margins of the journal over a period of several months many highly personal comments on thirty-eight members of the Kimball family.

Most of the comments are rather general—to the effect that so-and-so is "good," "faithful," "prayerful," "diligent," and "righteous." But some are specific enough to suggest the difficulties which had already developed in the Kimball family and the greater sorrows to come. In Hansen's opinion, for example, William "has but little faith and neglects prayers"; Helen "has but little faith and . . . is not always respectful of her parents . . . [and] is disobedient to her parents." Heber's young sons were "pretty good," "sassy," or "disobedient." Harriet Sanders was "inclined to jealousy," and Sarah Peak was "not very strong in faith" and was "proud and jealous."

At Garden Grove Heber learned that his home had been sold for thirty-five yoke of oxen, and wrote the church trustees to let the poor still in Nauvoo use them to come west. He added a comment indicative of the constant trouble the improvident Saints caused: "Here I am with thirty in my family and not one mouth full of meal nor have had for two weeks. . . . I am brought to this along with hundreds of others on account of so many coming on this journey without provisions to last them one week."[8]

When the camp moved out of Garden Grove on May 12, enough families were left behind to maintain the community and to help later Nauvoo exiles, of which there would be thousands. Six days and about thirty-five miles later they established another permanent camp and resting place. This site, on the middle fork (Twelve-Mile Creek) of the Grand River, was selected and named Mt. Pisgah by Parley P. Pratt, who, when he first saw it rising above the Iowa prairie, was reminded of the biblical Pisgah, where Moses viewed the Promised Land (Deuteronomy 3:27). There they built cabins and planted several thousand acres of rich bottomland lying to the west of the rise with peas, cucumbers, beans, corn, buckwheat, potatoes, pumpkins, and squash. Heber also took the opportunity to repair his wagons, tents, and other equipment.

Mt. Pisgah was maintained as a camp until at least 1852, and at its height had over 2,000 inhabitants, among whom may have been part of Heber's large family, left there until the future was more certain. Today little of this site remains but a cemetery, a monument to the hundreds who died there between 1846 and 1852, and a nine-acre park and picnic area. In 1929 the Daughters of the American Revolution placed a marker in this area to honor the "first white settlement" in Union County.

At Mt. Pisgah, after over two and a half months of Iowa mud, domestic problems, and the strain of leadership, Heber lost his customary good nature. He had had enough of whining and discontent. He assembled the camp in the shade of an oak and hickory grove, shucked his coat, and thundered that their lack of cooperation was holding the march back and that if they did not improve, the Twelve would go into foreign countries to preach the Gospel and raise up a body of people who *would* be willing to abide by council and act as becomes the Saints of God. The Saints, withered by Heber's denunciation, reformed. Old-time Mormons could repent in a hurry—like Heber's son Jonathan Golden, who was wont to say on occasion, "Hell, they can't excommunicate me, I repent too damn fast!" The people tried to do better, and their leaders sought divine help in a special manner. They withdrew to the isolation of the limitless prairie, clothed themselves in temple robes, formed a prayer circle, and invoked God for the good of the people and the success of the venture. All along the trek such special group prayers were held.

Late on June 2, the camp moved on toward Council Bluffs, 100 miles to the west, leaving behind enough people to improve and maintain Mt. Pisgah for the benefit of future Saints going west. This last section of the 1846 journey was relatively pleasant: the sun dried the roads, grass grew, and strawberries flourished. On Sunday, June 7, Heber cheered the people, or at least tried to, by reminding them that they were like the children of Israel going to an unknown land, and that they had already been greatly blessed.[9] A week later the camp reached the Council Bluffs area and the first portion of the march was nearly over.

From the bluffs Heber looked down on the remarkably wide floodplain stretching for over eight miles to the Missouri, which even then was known as "Old Muddy Face" and beyond which lay the Far West. But at Council Bluffs the Mormons were not yet really in the wilderness. The general area, up and down the river, had been an Indian trading site since at least 1804, when Lewis and Clark stopped there, military forts had been built there as early as 1824, steamboats from St. Louis reached there as early as 1819, and it was an established point of departure for Oregon and California. Downstream to Independence, Missouri, there were twenty-four inhabited sites on the river; upstream, eighty-one. There was a village and a steamboat landing on each side of the river, with service to Fort Leavenworth, Independence, and St. Louis, and regular mail service. Indian agents were located on one, sometimes both, sides of the Missouri, and a Presbyterian Indian mission was on the west bank. Many goods and services, including some medical aid, were available. Later missionaries were even dispatched directly to England from there. It was only 150 miles from Far West and about 60 miles from some Missouri settlements, where some Mormons went to find work. And although separated from Nauvoo by the memory of over three months of sorrow, one could, under extreme circumstances, cover the distance in as little as nine days.[10] Once, by driving night and day, it was done in six.

Soon after their arrival, Heber, part of his family, and many others visited "Indian Town" or Council Point (located near today's South Omaha Bridge). It was a straggling village on the Iowa shore inhabited mainly by halfbreeds and some French people who had been there when the area was part of the French empire in the New World, or had drifted up from Louisiana and St. Louis. The village and the Indian agency were there mainly to serve the Potawatomi tribe. Pitt's band played and a dance was held. Generally amicable relations were maintained with this settlement throughout the sojourn of the Mormons there.

During June the Pioneers settled temporarily in camps along the bluffs near Mosquito Creek and on the flats near the Missouri River just north of Indian Town.

In the Council Bluffs vicinity Heber and the Mormons in general had their first real and sustained contacts with the Indians. The Book of Mormons gave the Saints a unique attitude toward the Indians explaining the early and continued concern for their welfare. According to Mormon belief, many American Indians are descended from several groups of people in pre-Columbian America who had rejected God and fallen under a curse. This curse was to be removed eventually through the acceptance of true Christianity. Mormons felt it was their obligation to help the Indians, not only to "civilize" them but also to teach them about the Restoration and help them become a "fair and delightsome people."

Across Iowa the Mormons had been on Potawatomi lands since Mt. Pisgah. At Council Bluffs they met the Potawatomi chief, Pied Riche, called "the Clerk" by the French because of his education. The chief felt a kinship with the Mormons. In a welcoming speech he told them: "So we have both suffered. We must keep one another, and the Great Spirit will keep us both. You are now free to cut and use all the wood you wish. You can make your improvements and live on any part of our actual land not occupied by us. Because one suffers and does not deserve it, is no reason he should suffer always. I say, we may live to see all right yet. However, if we do not, our children will." [11] (The chief, like many Indians, was also a polygamist.)

The Indian agent in Council Bluffs, Major Robert B. Mitchell, was also friendly to the Mormons. He reported to the Superintendent of Indian Affairs in St. Louis: "I am gratified to say that since their arrival I have seen nothing to which exception could be taken. The principal men seem determined to hold themselves aloof from the Indians. They admit no intercourse after night particularly with the Indians. They complain that they have been badly treated, but declare their intentions to bear the American Flag to whatever country they cast their lot." [12] Much of the

Mormon aloofness may have stemmed from their concern that Indian hospitality sometimes included the offering of Indian women to visitors.

In July the Mormons established a third, more permanent camp on the Iowa shore north of Indian Town, a camp which became known as Kanesville, the origin of modern-day Council Bluffs. After this camp was made Heber Kimball and Brigham Young were immediately concerned over two major problems: sending an advance company to the Rocky Mountains, and locating a place for the main portion of the camp to build winter quarters until they, too, could go west in the spring.

On July 1, the first problem was solved by elimination. On that day Captain James Allen of the U.S. Army's First Regiment of Dragoons of Fort Leavenworth rode into the Mosquito Creek camp with a request from President James K. Polk for a battalion of 500 Mormon men to fight in the Mexican War, a generally unpopular war. Heber favored the action, however, and other church leaders concurred. Part of the agreement was that the Mormons would be permitted officially to camp on Potawatomi lands and, unofficially, allowed to move across the Missouri River and settle temporarily on Omaha Indian lands, which were closed to whites.[13] It was important to the Mormons to put one more river between them and the Gentiles. The next day, Heber and Brigham Young moved their families across the quarter-mile-wide river to Cold Spring camp—a temporary camp in what is now South Omaha.

On July 3 Heber, Brigham Young, and Willard Richards, acting as recruiting sergeants, started back with Allen along the line of march, 130 miles to Mt. Pisgah, passing en route more than 800 Mormon wagons on their way to Council Bluffs. At Mt. Pisgah the Saints were assembled in a hickory grove where the shirt-sleeved Heber, standing before a deal table and under the flag, gave them, in his rough-and-ready manner, what he thought was a pep talk. He said he did not think the men would have to fight, assured them their wives would be taken care of, that they would never want, and then, in a curious appeal to their faith and manhood, added, "If any of you die, why die away and the work will go on . . . we will go on and put in a crop."[14] In spite of, or perhaps because of, this talk their work of recruitment was a success. By July 12, they were back in Council Bluffs, and soon the battalion was mustered in and organized. On July 20 the new recruits started off for Fort Leavenworth, located 150 miles down the Missouri. Only one of Heber's extended family, John Forsgren, signed up.

There is still, as there was then, a widespread belief among Mormons that raising the Mormon Battalion was a great sacrifice on the part of the church to an undeserving government. Actually, the government was responding to the requests of Mormon leaders for "any facilities for emigration to the western coast which our government shall offer."

On at least two occasions, Heber referred favorably to the battalion incident. "These military affairs," he said on the following July 17, "is now found by most all of the people acknowledged to be one of the greatest blessings that the Great God of heaven ever did bestow upon the people." [15] In 1855, in Utah, he declared to veterans at a reunion of the Mormon Battalion, "I know that [the Battalion] resulted in the salvation of this people, and had you not done this, we should not have been here."

With the question of a pioneer group going west that fall eliminated by the formation of the Battalion, Young and Heber began in earnest to locate their winter quarters and to settle the Saints. Most of their searching was on the western side of the Missouri River on Indian lands disputed by the Omaha and Oto nations, the former having the best claim. The Omaha, unlike the Potawatomi, were indigenous to the Great Plains, having been there at least 200 years. They were a small tribe of only about 1,500 and were known for their consistent friendliness to the whites. The Otos, on the other hand, were considered by both Indians and whites to be a mean and thieving people. Both tribes were basically farmers living in permanent earthen lodge villages.

Chief Big Elk and the Omahas were agreeable to the Mormons settling among them: the Indians might benefit from Mormon expertise and what the Saints would leave behind, and the whites might afford them some help against an ancient enemy, the warlike Sioux, who frequently raided Omaha villages.

Two temporary camps were made opposite Council Bluffs. The first was called Cutler's Park, after Alpheus Cutler, Heber's father-in-law, who selected it that August. It was soon decided, however, that Cutler's Park was not suitable, and another campsite was selected in early September, three miles closer to the river. Here, in present-day Florence, Nebraska, the Saints finally built their Winter Quarters, the "Mormon Valley Forge." (A pretty story claims that the community was named after Brigham Young's favorite plural wife, but none of Brigham's twenty-seven wives was so named.) Winter Quarters was a city of 631 houses, some of logs and some of "prairie marble" or sod, and 3,483 people.

NOTES

1. The "Law of Adoption," which seems to have commenced in Nauvoo in 1842, permitted church leaders to graft onto their families other men and their

families in order to increase their posterity in this life and the next. Heber eventually adopted Hosea Cushing, William A. King, Howard Egan, Daniel Davis, James Smithies, Jacob Frazier, George Billings, Charles Hubbard, and three sailors from Denmark, Hans C. Hansen, Peter O. Hansen, and John Forsgren. Later during the Utah period too much competition in "Kingdom-building" grew out of this practice and it was abandoned. As late in 1880–82, however, Heber's son Abraham Alonzo had fifty-four men, women, and children posthumously adopted by his father. A. A. Kimball family records, in author's possession.

2. Watson, ed., *Manuscript History of Brigham Young, 1846–47,* 57–58.

3. Juanita Brooks, ed., *On the Mormon Frontier: The Diary of Hosea Stout, 1844–61* (Salt Lake City: University of Utah Press, 1964), 123n. See also Dale Morgan as cited by John D. Unruh, Jr., in *The Plains Across: The Overland Emigrants and the Trans-Mississippi West, 1840–60* (Urbana: University of Illinois Press, 1979), 422. Compare Deuteronomy 23:12–15. In reading more than 700 pioneer journals for the period 1831–69 I found no other reference to this matter, which Victorian Americans considered taboo.

4. Four horses, however, were lost through carelessness.

5. H. C. Kimball, Journal, Apr. 14, 1846, Church Archives.

6. H. M. Whitney, *Woman's Exponent,* vol. 12 (Jan. 15, 1884), 127.

7. *Ibid.* (Feb. 1, 1884), 135. What apparently was the first example of the blessing of sick animals took place earlier, on Feb. 14, when William Hall's horse sickened with bloating and colic. Citing the prophet Joel, who said that in the last days the Lord would pour out his spirit upon all flesh (Joel 2:28), some of the brethren laid hands on the animal and blessed it. It recovered. The much more famous similar incident involving the ox of Mary Fielding (one of Heber's wives) took place in 1848 (see below, p. 182).

8. H. C. Kimball to Joseph Heywood, May 12, 1846, typescript in author's possession.

9. H. C. Kimball, Journal, June 7, 1846, Church Archives.

10. "Brother Joseph Toronto, the only Italian man in the church, made mother a present of some lemons and oranges and a little wine; he had come from the City of Joseph in 9 days by hiring a man to bring him on." H. C. Kimball, Journal, June 23, 1846.

11. Leonard J. Arrington, *Charles C. Rich: Mormon General and Western Frontiersman* (Provo, Utah: Brigham Young University Press, 1974), 98.

12. Letters Received by the Office of Indian Affairs, 1824–81, M234, roll 216, Council Bluffs Agency, 1844–46, frame 497, June 29, 1846, National Archives, Washington, D.C.

13. To protect themselves the Mormons requested written permission from Allen. He gave them the following statement (which he also sent to Washington): "The Mormon people having on due application raised and furnished for the service of the United States a Battalion of Volunteers to move with the Army of the West in our present war with Mexico—and many of the men comprising the Battalion having to leave their families in the Pottawatomi Country—the written permission to a portion of the Mormon people to reside for a time on the Potta-

watomi lands obtained from the Indians on my request is fully approved by me and such of the Mormon people as may desire to avail themselves to this privilege are hereby fully allowed to do so during the pleasure of the President of the United States. July 16, 1846, Capt. James Allen." *Ibid.*, frame 539.

Despite Allen's assurances, there seems to have been some effort to remove the Mormons from these Indian lands, for on Aug. 14 the Superintendent of Indian Affairs in St. Louis wrote Washington, "If the Government decided to drive them from the Indian Country it has not the physical force at this time on the border, but I cannot believe that it is willing to force these poor, deluded people into the wild prairie to die of starvation." *Ibid.*, frame 504.

14. Arrington, C. C. *Rich*, 104.

15. H. C. Kimball, Journal 90, July 14, 1846, Church Archives.

CHAPTER 12

The Staging Ground at Winter Quarters

At Winter Quarters Heber first consolidated and housed his sprawling family and many dependents. Upon his arrival on the Missouri in June, Heber had twenty-two wagons and about twenty-eight people with him living in the wagons and tents. Among them were seven wives—Vilate, Christeen Golden, Sarah Ann Whitney, Sarah Lawrence, Harriet Sanders, Ellen Sanders, and Mary Houston; the other wives who had left Nauvoo with him were apparently scattered among different families. With him at Winter Quarters were also Vilate's four young sons, as well as William and his wife and daughter; Helen and her husband; Vilate's niece, Jennette Murray; several older adopted children; and a few others assigned to his care—Merrit Rockwell, brother of Orrin Porter Rockwell, one-time bodyguard to Joseph Smith and frontiersman extraordinaire, and some English converts of 1837, James Smithies and his wife and daughter Mary.

Also, from time to time, some of the wives and children Heber had left in Nauvoo came west. During that summer he was joined by Presendia Huntington and perhaps her son George, by another husband; Frances Swan and her daughter Margaret Jane; Lucy Walker and her daughter Rachel; Sarah Peak and her three daughters, Betsy and Harriet by a previous husband and Sarah Hellen, Heber's daughter; Clarissa Cutler and son Abraham; Emily Cutler and son Isaac; Mary Ann Shefflin; Ruth A. Reese; Mary Fielding; Mary Ellen Harris; and the sisters Ann Alice and Amanda Gheen. Heber's "camp" eventually consisted of 266 individuals over the age of twelve, 235 wagons, and some 1,600 animals.[1] By the end of 1846 Heber had at least twenty-five of his wives and twelve of his children with him in Winter Quarters, but not necessarily under his immediate care. Other wives were probably with him, but they are not mentioned in the records. In October Vilate's brother William and his wife arrived from Nauvoo. Throughout the period between leaving Nauvoo and settling in Salt Lake City, it is hard to keep track of just how many were in Heber's "family."

On the frontier Heber's full responsibility for the material and spiritual well-being of perhaps 300 people was exhausting. He was under constant strain. For his good as well as theirs he called a special family meeting, at which time he organized them, and rather patriarchally added, "I have become your father and I am your priest, your head, your prophet, your apostle and your revelator, and from no other man can you receive revelation, either now nor in eternity. And I want your prayers that I may have wisdom, and that I may have visions, dreams, and revelations, and that I may live long and your mother also."

Heber wore no hair shirt, courted no martyrdom. He wanted the best this life had to offer him and his. "I don't want to die," he said, "no I want [to] live and see all my children as rich so they can pay out gold by the bushels to pave the streets."[2]

To house such a large family, Heber eventually built one large two-story home and a series of single-story "row houses." The big house had four rooms on the first floor and two upstairs. The row houses were single rooms made of logs, with sod roofs, sod chimneys, and dirt floors; each room had one door and one four-pane window.

In the largest house Heber, Vilate, and their four little boys lived in one room; William, his wife, and their children in another; three young adopted men in one; two young adopted women in one; and two other wives in one. Just who lived in the row houses and exactly how many there were we do not know, but Mary Ann Sheflin lived in one, Sarah Ann Whitney had one, Helen and Horace had one, and another was used as a storeroom.[3] Christeen Golden apparently lived with the Grant family, Clarissa and Emily Cutler lived with their parents, Presendia Huntington kept house for Joseph and Henry Woodmansee, and Mary Ellen Harris stayed with Heber's son William. Other members of the family lived in tents and wagons. At one time Frances Swan, Laura Pitkin, and Presendia Huntington lived together.

Such crowded and primitive living conditions inevitably caused friction. Lucy Walker complained to William Clayton how some members of the Kimball family treated her; Sarah Lawrence left Heber's group and moved in with the Youngs; and one "female member of his family had spoken evil of him and opened her cares to other Woman or Women, who goes about for such purposes." Heber did not take such things casually. He chastized, counseled, and encouraged often that difficult fall and winter. He admitted fatigue from so many cares over the "wicked" and the "contrary spirit among the people."[4] The Saints were very human and the heads of polygamous households had much to contend with. The farther the modern Moses led the Saints from the comfortable homes they had been forced to abandon, the longer and more grim the sojourn in the wilderness, the more the followers questioned their leaders. In bad as well as good the Mormons were much like their ancient prototypes. Heber had to advise them against carelessness, improvidence, slothfulness, vanity, murmuring or complaining, and finding fault with him, their kindred, and each other. He spoke against the problem of slander and backbiting and urged the young girls to read the Book of Mormon, the Bible, or other good books instead of spending so much time in foolishness. These perorations always ended with his blessings for peace, prosperity, and salvation.[5]

The winter of 1846–47 was grim. At least 300 died from various causes, adding to the number already dead from malaria and other fevers. Heber was sick on occasion from the constant strain. There was also some trouble with the Indians—mainly stealing. Brigham Young, unaffected by either Rousseau's romantic concern for the Noble Savage or the cruel belief that the only good Indian was a dead one, wisely decided it was cheaper to feed them than to fight them; he also warned Big Elk, chief of the Omahas, that any Indians caught stealing would be whipped—the same punishment meted out to white malefactors. (Since the Mormons had no jails, they found it necessary to practice corporal punishment for a few years.) Even Heber's nephew Carlos Murray was given fifteen lashes for stealing cattle from some non-Mormons on the trail west in 1848.

Still, the Mormons made the best of things. They organized concerts, dances (even dancing lessons), songfests, feasts, festivals, and sleigh rides, and visited back and forth with the other whites across the river and downstream at Bellevue. On rare occasions they were treated to traveling entertainers. During February of 1847, for example, William McCarey, an "Indian Negro" and psychologically unbalanced Mormon claiming to be Adam, together with his wife played the flute, fife, saucepan, rattler, "36¢ whistle" and performed as mimics. The Saints also handcrafted things to sell, such as willow baskets and washboards.

And it is reassuring to know that life took its usual and ordained course even while crossing muddy Iowa in wagons, for on February 2 of that winter Vilate gave birth to another son, Solomon Farnham. She composed a revealing little poem after his birth:

> The Lord has blessed us with another Son which is
> the seventh I have born.

> May he be the father of many lives. But not the
> Husband of many Wives.[6]

In Winter Quarters Heber and Brigham received some unexpected
and welcome information regarding the Mountain West. That November
the famous Jesuit, Father Pierre Jean de Smet, stopped and visited with the
Mormons. He was en route to St. Louis after spending five years in the
mountains preaching to the Flathead Indians and was one of the few white
men who had visited the Great Salt Lake. Taking full advantage of this
good luck, the Mormons asked him every question they could think of. De
Smet took it goodnaturedly and some years later wrote a brief account of
this meeting.[7]

In early January, 1847, Heber and Brigham began readying a pioneer
company to start for the Rocky Mountains that spring sometime between
April 15 and May 30, which was the traditional time to head west. Part of
Heber's preparations for his family consisted in calling some special Sunday meetings.[8] In February he blessed six wives and their seven infants—
Sarah Peak with Sarah Helen, Clarissa Cutler with Abraham, Emily Cutler, with Isaac, Sarah Ann Whitney with David, Lucy Walker with Rachel,
and Vilate with Brigham and Solomon.

At another meeting he scolded them for "going to an extreme in
amusements, principally . . . dancing." He admitted that he himself loved
to dance, but that it should not be overdone. To encourage his family in
self-improvement he said, "Everyone has the greatest obstacle to govern
himself. I have greater trouble to govern Brother Heber, and put self down
than anything else."

Finally, on Sunday, March 21, he called his last family meeting. This
particular session was restricted to members of his immediate family,
which by this time consisted of about fifty individuals, including eleven
infants, and was for the purpose of giving instruction to those who would
follow the pioneer group west later that summer in the Second Division or
Big Company, as it came to be called.

William Kimball and his adopted brother Daniel Davis were given the
enormous responsibility of outfitting twelve of Heber's wives and eight
other families with wagons, teams, and supplies. Heber was most explicit.
With over 500 men away with the Mormon Battalion and nearly 150
more preparing to leave, there would be few ablebodied men left behind to
care for and protect the women and children. From this meeting we get
some idea of the women Heber felt first responsibility for: the wives listed
were Vilate, Sarah Peak, Sarah Ann Whitney, Ellen Sanders, Mary Ellen

Harris, Mary Ann Sheflin, Harriet Sanders, Christeen Golden, Presendia Huntington, the Gheen sisters, and Sarah Lawrence. Other women mentioned were Jennette Murray, Mary Forsgren (whose husband was with the Battalion), Melinda Miller, Alice Martin, Harriet Dilworth, a Sister Hess, and a Sister "Havath" (probably his future wife Elizabeth Doty Cravath Murray Brown). Why those particular women were specified is not known. Perhaps Heber thought they were those best able to spend that winter in the Valley and he planned on bringing the rest west when the final trip was made in 1848. Helen was to travel with her husband's family.

For reasons that are not at all clear, however, only three of his family went west in the Second Division. Perhaps at the last minute it was decided that none should be part of the Second Division save those able to sustain themselves in the Great Basin until a crop could be harvested. Or it might have been that William and Daniel failed to get wagons and teams ready in time, or perhaps the women, knowing Heber would not be staying in the Valley, wisely elected to spend that winter in the relative security of Winter Quarters and let him worry about getting them all west in 1848. (Davis's diary suggests that they were much too busy just staying alive to get ready to go west.)

In any case, from April, 1847, through September, 1848, the Kimball family was very scattered, and when Heber left Winter Quarters for the Great Basin in April, 1847, he took with him but one wife, Ellen Sanders; his son-in-law Horace Whitney; Vilate's nephew Carlos Murray; and five of his adopted sons, Howard Egan, William A. King, Hosea Cushing, George W. Billings, and Hans C. Hansen. Of this group, only Ellen Sanders and Hans Hansen remained in the Salt Lake Valley through the first winter. Only Mary Ellen Harris, Peter Hansen, and Mary Forsgren followed him west that year in a later company. Mary's husband presumably would be waiting for her in the Valley; Mary Ellen at the last minute decided to accompany her mother and stepfather; and Peter probably went along for adventure. The bulk of the Kimball family remained in Winter Quarters until the 1848 trek west.

Some idea of the staggering logistics of preparation for such a venture may be gained from the following inventory, detailed to the last half-cent, of just what Heber assembled and transported in his six wagons:

Teams belonging to H. C. Kimball: Horses 5, mules 7, oxen 6, cows 2, dogs 2, wagons 6. List of provisions: Flour 1228 lbs., meat 865 lbs., sea biscuit 125 lbs., beans 296 lbs., bacon 241 lbs., corn for teams 2869 lbs., buckwheat 300 lbs., dried beef 25 lbs., groceries 290¾ lbs., sole leather 15 lbs., oats 10 bus., rape 40 lbs., seeds 71 lbs., cross-cut saw 1, axes 6, scythe 1, hoes 3, log chains 5, spade 1, crowbar 1, tent 1, keg of powder 25 lbs., lead 20 lbs., codfish 40 lbs., garden seeds 50 lbs., plows 2, bran 3½ bus., 1 side of harness leather, whip saw 1, iron 16 lbs., nails 16 lbs., 1 sack of salt 200 lbs., saddles 2, 1 tool chest, 6 pairs of double harness . . . Total $1,592.87½.[9]

Apparently the original idea by design or accident (but in any case consonant with the tendency of Mormons to pattern themselves after the ancient House of Israel) was to hand pick and outfit 144 men—twelve for each of the Twelve Tribes of Israel. Not all of the men selected were Mormons, however, and there were also three black slaves or servants of southern members.[10] Collectively they had a variety of pioneering talents and skills. There were mechanics, teamsters, hunters, frontiersmen, carpenters, sailors, soldiers, accountants, bricklayers, blacksmiths, wagonmakers, lumbermen, joiners, dairymen, stockmen, millers, and engineers —varying in ability, temperament, and saintliness, they represented a cross section of humanity.

The numerical symmetry was not important. Even before the group left Winter Quarters three women and two children were added and a few days later one sick man returned to Winter Quarters. En route nineteen men left the Pioneers on other assignments and thirty persons were added. So the original 144 was augmented by 35 and decreased by 20, leaving a net gain of 15. Entering the Valley of the Great Salt Lake in July, 1847, was a final group of 159 members.

NOTES

1. H. C. Kimball, Journal 90, Aug. 18, 1846, Church Archives.

2. *Ibid.*, June 28, 1846.

3. H. M. Whitney, *Woman's Exponent*, vol. 13 (Feb. 15, 1885), 139.

4. From the H. C. Kimball Journal for that period.

5. *Ibid.*

6. Mary Haskins Parker Diary, Feb. 10, 1857, typescript, University of Utah, Salt Lake City.

7. As cited by Lelland H. Creer, *The Founding of an Empire* (Salt Lake City: Bookcraft, 1947), 167–68. De Smet almost visited the Mormons again. In 1858 he was one of three chaplains appointed to the army in Utah. He was, however, recalled en route in present-day Nebraska. One suspects that his presence in Utah would have bettered Mormon and army relations.

8. From H. C. Kimball Journal for that period.

9. Howard L. Egan, *Pioneering the West* (Richmond, Utah: Howard R. Egan estate, 1917), 24.

10. They were Green Flake, a member of the church who died in Idaho; Oscar Crosby, who died in Los Angeles in 1870; and Hark Lay, who lived for many years in Salt Lake City. In 1848 twenty-four Blacks came to Utah with the new settlers. Although it has been stated that one of these Blacks, Martha Crosby, who later married Green Flake, was brought to Utah by Heber C. Kimball (see Jack Beller, "Negro Slaves in Utah," *Utah Historical Quarterly*, vol. 2 [1929], 122–26), I have found no evidence to support this. Kimball did, however, employ Indians. An excellent study of Blacks in Utah is Ronald G. Coleman, "Blacks in Utah: An Unknown Legacy," in *The Peoples of Utah*, ed. by Helen Z. Papanikolas (Salt Lake City: Utah State Historical Society, 1976), 115–40. There is much confusion regarding whether these three black Pioneers were freed before or after the Great Trek. In another study, Coleman argues cogently that they were slaves. See his "Blacks in Pioneer Utah, 1847–69," *UMOJA: A Scholarly Journal of Black Studies*, n.s. 2, (Summer 1978), 96–110.

CHAPTER 13

Westward to Laramie

The 1847 Pioneer trek from "civilization to sundown" took a few days to get properly under way, as in 1846 when the Camp of Israel left Nauvoo. Heber moved three wagons out on April 5, but returned to Winter Quarters to meet with John Taylor, who had just arrived from England with some specially ordered scientific instruments for Orson Pratt. The elite, fast-moving, well-equipped, exploring band of Pioneers were not just taking themselves to the Valley, they were charting a road which the Saints and others would use for more than twenty years. For this they needed sextants, a circle of reflection, artificial horizons, barometers, thermometers, and telescopes. (The Mormons became very much a part of what is now known as the "Great Reconnaissance" of the Far West.) On April 14, Brigham and Heber left Winter Quarters and joined the main camp, which was waiting for them on the Platte River, forty-seven miles west, near present-day Fremont, Nebraska.

The unanticipated inclusion of three women and two children in an otherwise all-male venture was occasioned by the insistence of Brigham's younger brother Lorenzo that he be allowed to take his asthmatic wife, Harriet, and her two children, Isaac Decker (son by an earlier marriage) and John (Lorenzo's son). This of course necessitated including at least one or two other females to keep Harriet company. Fortuitously Brigham had married Harriet's daughter (also by the previous marriage) Clara Decker, so he took her. For Heber, taking Vilate was, of course, out of the question. She had five young sons, one of whom was an infant. So he took Ellen Sanders, his strong young Norwegian wife.

In the beginning Heber and Brigham, like Uriah, the Hittite, may have decided to deny themselves their conjugal rights, for they occupied the same wagon. By early May, however, Heber was in a private wagon with Ellen, and their child, Samuel Chase, born February 3, 1848, was one of the first white births in the Salt Lake Valley.

Ellen Sanders, née Aagaat Ysteinsdatter Bakka, had come to the United States from Norway in 1837 and settled in a Norwegian colony in Illinois, near LaSalle, where she and her sister Harriet Sanders converted to Mormonism. They moved to Nauvoo, where they both eventually married Heber in 1844.

These three women entered the Valley in 1847 with the Pioneers, but they were not the only women in the company. By then six females among the Mississippi Saints had joined them at Fort Laramie, so nine women and girls entered the Valley together. Unfortunately, history has recorded little of the activities of these women and children during the trek. In spite of the fact that most of Lorenzo Young's journal was kept by his wife, they remain only shadows. There are a few references to them—baking, washing, being sick, Ellen Sanders almost setting a wagon on fire, Harriet Young's children being unhurt when a wagon overturned—but that is about all. It may be assumed that they did most of the cooking, washing, sewing, and nursing for the company.

These women were not the first female pioneers; eleven women had been with Zion's Camp in 1834; seventy or so went with the Mormon Battalion; about thirty were laundresses.

At the Platte River camp the group consisted of 148 people, 72 wagons, 93 horses, 66 oxen, 52 mules, 19 cows, 17 dogs, and some chickens. There they organized paramilitary fashion into units of 50s and 10s, each with its respective leaders. Their marching orders included the following: reveille at 5:00 A.M., departure at 7:30, one hour for lunch, camp at 6:30 P.M., circle wagons, evening prayer at 8:30, and "taps" at 9:00. The Pioneers of 1847 were much better disciplined than was Zion's Camp of 1834 or the crossing of Iowa in 1846. This was largely the result of a revelation given by Brigham Young on January 14, 1847—the only revelation Young ever published. It began, "The Word and Will of the Lord concerning the Camp of Israel in their journey to the west," and is known today as Section 136 of the Doctrine and Covenants. Basically the revelation gave details on camp organization.

For a variety of reasons, including expense, the Mormons never used professional guides or outfitters. They preferred to "trust in the Lord" and pick up trail savvy as they moved along. Men were appointed to scout the trail and others to ride along the front, flanks, and rear—guarding and enclosing the moving camp in a box-like formation. Neither persons nor animals could be allowed to roam. Disreputable whites and thieving Indians had to be kept at a safe distance, and wolves had to be restrained from picking off stray or weakened animals.

The scouting assignment was vital. Not that there was much chance of getting lost on the established trails the Mormons used, but water, feed, grades, crossings, and whatever might prove dangerous to man or beast had to be anticipated, found, and reported. Heber, partly because of his excellent horsemanship, often rode ahead as guide. Eight men were appointed to hunt on horseback and eleven to hunt on foot. The Apostles were also permitted to hunt when they so desired.

At this camp on Sunday, April 18, Ellis Eames returned to Winter Quarters because of ill health, and Heber took this opportunity to send a letter back to Vilate. This letter is interesting enough to be presented in full. The situation was unusual to say the least. Heber was heading west with one wife on a trip of undetermined duration to an uncertain place, leaving behind his first wife with five children and perhaps twenty-five other wives and their children with little financial security or male protection. He obviously felt the need to try to cheer up Vilate, if not his entire family.

> Pioneers Camp on the Platt
> April 16
>
> My Dear Vilate
>
> One word by my own hand. I am well and in good spirrits. So is the camp. Now my dear Vilate I Love you as true as I am cable of Loving according to my capasity for you do have the Love of my [yo]uth which is first Last and now and fore Ever. So be of good cheer my dear girl for you are blest and shall Even be blest in time and in Eternity. This is your privit Epistle so keeps it to you self. I feel to bless the[e] with all my heart in the name of the Lord with all my family praying to my Father in heaven to incircle them all in his arms and let peas [peace] and hea[l]th and life be and abide with them for Ever. Let Jenet [Jennette Murray?] and Harriet [Sanders] stay with you. Let the rest come on in the Spring. Keepe my caul [council?] to your self. Without they refuse to obey, but you advise. Br. Whitney will ha[n]d Wm. one hundred dollars and one hundred to you. Pleas Keepe it privit from Wm. and all others. He has thirty or forty know [now]. With the one hundred more will pay all the demands. Keepe the rest till I com home without it is needed badly. If so hand out little at a time. If Hirum [Kimball] should send Enny [from Nauvoo] Keepe it. Use what you want fore your comfort. Take care of your self. I gave Sarah Noon five dollars. Keepe the presents Cournal [Thomas L.] Kane sent clost [close] till I come home. Without there is some choice thing you want fore [your] own dear self. All and Everything this Epistle contains and the contence keepe to your self and the articles I mention in it. Write when you get a chance. Tell the rest to do the same. Kiss and bless those little ones. Ellen [Sanders] wants [you]

should write a long Leter to hur. She ses give my kind love to you. Now I must Stop for time. Now fare ye well my dear. I still remain your true Husband and friend in time and Eternity in the New and Everlasting covenant.

H. C. Kimball

To Vilate Kimball

My dear Vilate since I rote this I have got a line from you. It was sweter than Honey to you[r] True Heber. My Lord bless the[e] with Every thing that can be bestowed on a woman. Thare is not a feeling but [the] finest the purest in this Brest towards the[e] my dear. My Soul ses bless the[e] fore Ever. Amen and Amen.

H. C. K.[1]

Contrary to myth and popular belief, this 1847 trek of approximately 1,073 miles and 111 days was not one long and unending trail of tears or a trial of fire. Over the decades Mormons have emphasized the tragedies of the trail, and tragedies there were. Between 1847 and the building of the railroad in 1869, perhaps as many as 6,000 died along the trail from exhaustion, exposure, disease, and lack of food. (Few were killed by Indians.) To the vast majority, however, the experience was positive—a difficult and rewarding struggle. Nobody knows how many Mormons migrated west during those years, but 60,000 in 10,000 vehicles is a close estimate.

It is a curious fact that the Mormons, who did not want to go west in the first place, were the most successful in doing so. Mormons were not typical westering Americans: where others went for adventure, furs, land, a new identity, or gold, Mormons were driven west for their religious beliefs. The first Pioneer group was not just concerned with getting themselves safely settled, but in making the road easier for others to follow. Furthermore, the Mormons transplanted a whole people, a whole culture, not just isolated, unrelated individuals. They moved as villages on wheels and differed profoundly from the Oregon and California emigrants. Mormons were the most systematic, organized, disciplined, and successful pioneers in U.S. history. As to the old question about whether the trail should be called rightfully the Mormon Trail or the Great Platte River Road, Oregon Trail, California Trail, or something else, Stegner has given the best answer. "By the improvements they made in it," he wrote, "they earned the right to put their name on the trail they used. . . ."[2]

The experience of the trail, the crossing of the plains, became a great event, not only in the lives of the pioneers, but in the minds of their descendants. It became a rite of passage, the final test of faith. The contemporary American Mormon is prouder of nothing more in his heritage than the fact that one or more of his ancestors "crossed the plains" for the sake of religious freedom before the coming of the railroad in 1869. (Those who came west by train are sometimes called "Pullman Pioneers.")

Today a special mythology and clouds of glory surround these Pioneers. Many Mormons belong to the Sons of Utah Pioneers or the Daughters of Utah Pioneers, whereas no similar societies exist for other important groups, such as the founders, the original Apostles, or the members of Zion's Camp. Throughout the world Mormons regularly celebrate July 24, when Brigham and Heber entered the Valley in 1847, as Pioneer Day.

The real beginning of the trek of 1847 and the whole trans-Missouri Mormon migration to follow was at 7:30 on the morning of Monday, April 19. The company moved out from their staging area west of Winter Quarters and the grand adventure began. Kimball's pioneer journal for that day reads, "The morning fine and pleasant. At half past 7 we continued our journey, the wagons traveling in double file by way of experiment . . . our route lay beside of a number of small lakes, where there were many ducks. The brethren shot some of them . . . at 6 P.M. formed our encampment in a semicircle, on the banks of the river, where we have a pleasant view of the majestic 'Nebraska' or Platte river, which at this place appears to be a mile wide but very shoal . . . the evening was fine and very pleasant."

During the "nooning" of that same day, Orrin Porter Rockwell, who had been sent back to Winter Quarters to pick up some presents, arrived in camp. The gifts (perhaps the same mentioned in Heber's letter to Vilate) were from Colonel Thomas L. Kane, who had visited the Mormons in Winter Quarters, to the Twelve and a few others. Kane's list of these gifts has survived, and from it we learn that he sent Heber a medical chest containing cinchona and morphia, the standard drugs for the treatment of fever and pain. Other gifts to the Twelve included whips, scientific instruments, pictures, fishing tackle, maps, guns, compass, stomach pump, gun cotton, and thirty bottles of brandy.[3]

The Platte River, rising in Colorado and one of the largest branches of the Missouri, is very broad and shallow, a meandering, braided river which oldtimers used to say "flowed upside down," a reference to the many visible sandbars. One disgruntled pioneer remarked that it would make a pretty good stream if it were turned on its side. Travelers seemed to enjoy thinking up insults for the Platte. The consensus regarding this river was that it was a mile wide, six inches deep, too thick to drink, too thin to plow, hard to cross because of quicksand, impossible to navigate, too yellow to wash in, and too pale to paint with.

For hundreds of miles the Pioneers hauled themselves across its flat, monotonous plain in present-day eastern Nebraska. During this phase of the trip, their journals are full of undramatic references to creeks, bits of wood they found, fish, birds, and game.

Heber's journal reveals clearly the high adventure of the Pioneer crossing of the plains. His positive reaction accords well with others who had similar experiences. A study of 135 Pioneer journals written between 1847 and 1866 found "that none contained a negative assessment of the Great Plains as a region . . . but all diarists commented positively on the entire plains area they traversed."[4] After it was over, Heber said, "It was pretty hard and laborious, I admit; but it was one of the pleasantest journeys I ever performed."[5]

Heber's journal during the trek, from which much of the following was taken, should really be called the Kimball-Clayton Journal, for at Heber's request, William Clayton kept a journal for him which unfortunately reads very much like Clayton's own famous journal, expressing few of Heber's private thoughts. From it, however, we do learn of Heber's great zest for life and adventure as they went along, of his sensitivity to nature and his love of the land. He went hunting, riding, fishing, exploring, he investigated caves, climbed vertiginous promontories, rolled stones down steep mountains, stood guard, scouted, fought quicksand and prairie fire, was chased by a she-bear, amused himself by naming several creeks, and became acquainted with the Indians and the buffalo—"the poetry and life of the prairie," as John C. Frémont noted. This journal recounts the music, singing, dancing, and horseplay in camp and the varied diet of game. We know little of the evening, the nights, or the sidereal splendors which, without modern haze and artificial light, must have been awesome. Characteristically, if Heber had any worries or troubles on the trail he did not record them. He seems to have enjoyed the trek.

There is some evidence that the Pioneers knew in advance that they were going into the Great Basin somewhere near its eastern rim, along the western slope of the Wasatch Mountains. As early as 1842, for example, Joseph Smith indicated that the Saints would go there, and as noted above, Brigham Young and Heber had studied Frémont's account and maps of the area. But into which of the several unclaimed valleys? En route, Brigham Young and Heber consulted with everyone they could about the area, including some famous mountain men—Moses Harris, Jim Bridger, and Miles Goodyear. It appears that as they moved toward and into the Great Basin they gradually decided to settle in the Valley of the Great Salt Lake. The camp moved deliberately, casually, about two miles an hour, and under little pressure. Their best distance for one day was twenty-three and three-quarters miles, but they averaged only ten miles a day. There was no need to get to the mountains before winter snows had melted.

The Mormons did very little trailblazing along the entire road from Nauvoo to the Valley. Wherever possible they followed existing roads and trails; most of their real pioneering was earlier, in western Iowa. West of Winter Quarters they followed generally what is sometimes called the Great Platte River Road, which from prehistoric times was known as the most advantageous approach to the easiest crossing of the Rocky Mountains, a trail which had been blazed by Indians, trappers, fur traders, and other emigrants. The Mormons were not looking for a place in history books. They had a job to do and they wanted to do it as simply, expeditiously, and conveniently as possible.

The first section of the Mormon Trail from Winter Quarters was generally along the north bank of the Platte River to near present-day Kearney, Nebraska. Up to this point in Nebraska the Mormon Trail and Oregon Trail were entirely separate. Along the second portion of the Mormon Trail, from Kearney to Fort Laramie, Wyoming, the Mormons remained on the north bank of the Platte and the Oregonians on the south. Since in the 1840s the commonly used route to Oregon and California was along the south bank of the Platte, it might appear that the Mormons had pioneered the less frequently used north bank trail, but actually during the 1820s and 1830s the north bank had been the preferred way used by fur trappers and missionaries. And the improvements the Mormons made on the north side by the 1850s made it again a popular route.

The third section of the trail was across modern Wyoming from Fort Laramie to Fort Bridger. Here the Mormons followed the Oregon Trail proper for 397 miles. The fourth and final section was from Fort Bridger, where the Oregon Trail turned north to the Pacific Coast and where the Mormons left the Oregon Trail and picked up the year-old Reed-Donner track through the Rockies into the Salt Lake Valley.

Topographically the trail led across the Central Lowlands, over the Great Plains into the Wyoming Basin, through the middle Rocky Mountains, into the Great Basin. The Mormons passed along river valleys, across plains, deserts, and mountains, several oceans of grasslands, sagebrush steppes, and through the western forests of Douglas fir and scrub oak. The modern traveler can still find many parts of the old trail. Much of the plains, deserts, mountains, steppes, and forests remain, but the Tallgrass Prairie is almost all gone, a victim of the white man's plow.

On April 21 along the Loup River, the Pioneers had their first meeting with a group of Great Plains Indians. Nomadic, warlike, mounted, powerfully built, and given to body paint and unusual hairstyles, they lived generally in graceful tepees rather than in permanent earthen lodges or flimsy bush wickiups. By the mid-nineteenth century, unlike most of the eastern Indians, who were already only a memory, those of the Great Plains were simultaneously at full flower and on the edge of extinction, for they lay across the path of Manifest Destiny, in the way of the white man's rule from sea to shining sea.

On this April day the Mormons met a band of Pawnees, the largest indigenous tribe in Nebraska, numbering as many as 10,000 people. The nation was centered on the Loup River near Fullerton and habitually demanded gifts from white travelers near Shell Creek. Its braves were easily identifiable by their plucked eyebrows, painted faces, and heads shaved except for a narrow strip of hair from forehead to scalp lock, which stood up like a horn. Relatively trustworthy, they were often hired as guides.

The Pioneers, who would meet other groups of Great Plains Indians such as the Sioux and the Crow, were entering the Great Plains at a time of great disorder and intertribal warfare. The inexorable push of the white man west had driven a jumble of eastern Indians onto the Great Plains, where they were considered invaders by the natives. During the period of the early Mormon migration, Indian life was further changed by military movements, the Mexican War, massive migration to Oregon and California, the forty-niners, disease, and the deliberate extermination of the great buffalo herds.

The Indian leader, Chief Shefmolan, rode up to Heber and demanded a gift. Wishing to be friendly and to establish good relations, Heber gave the chief some tobacco and salt. Whites usually considered the Indians to be beggars, but the Indians believed themselves to be merely extracting a sort of toll for permitting emigrants to cross their lands and disturb their game. The Plains Indians, furthermore, were open and generous with what they had and expected others to be.

The vast expanse of the plains permitted excellent astronomical observation. On the night of April 24, Orson Pratt set up his telescope and showed Heber and many others Jupiter's moons and probably the few celestial bodies mentioned in the Bible: Arcturus, Orion, and the Pleiades.

Perhaps the brethren debated which of all the visible stars might be Kolob, which, according to Mormon belief is one of the great governing stars, closest to the throne of God, so important that its revolutions determine "the reckoning of the Lord's time" at the traditional ratio of 1,000 years of earth time to one day with the Lord.[6]

Alternating with the beauty and majesty of the nights were the mundane realities of the days. Shortly after the astronomy lesson, when they were "scanted for wood," the Pioneers tried dry buffalo dung, euphemistically termed *bois de vache*, meadow muffins, or chips, for fuel.

When properly managed, the chips served as a very good substitute for wood. The main objection to them, other than the aesthetic one, was that they burned too fast. Collecting chips was considered woman's work and was commemorated (along with romance) in at least one trail song.

> There's a pretty little girl in the outfit ahead
> Whoa Haw Buck and Jerry Boy
> I wish she were by my side instead
> Whoa Haw Buck and Jerry Boy
> Look at her now with a pout on her lips
> As daintly with her fingertips
> She picks for the fire some buffalo chips
> Whoa Haw Buck and Jerry Boy.

Heber invented a new furnace for burning these chips more slowly. He first dug a hole in the ground about 15 inches long and 8 inches deep, into which the dried chips were piled. Then at each end and about 8 inches from this he dug another hole about the same size and depth, and at the bottom of the partition made a hole about 3 inches in diameter, which made a good draft.

On May 1 just west of what is today Kearney, Nebraska, the Pioneers sighted a herd (or, to pedantically use the proper noun of assembly, an obstinacy) of buffalo. Originally the animal had ranged from the Appalachians to the Rockies, but by 1820 had been driven west of the Missouri River. In 1847 the Mormons found them 200 miles farther west, along the Platte and Sweetwater rivers. A hunt was quickly organized and Heber decided to test his skills. According to one eyewitness:

> About this time Elder Kimball seemed to be inspired with the idea of chasing the buffalo and he immediately called for Egan's fifteen shooter and started with it on full gallop. . . . Heber joined just as the herd discovered them and commenced galloping off.
> At this time I got my glass and rested it on Brother Aaron Farr's

shoulder, determined to see as much of the chase as possible. . . . The hunters closed in on the first party and commenced their fire, especially at one cow which they finally succeeded in separating from all the rest, and determined to keep to her until they killed her. . . . The cow was now in close quarters and after she had been shot through two or three times, Elder Kimball rode close to her with his fifteen shooter and fired over his horse's head, she dropped helpless and was soon dispatched. At the report of the gun which was very heavy loaded, Elder Kimball's horse sprang and flew down the bluff like lightning and he having let go the lines to shoot, her sudden motion overbalanced him and his situation was precarious to the extreme. . . . However, being a good horseman, he maintained his position in the saddle and soon succeeded after some time in reining in his horse and returned to the rest unharmed and without accident.[7]

The Mormons usually boiled, fried, or roasted their buffalo meat or made it into jerky (Spanish *charqui*) by cutting the meat into thin strips and drying it for future use.

A few days later, on May 5, the Pioneers experienced another of the great natural phenomena of the plains—prairie fire, usually caused by dry lightning or Indians, a scourging wall of flame that, wind-driven, could reach a height of twenty feet, overtake a horse, and easily engulf a slow-moving ox train. Nebraska country was a great sea of grass which summer sun and winter frost regularly dried or killed, leaving it tinder to great fires every fall and spring. There are only two ways of fighting such a fire: with firebreaks or backfires. The Pioneers had time for neither. Heber, along with the others, quickly led his six wagons to a convenient island in the Platte and let the fire pass harmlessly by. The next day, although they may not have noted it, they passed the 100th meridian, beyond which there is insufficient rainfall for unirrigated farming, and entered the anteroom of the Great American Desert.

West of Ash Hollow, a famous camping site on the Oregon Trail, the Mormons entered the Broken Lands of the Upper Missouri Basin, and the terrain became increasingly more interesting and varied. For eighty miles to Scotts Bluff the Pioneers traveled through what might be loosely called a monument valley. Along this stretch on both sides of the river are some of the most famous and dramatic topographical features of the Mormon and Oregon trails. Courthouse Rock, Chimney Rock, and Scotts Bluff guarded the Oregon Trail while Indian Look Out Point and Ancient Ruins Bluff sentineled the Mormon Trail.

About twenty-one miles west of Ash Hollow, Heber killed two wolves, and the brethren found what they thought was the shoulder blade of a mammoth. They may have been right, for remains of both mammoths and mastodons were later found in many parts of Nebraska. The Pioneers were probably capable of recognizing the distinctive mammoth shoulder bone when they saw it, since some of them, including Heber, had visited St. Louis and may have seen Dr. Albert C. Koch's famous mammoth skeleton on exhibit there.

On May 22 they made camp near the most impressive topographic site along the entire Mormon Trail, a place the Mormons called Ancient Ruins Bluff, located about eight miles northeast of present-day Lisco, Nebraska, on U.S. Highway 30. On Sunday, May 24, Brigham Young and others climbed the main bluff. While there, they wrote their names on a buffalo skull and left it on the southwest corner. Although not of a philosophical or reflective nature, Heber may well have stood at that corner, from which one can look farther yet see less than at any other site along the trail, and mused on what had brought him to that place, on his family in Winter Quarters, on the desolation of the country in which he must find a new home, and above all, on the mind and will of God and his relationship to Him.

Later that Sabbath, Heber and Clayton walked about a quarter of a mile away from camp, where Heber looked over the journal Clayton was keeping for him. Then, as they kneeled down and prayed, a gust of wind carried Heber's hat away, but rather than interrupt their prayer, the devout Heber let it go. Afterwards, he had to chase it for nearly a mile.

Along this same portion of the trail they engaged in some mock trials and elections. James Davenport, for example, was accused of "blocking the highway and turning ladies out of the way," and "Father" Chamberlain was voted the most even-tempered man in camp —*always* cross and quarrelsome.[8]

On May 24, at their camp opposite Courthouse Rock, so named from its fancied resemblance to the St. Louis Courthouse, the Pioneers were visited by a party of Sioux, certainly the largest of the Great Plains tribes and perhaps the most dominant. Proud, ferocious at times, the Sioux had developed more than other tribes that system of "feather heraldry" by which eagle plumes proclaimed a brave's achievements; the shaping of a single eagle feather could denote any of seven different brave acts.

"They all appeared well-dressed," noted the Kimball-Clayton Journal, "in blankets and robes, variously ornamented with beads and paintings. All look clean and neat and are very noble looking men. Some had nice large shells suspended from their ears, and all well-armed with rifles, muskets, etc. Their moccasins are very neatly made, clean, sit tight to the foot and ornamented with beads, and to view them from head to foot, for neatness and cleanness they will vie with the most tasteful whites."

On May 26 they passed Chimney Rock—a principal milestone which (though only 425 miles from Winter Quarters) came to be considered sort of a halfway mark. This most familiar sight on the Oregon Trail was an eroded tusk of Brule clay jutting some 500 feet above the Platte. No one is known to have successfully climbed it, but there is one legend that an Indian Brave, to win a bride, did reach the top, only to plunge to his death.

On Friday, May 28, while opposite the massive formations of clay and sandstone called Scotts Bluff, Heber walked around the wagons of his division and was disturbed by the levity, gambling, and profane language he witnessed. By the time he had reached Appleton Harmon's wagon he had had enough. Calling the men together, he dressed them down "in language not to be misunderstood" and persuaded them "to conduct themselves like men of God, or they would be sorry for it."[9]

Upset and not feeling well, Heber retired early. Later on, Brigham Young sent for him. Heber arose, dressed, and went over to Young's wagon, where Brigham told him of a revelation he had had in which he had been constrained by the Spirit "to call the camp to repentence."[10] Heber then told Brigham what he had just done, and they discussed the matter until after midnight. They decided to call the whole camp to repentence on the morrow. Then they slept.

The next day the two leaders remonstrated with those brethren who were giving way to trifling, dancing, and card playing and warned them in the name of the Lord against the spirit which many of the camp possessed, and called upon them to cease their folly and turn to the Lord their God with full purpose of heart to serve him.[11] Thereafter a more saintly atmosphere prevailed in camp. These typical old-time Mormons could take, even thrive on, chastisement from the proper authority.

The following day was Sunday and, just east of today's Wyoming state line near Henry, Young convened a special meeting of the Council of Fifty, of which at least eighteen of the Pioneers were members. They went out on the bluffs, clothed themselves in their temple robes and held a prayer circle to pray for guidance.

That same day they spotted the pyramidal bulk of Laramie Peak looming regally above the "Black Hills" today's Laramie Mountains—the first mountains seen by westering Americans. A day later they passed out of present-day Nebraska and came upon a wagon track which led them to Fort Laramie thirty miles farther west.

NOTES

1. H. C. Kimball to Vilate Kimball, Apr. 16, 1847. Original in possession of Mrs. Elwood G. Derrick. Used by permission.

2. Stegner, *The Gathering of Zion*, 12.

3. "For Whom of My Friends Each Intended," T. L. Kane Papers, Church Archives.

4. Richard Jackson, "Mormon Perception and Settlement of the Great Plains," paper read at Images of the Plains Conference, Apr., 1973, University of Nebraska, Lincoln.

5. *Journal of Discourses*, vol. 5 (Aug. 2, 1857), 132.

6. *Pearl of Great Price*, rev. ed. (Salt Lake City: Deseret Books, 1952), Abraham 3:4. Cf. 2 Peter 3:8.

7. *William Clayton's Journal* (Salt Lake City: Clayton Family Association, 1921), 118–21.

8. *Ibid.*, 176.

9. H. C. Kimball Journal, May 28, 1847, Church Archives.

10. Fred C. Collier, comp., *Unpublished Revelations of the Prophets and Presidents of the Church of Jesus Christ of Latter Day Saints* (Salt Lake City: Collier's Publishing, 1979), 109.

11. Watson, ed., *Manuscript History of Brigham Young: 1846–47*, 555–56.

CHAPTER 14

. . . And on to the Valley

Fort Laramie has had at least three names. Founded in 1834 as Fort William, later called Fort John, by which name Heber knew it, it finally in 1849 became Fort Laramie, after a French trapper, Jacques LaRamie. Thus far the Pioneers had suffered no deaths, little illness, and the loss of only four horses, two to the Indians and two accidentally killed—one was shot (loaded firearms kept in jolting wagons or held while on horseback claimed many a life needlessly on the frontier), the other fell into a ravine while tethered and broke its neck.

While there in 1847 they rested their animals and themselves and prepared to pick up the Oregon Trail. This famous trail, the longest wagon road in history, the Main Street to the West, stretching over 2,000 miles from Independence, Missouri, to the Columbia River, had been blazed by Indians, trappers, and traders between 1811 and 1839, by which time there were about 100 Americans in Oregon; by 1843 there were perhaps 1,200. Thereafter, tens of thousands used the trail annually on the way to Oregon and California—perhaps as many as 350,000 to the coming of the railroad in 1869. Those going to California left the Oregon Trail at Soda Springs (in present-day Idaho).

While at the fort the Pioneers were joined by seventeen advance members of the "Mississippi Saints" from Monroe County, Mississippi, who had been waiting for them for two weeks. Among this advance group were six females: Elizabeth Crow and her five daughters, four of them married. Their arrival probably pleased Heber's wife Ellen. From these Mississippi Saints it was learned that most of their group and the soldiers of the Mormon Battalion too sick to pursue the march any farther (commonly called the Sick Detachment) were still at Fort Pueblo in modern Colorado. To help this group join the Pioneers in the Valley, Young dispatched four men to Fort Pueblo. This meant a net gain of thirteen individuals, bringing the number of the Pioneer group to 161 people and seventy-seven wagons.

On Saturday, June 5, the Pioneers were ready to leave for the continental divide at South Pass and Fort Bridger, which was 397 miles west. For a little over one month the Pioneers would be on the Oregon Trail along with several other "Gentile" companies with whom they would vie for the best campgrounds, feed, and priority in fording rivers. They would pass Mexican Hill, Register Cliff, Warm Springs Canyon, Laramie Peak, Red Buttes, the Avenue of Rocks, Independence Rock, Devil's Gate, Split Rock, the Ice Slough, Rocky Ridge, South Pass, Pacific Springs, and Church Butte (so named because Mormons are said to have held church services there). They would help deepen the now-famous trail ruts near Gurnsey, Wyoming, pass by the sites of the future handcart tragedies of 1856, improve the road, and establish ferries on the Platte River at modern Casper and on the Green River.

On their first day out from Fort Laramie they came to what is now called Mexican Hill. Heber may have been familiar with the frontier hyperbole regarding this steep cut down the bluffs to the river. While descending, so the story went, if a tin cup fell out of a wagon it would land in front of the oxen. Two days later, near Horseshoe Creek, Heber discovered a large spring which he named after himself.[1] On Sunday, June 13, while at their ferry on the Platte (frequently referred to as "Last Crossing"), they established a permanent ferry, for the Saints who would follow and as a money-making venture. Ten men were left behind to operate and maintain what soon became known as Mormon Ferry.

When the Pioneers left on June 19, they quit the Platte for good. From the Elk Horn to Last Crossing they had generally followed its gentle valley for more than 600 miles. The easy part of the trek was over, as the next fifty miles would prove. The stretch from Last Crossing through Emigrant Gap to the Sweetwater River near Independence Rock was the worst section of the whole trail between Nauvoo and Salt Lake Valley: a "Hell's Reach" of few and bad campsites, bad water, little grass, one steep hill, swamps, and stretches of alkali flats. The cattle had poor purchase; their tender hooves cracked, and some, including the ox of Mary Fielding, almost gave out in 1848 on this part of the trail, where desiccated oxen carcasses soon became a familiar sight. But the Pioneers endured and lived to enjoy refreshing draughts of the Sweetwater River, which acquired its name either from American trappers because of its contrast with the other brackish streams in the vicinity, or from French *voyageurs*, who called it the *Eau Sucrée* because a pack mule loaded with sugar was lost in its water. This small, gentle, beneficent river, which all Oregonians and Mormons followed for 109 miles to South Pass, made it possible for travelers to reach their destination in one season, avoiding a winter in such hostile country.

Like all travelers before and after them, the Pioneers stopped to climb the huge turtle-shaped Independence Rock; some carved or painted their initials or names into and on it.

Four and a half miles west was the equally famous Devil's Gate, another popular resting place on the trail. Its name derives from the notion that the formation bears the profiles of twin petrified genii. It is a 1,500-foot-long, 370-foot-deep gap in a rocky spur through which flows the Sweetwater. Heber tried to ride his horse through it but the current was too fast. He humorously commented that the devil would not let him. According to Shoshoni and Arapahoe legend, the gate was formed by an evil spirit in the form of a tremendous beast with tusks which, when trapped by the Indians, ripped open the gate and fled. (An earthquake is the more probable and prosaic cause.)

Emigrant children, including the Mormons, had great fun here, climbing to the top of the gate and tumbling rocks down into the river, firing guns to hear the marvelous reverberations, or leaning over the side and trying to see the bottom. This last feat was particularly dangerous—to do so several individuals had to form a human chain holding hands, permitting the end person to hang over the precipice at a perilous angle.

On June 27 they crossed the flat, almost imperceptible 7,750-foot-high continental divide at South Pass, the "Cumberland Gap" of the Far West. Travelers had to reach this pass by July 4 in order to get to their destination in Oregon before winter. At Pacific Springs, immediately west of South Pass, the Pioneers refreshed themselves and their animals. These famous springs, so named because their waters flowed to the Pacific Ocean, were the recognized beginning of the sprawling and ill-defined Oregon Territory. A few miles farther on the aptly named Dry Sandy, they met the first of the mountain men, Moses Harris, with whom they consulted about their destination. Harris, who had roamed the West for twenty-five years, did not think much of the country around the Great Salt Lake; he said it was barren, sandy, and destitute of timber and vegetation except wild sage. Heber learned quickly to approach most mountain men upwind, for they generally considered cleanliness as bad as godliness; their idea of a bath was to place their clothing on an anthill and let the ants eat off the lice and nits. On the next day, still on the Dry Sandy, the Pioneers met the famous Jim Bridger, who was on his way to Fort Laramie, and spent some time with him discussing the Valley of the Great Salt Lake. The great scout, who had gone west in 1824, could neither read nor write, and was so "likered up" he could hardly sit on his horse. The Pioneers could not make much out of what he tried to tell them. Literally and figuratively in good spirits, Bridger undoubtedly told Heber and others one or more of his famous tall tales, like the one about the glass mountain strewn about with the corpses of animals which had killed themselves running into it headlong, or the one about petrified birds singing in a petrified forest, perhaps the one about a stream which ran so fast it cooked the trout in it, or about the day he threw across the Sweetwater a rock which just kept on growing until it became Independence Rock, and maybe the story of the time some Indians chased him up a narrow canyon closed at the head by a 200-foot-high waterfall. "And how did you escape, Jim?" the Mormons may have asked. "I didn't," he'd have answered, "they scalped me."

This camp was also the setting of Bridger's well-known challenge that he would give a thousand dollars for a bushel of corn raised in the Great Basin. For his help Young gave Bridger a pass for the Mormon ferry on the Platte.

June 29 was a banner day: the Mormons made the best distance of the whole crossing—twenty-three and three-quarters miles, against an overall average of ten miles per day. Such a distance was covered only because there was no water between the Dry Sandy and the Sandy.

By July 3 at the Green River camp, Heber had seen enough of what they called "camp or mountain fever" to become alarmed. He rushed a letter of warning and advice back to the Second Division, where he assumed some members of his family were. "It affects," he wrote, "the eyes, back and in short the whole system with aches and pains, in most cases accompanied with a sickness at the stomach; it has no appearance of being fatal, and only lasts generally from 1 to 3 days; as far as we can judge it is brought on or caused mainly by the sudden change from hot to cold and from too hot to cool, against which we have not been sufficiently on our guard."[2] Heber himself was spared, but not Brigham Young. This dreaded fever was almost undoubtedly Colorado tick fever—an acute infection bringing on chills, fevers to 104 degrees, pains in the muscles and joints, and the eruption of a rash of livid spots—and not the more serious Rocky Mountain spotted fever.

On July 4 the number of Pioneers was reduced by another five men, who returned to help guide the other companies which were following into the Valley. (For some reason, probably haste, it appears that the Pioneers did not celebrate the Glorious Fourth.) On the next day they were joined by thirteen members of the Mormon Battalion Sick Detachment—bringing the total to 159 souls.

Finally, on the afternoon of July 7, they arrived at Fort Bridger, a poorly built ramshackle adobe establishment on Blacks Fork of the Green River put up in 1842 to service emigrants on the Oregon Trail. The Pioneers tarried at this straggling place just long enough to do some trading and repair their wagons, especially the running gear and wheels. Heber "chored around," carefully checking for loose tires, cracked or broken spokes and felloes, weakened axles, loosened bolsters, broken braces and chains, worn hubs and brakes, and broken bows and torn tops. He also exchanged two rifles for twenty buckskins, which he considered a good trade.

At 8:00 A.M. on Friday, July 9, the Pioneers quit the Oregon Trail, which there turned north, and began the last leg of their journey, following Hastings Cutoff, the barely visible track left through the Rockies by the Reed-Donner party of 1846, which perished in the Sierra snows. Even with the trailblazing done by the Reed-Donner party, it took the Pioneers sixteen days and ten camps to traverse the 116 miles between Fort Bridger and the Salt Lake Valley.

Their second day out of Fort Bridger they met a third mountain man, Miles Goodyear, passed a pure-water spring, a sulphur spring, and an oil spring. (All that this oil meant to Heber was something with which to lubricate his wagon wheels—the commercial use of black gold lay some dozen years in the future.) Then they entered the beginning of a ninety-mile-long natural highway, a chain of defiles (including Coyote Creek Canyon, Cache Cave Creek Draw, Echo Canyon, Weber River Valley, Main Canyon, East Canyon, Little Emigration Canyon, and finally Emigration Canyon) which meandered through the forbidding Wasatch Range of the Rockies into the Valley as if an ancient Titan had dragged a stick through the area.

By noon on July 12, they had made midday camp along Coyote Creek, about one mile east of a prominent and strange formation of conglomerate rocks called the Needles, or Pudding Rocks, and about one and a half miles east of the present Wyoming-Utah border. Here Young was suddenly stricken with tick fever. He remained ill for nearly two weeks, during which time Heber took over the direction of the Pioneer camp. In the hope that Young would be well enough to travel the next day, Heber and a few others remained at the Coyote Creek camp and sent Parley Pratt and the main company on. On July 13, however, it was obvious that Young was worse, not better. Heber then rode forward to the main camp six and three-quarters miles ahead near Cache Cave and suggested that Pratt drive on to hunt out and improve a road.

For the rest of the journey the Pioneers split into three groups— Pratt's vanguard blazing the trail, the main portion following, and a rear guard which stayed with Brigham and Heber. Pratt's company sighted the Valley on July 19 and scouted it on the 21st; on the 22nd at about 5:30 P.M. the main company arrived in the Valley via what came to be called Emigration Canyon. Early the next morning the group moved about two miles northwest and made camp on the south fork of City Creek, in the area of today's City Hall Park. There they dammed up the water and began plowing, planting potatoes, and irrigating.

Meanwhile, back on Coyote Creek, Heber and a few others went to the top of the Needles and offered up prayers for the sick, and on July 15, Young was well enough to travel in Wilford Woodruff's carriage. Shortly thereafter they crossed Hog's Back at the summit of Main Canyon (west of present-day Henefer) and caught the traveler's traditional first view of the continent's backbone, the Wasatch Range of the Rocky Mountain cordillera. Despite this disheartening assurance that the worst of the mountain passes still lay ahead, Heber probably thrilled at this awesome sight of nature in her western majesty and realm, this view of light playing on distant peaks.

On the morning of July 23, the Young-Kimball detachment left Mormon Flats on East Canyon Creek and began the final section of the trail— up Little Emigration Canyon and over Big Mountain Pass, over Little Mountain, and down Emigration Canyon. The Kimball-Clayton Journal noted, "The road [up Little Emigration Canyon] in some places is rough and rocky and on side hills which makes bad traveling. The road lays through many thickets of underbrush, and forests of hemlock and poplar trees. After traveling 4¼ miles we arrived at the summit of the mountain [Big Mountain] from whence we had a fine view of the snowy mountains and the valley of the Salt Lake in the distance south west."

As Heber crossed the 7,400-foot-high Big Mountain pass he entered his new homeland, the Great Basin—a vast and forbidding area of over 200,000 square miles lying generally between the crests of the Sierra Nevada and the Wasatch Mountains, including parts of Utah, Nevada, California, Oregon, and Idaho, and inhabited only by various tribes of Great Basin Indians. It is a natural basin. What streams and rivers there are, such as the Humboldt, Jordan, Provo, and Weber, have no access to the sea. They flow into the Great Salt Lake, into sinks, or disappear by evaporation and percolation. The area is spotted with such unattractive places as Salt Marsh Lake, Little Salt Lake, Fossil Lake, and the Humboldt Sink.

Until the Mormons arrived this region had never known a white master. Imperial Spain, which had claimed it by right of discovery, had done nothing with it for centuries. England and France had never even fought for it. The Mexicans, who took it from Spain in 1821, generally considered it a worthless waste separating more desirable lands. For perhaps four billion years the Great Basin had bent all to its inexorable will—adjust or perish. In 1847 the Mormons decided to make the Great Basin serve them, and they did it on ancient principles worked out in Mesopotamia and among the Incas—centralized organization, division of labor, and a chain of command, all on an agricultural basis with controlled irrigation at its heart.

Roughlocking their rear wheels with chains and attaching drag shoes (wagon brakes were not then in general use), the Pioneers slid down Big Mountain and a few hours later ascended Little Mountain. At 5:00 that afternoon, suffering much from heat and dust, they were in Emigration Canyon, at Last Camp.

The next day was July 24—the second most important day in the Mormon calendar—the marking of the official entrance into the Valley. (The first is April 6, the day Joseph Smith formally organized the church and the day on which Mormons believe Christ was born.) Of this day the Kimball-Clayton Journal recorded: "*Saturday 24.* We started early this morning and found the road very rough and uneven to the mouth of the Kanion which is 4¾ miles from where we started . . . we beheld the Great Valley of the Salt Lake spreading before us . . . we arrived amongst the brethren at a quarter past 12 having traveled today 12¼ miles . . . we found the brethren very busy stocking and preparing plows, and several plows to work."

Young's own journal entry was equally prosaic. "I started early this morning," he wrote, "and after crossing Emigration Kanyon Creek eighteen times emerged from the kanyon. Encamped with the main body at 2 P.M."[3] Likewise Wilford Woodruff, an indefatigable diarist, noted only that "President Young expressed his full satisfaction in the appearance of the Valley as a resting place for the Saints, and was amply repaid for his journey."[4] It was a few days, however, before the final decision was made to settle where they were. On July 25 William Clayton noted in his journal, "We shall go tomorrow if Brigham is well enough, in search of a better location—if indeed such can be found—if not we shall remain here." Brigham Young's illness prevented any further searching and by July 28 Clayton recorded, "The brethren are more and more satisfied that we are already on the right spot," and Norton Jacob noted in his journal that Young said, "I know this is the right spot. I knew this spot as soon as I saw it." Thirty-three years later, after Young was dead, during the excitement of Mormonism's fifty-year jubilee in 1880, Woodruff embellished the events of July 24, 1847, with the following afterthought: President Young

"was enwrapped in vision for several minutes. He had seen the Valley before in vision, and upon this occasion he saw the future glory of Zion and
of Israel, as they would be, planted in the valleys of these mountains.
When the vision had passed, he said: 'It is enough. This is the right place,
drive on.'"[5] Such was the origin of the most famous single statement in
Mormon history (but little known in Young's day): "This is the place."

The event is commemorated today by a large granite monument at the
mouth of Emigration Canyon honoring the Pioneers and pre-Mormon explorers and trappers. Atop a huge shaft thrusting from the center of the
base stand larger-than-life-sized figures of Brigham Young, Heber C. Kimball, and Wilford Woodruff, serenely and eternally contemplating their
work.

July 24, 1847, is the traditional pivot in Mormon history—everything is related to and from this date. The return trip to Winter Quarters,
the winter there, and especially the 1848 trek west are usually ignored in
Mormon historiography. But Heber and Brigham and most of the original
Pioneers spent only thirty-three days in the Valley in 1847. This biography
must follow Heber for another fourteen months before the Utah part of
his story can properly begin.

Place of revelation or not, the Valley was the first site suitable for
Kingdom-building which the Pioneer leaders had seen since Nauvoo. It
was vast, isolated, and fertile enough to look like the "Promised Valley" of
twentieth-century Mormon lyric theatre. They were impressed with its
beauty, streams, and vegetation, and they set about earnestly and immediately to tame it. At least two women (and perhaps some of the men),
however, had a different reaction. They saw only a wilderness, a reptile's
paradise. "I have come 1,200 miles to reach this valley and walked much
of the way," Clara Decker said, "but I am willing to walk 1,000 miles farther rather than remain here."[6] Her mother, Harriet, echoingly said, "We
have traveled fifteen hundred miles over prairies, desert and mountains,
but, feeble as I am, I would rather go a thousand miles farther than stay in
such a place as this."[7] Nevertheless, they stayed. From their disappointed
reactions, however, originated the enduring misconception that the Valley
was desolation. There is also some evidence that in order to persuade later
emigrants of the feasibility of settling the drier parts of southern Utah,
church leaders consciously or unconsciously fostered the impression that
the Wasatch oasis, which had "been made to blossom as the rose," had
originally been a desert.[8]

Since Young was still sick with mountain fever, it was Heber who assembled the camp on July 25 to give thanks for their safe arrival and the
good prospects of the Valley. From the back of Brigham Young's wagon,

drawn up in some shade, Heber again exhorted the Pioneers to be faithful and obey counsel. Afterward he called his "family" together around his wagon and advised them to help each other, to be prudent and take care of all things entrusted to their care, and suggested that some should go back to the Sweetwater to kill some buffalo and dry the meat for winter consumption. He advised them to build an enclosure for the horses and cattle, watch out for Indians, keep the Sabbath day holy, plant peach stones and apple seeds, and make clothing out of the buckskins he had purchased at Fort Bridger.[9]

On July 26 Brigham Young was better, and along with Heber and a few others he rode and walked to the summit of a low mountain north of their camp. Despite recurrent and persistent rumors, however, no U.S. flag was hoisted that day. Heber, probably remembering Isaiah's prophecy regarding an "ensign to the nations," did say that someday an ensign would be flown there, but on that particular day all that was left fluttering in the breeze was one of his yellow bandanas. (The promontory, of course, was immediately designated Ensign Peak.)

The best way to visualize what the Valley looked like to Heber in 1847 is from this same summit. Heber described it as an

> extensive, level looking valley . . . which lays about 25 miles to the west, and runs south about 40 miles . . . bounded by high mountains. . . . The valley looks exceedingly rich, of a loose black soil. . . . There are a number of small creeks . . . from the mountains on the East watering the valley. . . . On these creeks there is a little timber, but the valley itself looks bare of timber. . . . The part of the valley which lays on the north is mostly naked . . . is not calculated for cultivation except for a few miles north of the camp. At the edge of the mountain running north from here there are many warm sulphur springs.[10]

Heber was a little off in his estimation of distances. The Valley is oblong, closer to fifteen miles wide by twenty long, bounded on the west by the Great Salt Lake and the Oquirrh Mountains, pinched off in the south by Point of the Mountain, and defined on the north and east by the Wasatch Front. Geologically it is a sagebrush plain delimited by mountains.

While the Mormons were the first to settle the Valley, they were far from being the first whites to see or visit it. The famous Spaniards, Fathers Escalante and Dominguez, got as far north as Utah Lake in 1776. The Valley itself had been explored and traversed since the 1820s by mountain men and explorers.

Thereafter, the days of Heber and Brigham were crowded with the

supervision of laying out a city, planting potatoes, corn, beans, peas, buckwheat, and other crops, assigning building lots, dealing with the Indians,
building homes, a fort, a bowery, and fences, repairing equipment, and exploring. They worked in a little recreation by bathing in the warm springs
at the base of Ensign Peak and at a place they called Black Rock by the
Great Salt Lake. The warm springs (today's Wasatch Springs) have a temperature of 109 degrees and are quiet evidence of Utah's early volcanic history. Black Rock was later developed as a beach resort and the formation
still stands. (Heber eventually built a ranch house there—see below, p.
222.)

On July 29 the rest of the Sick Detachment of the Mormon Battalion
and the Mississippi Saints arrived in the Valley and swelled the population
to about 400.

On the first Sabbath following the arrival of these two companies,
some overall plans and rules were formulated. "Elder Kimball . . . rose to
lay before the brethren some items of business, whereupon it was decided
that the three companies [the Pioneers, the Battalion, and the Mississippi
Saints] form into one camp and labor together, that the officers be a committee to form the corral. . . . That horses and mules be tied near the camp
at nights . . . that we go to work immediately putting up houses . . . that
the houses form a stockade or fort to keep out the Indians; that our
women and children be not abused and that we let the Indians alone." [11]

Subsequently the Pioneers renewed their religious covenants by being
rebaptized in City Creek and then set to work building the fort and their
homes. By August 12 seventeen homes were under construction, five of
which belonged to Heber. The fort was built of adobe and covered ten
acres—where Pioneer Park is today. Its walls were nine feet high and
twenty-seven inches thick. The houses were roughly fourteen by sixteen
square feet, built next to the wall facing a common green.

Heber's four rooms (one of which was a good-sized storeroom) were
built in a row on the east side of the stockade (on the west side of today's
Second West Street between Third and Fourth south streets). His complex
was for years the largest structure in the Valley and was used as a school,
for religious meetings, and for nearly all civic and legislative meetings until at least August, 1853.

By Sunday, on a hot August 22, it was time to return to Winter Quarters to prepare for the final migration the following year. On this Sunday a
special conference was held in the Bowery, a temporary shelter which had
been erected on the block Young had designated for building a temple.
Brigham presided, but Heber conducted the extensive business which remained to be transacted. While the assembly sat quietly on rude benches,

he said, "These are matters for your consideration—if the brethren have any interest, we want an expression of it—if they have not, be silent and [we] will transact the business"—a typical example of Mormon democracy.

Fanning himself with his hat, Heber then gave the faithful a pep talk to forge them into a cooperative unit and to steel them for the rigors of the forthcoming winter. "I wish to God we had not got to return," he said. "If I had my family here, I would give anything I have. This is a paradise to me. It is one of the most lovely places I ever beheld."[12]

Before the meeting was over it was decided to fence part of the crops, to call the community the Great Salt Lake City, and to name a number of streams. Heber is credited with the felicitous thought of naming the river to the west (which connected fresh-water Utah Lake with the dead Great Salt Lake) the Jordan.

The people were then organized into wards and a stake. (A ward, a term borrowed from politics, is a congregation; a stake, a reference to the wooden stakes which supported the tents and tabernacle of ancient Israel [Isaiah 33 : 20, 54 : 2], is a group of wards; cf. diocese.) John Smith, uncle to Joseph Smith, who was then en route to the Valley, was named and sustained as stake president. (After he arrived in the Valley that September he selected Charles C. Rich and John Young as counselors and organized a twelve-man High Council. This organization cared for the approximately 1,600 who were in the Valley by that winter and formed the basis for government in Utah until January, 1849.)

Five days later Heber bade farewell to Ellen Sanders, then four months pregnant. Undoubtedly he arranged for Harriet, who was also pregnant, and Clara Young to look after Ellen as her time drew near. (Ellen survived that first winter in the Valley, but her son did not, and Heber never saw the child.) That same day Heber turned his affairs in the Valley over to the stewardship of Edson Whipple, saddled up and left with Young and 106 others for Winter Quarters. Over 100 Pioneers, including all the women, remained in the Valley. Since William Clayton had already departed (with the ox teams), Horace Whitney kept Heber's journal on the return trip.

Heber's return was much the same as coming out except that the newness had worn off, and his party, unencumbered with slow-moving oxen, made the journey in only sixty-six days. En route they met each of the ten companies and 1,553 Saints of the Second Division heading for the Valley. At Pacific Springs Heber met the three members of his family who had followed him west. How he reacted to the fact that so few had followed his advice is unknown.

On September 9 the Pioneers encountered a party of Crow Indians, far to the south of their homeland along the Yellowstone River. It was a raiding party willing to risk stealing horses even from the ferocious Sioux. Once they saw the Mormons, however, they promptly forgot the Sioux and stole forty to fifty head from the Pioneers. Although the Mormons gave chase, only five were recovered, and Heber lost his own chestnut.

The wealth and prestige of the Red Knights of the Plains was measured by horses: they paid debts with horses, bought wives with horses, made war on horseback, ate horses if necessary, and would risk their lives to steal horses. An armed, mounted Plains Indian was the perfect horseman, the ultimate fighting machine of his age. At full gallop he could carry and shoot up to 100 shafts, over or under his horse's neck, fast enough to keep one or more in the air at all times and powerfully enough to kill a buffalo. For fun and under ideal circumstances he could keep as many as eight arrows aloft at one time.

While the Mormons seldom fought the Plains Indians, they were certainly briefed on this formidable foe. The wisest course of action was always to avoid conflict or outrun it if possible, but once a fight commenced, they were advised to fight to the end, never surrender, never retreat, and save the last bullet for themselves, for many Indian tribes had raised torture to a fine art to honor the bravery of their captives.

Two weeks later, the Sioux stole eleven more horses from the seemingly careless Pioneers. This time Heber and Brigham were among those racing across the sage-covered plains in pursuit. They soon discovered that the horses had been stolen by the same band of Sioux they had met on their outward journey and that they knew the chief. The chief returned the eleven horses and then bragged that his braves had recently stolen forty-five horses from some Crows. Whether the old chief knew that these were the Mormon horses is not known.

In an attempt to regain more animals, Heber went to see the chief again. In front of the chief's tepee the unsmiling Heber demanded more horses—and got them. "I verily believe," he later commented, "that if I had had a few men with me of sufficient energy and resolution while at their camp, I could have secured all of the stolen horses."[13]

In between these Indian troubles Heber and Brigham had a run-in with *Ursus horribilis*, a grizzly bear, the most dangerous animal in western America. (Once in the early days of San Francisco some "sports" arranged a contest between a tiger and a grizzly. The bear cuffed and bit the great cat to death in less than a minute.) While they and a few others were walking along Deer Creek, just east of today's Glenrock, Wyoming, searching for veins of coal, they flushed a sow and her two cubs. One of the party, rather unnecessarily it appears, shot three times at her. The rifle misfired but drew the attention of the bear, which charged the company. By the time Heber and Brigham got off two ineffective rounds the bear was within about thirty feet of them. They quickly scrambled up the high rocky bank of the creek to safety. Seeing them out of reach, the sow ambled off.[14] Luckily for Heber, the grizzly is the only member of the bear family that is a poor climber.

At Fort Laramie they met Commodore Robert Field Stockton of the U.S. Navy. He and his men, who had recently fought in the Mexican War, joined the Mormons and traveled with them to six miles west of Chimney Rock, where he crossed the Platte to the Oregon Trail.

The remainder of the return proceeded without incident. On October 31, about one mile from home, Young called the men together and gave them well-deserved praise, which could be as sweet as his chastisement was sharp: "Brethren . . . I wish you to receive my thanks for your kindness and willingness to obey orders; I am satisfied with you; you have done well. We have accomplished more than we expected. Out of one hundred forty-three men who started, some of them sick, all of them are well; not a man has died; we have not lost a horse, mule, or ox, but through carelessness; the blessings of the Lord have been with us. . . . You are dismissed to go to your own homes."[15]

About sunset they drove triumphantly into town, to streets crowded with people, and many happy reunions were effected. A journey of over 2,200 miles and nearly seven months was successfully and finally completed. A road had been charted and a colony planted. Heber could now spend a relatively quiet fall and winter in Winter Quarters before making the return trip the following summer.

NOTES

1. Heber's Spring, known locally as "Mormon Spring," is located in the extreme southeast corner of section 36, nine miles west of Glendo on Horse Shoe Creek Road, between the creek and the road. The spring still appears as it did in Heber's day—covered with scum and alive with frogs.

2. James Smithies Diary, 41, typescript in author's possession.

3. Watson, ed., *Manuscript History of Brigham Young: 1846–47*, 564.

4. Wilford Woodruff Journal, July 24, 1847, Church Archives.

5. From Woodruff's sermon, July 24, 1880, as cited by Preston Nibley in *Brigham Young, the Man and His Works* (Salt Lake City: Deseret News, 1937), 98–99.

6. William E. Berrett, *The Restored Church* (Salt Lake City: Deseret Book Co., 1944), 383.

7. Orson F. Whitney, "Pioneer Women of Utah," *The Contributor*, vol. 11 (Sept., 1890), 405. These statements are so similar it may be that only one of the two women actually voiced this sentiment.

8. See Richard H. Jackson, "Mormon Perception and Settlement," *Annals of the Association of American Geographers*, vol. 68 (Sept., 1978), 317–34.

9. H. C. Kimball, Journal, July 25, 1847, Church Archives.

10. *Ibid.*, July 24, 1847.

11. *William Clayton's Journal*, 336–37.

12. H. C. Kimball, Journal 94, Aug. 22, 1847, Church Archives.

13. *Ibid.*, Sept. 21, 1847.

14. *Ibid.*, Sept. 18, 1847. Deer Creek is located immediately east of Glenrock, Wyoming. The rocky heights, about a quarter-mile south of the main highway, are clearly discernible.

15. *Ibid.*, Oct. 30, 1847.

CHAPTER 15

The Return

During Heber's absence there had been three deaths in his family—Helen's infant, Helen Rosabelle, Sarah Ann Whitney's little David, and Vilate's brother William, who had died while working in Missouri. When Sarah Ann's child was dying, Vilate's loving generosity revealed itself: her Solomon was ill at the same time and both infants appeared near death. Sarah Ann's grief for her firstborn was such that Vilate, mother of seven living children, prayed that if God required one, he would take hers and spare Sarah Ann's. Such were the bonds of love which could exist between "sister wives" in the Mormon system of plurality. Even so, Vilate's child lived and Sarah Ann's died of the dread cholera.[1]

During his absence Heber's wives had not only generally tended to their own material wants—Vilate had earned a little money by renting her dining room to two non-Mormon merchants from Nauvoo who had freighted out a line of goods, groceries, and fine wines and liquors—but also to their spiritual needs. They had held meetings with each other and enjoyed several spiritual experiences. On at least one occasion Vilate and Presendia were present when the gift of tongues was manifest. At least twice, several of them, including Vilate, Presendia, and Laura, administered to sick babies. From the beginning Mormons believed that the sick could be healed by the laying on of hands and the giving of blessings, or "administering," as this act is still called. On the frontier and especially under polygamy, Mormon women were much more engaged in such spiritual acts than today. They were not only permitted but encouraged to pray with their families and to administer to the sick.

These women were convinced that the "destroyer" was present and waiting to snatch infants away. Once they believed they saw the face and shoulders of Satan through a window. To them such trials were necessary to fit them for the highest degree of post-mortal exaltation, and they practiced humility, prayer, and fasting to overcome the adversary.

On the first Sunday after the return, Orson Pratt was assigned to give an account of the Pioneer journey and to describe for all their new home. Thereafter many meetings were held to bring the Twelve up to date on past and present problems. All kinds of things demanded their attention—looking after the poor in Winter Quarters, especially the families of the Mormon Battalion; consolidating scattered graves into one central cemetery; petitioning the Iowa legislature for a post office and county government; supervising the activities of the church trustees in Nauvoo, especially the disposition of the temple; directing the activities in the four mission fields of that day—England, the Pacific Islands, the southern states, and the eastern states; and, above all, preparing for another winter.

In the midst of all these and other activities one long-delayed act of church organization finally took place. Since the death of Joseph Smith, Brigham Young had led the church in the capacity of president of the Quorum of the Twelve Apostles. This had worked well; few questioned his authority. Indeed, some considered the Quorum of the Twelve enough leadership. In December, 1847, however, the First Presidency was reorganized. There seems to have been neither revelation nor pressing need for this move, and the sources do not make it clear why the reorganization took place when it did. In a forthcoming dissertation, however, Ronald Esplin has pointed out that Young had said, since leaving the Valley of the Great Salt Lake, that the spirit had whispered to him repeatedly that the presidency must be organized and the Twelve dispersed throughout the world on missions—which they were during February 1849. One other reason, perhaps, was that for the first time since the death of the Prophet the Saints were enjoying relative peace and security. No one was threatening them, a new home had been found and colonized, and church leaders were able to concern themselves with less pressing matters.

Brigham Young first suggested forming a separate First Presidency in October, and the proposal was discussed formally in a November meeting of the Quorum of the Twelve Apostles. Several were against it. They believed that a First Presidency could not be appointed without revelation. There was also the feeling that the creation of a separate First Presidency might diminish the role of the Quorum of the Twelve. Orson Pratt, one of the main dissenters, complained that the subject "has been thrown in incidently in conversation."[2] After several more discussions, a final meeting was held on December 5 at the home of Orson Hyde, leader of the Iowa Saints, a few miles south of Kanesville. In Hyde's comfortable living room, Young again presented the question of reorganization to the nine Apostles present. When the question of power and authority came up, sitting back in his chair and glancing around the room at Orson Pratt, Heber commented, "I don't consider it would give any more power [to Young, Richards, and himself] than they have now," and ingenuously added, "I have all the power I can handle."[3] After thorough discussion, the proposal passed unanimously. Hyde, who would later succeed Young as President of the Quorum of the Twelve, then moved that Young be sustained as President of the church. To the surprise of few, Young promptly selected Heber as his First Counselor and Willard Richards as his second. On the following December 27, this reorganization was sustained by the general membership of the church in that area during a general conference held in Kanesville. After three and a half years the Saints again had a First Presidency, and Young, the dynamic, pragmatic "Lion of the Lord," led as chief executive.

There were certainly more capable and better educated administrators Young could have chosen for a first counselor than Heber—Wilford Woodruff and John Taylor, for example, who eventually did head the church. If one accepts the imperative in Heber's 1842 patriarchal blessing—"Thou shalt attain to the honor of the three"—and the principle of revelation, then his selection can be considered providential. Moreover, Young knew Heber from years of totally dependable friendship, proven loyalty, well-tried faith, compatability, spiritual energy, and unquestioning obedience to authority. As already noted, Brigham, Heber, and Willard had been functioning as a sort of executive committee since 1844. In any event, never did Young seem to have regretted his choice. Heber remained loyal until death.

As a cousin and convert of Young, longtime Apostle, secretary of the Quorum of the Twelve, and Heber's companion during the first British mission, Willard Richards was close to Brigham Young and to Heber, and was thoroughly conversant with church affairs. He was also relatively well educated, a superb recorder and secretary, and the essence of obedience and submission.

Prior to his conversion in 1836, Richards toured with his "Electro Chemistry" show in the 1820s, became interested in herbal medicine, and in 1833 joined the Friendly Botanic Society. The following year he went to Boston to take a six-week course with Samuel Thompson, founder of the Thompsonian method of herbal medicine, and became "Doctor" Willard Richards—the title is invariably used in Mormon literature. (Several "Botanic Family Physicians" were attracted to Mormonism and rose to positions of influence. Besides Willard there was his brother Levi, who became Joseph Smith's personal physician; Frederick G. Williams, a counselor to Joseph; Sampson Avard, leader of the unauthorized Danite Band; Isaac Galland, a land speculator from whom Joseph purchased the site of Nauvoo; and John C. Bennett, one-time mayor of Nauvoo.[4] Probably Mormons were attracted to these men for their use of herbs rather than drugs.)

Thereafter Richards served the church faithfully in many assignments as a clerk. He kept Joseph Smith's private journals and was with the Prophet at the time of his assassination in the Carthage jail. He became church historian in 1842, and even while a member of the First Presidency, he was primarily occupied with the business of record-keeping, continuing to serve as Church Historian, Church Recorder, and, later in the Great Basin, as editor of the *Deseret News*. Perhaps it was for these skills that Young chose him as Second Counselor. Certainly it was not for executive assistance: Young delegated few of his executive prerogatives and responsibilities to anyone.

Most of the late winter and early spring was spent in preparation for going west, relocating in Kanesville those who would not or could not go, and "setting in order the things of the kingdom." At the general conference of April 6 Elders Orson Hyde and George A. Smith were appointed to remain in charge of the Saints in Kanesville. Heber's father-in-law Alpheus Cutler may have been appointed to supervise the winding down of Winter Quarters. He became disaffected, never went west, founded the "Cutlerlite" church, and his two daughters, wives of Heber, remained with him.

Sometime during this spring, Heber called a meeting of all the male (mostly adopted) members of his family. They all came together in his two-story log home, where, after the usual exhortations to be faithful, obedient, and industrious, he encouraged them all to go west with him. He regretted that he was in debt himself and could not help them much, but said he would do what he could, even to sending his teams back to pick them up once he had reached the Valley. "In five years," he promised them, "you will [be] better off than when in Nauvoo. . . . I hope . . . to see Israel gathered, Zion established, the Saints settled in peace. I can then lie down for a season. I want my family to gain riches, be honorable and . . . independent."[5]

By May the Saints had been divided into three great companies totaling 2,408 people to be led by Young, Kimball, and Richards and Amasa Lyman. On May 26 Young left Winter Quarters to join his company, which had left previously and was waiting for him west of the Elk Horn River; this company consisted of 1,220 people, 397 wagons, and 2,251 horses, mules, and cattle.

Heber left Winter Quarters May 29, with his company of 662 people, 226 wagons, and 1,253 horses, mules, and cattle, plus sheep, pigs, chickens, cats, dogs, goats, geese, doves, a squirrel, and some beehives. (Richards's and Lyman's company of 526 left in July.) The sources indicate that Heber had about sixty-six members of his family with him—at least twenty-six wives, nine children, some grandchildren, a number of adopted sons and their wives, a niece, and several children of his wives by previous marriages. As in 1846, his daughter Helen and his wife Sarah Ann Whitney were pregnant.[6] Winter Quarters was soon lost to view. Heber hardly looked back; the rest of his destiny lay to the west.

The 1848 trip west was not made by a hand-picked group of skilled men as in 1847, but by a congress of old and young men and women and children. It was more like the companies which had left Nauvoo in 1846. Still, as a result of experience and discipline, the three companies made the trek surprisingly well and fast. Heber's section took 114 days to make the journey, only three days over what the unencumbered Pioneers had required. Young arrived in the Valley September 20, Heber on the 24th, and Richards on October 11. It appears that Heber followed the route of 1847 with but one exception—on July 17, six miles west of Chimney Rock at an old buffalo ford, he crossed the Platte and followed the Oregon Trail to Fort Laramie via Robidoux Pass just south of Scotts Bluff, saving about ten miles. Even though each company was assigned one or more blacksmiths, he may also have taken this route to visit the smith the Robidoux family maintained in the pass. Maybe it was simply an attempt to find better feed for his animals.

It was only natural, with a larger company including many women and children, that there would be more deaths, accidents, loss of cattle, and Indian troubles than in 1847. While Heber's company had still been on the Elk Horn, some Otos and Omahas drove off a few head of cattle. Later, many of the oxen gave out, some falling dead in their yokes. More than thirty, for example, expired along the Big Dry Sandy, just beyond Pacific Springs.

Heber, protective, concerned, and perhaps a little officious, carefully looked after the women in his company. He scolded some of them for bathing in the Platte at a late hour (with little brush or timber lining its banks, when else could they have bathed?), and admonished them not to "ramble away from camp," or go visiting from wagon to wagon, but to stay home and keep themselves clean and their children and wagons clean.

Of the four recorded female deaths on the 1848 trek, the saddest was along the Loup River. Six-year-old Lucretia Cox in Heber's company fell off the wagon tongue and was crushed by the fore wheel of the wagon. Her pitiful screams brought her parents, but she died quickly. Heber came as soon as he was informed and tried to comfort the parents. Unfortunately such deaths were not uncommon. Children, probably including Heber's, could not resist the temptation to ride between the oxen, balancing on the wagon tongue. Heber, shaken by this tragic loss so soon after his admonition to the women, on the following Sunday scolded, "It is better for mothers to tie up little children in the wagons than bury them. Mothers don't half the time know where their children [are]."[7]

Perhaps he was a bit unfair. Some of the women were as busy as the "dear brethren." Heber's wife Mary Fielding (widow of Hyrum Smith) and her stepdaughter Jerusha drove their own wagon, for example. And somewhere along that dreadful stretch between Last Crossing and the Sweetwater was where Mary's renowned ox lay down in its yoke and refused to move. But after being administered to, it got up and pulled the wagon of this famous early Mormon widow safely into the Valley.[8]

There were also births, at least ten in Heber's group. Sarah Ann Whitney gave birth to David Orson on August 26 along the Sweetwater River, and Heber's daughter Helen had a son, William Howard, on August 17, also on the Sweetwater one mile west of Sage Creek. But William died five days later at 9 P.M. on August 22 on Helen's twentieth birthday, and was buried the next day in a curve of Spring Creek one mile west of the Sweetwater near South Pass. This infant's death was Heber's greatest trial during the 1848 trek, indeed one of the greatest trials of his life. Helen had already lost an infant daughter at Winter Quarters while her husband was with the Pioneers of 1847. Another loss, so soon after her first, prostrated her with grief and with what Priddy Meeks, still another botanic doctor, diagnosed as a *prolapsus uteri*, a fallen uterus. There was so much concern over Helen's condition that the whole camp laid over August 24. On that day Helen's husband Horace and Heber even took the extreme measure of disinterring the infant to determine whether it might have been prematurely buried. It had not been.[9]

Helen herself was convinced she was dying. As she lay in her wagon in the August heat and dust she gave parting kisses to her husband, mother, and father, and told her mother not to mourn for she would soon follow. This shook Heber out of his cocoon of sorrow and he cried out, "Vilate, Helen is not dying!"[10] He then administered several times to the prostrated daughter and her distraught mother and somehow, largely through will and faith, got them to the Valley, where they both eventually recovered in mind and body.

It was a Sunday, September 24 when Heber's company finally reached the Valley. Brigham Young and many others were on hand to greet them.

Church services had been held up pending their arrival. After a 3:00 P.M. meeting at which "Brother Brigham spoke until nearly dark," Heber and six wives—Vilate Murray, Christeen Golden, Lucy Walker, Harriet Sanders, Francis Swan, and Mary Ann Shefflin—"partook of a most excellent supper" prepared by the two wives who had come west in 1847, Ellen Sanders and Mary Ellen Harris. Heber's pioneering days were over for good.[11]

NOTES

1. H. M. Kimball, *Woman's Exponent*, vol. 14 (Jan. 1, 1881), 118.
2. Brigham Young Papers, Council Minutes, Nov., 1846, Church Archives.
3. *Ibid.*, Dec. 5, 1846.
4. See Robert T. Divett, "Medicine and the Mormons: A Historical Perspective," *Dialogue: A Journal of Mormon Thought*, vol. 12 (Fall, 1979), 16–25.
5. H. C. Kimball Papers, Church Archives. The date has been torn off this document.
6. The best source for this 1848 trek is William Thompson, clerk of Heber's division, "Journal of the travels of H. C. Kimball's Division, from Winter Quarters to Salt Lake, 1848," H. C. Kimball Papers, Church Archives, and "Journal History of the Church, Church Emigration Second Division, First Counselor Heber C. Kimball in Charge," May 29–Sept. 24, 1848, Church Archives.
7. Brigham Young Papers, Council Minutes, June 18, 1848, Church Archives. Some women likewise perished or were injured. Their totally inappropriate clothes caused them to fall or be dragged under the wagon wheels—such was the force of fashion and modesty. Several brave souls wore the safer "bloomers."
8. The most famous of all Mormon widows was, of course, Emma Smith, wife of Joseph, but she refused to go west. In spite of all the inducements and offers from Brigham Young and Heber she preferred to remain in Nauvoo and make the best of things. She eventually married a non-Mormon in 1847, applied for membership in the Methodist Episcopal Church (her pre-Mormon faith) in 1848, and her eldest son, Joseph Smith III, became the first president of the Reorganized Church of Jesus Christ of Latter Day Saints. See Almon W. Babbitt to H. C. Kimball, Jan. 31, 1848, H. C. Kimball Papers, Church Archives.
The traditional heroic view of Mary Fielding as a lone widow left to her own devices from Nauvoo to the Valley is not quite correct. In the first place she was no longer a widow but a wife of Heber; furthermore she traveled with her brother Joseph. Both Heber and Joseph (and others) provided her with a great deal of help and encouragement along the trail.
9. Daniel Davis Diary, Aug. 24, 1848, Church Archives. It was most unusual to stop even small companies, let alone the great company Heber was leading, for deaths.

10. Crocheron, *Representative Women*, 111–12. Helen lost her first four children.

11. Daniel Davis Diary, Sept. 24, 1848, Church Archives. Mary Ellen recorded a pretty little incident when she entered the Valley with the Second Company. "I found Ellen Sanders with supper ready. How charming to walk into a house and sit down to a table once more. . . . She told of her travels and I told mine until a late hour, but we finally slept and rejoiced together that so goodly a number of our friends had arrived safely." Mary Ellen Able [Harris], Kimball Pioneer History, 28. Church Archives.

PART IV

THE KINGDOM-BUILDING
AND FIRST PRESIDENCY YEARS
1848–68

I know you will prosper, and live in peace in the mountains
of the Great Salt Lake, and be perfectly independent.
Journal of Discourses, Aug. 13, 1853

CHAPTER 16

A New Beginning in Deseret

With Heber's second arrival in the Valley in 1848 a new and final phase of his career and life began. He never again left the Mountain West, and only once during the last twenty years of his life did he leave the area of present-day Utah. From his baptism in 1832 Heber had been generally an independent missionary and Apostle, but after he became First Counselor to Brigham Young in 1846 he went on no more missions. All of his zeal and energy were gradually funneled into devoted support of Young and directed toward the building of what twentieth-century Mormon historian Leonard Arrington called the Great Basin Kingdom.

While he became a devoted counselor, he instinctively realized that friendship in the fullest sense can exist only between peers; furthermore, Heber had no intention of becoming lost in Brigham's shadow. He succeeded in maintaining his independent spirit, rugged individuality, and parity through his increasingly powerful and outspoken preaching style and his penchant for prophecy—two traits which made Heber nearly as well known as Brigham.

In Utah Heber became as important and as influential as it is possible in the Mormon Church for anyone, other than the Prophet, to become. It could be argued that of all the men who have ever served as counselors to the various presidents of the Mormon Church, Heber is the most well known; certainly he is among the best remembered.

To 1848 there had been many rifts in his life, created by his various missions and the troubles which had caused him to move from state to state. Once in the Salt Lake Valley, however, these ceased, and his life became more routine and predictable—and harder to chronicle. The sources are scantier: he stopped keeping journals and wrote fewer letters to Vilate detailing his activities. For the rest of his life he devoted his energy and talents to building what he considered to be the earthly kingdom of God (to him Salt Lake City was to become the center of a worldwide kingdom directed by the First Presidency and the Quorum of the Twelve Apostles), caring for his enormous family, helping settle the thousands of emigrants who flooded into the Valley annually, and looking after a host of ecclesiastical and political duties.

This last phase of his life does, however, divide conveniently into three political periods: (1) the State of Deseret, 1849–51; (2) the Territory of Utah I, 1851–58 (to the end of the "Utah War" and Brigham Young's governorship), and (3) the Territory of Utah II, 1858–68 (from the beginning of the non-Mormon governorships to Heber's death). Throughout these periods he engaged in many simultaneous political, economic, social, and cultural activities, making it difficult to present his life in a strictly chronological manner.

The members of the First Presidency, the troika of Mormon leadership, shared some features: all were in the prime of life and clean-shaven. But they differed in other respects. Heber was balding with sideburns, while Young's and Richards's collar-length hair was scrolled under or curled at the ends. And while Heber and Young were powerfully built, Richards was a twinkle-eyed, roly-poly, double-chinned cherub.

In the Great Basin Young stamped his personality and will on everything—all political, social, economic, and cultural life. As chief executive he delegated little decision-making to others. The power of the ancient formula "Verily, verily, thus saith the Lord" was stated or implied by Young in most of his public utterances. Richards, probably due to lingering palsy and dropsy, remained a clerk and recorder, a man behind the scenes, inconspicuous, retiring, but powerful with the pen, the drafter of most of Young's church and state papers, and editor of the church-owned *Deseret News*. Heber, a modern Jonathan, was as loyal a friend, follower, and supporter as any man could be, and was clearly the second in command.

During the first few years in the Great Basin the members of the First Presidency were paternalistic, authoritarian, and not only tried to do everything all at once, but succeeded rather well. They addressed themselves to cultural and social problems as well as to the more pressing and immediate economic and administrative necessities. Authority was concentrated in a few hands.

When the members of the First Presidency arrived for the second time in the Valley, they found about 5,000 people living there, and there were shops, mills, bridges, and more than 1,000 acres of land under cultivation. There had been 15 deaths (including Heber's son Samuel Chase, who died February 3, 1848) and 120 births. The church organization had worked well and had provided adequate civil and religious leadership.

The now-famous cricket scourge and the seagulls which had eaten the crickets and saved some of the crops had occurred during the preceding May and June. Curiously, despite the miraculous nature of this event in current Mormon thought, it was not commented on much at the time and was hardly mentioned in the *First General Epistle of the First Presidency* of April, 1849. Cricket and grasshopper plagues were common terrors for many years in Utah. (One invasion took place on the day of Heber's funeral.)

Among the initial activities of Heber and Brigham Young was distribution of additional city and farm lots. In 1847 they had already allotted 114 ten-acre blocks. By October they had organized an additional sixty-three ten-acre blocks and had apportioned over 11,000 acres by lot to 863 applicants for city and farm sites. Among the first lots thus distributed were the prized "inheritances" around the temple block that had been reserved since August, 1847, for the First Presidency and other prominent Pioneers. Heber, perhaps because of his large family, received the largest portion—almost the entire ten-acre block northeast of the temple block.

The First Presidency encouraged farming, animal husbandry, even bee- and poultry-keeping, and pushed to the limit all activities which would maximize self-sufficiency—not only to supply the basic needs of those already in the Valley and the anticipated thousands of emigrants to come, but to preserve their independence from the Gentiles and to save the cost of freighting.

It was also necessary to formulate policies for the natural resources in the area and to begin their development. There would be no private ownership of water and timber (and later minerals). These were to belong to all. No one would be allowed to carve out huge cattle baronies, as later happened in Colorado or Wyoming, simply because the early settlers first gained control of the few water resources.

Water was also harnessed for grist, linseed oil, molasses, and sawmills; coal, lead, plaster of paris, and sulphur were mined and dug; salt was refined; lime was burned for mortar and cement; carding machines, tanneries, a pottery, blacksmithies, a foundry, a blast furnace, a printing press, and several machine shops were set up. A number of consumer goods were manufactured: combs, cutlery, shingles, nails, paper, cloth, hats, cordage, brushes, soap, crockery, locks and hinges. The Saints built bridges, canals, miles of walls, fences, ditches, and roads; surveyed a railroad; built chapels, schools, and shops, a council house, bathhouse, statehouse, tithing storehouse, Seventies' Hall, Tabernacle, social hall, endowment house, arsenal, courthouse, warden house, and penitentiary. To hasten the erection of some of these necessary buildings, and to give work

to the needy, a public works program was set up under the general direction of Daniel H. Wells—a dynamic personality who later became a member of the First Presidency.

The Mormons even printed their own paper money and coined some
gold pieces from the gold dust brought into the Valley by the Mormon
Battalion. Between January 2 and 5, 1849, Young, Kimball, and Newel K.
Whitney signed 1,565 notes (in denominations from fifty cents to five dollars) and reissued 256 Kirtland Safety Society Bank notes with a total face
value of $5,529.50.

But food, clothing, and shelter were in short supply during the extremely harsh winter of 1848–49. When a gaunt Heber stood up in a
gathering of men whom he knew to be feeding their families on beefhides,
wolves, dogs, even skunks and dead cattle and said, "Never mind, boys, in
less than one year there will be plenty of clothes and everything that we
shall want sold at less than St. Louis prices," even he considered it "a very
improbable thing." Charles C. Rich told him that he "had done up the job
at prophesying that time."[1] (Heber and Charles must have forgotten 2
Kings, where there is described, at the time of the Syrian Wars, a famine so
terrible that people ate asses' heads, doves' dung, even their own children.
At the height of this crisis, Elisha prophesied a miraculous end to the famine, and the next day the Syrians, leaving behind all their stores, fled before the rumor of approaching Hittite and Egyptian mercenaries.)

Heber's daring prophecy was fulfilled, not quite so dramatically, by
the Gold Rush, when some 50,000 gold-seekers went overland to California in 1849. From 15,000 to 20,000 passed through Salt Lake City in need
of fresh supplies, ground grain, wagon and harness repair, and help in
lightening their loads. The Mormons were in a position to provide the necessary goods and services, and the rate of exchange greatly favored them,
as they were able to trade at one-fifth to one-half of eastern market value.
Three heavy wagons went for one light one, and sometimes a team of oxen
would be thrown into the deal; a wagon could be bought for half what the
iron would cost in St. Louis; horses and mules rose to $200 a head.

The Saints benefitted not only from forty-niners hastening to the gold
fields, but also from merchants rushing goods to California. Near Salt
Lake City many merchants, hearing that goods were being sent to California in ships, feared the market would be glutted before they got there and
sold out cheaply to the Mormons. Some of these travelers gave up the
quest and stayed over in the Salt Lake Valley, some even joining the
church.

To dissuade the Saints from joining this mad rush, leaders told them
that the proper use of gold was for paving streets and making culinary

dishes(!), that gold was a good servant but a terrible master, and that when they had preached the Gospel and built up the Kingdom, God would give them all the gold they wanted. Few went; most stayed to build.

To facilitate the immigration and settling of thousands of annual converts from Europe which this expanded missionary program generated, and to help bring the remaining impoverished Saints from Iowa, the Perpetual Emigration Fund was organized. Heber was one of its founders and original directors. During the October, 1849, conference, he reminded the people that in the Nauvoo temple they had convenanted "that they would not cease their exertions until the poor were gathered," and urged them to contribute of their means to this end.[2]

The fund, formally created in September, 1850, was raised by voluntary subscriptions and based on the idea that money advanced to immigrants would be repaid by them after they settled in the Valley and thus the fund would be perpetuated. The fund accomplished its main purpose well. Between 1850 and 1859 the society brought to Zion 4,769 immigrants at a cost of $300,000,[3] and in forty years at least 80,000 came.

As thousands of new converts from all over the world inundated the Valley, Heber and Brigham Young were busy overseeing the work of exploring the area, colonizing, and settling the new arrivals. The actual locating and planting of colonies was delegated to the Apostles, but Brigham Young and Heber spent much time supervising and visiting the established colonies.

Very little was left to chance. After the sites had been carefully selected, equal attention was given to the choice of the leaders, and the first settlers of these colonies themselves were often "called." For the last twenty years of Heber's life, colonizing continued unabated. It was part of the basic doctrine of the "gathering." Within five years eight counties and forty-nine wards were organized, and during the first decade ninety-nine colonies had been planted in the Great Basin throughout an area extending 1,000 miles from north to south and 800 miles from east to west. Settlements ranged from Fort Lemhi (then in Oregon Territory, now Idaho) on the north to Parowan on the south and as far west as San Diego. The first major settlement after Salt Lake City was Brownsville (now Ogden), thirty-eight miles north of Salt Lake City, originally settled by Miles Goodyear before the Mormons arrived. In 1849 Brigham, Heber, and others planned the city and organized the second stake in Utah. The next large settlement was Provo, about forty-five miles south of Salt Lake City, which Brigham and Heber established during the spring of 1849.

By the time of Heber's death in 1868, 237 colonies had been planted, and he had made over forty visits to these settlements. The shortest was a one-day trip to Farmington, Davis County, in 1866, and the longest was a thirty-three-day trip to Fort Lemhi, 380 miles north of Salt Lake City, in 1857.

Some of these many trips provided rest, relaxation, adventure, and a change of pace and scenery. As in 1847–48 while crossing the plains, Heber was greatly interested in the flora, fauna, mineral deposits, topography, and indigenous population of his new homeland. He usually traveled without members of his family, but occasionally he would take a son or wife along. Some of the expeditions were rather large. The June, 1857, trip to Fort Lemhi, for example, included 142 men, women, and children, 54 wagons, 168 horses and mules, and 2 boats. Another trip to Cache Valley in June, 1860, totaled 116 men, women, and children.

The *Deseret News* frequently printed glowing accounts of the good done for the scattered Saints by these visits. A typical one of August 21, 1852, reported rather tendentiously that the First Presidency "enjoyed a very pleasant trip, . . . realizing that the Saints have learned wisdom and truth, and observed an increased desire in them to do better. . . . In every place visited, they rejoiced for the privilege of receiving instruction and manifested by their works that they would live accordingly."

On one such trip in 1851, Heber encountered the practice of Indian slavery. This evil had been going on since before 1800 and was so lucrative that the Indians even preyed on one another to acquire captives, mainly children, to sell to the Mexican traders for horses and mules. On November 3, near Manti, Heber and the Mormons came across Pedro Leonard and a small party of Mexican slavers from Santa Fe with a license from Governor Calhoun to carry on such traffic. They were buying Indian children from Chief Walkara's band of Utes. Young was disgusted, and by his authority as governor of Utah Territory and superintendent of Indian affairs he pointedly forbade the practice and declared their licenses invalid in Utah Territory. But despite his opposition the trade continued into the 1860s.

Up to 1848 Heber and the Mormons had been acquainted mainly with Plains Indians; the Great Basin Indians were much more primitive. Those near the early Mormon settlements were Utes, Gosiutes, and Paiutes, short-legged and dark-skinned desert gatherers of Shoshonean stock. The Gosiutes, who lived closest to the Mormons, were commonly and pejoratively called Diggers by the Whites because they grubbed for roots. Collectively they were desperately poor, weak, and peaceful. They lived in the most primitive of dwellings, flimsy brush wickiups, and existed chiefly on seeds, berries, roots, greens, grasshoppers, and lizards.

In Winter Quarters and along the trail west Heber had urged and Young had decreed only peaceful and fair dealing with the Indians. This was done for a variety of reasons, mainly to help insure the safe passage of the thousands of Saints who would follow. Before the Saints ever arrived in the Great Basin, the basic policy of Mormon-Indian relations—"it is cheaper to feed them than to fight them"—had been well established.

The First Presidency also urged compassion, not heavy-handed treatment, a slow process of civilization, and a gradual change prompted by good example and patience to demonstrate a superior way of life the Indians could imitate. Mormons were advised that the "Lord had a purpose to subserve by these long degraded, and often much abused descendents of Abraham," that the church "could hardly send missionaries to the ends of the earth and neglect . . . our immediate brothers," and that "we have in our very midst a people just as worthy and intelligent, just as capable, and everyway as much entitled to receive the Gospel" as anyone in the world.[4] The Saints were to become *Kulturträger*, not conquerors.

Mormon-Indian relations in Utah generally remained good and peaceful, but there were intermittent troubles for about twenty years— from some horse-stealing in 1849 through the Black Hawk War of the 1860s. By some force and great patience, however, the First Presidency was able to keep such trouble to a minimum. Their adoption of some Indian ways may also have helped. When occasion demanded, Heber, Brigham, and others would sit cross-legged in a circle with the chiefs, discuss problems, come to an understanding, and then smoke the pipe of peace. Heber participated in this unsanitary—to the white man—but now highly romanticized Indian ceremony, for to do otherwise would have offended the Indians.

Throughout the early Utah period Mormons would take Indian children into their homes—especially rescued or ransomed slaves—and some Indians played on their heartstrings. They would offer a captured child for a rifle or money, and if refused, would torture the child until the Mormons could stand it no longer and would agree to the trade. The Kimball family raised several such children. William, for example, ransomed five young Indians. Once for $50 he bought from the Shoshones a little Ute boy whom he named David Eagle Kimball. Many years later he returned to his people in Skull Valley west of Salt Lake City and became a chief. A daughter-in-law, Caroline (Mrs. David Patten Kimball), reared a young Piede Indian girl named Viroque, whom her father had ransomed, to become an expert housekeeper, and Heber himself employed Chief Tabby to oversee his horses on Kimball (or Stansbury) Island in the Great Salt Lake. Tabby (Tabiyuna or Tabinaw) was a Ute chieftain and brother to the more important leaders Arapeen and Walkara. The latter, called Walker by the whites, was an authentic Indian hero of the caliber of Sitting Bull, Crazy Horse, Geronimo, and Chief Joseph and deserves to be better remembered. He was certainly the most important Indian with whom Heber dealt.

Heber also had at least one Indian woman, named Kate, working in his home. "She lived in the big house," noted one of his wives, "would help the folks when needed, but did not have to work hard, was treated kind by all."[5] She was eventually buried in the family graveyard.

Sometimes such considerate treatment of the Indians paid surprising dividends. In September, 1858, Heber's son David Patton (whose wife had adopted an Indian girl) was returning to Salt Lake City from freighting on the Humboldt River when his party was attacked by Indians. As soon as the Indians discovered the party was Mormon they became friendly. "They said they liked the Mormons, but not the gentiles. Upon being asked the reason why they did not like the gentiles, said they called them hard names such as damned sons of bitches which the Mormons never did."[6] The Indians also introduced the Saints to wild artichokes, segoes, and other palatable roots, pinenuts, serviceberries, chokecherries, and other wild fruits and thereby made a contribution to Utah larders in times of poor harvests.

Although the Mormon policy of peace and friendship worked well, it did not entirely prevent Indian troubles. During the summer of 1853, for example, the Walker War broke out, during which at least nineteen white men lost their lives, including William Hatton at Fillmore. (Later his widow, Adelia Wilcox Hatton, became a plural wife of Heber.)

About ten months after the Walker War began, the Indians were ready to discuss peace. During May, 1854, Brigham and Heber visited the Ute camp to talk with Chief Walkara, who was also a Mormon Elder. The chief's daughter was sick, and he had ordered that if the child died, an Indian woman must be killed to accompany her spirit to the next world. This was no idle threat, for Walkara, on at least one previous occasion, had had two captive children killed in the hope of relieving his own pain. At times the Utes even buried live children with a corpse to keep it company and to be servants in the next life. When Walkara did die eight months later, two Indian women, three children, and twenty horses were slain and entombed, along with one live boy, as Walkara's companions to the Happy Hunting Ground.[7] Under considerable pressure, then, Dr. S. D.

Sprague, close companion of Brigham Young and an official camp physician, attended to the child, and Heber, kneeling down in the dirt in the wickiup, laid his hands on the girl's head and gave her a blessing. After her recovery, the old chief softened and the Utes were less troublesome thereafter. But Indian troubles did not end. There were difficulties in 1855 near Moab, the Tintic Indian War in the Utah, Cedar, and Tintic valleys in 1856, and finally the Black Hawk War of 1865–68.

NOTES

1. *Journal of Discourses*, vol. 10 (July 19, 1863), 247.

2. *Second General Epistle*, Oct. 12, 1849, *Millennial Star*, vol. 12 (Apr. 15, 1850), 118–22.

3. According to a report by John T. Cave, Feb. 1, 1860, to Governor Cumming, U.S. State Department, Territorial Papers, Utah 1853–73, M12, roll 2, 477, National Archives, Washington, D.C. The Saints, however, were slow in paying back their advances. By 1877 $1,000,000 was owing the fund. Many of these debts were written off during the Jubilee Year of 1880.

4. *General Epistles* 10, 11, and 13; *Journal of Discourses*, vol. 1 (July 31, 1853), 171. As Howard A. Christy has pointed out, however, in practice this initially enlightened Mormon attitude toward the Indians was not successful in the long run and the Mormons offered mailed fists as well as open hands. "Open Hand and Mailed Fist: Mormon-Indian Relations in Utah, 1847–52," *Utah Historical Quarterly*, vol. 46 (Summer, 1978), 216–35.

5. Adelia Almira Hatton Memoirs, 23, in author's possession. Typescript copy in Church Archives.

6. "A Sketch Pioneer History: A Sketch of Our History in This Valley by M. E. Kimball, September 26, 1858," typescript, 34, Mary Ellen Kimball Papers, Church Archives.

7. Thomas Bullock Journal, May 12, 1854, Church Archives; *Journal of Brigham Young*, Jan. 29, 1855, 3.

CHAPTER 17

Administering the Kingdom

When the Mormons entered the Salt Lake Valley in July, 1847, they were in territory claimed by both Mexico and the United States. Temporarily, for self-government purposes and to hasten the orderly extension of civilization in the Great Basin, they simply and naturally extended their priesthood organization much as had been done previously in Nauvoo and in Winter Quarters in the form of a social contract. Civil authority was held by the First Presidency but was generally administered through the Bishops and the High Council. From July 24, 1847, through March, 1849, a theo-democracy existed. Leaders were appointed, but always subject to a vote of approval by the people. Revenue came from tithes and offerings; lawmaking power was vested in the High Council; the courts were administered and formed by Bishops, the High Council, the Quorum of the Twelve, and the First Presidency; and the law was executed by the Nauvoo Legion. This fusion of church and state, anathema in American history and tradition, came naturally to the Mormons. Their task was to build the Kingdom of God on earth: what better leaders than God's anointed, and what better system than God's own Priesthood? The Mormons, furthermore, had found little justice from regularly elected state and federal officers. What is more, their theo-democracy worked. Justice was done and the mundane affairs of the Kingdom were administered. This system was to be of short duration, however; it lasted only until the Mexican War was ended and a regular territorial government could be set up.

By the time of Heber Kimball's second entrance into the Valley, the treaty of Guadalupe Hidalgo had been signed on February 2, 1848. This ended the Mexican War and transferred the Great Basin to the United States. The 1848 treaty and the discovery of gold in 1848 placed the Mormons squarely in the path of the surge to the west, and Mormon and Gentile ways were to continue to clash. However strong the Mormon desire to live their religion in peace, they had no intention of establishing a separate nation. As soon as possible the First Presidency commenced preparation to gain statehood and enter the Union.

By January 6, 1849, a constitution had been drafted, a delegate to Congress selected, and a petition for statehood prepared. Without waiting for Washington's response to this petition, the First Presidency opted to move ahead and create their own provisional State of Deseret (which they in no way intended to become an independent Mormon republic in the Texas manner). It was just as well they did, for President Zachary Taylor, who succeeded Polk in 1849, temporized. He worried over the rumors about Mormon "sedition" and polygamy and the larger issue of a balance between slave and free states. A year later the Compromise of 1850 was hammered out, which admitted California into the Union as a free state, but granted only territorial status to Utah and New Mexico, a situation that continued for Utah until 1896, after thirteen other territories had preceded her into the Union. Utah's admission was finally effected after the 1890 Manifesto ended Mormon polygamy and broke the deadlock between the church and Washington. Only three of the first forty-eight states came into the Union after Utah: Oklahoma, Arizona, and New Mexico.

The First Presidency drew the boundaries of their proposed state rather generously—including what came to be Utah, most of northern Nevada and Arizona, much of Wyoming, Colorado, and New Mexico, and a small portion of Oregon, Idaho, and southern California (to secure access to the sea at San Diego)—an empire of about 490,000 square miles, or an area the size of today's France, Germany, Italy, Belgium, and Holland combined. The name they chose, Deseret, is from the Book of Mormon and means honeybee, suggesting industriousness. The Mormons were not unique in their attempt to independently create a state: at least five other such attempts are recorded—Texas, Franklin (Tennessee), Oregon, Jefferson (Colorado), and California.

A political convention was scheduled to meet in Salt Lake City during March, 1849, and a notice was sent to "all citizens of that portion of Upper California lying east of the Sierra Nevada mountains." This convention adopted a constitution, provided for a bicameral legislative body, and conducted elections. It was hardly democratic by any American standards—out of a total of nearly 5,000 persons only 674 voted, and they voted for only one slate of candidates. This seems to have caused little if any disturbance—Mormons were used to authority and rule by the priesthood.

Predictably the three top offices were filled by the First Presidency: Young became governor; Kimball, chief justice; and Richards, secretary of state. The government lasted just two years and most of its deliberations were held in Heber's home in the original fort.

Heber and his associate justices, Newel K. Whitney and John Taylor, served as the Supreme Court of Deseret and the main conservators of the peace for one year, after which they turned over their duties to Daniel H. Wells, Daniel Spencer, and Orson Spencer, who were somewhat better qualified. During his one year on the bench Chief Justice Kimball had little to do, as the Mormons were generally law-abiding and were encouraged to use their own ecclesiastical or bishop's courts. Only one known case came before Heber—the case of the kidnapping of a daughter of Orrin Porter Rockwell in 1849. The results of this action are unknown.

Even non-Mormons, especially passing emigrants, appealed to the Mormon courts, and found their decisions for the most part remarkably fair and impartial. In those days territorial justices were not held in high repute; since no minimal standards for appointments existed, many bumblers, drunkards, and flamboyant eccentrics were appointed to office. It is not surprising that the Mormon judiciary was considered exemplary.

The provisional legislature was duly established. At the first meeting of the general assembly, held July 2, 1849, the previous elections were recognized and one oversight was corrected by electing Heber to the vacant office of lieutenant governor. In this capacity he also served as ex-officio president of the senate. If he had little to do as chief justice, his responsibilities as president of the senate were more demanding. He supervised the division of the state into counties; the incorporation of cities; the establishment of county courts with judges, clerks, justices, constables, and sheriffs; the creation of a state militia and the University of the State of Deseret (later the University of Utah). He was also concerned with mail service, roads, bridges, ferries, taxes, prisons, the chartering of companies, and a host of similar social needs.

Another immediate concern of the First Presidency was church organization and administration. They completed the reorganization of the Quorum of the Twelve and the First Quorum of Seventies, called patriarchs, increased the number of wards outside Salt Lake City, built a suitable bowery for public worship services, and established a satisfactory way of collecting and distributing tithing donations.

Four additions to the Quorum of the Twelve were necessitated by the creation of the First Presidency and the disfellowshipping of Lyman Wight for apostasy. The new apostles chosen were Charles C. Rich, Lorenzo Snow, Erastus Snow, and Franklin Dewey Richards. Immediately following their appointment and while they were glowing with pride and pleasure and receiving felicitations, Heber stepped forward and in his typically blunt manner announced, "I'll tell you one thing [you] don't know the difference between [a] Dutch Penn harness from [and] a light harness. You were free men before, but you will get heavy harness on [now]. . . ."[1]

The charge to take the Gospel unto every kindred, tongue, and people weighed heavily on the First Presidency. Within a short time they had selected, interviewed, set apart, instructed, and sent missionaries to many places in the United States, Europe, the Pacific Islands, Australia, South Africa, Thailand, Ceylon, Malta, Iceland, India, China, the West Indies, and British Guiana. By 1856 the Book of Mormon had been translated into Danish,[2] German, French, Italian, Welsh, and Hawaiian, and church newspapers published in St. Louis (*The Luminary*), New York City (*The Mormon*), San Francisco (*Western Standard*) as well as Salt Lake City (*Deseret News*).

In addition to his normal share of organizing and administering this expanded proselytizing program, Heber, as "Father of the British Mission," generally supervised all missionary efforts in that, the largest of all missions. He sent eight of his sons (three natural and five adopted) there on missions; other British missionaries sent him reports and letters; members wrote to him requesting various favors; and many British immigrants sought him out upon their arrival in the Valley.

A major part of Heber's church administration was presiding over all temple ordinances in Utah until his death in 1868. Throughout his life in the church he was closely connected with temple work. Prior to the Great Basin period he had contributed money to and worked on the Kirtland temple, had helped dedicate the Far West (Missouri) temple site, and had helped build and officiate in the Nauvoo temple. In February, 1853, he participated in ground-breaking for the Salt Lake City temple, offered the prayer consecrating the site, and on April 6 of that same year gave the dedicatory prayer for the main or southeast cornerstone.

During Heber's lifetime in the Great Basin, temple work was done in Young's office, in the new Council House, and in the Endowment House on the northwest corner of Temple Square. The first real temple in Utah (in St. George) was not dedicated until 1877, nine years after Heber's death, and the Salt Lake City temple was not dedicated until 1893.

Heber usually spent from one to three days a week giving instruction and administering the ordinances to as many as 200 individuals a week. The work was demanding and tiring. "Through my labors," he once said, "in giving the brethren and sisters their endowments and superintending the labors from the different Wards, in addition to seeing to those affairs more directly personal, my body is considerably wearied. . . ."[3]

To lessen the work he requested the bishops of the various wards to take care of all the preliminary work of calling and interviewing appropriate candidates and arranging for their presence with letters of recommendation and temple clothing at the Endowment House at the proper times. "These men and women," he wrote the bishops in 1856, "who you recommend for their endowments must be individuals who pay their tithing from year to year; who pray in their families; and do not speak against the authorities of the Church and Kingdom of God; nor steal; nor lie; nor interfere with their neighbors wife, or husband; who attend strictly to meetings and prayer meetings and those who pay due respect to their presiding officers and Bishops and those who do not swear."[4] As strict as these standards were, modern Mormons will note that today's stringent health requirements are not mentioned.[5]

Heber must have wondered how much attention was paid to his instructions. "I have a great chance to learn the state of the people," he noted in 1866; "out of one company of thirty-five men there were only seven that prayed; this company were well recommended by their Bishops. . . . This tells you how some live when they are here in Zion."[6]

In those days it was possible to receive one's endowments at the age of fourteen. As early as 1855 Heber said to the young men, "Take unto yourselves wives of the daughters of Zion, and come up and receive your endowments and sealings, that you may raise up a holy seed unto the God of Abraham. . . ."[7] He urged young people to get married and do their courting afterward, for the money spent on pleasing the young lady beforehand would go far toward outfitting a new home. Couples were also advised to keep romance alive after marriage. Then, as now, great emphasis was placed on marrying within the church. Heber is supposed to have said, "An Elder or saint that honors his place will never marry a wife out of the church. A man that marries out of the church is a fool. . . . Let men be Baptized & prove themselves four years before a sister marries him."[8]

Heber saw to it that his own children went for their temple ordinances early. "I desire to refer back to a time when I was about thirteen years of age," one son recorded, "when Heber C. Kimball sent word to me and my brother Joseph Kimball . . . to come to his office. When we arrived there, mere boys, he said to us: 'If you want your father's blessing you be at the Endowment House in the morning and have your endowments.'"

"Of course we were frightened nearly to death," he added. "I do not know how people feel when they are going to be executed, but I suppose that is the sort of feeling I had, not knowing and having no conception of what it all meant. However, we were there, and we had our endowments. I did not remember much that transpired, but I was awed, and the impression was burned into my soul of the sacredness of that place, and the sacredness of the covenants which I entered into when almost a child."[9] To Heber the giving of endowments to such young people was "like catching a calf while we could catch it."[10]

In addition to Heber's temple concerns in Salt Lake City, two stories are recorded about him of the future Manti and St. George temples. In 1850, when the site for the settlement of Manti was being selected, he predicted that a temple would be built on a nearby hill. Some did not think anything would ever be built in that area. "Well it will be so," he declared, "and more than that, the rock will be quarried from that hill to build it with, and some of the stone from that quarry will be taken to help complete the Salt Lake Temple." And so it came to pass. And during May, 1855, while in Harmony in southwestern Utah, on one of his many trips among the settlements, "Bro. Kimball tried to avoid prophesying," it was reported, "and twisted to get around it, but out it would come, and at length it came forth that soon we would [have] thousands of the Indians around us at Parowan."[11] While the spirit of prophesying was upon him he also revealed "that a wagon road would be made from Harmony over the Black Ridge; and a Temple would be built in the vicinity of the Rio Virgin, to which Lamanites would come from the other side of the Colorado and would get their endowments in it."[12] At the time the building of such a road was considered impossible, but eventually the road was built, the site of the St. George temple on the Rio Virgin was dedicated in 1871, the temple itself was dedicated in 1877, and many Indians have attended its sessions.

In connection with his temple work he was consulted in reference to plural marriage. In 1857, for instance, John S. Fuller of Spanish Fork wrote to him for permission "in obtaining more wives," and offered his fifteen-year-old daughter Adelaid as a wife to Heber's son William, assuring him that it was agreeable with Adelaid and her mother.[13] (William eventually took five wives, but Adelaid was not one of them.) And in 1861 Heber wrote John A. West of Parowan, "The letter you wrote me requesting the privilege of yourself and wife receiving your endowments and also taking another wife, has been submitted to Pres. B. Young. He has given his permission; for you [to] take another wife; and I also privilege you and them to receive their Endowments. Be here some Friday as the Endowments are given on Saturdays. Be there by 7 A.M. with clothing and oil."[14]

In spite of the awesome responsibility of seeing after the temporal and spiritual needs of the people, the First Presidency promoted cultural and educational affairs, especially those useful in Kingdom-building. Heber was fond of the theater and music. He loved parties and especially dancing "to the Lord, to His glory," *ad majorem Dei gloriam* as it were. Sometimes he took his combined families to the production of the Deseret Dramatic Association in the Social Hall, the first theater west of the Missouri. For one opening night he was given fifty complimentary tickets. Three of his favorite plays were *Still Waters Run Deep*, *Pizarro*, and *The Honeymoon*. Generally he preferred comedies, believing that there was enough tragedy in real life.

Education was encouraged. It stretches credibility to learn that during the winter of 1848–49, English, Greek, Latin, Hebrew, French, German, and Tahitian were taught in the Great Basin. Later, Spanish and Indian dialects were also offered. Since there were few books available, classes must have been taught by the rote method. Aside from the cultural advantages of these languages, some, of course, had direct proselytizing value.

Among the first buildings erected were common schools in each of the wards, and Heber and others also built private schools for their large families. By 1854 there were 226 schools of various kinds in the territory, and Mormon illiteracy was probably the lowest in the West. A university was chartered and adult education was fostered by evening lectures and language classes.

Under such leadership, by 1863 Utah not only had more than 200 schools, and scattered choirs and bands, but also a social hall, the Salt Lake Theatre, a musical and dramatic society, the Deseret Academy of Fine Arts, the Salt Lake Tabernacle Choir, the Seventies' Hall of Science, a horticultural society, the Universal Scientific Society, the Deseret Philharmonic Society, the Deseret Typographical Union, the Deseret Theological Institute, and the 5,000-volume Utah Library. (One visitor to Utah claimed to have met Heber in the Utah Library and discussed at length with him Homer, Plato, Phidias, Praxiteles, Cicero, Virgil, Dante, and Goethe. If such an encounter ever took place, the visitor surely must have confused him with someone else, such as Orson Pratt or John Taylor,[15] since there is no evidence that Heber ever studied the classics.)

Not all cultural and intellectual efforts succeeded. One student of early Utah culture has concluded, "Frontier Utah had little respect for the ivory tower intellect, male or female . . . the arts, except for the easy diversion of the theatre, were not useful in kingdom building."[16]

Some of the leaders seem especially to have downgraded female intellectual organizations. In 1850 a group of Mormons organized the Elocution Society. Heber, for one, could see no practical or positive good in such activity and was disturbed when some of his wives joined. He much preferred that they learn practical skills. His forthright solution was simply to ask one of the leaders to resign. "Elder Kimball," Martha Heywood sadly recalled, "called here on Monday to express to me his wish that I would withdraw from the Elocution Society, that it might be the means of breaking up the Society or drawing away his wives. . . ."[17] That seems to have been the effective end of the society.

The Polysophical Society for the advancement of cultural and intellectual life organized in 1854 was another casualty. Even though Heber's favorite daughter Helen was a member, it succumbed to the religious and intellectual retrenchment of the Reformation. Heber is reported to have considered it a "stink in his nostrils," and believed that there was an "adultrous spirit in it"[18]—a curiously strong reaction. Was it thought to be merely a waste of time or were some of the members putting on airs, creating more class distinction than was wanted in the church? Were "undesirable" works of literature discussed? Whatever the reasons, the society was disbanded.

This selective zeal for culture and education drew the First Presidency into an attempt in 1853 to reform English orthography—a thankless and impossible job that no one before or since has ever come close to accomplishing. The First Presidency, never daunted by any task, sponsored the strange experiment known as the Deseret Alphabet. Perhaps the most unusual assignment in Heber's life was to serve on this committee along with Parley P. Pratt and George D. Watt. Although Heber had studied phonography (shorthand phonetics) with Watt in 1845, he had no special talents for this sort of endeavor, and his appointment to the committee as a representative of the First Presidency only suggests the importance Young gave to this project.

The Deseret Alphabet was an attempt to make the reading and writing of English simple for the hordes of European immigrants gathering in Utah and to facilitate their complete assimilation into a western American milieu.

No one knows the origin of its strange characters, but certainly Watt's knowledge of phonography was fundamental. After the thirty-eight-character alphabet (including the Latin letters C, D, L, O, P, S, W) was devised, the committee had a type font cast in St. Louis and some printing was done with it. A *First Reader*, in an edition of 10,000 copies, was published, as well as 10,000 copies of a *Second Reader*, and 8,000 copies of part of the Book of Mormon were also printed. The experiment was finally abandoned in 1869, a year after Heber's death. There is no evidence that Heber ever learned the alphabet.[19]

NOTES

1. Brigham Young Papers, Council Minutes, Feb. 12, 1849, Church Archives.

2. This translation was made by Kimball's adopted son Peter Hansen in 1851. He was so proud of this that when he died in 1895 in Manti his tombstone commemorated this achievement.

3. *Journal of Discourses*, vol. 3 (Mar. 23, 1856), 268.

4. H. C. Kimball Papers, May 19, 1856, Church Archives.

5. Many sources indicate that while Heber was generally against the use of "hard" liquor, neither he nor his family regarded the proscriptions of tea, coffee, tobacco, or "soft" liquor as absolute. In his day Mormon standards of health had not become today's *sine qua non* of orthodoxy. It was not until the administration of President Heber J. Grant (1918–45) that compliance with this principle of health became a formal prerequisite to advancement in the church and entrance to the temple.

Unfortunately the only thing too many people know about Mormonism is the Word of Wisdom, that good members are not supposed to use tea, coffee, liquor, tobacco, or drugs. Often the weightier matters of the faith are overlooked. This is not likely to change, so perhaps it will not be amiss to explain what the salutary Word of Wisdom really is. Officially it is known as Section 89 of the Doctrine and Covenants, a revelation given to Joseph Smith Feb. 27, 1833, in Kirtland, Ohio. It consists of three parts. One stresses the use of herbs, fruit, grain, vegetables, and meat (but sparingly); the second warns, "in consequence of evils and designs, which do and will exist in the hearts of conspiring men in the last days," wine, strong drink, tobacco, and hot drinks [interpreted to mean tea and coffee] "are not for the body or belly." The third part contains the promise to the obedient: "And all saints who remember to keep and do these sayings . . . shall receive health in their navel and marrow to their bones; And shall find wisdom and great treasures of knowledge, even hidden treasures; And shall run and not be weary, and shall walk and not faint."

Originally in 1833 the revelation came "not by way of commandment or constraint," and many from that day to the 1920s considered its observance optional. More zealous Mormons from that day to this, stressing the fact that the revelation also showed "forth the word and will of God in the temporal salvation of all saints in the last days," and that the principle was "adapted to the capacity of the weak and the weakest of all saints, who are or can be called Saints," have regarded the revelation as law. Joseph's brother Hyrum was among the earliest to do so. As late as 1861 Brigham Young said, "Some of the brethren are very strenuous upon the 'Word of Wisdom'; and would like to have me preach upon it, and urge it upon the brethren, and make it a test of fellowship. I do not think that I shall do so, I have never done so" (*Journal of Discourses*, vol. 9 [Apr. 7, 1861], 35). He never did. In time, however, the Word of Wisdom slowly evolved into a test of fellowship, which it remains to this day. See Leonard J. Arrington, "An Economic Interpretation of 'The Word of Wisdom,'" *Brigham Young University Studies* (Winter, 1959),

37–49, and Paul H. Peterson, "An Historical Analysis of the Word of Wisdom" (unpublished M.A. thesis, Brigham Young University, 1972).

6. H. C. Kimball to Brigham and Isaac Kimball, Dec. 7, 1866, *Millennial Star*, vol. 24 (Jan. 26, 1867), 59.

7. *Thirteenth General Epistle*, Oct. 29, 1855, *Millennial Star*, vol. 28 (Jan. 26, 1856), 49–55.

8. John Pulsipher Scrapbook, Feb. 3, 1855, Church Archives.

9. Claude Richards, *J. Golden Kimball* (Salt Lake City: Deseret News Press, 1934), 274–75.

10. H. C. Kimball to David Kimball, July 17, 1865, H. C. Kimball Papers, Church Archives.

11. Thomas D. Brown, *Journal of the Southern [Utah] Indian Mission: Diary of Thomas D. Brown*, ed. Juanita Brooks (Logan: Utah State University Press, 1972), 35.

12. James G. Bleak, "Annals of Southern Utah Mission," vol. 1 (Book A), typescript, 14–15, copy in Utah State Historical Society, Salt Lake City.

13. John S. Fuller to H. C. Kimball, Mar. 10, 1857, H. C. Kimball Papers, Church Archives.

14. H. C. Kimball to John A. West, Mar. 27, 1861, H. C. Kimball Papers, Church Archives.

15. Austin and Maria N. Ward, *Husband in Utah* (London: James Blackwood, 1857), 185–86.

16. Maureen Ursenbach, "Three Women and the Life of the Mind," *Utah Historical Quarterly*, vol. 43 (Winter, 1975), 40.

17. *Ibid.*, 31.

18. *Ibid.*, 32.

19. Contrary to popular belief, the Deseret Alphabet was not a device for the keeping of Mormon "secrets." Such an attempt at that time in the Great Basin seemed so bizarre that some non-Mormons sought a deeper meaning. Except for their sacred temple ceremonies, Mormons really do not try to keep secrets, in fact they expend enormous time and treasure trying to share their "secrets" with the world.

Some wags have commented that a printed page in the Deseret Alphabet resembles a Turkish tax list more than anything else. More serious observers have guessed that it may derive from Isaac Pitman's *Stenographic Soundhand* of 1837 or his *Phonographic Journal* of 1842, or from an Ethiopian alphabet, or even from the Book of Mormon "reformed Egyptian."

CHAPTER 18

Defending the Kingdom

In September, 1850, Millard Fillmore and Congress established the Territory of Utah. Because of Utah's remote location, however, the territorial government was not effected until March 26, 1851. According to law, when a territorial government was set up, Washington appointed the executive and judicial officers (the governor, secretary of state, three judges, a marshal, and an attorney), and the people of the territory elected the members of their legislature and their one delegate to Congress. The Mormons felt justified, however, in sending President Fillmore their own proposed list of territorial officers—Brigham Young for governor, Willard Richards as secretary of state, Zerubbabel Snow[1] for chief justice, Heber C. Kimball and Newel K. Whitney for associate justices, Joseph L. Heywood for marshal, and Seth M. Blair for attorney.

Fillmore was surprisingly agreeable and accepted four of the seven—Young, Snow, Blair, and Heywood. Broughton D. Harris was appointed as secretary of state and Joseph Buffington as chief justice, with Snow and Perry G. Brocchus as his associates. Heber, lacking any formal training in jurisprudence, received no appointment of any kind.

Fillmore had considerable trouble with his justice appointees, as these positions were not popular. In all there were six chief justices and seventeen associate justices appointed to serve in Utah between 1850 and Heber's death in 1868.[2] Heber, however, was never appointed to any of these many vacancies, although on at least one occasion he formally petitioned for one.

Although no longer chief justice, Heber did remain politically active. He served as a councilor (senator) representing Salt Lake County in the territorial or legislative council (senate). Through 1858 he also served as president of this thirteen-man body and worked on two of its standing committees—the judiciary and the committee on herding.

The first session of the new territorial legislature convened September

23, 1851, in the Social Hall in Salt Lake City and immediately got off to a bad start with the departure for Washington, four days later, of Brocchus, Harris, and Lemuel G. Brandebury, who replaced Buffington as chief justice when the latter refused to serve, all three of whom returned to Washington. They promptly announced that they had been compelled to leave Utah because of the illegal and seditious acts of Governor Young, that Young was wasting federal funds, and that the Mormons were immoral and polygamous. This was the beginning of many years of misunderstandings between the Mormons and Washington-appointed territorial officers.

Heber's typical response to their departure was to rise in the Social Hall and propose to the council that "we the Elders of Israel, agree to deliver the United States officers now about to leave the Territory into the hands of Satan that he may have power to buffet them until they shall be devoid of reason and have no power to injure any one."[3] This motion, of course, carried unanimously.

Heber took his position as a councilor and as president of the council seriously and had no intention of being a mere figurehead, tolerated simply because he was a member of the First Presidency. "I want to speak," he insisted, "and not be here like a dumb dog. I am ignorant of many technicalities, but . . . I know the truth. . . ."[4] On a freezing January 13, 1852, he spoke sternly against a bill requiring code commissioners to be learned in the law and argued that any good man could be a lawyer in Utah, not just those with training. "I am not learned in the law, and I want to get a salary and sit on my h——s [harse?] the same as other men, let us not make laws that will prohibit ourselves from such privileges. . . ." He went on to add, "Now the most of these learned lawyers are as ignorant as I am, and I tell you, if I sat upon the bench, and they treated me as they treat Judge [Zerubbabel] Snow I would knock them down. He is learned in the law and must submit to have the nasty curses shame him and they will call him a nasty shit. Then I say let us poor ignorant fools have a chance to get salaries."[5]

Although he took political life seriously, Heber was not loath to take advantage of his positions as a member of the First Presidency and president of the council to preach to either that body or the house when he felt the need to. When someone fussed over his insistence on prayer and the role of the Priesthood in the legislature he let it be known that the "brethren were to be brethren," that if the Priesthood were not present and honored he would leave. To him the legislators were to "make the laws for Israel," like the Seventy selected by Moses and the Council of Fifty chosen by Joseph Smith.[6] Heber was especially insistent during the Reformation of the mid-1850s. On December 30, 1855, for example, he advanced a resolution to the general assembly: "This is a day of reformation and we of the Council cannot do business until the work of the reformation goes through and all repent and are baptized for the remission of sins, that we may have the Holy Ghost to be in us and over us."[7] On the next day he had John 15 read to the group to buoy them up spiritually.

A year later Heber made a speech to the council, calling every member to repent of his sins and be baptized for the same, whereupon the group adjourned to the Endowment House.[8] Two weeks later on New Year's Eve, he addressed a joint session of the legislature regarding order, discipline, and righteousness: "I would positively motion that every house that is not a House of God should be removed destructively, as Hosea says . . . 'If there is not a known tribunal to put these things into force there should be a tribunal unknown to do it.'. . . We should be organized precisely after the order of God." He further charged them to be different in preventing wickedness. "We are minute men, all of us, from this time henceforth and forever, to spy out the liberties of our enemies in our midst, upset their nastiness, upset their wicked combinations, and cast out their nuisances."[9]

This reference to a "tribunal unknown" may have been a veiled allusion to the Council of Fifty. Such statements may be one source of non-Mormon rumors of "avenging angels" and the like. Certainly his citing the fiery minor prophet Hosea was strong language to men who knew their Old Testament. In this same joint session of December, 1856, which was one of his last, he let all the delegates know in unequivocal terms that the church ruled the legislature. "Ain't we got authority," he said, "to cut you off the Church here just as much as in a Church capacity? Why Gentlemen I can turn this assembly into a [church] Council in a moment."

In 1854 Willard Richards, Second Counselor to Young in the First Presidency, died. Young, feeling the burdens of administration, replaced the clerk and recorder with an executive, the young, dynamic, thirty-nine-year-old Jedediah Grant, who, despite a broken nose, somewhat resembled Andrew Jackson in appearance. Grant had joined the church when only eighteen, had participated in Zion's Camp, had fulfilled several successful missions, had been ordained in Nauvoo as one of the Seven Presidents of Seventy, and had led a company across the plains in 1847. In Utah he had served as major general of the Nauvoo Legion (the territorial militia), speaker of the house in the legislature, and superintendent of public works in Salt Lake City, and was an obedient polygamist with three wives. Grant's great promise remained largely unfulfilled, however; two years and eight months later he died—a death generally ascribed to exhaustion.

His major accomplishment in the First Presidency was directing a reform among the Saints. The Reformation movement commenced in 1855 and swept throughout the church. There was much need for a moral and spiritual awakening by that time. For ten years the Saints had not lived under normal conditions; soldiers, merchants, travelers, and emigrants were spreading "Gentile wickedness." Regularity and discipline needed to be reintroduced. The practice of plural marriage was also reemphasized. Heber, to lead the way, took his last five wives during this period; President Young took two.

The Reformation resulted in more than just widespread repentance and rebaptism and cultural retrenchment. Some unusual doctrine emerged also. It is clear, for instance, that Heber sometimes used the word "God" to refer to superior human beings (a usage justified by John 10:34-35); he also seems to have thought that "Adam" was one of the proper names of God the Father.[10] Such ideas may be part of the misunderstanding which led listeners to suppose that he and Brigham Young believed that the Adam of the Garden of Eden was God the Father.

In 1852 Heber stated, "Some have said that I was very presumptuous to say that Brother Brigham was my God and Saviour; Brother Joseph was his God; and the one that gave Joseph the keys of the kingdom was his God, which was Peter.[11] In a moment of reverie Heber said, "Brother Brigham, I have an idea that Adam is not only our Father, but our God.[12] In 1856 he added, "Brother Brigham is my President; he is my Governor, he is my prophet, he is my apostle, he is my Priest, and if you please he is my God. . . ."[13] Apparently this was still considered by some as presumptuous, for about two weeks later Heber somewhat backtracked: "I have called Brother Brigham a God to me—well, he is a son of God. I won't do so any more, or if I do I will take it back again."[14] Seven years later he confided in a private memorandum book, "April 20, 1862, The Lord told me that Adam was my father and that he was the God and father of all the inhabitants of this Earth."[15]

Precisely what was meant by these allusions is not known, but he certainly did not believe or teach that God the Father (Elohim) and the Adam of the Garden of Eden were the same being (see p. 274). Heber and other individuals, in and out of the church, recognized this as incorrect doctrine, and it never became widely taught or accepted.

The Reformation also produced statements which might imply the widely decried doctrine of "blood atonement." A close reading of the sources makes it clear that while Brigham Young accepted the Old Testament doctrine that under certain circumstances the shedding of one's own blood might contribute to complete atonement, he emphatically taught that by sincere repentance the ultimate violence could be avoided. Certainly he did not advocate the *practice* of blood atonement—a distortion that some writers continue to propagate.

Most of Heber's printed sermons for that period are free of sensational doctrine. They were calculated, rather, to raise the spiritual tone of the whole church. "You will be tested," he warned, "as to whether you are of the religion of Christ or not. . . . I have said that the scarcity of bread was nothing in comparison to what is coming: and for this reason the Lord wants this people to repent, reform, and live their religion; to learn to be punctual, true, and humble; and those who do not will go overboard." [16] He reproached lax priesthood leaders for not trimming their quorums. "Wake up ye Elders of Israel, and purge youselves, and purge out the filth that is in your Quorum, for we will not countenance unrighteousness in our midst. Why pursue this course? To cleanse Israel and qualify and prepare them, for there is going to be a test, A Test, A TEST: and if you do not forsake your wickedness you will see sorrow, as the children of Israel did in Jerusalem." [17]

Another important event of 1856 was the arrival on September 26 in the Valley of the first of the handcart companies. Although the Mormons did not invent this method of crossing the plains, some gold-rushers had used wheelbarrows and handcarts as early as 1850; their development of this method is considered to be the most remarkable travel experiment in the history of the Old West. As soon as it became possible in 1856 to travel by rail from the East Coast to Iowa City, that railhead became the point of departure for the Valley. By 1858 it was possible to take trains as far west as the Missouri. In both places the Mormons secured handcarts from emigration agents and pushed and pulled them to Zion.

The first company to arrive was Captain Edmond Ellsworth's, which had made it successfully from old Winter Quarters in 110 days, supporting the sanguine hopes of the First Presidency that this mode of migration would be faster, better, and cheaper than by the usual slow ox-team method. Brigham and Heber went by coach up Emigration Canyon to the foot of Little Mountain to greet this company, which came in singing "The Handcart Song":

> Ye Saints that dwell on Europe's shores,
> Prepare yourselves with many more
> To leave behind your native land
>   For sure God's Judgements are at hand.

> Prepare to cross the stormy main
> Before you do the valley gain
> And with the faithful make a start
>> To cross the plains with your hand cart.
>
> CHORUS
> Some must push and some must pull
>> As we go marching up the hill,
> As merrily on the way we go
>> Until we reach the valley, oh.

Three days later Heber spoke eloquently of this accomplishment and expansively predicted that "millions would come by hand-carts."[18] As a matter of fact the handcart era lasted only five years, but during that period ten companies brought a grand total of about 3,000 Saints to the Valley that way. (Thereafter until the coming of the railroad most emigrants were brought into the Valley in great church wagon trains.[19] Eight of these handcart companies arrived safely with minimal difficulties along the trail. Two companies in 1856, however, the fourth and the fifth, started too late and suffered terrible hardships in Wyoming snows. Nearly 200 people perished along the frozen Sweetwater.

During these two tragedies there was a protest and criticism of the First Presidency. Heber vigorously defended the handcart policy. "Let me tell you, most emphatically," he said once, "that if all who were entrusted with the care and management of this year's immigration had done as they were counseled and dictated by the First Presidency of the Church, the sufferings and hardships now endured by the companies on their way here would have been avoided. Why? Because they would have left the Missouri river in season and not been hindered until late September."

Because of their murmuring, he said threateningly, using the full power of his ecclesiastical position against them, "The heavens are closed against you. . . . I cannot account for the barrier that is between you and the Lord in any other way, only that there is quite a sympathy at work against br. Brigham and his Council. . . . We have to acknowledge the hand of God in all things; and that man or woman that feels to murmur and complain is in the gall of bitterness and the hands of iniquity, and does not know it. May God have mercy on you. Amen."[20] As would be expected, this silenced most critics. Those who censured him or his leader found they had picked up a two-edged sword which Heber skillfully turned back on them. Recourse for dissenters was to leave the church or remain silent; open dissent was inconsistent with membership in a society based on acceptance of authority.

Early in 1857, following the death of Grant, Young selected as his Second Counselor the forty-three-year-old Daniel Hanmer Wells, another able executive. Young was fond of saying Heber was the prophet and Wells his statesman. A craggy, full-maned, Lincolnesque figure, with jutting chin whiskers and a cast eye, Wells had been a pre-Mormon resident of Nauvoo. He joined the church in 1846 and during the 1848 trek west served as Young's aide-de-camp, becoming a favorite of the President.

In Utah, before becoming a member of the First Presidency, Wells served in the territorial legislature, as attorney general of the State of Deseret, major general of the militia, superintendent of church public works, and member of the city council. He was also a polygamist who eventually had six wives and thirty-seven children.

In the same year that Wells became a member of the First Presidency the "Utah War" commenced. This trouble broke out partly as a result of anti-Mormon furor following the public announcement of polygamy in 1852, but more directly it arose out of an attempt to weaken the power of the church in the territory. It may even have been a ruse to get the nation's mind off the growing slavery problem. Whatever the reasons, the new administration of James Buchanan (as of March 4, 1857), receiving many unfavorable reports about affairs in Utah, decided to send a military expedition to install a new governor and to insure obedience to federal laws.

The following July 18, 2,500 troops, led first by General W. S. Harney and later by Colonel Albert S. Johnston, began to march secretly to Utah from Fort Leavenworth, Kansas Territory, along the Oregon Trail. This figure, swelled by civilian employees and camp followers, grew to nearly 5,000 by the time Utah was reached.

By July 24, however, Young had already learned of the army's approach. Mormon mail-carriers in Independence, Missouri, divining the army's intention, had rushed the message to Salt Lake City. The First Presidency immediately ordered a total defense movement against what they considered to be a declaration of war. Wells, still commanding officer of the Utah militia even after he became a member of the First Presidency, was placed in charge of all military operations, and all Saints were ordered to be prepared to protect themselves. Wells ordered his men to avoid bloodshed at all costs, to harass and burn the army's supply trains, and to build breastworks at the mouth of Little Emigration Canyon and along the narrow parts of Echo Canyon (the Mormon Thermopylae)—breastworks that are still visible.

Heber participated fully in defense preparations, but he did manage to keep cool, inject a little grim humor into the situation, and even see some possible advantages for the Saints. In his many recorded sermons of that time he said such things as "I have about a hundred shots on hand all the time; three or four fifteen shooters, and three or four revolvers right in the room where I sleep."[21] He advised the Saints to "go and get your butcher-knives, your bowie knives and sharpen them," or to "buy . . . a good dirk, a pistol, or some other instrument of war," and "to get a good blanket, a gun or a sword." He admonished the ladies to provide themselves "with weapons . . . be ready to defend" themselves. In derision of the army he announced, "Good God, I have enough wives to whip out the U.S. army for they shall whip themselves."[22]

Echoing Heber's disdain are two Mormon songs of the period, the first based on Stephen Foster's "Camp town Races," the second "A Song of 1857."

Doo-Dah-Day

Come brethren listen to my song, Doo-dah doo-dah,
I don't intend to keep you long, Doo-dah doo-dah day,
'Bout Uncle Sam I'm going to sing, Doo-dah, doo-dah,
He swears destruction on us he'll bring, Doo-dah, doo-dah day
Then let us be on hand, by Brigham Young to stand,
And if our enemies do appear, We'll sweep them from the land.

Chorus:

I'se gwuine to run all night,
I'se gwuine to run all day,
I'll bet my money on a bobtailed nag,
Who dar bet on de bay.

So here's long life to Brigham Young, Doo-dah, doo-dah,
And Heber too, for they are one, Doo-dah, doo-dah day,
May they and Daniel live to see, Doo-dah, doo-dah,
This people gain their liberty, Doo-dah, doo-dah day
Then let us be on hand, by Brigham Young, to stand,
And if our enemies do appear, We'll sweep them from the land.

A Song of 1857

When Uncle Sam, he first set out his army to destroy us:
Says he, "The Mormons we will rout, they shall no longer annoy us,"
The force he sent was competent to "try" and "hang" for treason,
That is I mean it would have been, but don't you know the reason?

Chorus:

There's great comotion in the East, about the Mormon Question,
The problem is to say the least, too much for their digestion.

As they were going up the "Platte" singing many a lusty ditty,
Saying we'll do this and we'll do that, when we get to Salt Lake City,
And sure enough when they got there, they made the Mormons stir Sir.
That is I mean they would have done, but oh, they didn't get there.

Chorus:

When they got within two hundred miles, the old boys they were saying,
"It will be but a little while, till the Mormons we'll be slaying
We'll hang each man who has two wives, we've plenty of rope quite
     handy."
That is I mean they would have had, but Smith burned it on "Sandy."

Chorus

Then on "Ham's Fork" they camped a while, saying we'll wait a little
     longer,
"Till Johnston and his crew come up, and make us a little stronger.
Then we'll go on, take Brigham Young, and Heber his companion,"
That is, I mean they would have done, but were afraid of Echo Canyon.

Chorus

In a more serious mien, Heber declared that the government would
have "to pay all the debts of the trouble that they had brought upon the
innocent from the days of Joseph to this day, and they cannot get rid of
it." [23] Characteristically he prayed that the Almighty would "curse such
men, and women and every damned thing there is upon the earth that opposes this people." [24] Of those who opposed the First Presidency in their
preparations and policy, he wrathfully declared, "I wish there was a magazine in you, and we could touch you off. You are not fit to live in hell. . . ." [25]

In reference to how the government might pay for all the wrongs it
had laid on the Saints in the past, he said shrewdly, "Will we have manna?
Yes. The United States have 700 wagons loaded with about two tons to
each wagon with all kinds of things, and then 7,000 head of cattle; and
there are said to be 2,500 troops, with this, and that, and the other. That is
all right. Suppose the troops don't get here, but all these goods and cattle
come; well, that would be a mighty help to us. . . ." [26] (For a close approx-
imation of this circumstance, see below, p. 263.)

The Utah militia was so successful in its bloodless guerilla tactics that it forced the army to winter 115 miles short of Salt Lake City in Wyoming, near Fort Bridger, which the Mormons had first bought, then burned. This respite gave cooler heads in Washington time to reconsider. It also gave the church an opportunity to send a "memorial" to Congress. While the army was in its winter quarters, Heber and others drafted the memorial, denouncing the sending of the expedition, interference with the eastern mails, and the appointment of officers without reference to the wishes of the people of Utah. The memorial pointed out Mormon service in the war with Mexico, Mormon efforts in suppressing Indian hostilities and maintaining peaceful relations with the native tribes, and asked that the Saints be treated as friends and citizens and not as "alien enemies." The Mormons claimed "that we should have the privilege as we have the constitutional right, to choose our own rulers and make our own laws without let or hindrance." The memorial closed, "Withdraw your troops, give us our *constitutional rights*, and we are at home." [27]

As a reult of Mormon military determination, this memorial, an on-the-spot investigation, the work of the territorial delegate John M. Bernhisel, a report of Colonel Thomas L. Kane, who visited Utah in February, 1858, and the peaceful acceptance of the new governor, Alfred W. Cumming, actual war was averted. Also favoring a peaceful solution was a growing public opposition to the expedition. A letter from Vilate's sister-in-law Laura in Rochester reflected public opinion. "Be assured," she wrote, "we have stood appalled and trembled for your safety at the near approach of so formidable a foe as this blood thirsty government having at their command the U.S. Army and Navy." [28]

The new governor, who had spent an unpleasant winter with the army in Wyoming, arrived in Salt Lake City on April 12 and was accorded all due respect. Shortly thereafter Buchanan's peace commission arrived in Utah and arrangements were made to end officially the Utah War, by that time termed "Buchanan's Blunder." In the end the Mormons agreed to accept a "pardon," receive a Gentile governor, and allow the army to enter the Valley peacefully.

To show their determination, however, and to insure that the army would in no way molest the people, the First Presidency threatened the army with a scorched-earth policy. The Saints were instructed to prepare their homes to be burned if necessary and to move south into Utah Valley. This policy required nearly 30,000 people once more to abandon their homes and farms. Another diaspora commenced. From April 1 through the end of May Heber Kimball moved his family south along the State

Road and resettled them variously in American Fork, Provo, and Spring-ville.

When all was in readiness, the people safely in the south, and homes prepared for the torch, the troops were allowed to pass through the abandoned city on June 26. The passage was without incident. Their camp in Cedar Valley, adjacent to the hamlet of Fairfield thirty-five miles southwest of Salt Lake City, was named in honor of John B. Floyd, secretary of war. Camp Floyd and Fairfield grew to a community of nearly 7,000 soldiers, camp followers, and civilian employees. It became the third largest city in the territory (after Salt Lake City and Provo) and the largest military installation in the country until it was abandoned at the beginning of the Civil War.

A woman's version of this Mormon exodus was recorded by one of Heber's wives, Adelia Wilcox.

> The Winter passed by without anything of note occuring to disturb the people, but along in April [1858] President Young told the Saints to vacate the City before the army came in. Mr. Kimball loaded up some of the members of his family and sent them to Provo. I was one of the first that went. Christeen [Golden] and I had a room in Brother Redfields house. Here we lived for several weeks until he moved all of his family and rented a place called 'The Grove.' I was then moved there and lived with some of the other members. The time passed slowly by and it always seems long when a person is not settled down and doesn't know what they are going to do and this was the condition we were in until along in July when the glad and joyful word came, 'Saints return to your homes.' And it was a welcome sound to all for they had been deprived of this blessing just long enough to know how to appreciate it.[29]

Thousands of Saints then began to trudge back to their abandoned homes and fields, back to a new era of Gentile governors. In a pointed reference to the many times the Saints had been driven from their homes, Heber humorously remarked to Brigham Young that in the future they should build their homes on wheels so they could flee their enemies more readily.[30]

NOTES

1. A brother of Apostle Erastus Snow, former member of Zion's Camp: he drifted away from the church, remained in Ohio, was reactivated in 1850 by Erastus, and had some legal training.

2. Records Relating to the Appointments of Federal Judges, Attorneys, and Marshals for the Territory and State of Utah: 1853–1901, M680, roll 1, National Archives, Washington, D.C.

3. "Speech in Legislative Council," Sept. 27, 1851, H. C. Kimball Papers, Church Archives.

4. Historian's Office Journal, Dec. 20, 1854, Church Archives.

5. "Speech in Legislative Council," Jan. 13, 1852, H. C. Kimball Papers, Church Archives. It would be unfair to judge Heber's irate frontier language among a group of close associates by our own standards of what is appropriate. Heber once complained to this same Council that he "could not preach *half* to the Saints in the Tabernacle." He was much more at liberty in such Council meetings. Thomas W. Ellerbeck Diary, Dec. 28, 1852, Church Archives.

6. Historian's Office Journal, Dec. 20, 1854, Church Archives.

7. Resolution in the General Assembly, Dec. 3, 1855, H. C. Kimball Papers, Church Archives.

8. Gustive O. Larson, "The Mormon Reformation," *Utah Historical Quarterly*, vol. 26 (Jan., 1958), 59.

9. "Remarks by Prest. Heber C. Kimball," Dec. 31, 1855, H. C. Kimball Papers, Church Archives. This quote is not found in Hosea.

10. Wilford Woodruff Journal, Apr. 9, 1852, Church Archives.

11. *Ibid.*

12. T. B. H. Stenhouse, *The Rocky Mountain Saints: A Full and Complete History of the Mormons* (New York: D. Appleton, 1873), 561.

13. Brigham Young Addresses (unpublished), Dec. 18, 1856, Church Archives.

14. *Ibid.*, Dec. 30, 1856.

15. Private Memorandum Book, Apr. 20, 1862, H. C. Kimball Papers, Church Archives.

16. *Journal of Discourses*, vol. 4 (Dec. 21, 1856), 139, 141, 143.

17. *Ibid.*, vol. 4 (Dec. 21, 1856), 141.

18. *Ibid.*, vol. 4 (Dec. 28, 1856), 106.

19. As would be expected, sometimes Heber's utterances did not come to pass (or at least have not yet come to pass). In anger over Buchanan sending an army to Utah, he predicted that the President would die an "untimely death." Buchanan, however, lived until he was seventy-seven, dying in 1868, the same year as Heber. Heber also believed that the Saints would be "blessed, and you will see the day when President Young, Kimball, and Wells, and the Twelve Apostles will be in Jackson County, Missouri laying out your inheritances. In the flesh? Of course. We should look well without being in the flesh! We shall be there in the flesh, and all our enemies can not prevent it. Brother Wells, you may write that: You will be there, and Willard will be there, and also Jedediah, and Joseph and Hyrum Smith and David, and Parley: and the day will be when I will see those men in the general assembly of the Church of the First-Born, in the great council of God in Jerusalem, too." Mormons may one day return to Missouri, but none of Heber's

generation did. There is no evidence, however, that these prophetic "misses" affected the Saints adversely. Next to Joseph Smith, Heber made more recorded prophecies than any other major Mormon leader. Some of Joseph's prophecies have also yet to come true, but this has bothered few.

20. *Journal of Discourses*, vol. 4 (Nov. 1856), 66.

21. *Ibid.*, vol. 5 (Aug. 30, 1857), 164.

22. *Ibid.*, vol. 5 (July 26, 1857), 95. Some members of the eastern press, ever anxious to exploit a *double entendre*, ran cartoons showing Brigham Young urging his wives, holding infants high, to charge the U.S. soldiers. Such cartoons were titled "Brigham's Breast-works."

23. *Ibid.*, vol. 5 (July 26, 1857), 94.

24. *Ibid.*, vol. 5 (July 12, 1857), 32.

25. *Ibid.*, vol. 5 (July 26, 1857), 89.

26. *Ibid.*, vol. 5 (July 26, 1857), 94.

27. U.S. State Department, Territorial Papers, Utah 1853–73, M12, roll 1, 104–5, National Archives.

28. Laura Murray to Vilate Kimball, June 23, 1858. Original in possession of Spencer W. Kimball. Used by permission.

29. Adelia Almira Hatton Memoirs, 20. Heber later remarked, "We are richer now for moving to the south than we should have been if we had not moved. What did we save by it? It saved that difficulty that would have brought you into sorrow, probably, all the days of your life, if you had withstood that army and shed blood. But by that move you saved your blood and the blood of your enemies, and in this you did a good deed. It cost considerable, but Father booked it against them, and he will make them pay the debt." *Journal of Discourses*, vol. 9 (Apr. 7, 1861), 27. For a probable fulfillment of this prediction see below, p. 263.

30. John O. Ellsworth, *Our Ellsworth Ancestors* (privately printed, 1956), 112–13.

CHAPTER 19

Kimball's Plantation

"Nobody pays my bills nor my expenses for me," Heber wrote some absent son. "I pay or go without."[1] To care properly for his families' physical wants, he worked hard, protected what he had, was enterprising, and engaged in many different kinds of economic activities. Although a member of the First Presidency, he was expected to support himself. Because of his industry he was able to assure his brother Solomon back in New York that he had plenty of groceries, wheat, cheese, beef, pork, potatoes, "and almost every luxury you can obtain in the states."[2] "I have everything here almost for my comfort and the comfort of my family that you have in that land"—flour, cornmeal, every kind of vegetable, peaches, apples, pork, beef, cakes, fritters, sugar, tea, coffee, and rice. "I can say," he added, "I am about ten times better off and more comfortable than I was in Mendon."[3]

His immediate economic concern was, of course, his "plantation" (as he liked to call it), his ten-acre lot, which he developed agriculturally and industrially. He was proud of his plantation and improved it in many ways, planting shade and fruit trees and gardens, surrounding it with a cobblestone wall, and building several barns and storehouses on it.[4] Later a family cemetery was set aside. (Today this 82-by-75-foot cemetery is all that remains on this site from Heber's day.) He enjoyed showing off his industry.

Several non-Mormon visitors were impressed with Heber's garden. During the summer of 1859 Horace Greeley paid Heber a visit while en route to California. Heber proudly showed Greeley around and pressed fruit, berries, and doctrine on his guest. Greeley later wrote that it was the "most magnificent garden I have been invited to visit."[5] A New York writer, Fitz Hugh Ludlow, also treated to fruit and exhortations, was unsparing in his praise: "I must confess," he wrote, "that if there ever could

be any hope of our conversion, it was just about the time we stood in
Brother Heber's fine orchard, eating apples and apricots between exhortations, and having sound doctrine poked down our throats, with gooseber-
ries as big as plums, to take the taste out of our mouths, like jam after
castor-oil."[6]

Ludlow left behind a detailed description of this plantation which is
worth recording in full:

> Mr. Kimball's city establishment (he is a large property holder else-
> where) is situated on a rise of ground but a few rods from the Temple
> corner and the Presidents inclosure. . . . [His house is] neat and com-
> modious but, unostentatious, like the residence of some principal se-
> lectman in a New England village. Utah has not yet had time to grow
> the noble elms which shade such a residence; but everything which
> money, keen business tact and indomitable energy can do has been
> done by Heber Kimball at least, to make his place a paradise of lux-
> uriant vegetation. In picturesquely selected places he has contrived to
> create pretty little groves of maple, poplar, acacia, and box elder,
> transplanting the young trees from the Wahsatch cañons, and by plen-
> tiful irrigation making them grow so rapidly that they had already
> attained the respectable height of twenty-five or thirty feet.
>
> In this matter of irrigation I noticed that both Brothers Brigham
> and Heber seemed to be "not under the law, but under grace." The
> chief water supplies of the Mormon city may without metaphor be
> said to run through each apostle's back yard, and no hand but their
> own shuts the gate on their trenches. The lower level of Heber Kim-
> ball's place, toward the city, is a garden laid out under its owner's su-
> pervision by an old Mormon gardener. . . . The plan of the garden is
> as simple and natural as a path through the woods, the walks wander-
> ing hither and thither among intersecting rivulets, and under green
> arches of apricot, apple, peach, plum, and nectarine, whose pleasant-
> scented fruit, ripe already or mellowing to ripeness, bowed their over-
> weighted branches together above our heads.
>
> Heber's melons and cucumbers were very thrifty: Indeed, the soil
> and climate of Utah are finely suited to the cultivation of all gourd
> fruit. It was a week too late for strawberries, or, Heber told me, I
> should have seen a sight,—Brother Brigham's crop had amounted to
> over eighty bushels, and he had gathered an almighty lot himself.
> Heber was cultivating a kind of currant which he had introduced
> from the cañons, and which by high science had been so far domesti-
> cated and improved that its fruit was very pleasant having an abun-
> dant juice, less acid, and a flavor no less pronounced, than our own
> large white currants at the East; furthermore, attaining the weight of
> a good-sized gooseberry.[7]

Utilizing the power of City Creek, Heber was able to develop on this lot one of the earliest "industrial centers" in Utah. He first built an oil mill or press to make linseed oil out of flax seeds.[8] Heber got off a little joke in reference to this mill. "A gentleman," he related, "desired to inform me, the other day, how to adulterate my oil with lye; but as I did not believe in *lying*, I did not procure the recipe."[9]

To the *Deseret News* this was "another step towards that social independence so much desired by all who know the blighting consequences of importing, instead of manufacturing those things that are necessary to the comfort, existence and happiness of the people."[10] This comment suggests clearly what Mormondon's greatest economic problem was—no exports. An imbalance of imports over exports leads to a weak economy, and was the economic reason for the Isaiahan denunciations from the pulpit of female finery, as well as tea, coffee, tobacco, and all other nonessentials. Such imports drained Utah of specie.

To this oil press he later added a run of stones to grind wheat, a cane mill, and a circular saw. Ludlow described Heber's industrial complex:

> We visited upon the same grounds, on the bank of one of those streams heretofore mentioned as traversing apostolic back yards, a cider-mill, a grist-mill, a feed-grinder, a workshop with lathes, belts, and shafting, and almost every conceivable mechanism for economizing human power in the management of a large estate demanding constant supplies and repairs. . . .
>
> Among other apparatus operated by Heber's waterwheel I observed a carding-machine, and was told by the proprietor that he had the entire gear of a woolen factory on a small scale, and when it was set, could manufacture from the fleece excellent yarn and durable cloth, sufficient at least for all household uses.[11]

Prior to the development of his mills in Salt Lake City, Heber had built in 1852 a gristmill a few miles north in Bountiful, Davis County, where much grain was then grown. In seeming contradiction to the policy that water and timber should not be privately owned, the general assembly granted him exclusive rights to North Mill Creek Canyon—the first good canyon for water and timber north of Salt Lake City. Such grants, however, gave the grantee development and regulatory rights only. This mill at the mouth of his canyon was a burr type, two stories high, and powered by an over-shot wheel. It was the largest in the territory and stood until 1892. The ruins are located at approximately the intersection of Fourth East Street and Ninth South Street and are marked by a plaque. Also, in order to develop the timber resources of this broad and gentle canyon, in 1849

Heber built a two-and-a-half-mile road and extracted a toll of 25 percent of all wood and poles taken out of it. (The upper canyon is known as Mueller Park today.)

In addition to the ten-acre lot and eleven building lots in Salt Lake City mentioned above, Heber acquired other land for homes, farming, and ranching. Near present-day Twenty-third South and Third East streets he owned twenty-seven acres, and north of his home he took a section of bench land, on Capitol Hill, which no one wanted. Often when poor emigrants came into the valley he permitted them to build homes on this bench property at no cost or for very little. After his estate was partially settled in 1875, deeds were issued to fifty-four individuals who had built on this and other Kimball property.[12] This part of Salt Lake City today is known picturesquely as the Marmalade District because at one time a number of short streets there were named after such fruits as apricot, plum, cherry, and peach. Heber also owned a meadow, a building lot, and a home in Provo, and part of the "Big Field" in Brigham City, fifty-five miles north of Salt Lake City.

Heber was also involved extensively in ranching. He ran cattle, horses, and sheep in Cache Valley, Grantsville, on Kimball (Stansbury) and Antelope islands in the Great Salt Lake, and at Black Rock on the shore of the Lake. He was grazing cattle near Black Rock as early as 1849. Today copper smelters give the area the look of the sixth and seventh circles of the *Divina Commedia*, but then meadows flourished near the springs at the base of the Oquirrh Mountains. By 1860 Heber had built a substantial ranch house, bunkhouse, barns, and other buildings out of rock, all surrounded by a rock fence. (The ruins of this ranch house were destroyed by Interstate 80.)

Heber had at least two brand marks. The first, a simple *H* placed on the left hip, was recorded on December 29, 1849. Since other cattlemen soon had the same brand and applied it on the left shoulder, right shoulder, right hip, and left thigh, Heber may have changed brands to avoid confusion. (This heraldry of the range evolved into a near science, and there was many a bunkhouse genealogist in the Old West.) In 1852 the *Deseret News* pictured his brand thus $\rightthreetimes$, probably a fancy *H* on its side, in cowboy lingo a Lazy H, or maybe an attempt to make a monogram out of his initials.

In the mid-1850s he had about sixty head of cattle and eight horses, along with the church herds, in Cache Valley. Kimball Island, about fourteen miles north of Grantsville, Tooele County, does not seem to have been grazed extensively. More important was Antelope Island, which was reserved mainly for the benefit of the Perpetual Emigration Fund, but Heber and Brigham also kept cattle and sheep there. The island was a particularly good winter range, for the winds blew the snow off the low mountaintops, exposing the grass. He also did some ranching in Parley's Park about twenty-five miles east of Salt Lake City. In 1855 the legislature granted him, Jedediah M. Grant, and Samuel Snyder the area as a herd ground. Heber's son William later operated a stone hotel there (which is still standing). It became a regular stop on the Overland Stage, and Horace Greeley, Walt Whitman, Mark Twain, and many others stayed there.

Heber's most extensive ranching was done seven miles south of Grantsville, about forty miles southwest of Salt Lake City. In 1856 the territorial legislature granted him and William McBride a twenty-five-square-mile herd ground.[13] Heber built a ranch house there, and two of his sons, David Patton and Abraham, lived there at different times. By 1866, the property was pretty much run down, as Abraham quickly discovered. He had injured his lungs in his father's carding mill, and two Salt Lake City physicians had ordered a change of climate. Accordingly Heber, first observing that "he did not care what any D—— Doctor said, remarking if I [Abraham] did what was right, I would live long enough any how," lent his son a wagon and team and sent him to take charge of the Grantsville property. On Sunday, April 9, Abraham, his wife, daughter, and mother-in-law saw their new home—such as it was. The two-room log cabin had been used as a stable and had manure in it six inches deep.

Abraham dug a hole in the dung, set up a stove, and, while the women prepared something to eat, began hauling off dead cattle. The hard winter had left twenty-eight carcasses around the house and stockyard. "Some of them were fearful dead and mellow," the sick man recalled, "hardly holding together long enough to haul them off."[14]

In addition to farming, ranching, and milling, Heber was involved in freighting. In 1855 he became one of the several vice-presidents in the Brigham Young Express and Carrying Company (popularly known as the Y. X. Company). Later, after the U.S. Army settled in Utah, he and some of his sons kept several wagons busy carrying freight for the army. Such trafficking with the Philistines was frowned on by some, and Heber wanted it understood that he was not selling the army any locally needed supplies, especially wheat. "I have hauled wheat to the camp," he explained, "that the merchants have bought of this people, and I have got my pay for it."[15] If some of the Saints insisted in going against church policy and selling wheat to the army, then others in the church, including himself, might as well profit from the freighting as did the Gentiles.

On top of all these activities, Heber, along with a few others, in 1853 privately incorporated the Great Salt Lake Water Works Association to pipe water to homes and businesses in the city. Its shares were offered at $100 each.[16]

Not only did he strive to support his own family well, but he helped and encouraged others to do likewise. A consistent advocate of self-sufficiency and "home manufacture," he believed the Saints in Utah could become self-sufficient and preached this theme often, from the pulpit and the senate. On January 6, 1852, for example, he made a powerful and enlightened speech in the council advocating home manufacture.

> It is my opinion that measures can be entered into for the encouragement of home manufacture, by nourishing men that have a disposition to go into business, with public funds of either the church or state. . . . I know of a great many men that seem to be anxious to do something in this way, but have nothing to help themselves with. . . . I have this disposition as well as any other man. I am trying with all my might to dispose of all of the capital I can raise to lay the foundation for my existence, and for the existence of my family, that they may be independent.
>
> Until we take a course to assist such men, and nourish and cherish them we shall [not] accomplish anything. . . . If there is anything we can manufacture ourselves let us go at it right straight and not sit here on our harses doing nothing. . . . Let those who have surplus property, let us lend it to the state, and by and by the state will pay it back with usury, or lend it to the Church and the Church will turn around and pay you again.

In this same speech he not so enlightenedly criticized the sisters for insisting on expensive imports in favor of homemade items and accused them of "teasing us all the time to buy such little nasty shitten things."[17] Most of the assembled brethren probably enthusiastically agreed.

He was also greatly concerned with the storing up of food stuffs, especially grain, against poor crops and famine. For years he preached preparedness. On August 13, 1853, for example, he warned the Saints to take care of their grain "for you will see hard times."[18] When a near famine did come in 1856 he had to put his own family on half-rations in order to feed the heedless.

Along with President Young, Heber pushed hard for economic self-sufficiency. All kinds of enterprises were fostered, and many men and families were called and sent on economic missions to develop lead and coal mines, to grow cotton, tobacco, figs, grapes, and other fruits, to manufacture molasses, to navigate the Colorado River, or to grow silkworms.

Some of these missions worked, some did not. Experimental farms were more successful.

Heber supported the organization of the Deseret Agricultural and Manufacturing Society which the general legislature organized in January, 1856, "to promote the arts of domestic industry, and to encourage the production of articles from the native elements." This society lasted until 1907, when it became the Utah State Fair Association. In recognition of his own economic enterprise, Heber was made an honorary member from the beginning.

NOTES

1. H. C. Kimball to David, Charles, and Brigham Kimball, Nov. 20, 1864, H. C. Kimball Papers, Church Archives. Daniel Davis's journal makes it clear, however, that Kimball did receive supplemental help from the church. The porch on his home may also have been built from temple materials. Salt Lake Temple Stonecutters Record, 1852–57, 1870–75, March, 1855, Church Archives.

2. H. C. Kimball to Solomon Kimball, Feb. 29, 1852. Original in possession of Spencer H. Kimball. Used by permission.

3. H. C. Kimball to Solomon Kimball, Jan. 2, 1857, H. C. Kimball Papers, Church Archives.

4. He sometimes overextended himself. Once he bought 5,000 peach trees and then according to the *Deseret News*, Mar. 11, 1857, offered to dispose of them "at the rate of one-half less than he paid two or three years ago."

5. Horace Greeley, *An Overland Journey from New York to San Francisco in the Summer of 1859* (1860; reprinted New York: Alfred A. Knopf, 1964), 204–5.

6. Ludlow, *The Heart of the Continent*, 347.

7. *Ibid.*, 348–49. On at least one occasion in 1855 Heber did use too much water, but Water Master Phineas W. Cook was afraid to fine him. When Heber heard of this, he told Cook he "would cuff his ears if he did not fine him, told him not to be afraid of the big men, he was Water Master and expected to act like it." Heber paid the fine. *The Life and History of Phineas Wolcott Cook*, n.p., n.d., 81–83. Utah State University Library.

8. Kimball said he was using the hydraulic presses "brother Taylor brought into this country, and they are performing wonders. They will each press equal to a hundred and twelve tons weight." *Journal of Discourses*, vol. 9 (Apr. 7, 1861), 28. These were probably the same presses which had been imported from France in an unsuccessful attempt to make beet sugar.

9. H. C. Kimball to "Brothers," May 15, 1861, *Millennial Star*, vol. 23 (July 27, 1861), 478.

10. *Deseret News*, June 20, 1860.

11. Ludlow, *The Heart of the Continent*, 349–52. Heber later built a second carding machine on Fifth North between Second and Third West.

12. H. C. Kimball Estate Papers, Order Confirming Acts of Administration, Utah State Archives, Salt Lake City.

13. *Journal of the Legislative Assembly of the Territory of Utah, 1856–57*, 14, 24.

14. A. A. Kimball Journal, 334–35, in author's possession, Typescript in Utah State Historical Society, Salt Lake City.

Abraham seemed destined for bad luck. Following lung problems in Salt Lake City and the wretched experience at Grantsville, two years later he was sent to Utah's "Dixie," south of St. George. There he and his family had to contend with wind, dust, scorpions, tarantulas, rattlesnakes, and heat—heat so oppressive he declared that he would bathe at night in ditches, onions would cook in the sand, coffee and cold water placed in a canteen in the sun would steep itself, and if carrots were watered in the morning they would be so cooked by noon that their skins slipped off when they were pulled.

15. *Journal of Discourses*, vol. 8 (July 1, 1860), 109.

16. *Deseret News*, Mar. 5, 1853. Nine men bought thirty-four shares, of which Heber acquired three. See Ledger A, Great Salt Lake City waterworks Assn., Church Archives.

17. "Speech by Counselor Kimball. . . ," Jan. 6, 1852, H. C. Kimball Papers, Church Archives.

18. *Journal of Discourses*, vol. 2 (Aug. 13, 1853), 105.

CHAPTER 20

Reluctant Polygamist

Sharing the reticence of most polygamists to speak of their family lives, Heber recorded little of it. From scattered jottings, letters, journals, and memoirs of his wives and children, however, it is possible to partially reconstruct it to get an inside view of what sensational writers like to one-sidedly exploit. Of romance and passion there is little to report. We have already noted that Heber was a reluctant polygamist in the first place, that his first choices for plural wives were two spinster sisters, and that most of his first thirty-eight wives were sealed to him immediately prior to the exodus from Nauvoo and therefore were more family wards than wives. In Utah he married five times. Two were spinsters and two were widows with small children—more wards. Only once, after his first marriage, does something more than obligation and duty seem to have surfaced. The fifth Utah bride and last of all his wives was an English teenager.

At best it is difficult to account for the number of Heber's immediate family at any given time. He was of little help. "I have a good many wives," he once said. "How much would you give to know how many? If I were to tell you, you would not believe it." At another time he said, "I have sixty to seventy subjects," or "I have twenty-three boys living and ten dead, and lots of girls."[1] One Mormon woman, disenchanted with polygamy and therefore not an entirely credible witness, asked him once, after meeting a number of his wives, "Are these all you have got?" He allegedly replied, "Oh dear no, I have a few more at home, and about fifty scattered over the earth somewhere; but I've never seen them since they were sealed to me in Nauvoo, and I hope I never shall again."[2] This figure of fifty may be wildly incorrect, but the anecdote could be an accurate reflection of his feelings regarding the ten wives who left him and the six unaccounted for after Winter Quarters.

Prior to Utah he had been sealed to thirty-eight wives and had eighteen children. Of this total there were about thirty-seven family members with him in the Valley in September, 1848—twenty-six wives and eleven children. Some wives and children had died or did not come west. After his arrival in Utah he married five more wives and sired forty-seven additional children, for a grand total of forty-three wives and sixty-five children, or 108 dependents. (For comparison's sake, Brigham Young had twenty-seven wives and fifty-seven children, John D. Lee eighteen wives and sixty children, John W. Hess, the author's maternal great-grandfather, seven wives and sixty-three children, and Christopher Layton ten wives and sixty-five children.)[3]

Because of deaths, marriages, and separations, it appears that Heber never had more than seventy in his immediate family at any one time. This is the figure credited him in an 1860 census.[4] In that year I can account for twenty-four wives and thirty-four under-age children with him. This means that he probably counted about twelve adopted or foster children as part of his family. He may have considered other adopted and foster children as partly his responsibility. Ten of his wives collectively had at least fifty-three children before their marriage to him. Most assuredly he was never even partially economically responsible for more than twenty-five of these children, and only three are mentioned in the sources.

The following charts will help in understanding this complicated family. (See Appendix A for details on Heber's wives and children.)

Number of Wives

Wives who came west		28
Wives married in the West		5
Wives who died at Winter Quarters		2
Wives known to have remained at Winter Quarters		2
	subtotal	37
Wives unaccounted for in Utah		6
	total	43
Wives who bore Kimball children		17
Wives who left Kimball		16

Number of Children

Children by wives known to have remained in Winter Quarters		2
Children by other wives known to have left Kimball		1
Children by Kimball's "basic family" of twelve wives		57
Children by the fourteen wives Kimball partially supported (one of these wives had the five children)		5
	total	65
Number of children who lived to maturity		43

By the mid-1850s Heber's plural family life had pretty well stabilized. A typical day would start out with early prayer, breakfast, consultation with members of his family, and an ordering of the day's work on his plantation and at his other enterprises. About nine o'clock he would walk cross-lots about 200 yards to President Young's office for council meetings, general discussion regarding the church and Kingdom, or meetings with visitors. Later he might go across the street to the Church Historian's Office (which was also a semi-official chancery) to dictate letters, sign documents, or check copies of his sermons for publication. Several times a week he would spend part of the day in the Endowment House supervising temple ordinances. At other times he might tend to some aspect of colonizing, or missionary work. Lunch was usually away from home. Evening would find him with one family unit or another and sometimes at the theatre or a party.

His immediate family consisted of a core of twelve units—twelve wives and eighteen children, or thirty individuals. In 1854, for example, he wrote a son, "I furnish the wood and fuel, bread, and vegetables, for twelve families, and the most of them their clothing. . . ."[5] On another occasion he compared his wives to "twelve teapots each holding equal quantities of good tea, yet differing in form." Just so with his wives, differing in age and exterior, yet each of equal worth.[6] In 1855 William, from England, sent greetings back to twelve of his father's wives.[7]

In 1855 this basic group probably consisted of Vilate, forty-nine years old, and her sons David, Charles, and Solomon; the thirty-six-year-old childless Mary Ellen Harris; twenty-seven year-old Ann Alice Gheen and Samuel Heber; Amanda Gheen, twenty-four-year-old mother of William and Albert; thirty-two-year-old Christeen Golden and Jonathan Golden; Sarah Peak, his forty-three-year-old first plural wife, and her children Henry and Sarah Helen; Ruth A. Reese, thirty-seven years old with Jacob; his twenty-nine-year-old Pioneer wife, Ellen Sanders with twins, Joseph and Augusta, and Rosalia; her thirty-year-old sister Harriet, whose only child had died the day it was born; and three widows of Joseph Smith, the twenty-eight-year-old Lucy Walker with John Heber and Willard Heber; twenty-seven-year-old Sarah Ann Whitney and David Heber and Newel Whitney; and the forty-four-year-old Presendia Huntington with her son Joseph Smith. In addition to this core group he apparently was also supporting nine other wives—all of whom may have been nonconnubial (i.e., wards): Laura Pitkin, Martha McBride, Mary Houston, Hulda Barnes, Mary Fielding, Theresa Morley, Rebecca Swain, Nancy Maria Winchester, and Sara Schuler. None of these bore him any children.

Of the remaining seventeen wives he had married prior to 1855, some of whom may have been nonconnubial, two had remained in Winter Quarters with their father (Clarissa and Emily Cutler) and two had died there (Abigail Pitkin and Sophronia Harmon). Eight others left him for one reason or another—Ruth L. Pierce may have left as early as 1846 and appears to have remarried; Sylvia Porter Sessions separated in 1847 and remarried; Charlotte Chase left in 1849 and remarried in California; Elizabeth Hereford apparently left in 1850 and nothing further of her is known; Mary Ann Shefflin left in 1850 and remarried; Sarah Lawrence formally divorced Heber on June 18, 1851, and apparently died in California; Frances Swan seems to have left Utah in 1854; and Nancy Maria Winchester separated from Heber in 1865 and remarried. (Note that Nancy Maria Winchester has been counted twice: as a wife up to 1865 and as a separatee after 1865.) The evidence suggests that such separations were agreeable and not limited to the Kimball household. Recent studies show that seventy-two early Mormon leaders collectively experienced eighty-one broken marriages and that Young granted 1,645 polygamous divorces.[8] Since the marriages were never recognized by the law of the land there was no need for divorce formalities, though ecclesiastical bills of divorce were often issued. Polygamous Mormon divorce was as easy for the wife (but not the husband) as among polygamists in the Old Testament.

Only three of these twelve wives bore Heber any children. Clarissa Cutler had one son, Abraham, and her sister, Emily, also had one son, Isaac. Both sisters remarried and apparently died in Indian Territory, now Jefferson County, Kansas, in the early 1850s. Years later both sons, raised by maternal grandparents, joined their father in Utah. Frances Swan had an infant daughter, Margaret Jane, who died at Winter Quarters.

Six other wives, Abigail Buchanan, Mary Dull, Margaret McMinn, Sarah Scott, Sarah Stiles, and Ruth Wellington, are totally unaccounted for after 1846. Perhaps they never left Nauvoo; or, after the hard winter in Winter Quarters, perhaps they returned to relatives in the East.

In Utah during the Reformation Heber married five wives, four in 1856—two spinster sisters, fifty-four-year-old Hannah Moon and fifty-two-year-old Dorothy, daughters of one of his English converts; and two widows, the thrice-married forty-eight-year-old Elizabeth Doty and the twice-married twenty-eight-year-old Adelia Wilcox, whose husband had been killed by Indians in 1853. Finally, in 1857, he married his last wife, nineteen-year-old Mary Smithies, the girl he had blessed as an infant in England in 1837. Of Elizabeth Doty and the Moon sisters little is known. Adelia became a member of Heber's immediate household but bore him no children; and Mary gave him five children, of whom Abbie Sarah, born in 1865, was his last. Also, during the Reformation, Heber was sealed to two deceased sisters, Charlotte and Clarissa Young, who were nieces of Brigham.[9]

There is a family story that, during the Reformation, Heber preached that unmarried women who wanted to get married should seek out a good man and ask to be sealed to him. It appears that Adelia Wilcox took his advice; perhaps the Moon Sisters did also. A similar tale has Heber, when two women knock on his door, hiding in a closet for fear they have come to request that he marry them.

The governing and support of such a large family even under ideal circumstances would have greatly taxed Heber's wisdom, time, patience, and financial resources and complicated his personal relationships. Heber, a grandson noted, "was often heard to declare that the plural order of marriage, with its manifold cares and perplexities, had cost him 'bushels of tears.'"[10] Part of the problem was that, while the puritanical Heber maintained a close and loving relationship with his first family (Vilate and her children), he seemed to have less close ties with his plural wives and their children. One reason for this detachment and the second part of the problem was that all concerned were called upon to compromise the most deeply held personal beliefs and strongest cultural traditions regarding marriage and family life. Not even the weight of divine revelation, approbation, even command, eased the difficult transition from monogamy to plurality. There was also the question of time and energy. With his manifold church duties he did well to keep close to one family.

Death, uncooperative wives, and disobedient children brought him much grief. Prior to 1848 four of his children had died. In Utah he lost eighteen more children and ten wives, and as just noted, eight more wives left him (bringing the total to eighteen). Others were uncooperative. As early as 1849 he wrote to Vilate, "Your duty is to look after your children and teach your sisters [his plural wives] . . . to mind thare own business and to treet thare husband with respect and let my business alone and hold thare toungs when they want to speak evil to me. . . ."[11] On February 3, 1852, he confided in a private memorandum book, "The Spirit said I should devote my time to the church of Jesus Christ of Latter day Saints and I should not be under the Law of Lawless women any more in time as I have fulfilled the Law and am now free from such Spirits. . . ."[12]

In some of his public sermons we find references to domestic discord. He said that he would deed his property to the church so that his family would not quarrel over it; that he was not always responsible for his wives; that wives should not rebel; that he had one or two wives he could not control; and that he was not so foolish as to quarrel with women.[13]

In 1857 he became convinced that Christeen Golden was "not one with him." It was Heber's custom to bless his infants and give them a name while their mothers were present. He named his children after good people and anticipated that the power and spirit of those good people would influence his children. He claimed that he could "read its [the child's] spirit when alone with the child or in company with those who were of the same spirit as himself."[14] Apparently something unfortunate happened at the time he blessed Christeen Golden's infant son, Elias, for afterward he said he had never "desired to bless his children in the presence of their mothers since; and did not believe he would should he live a thousand years. He said the observations that several of his wives made at that time wounded his feelings severely and grieved the spirit of the Lord. And the day would come when they would feel sorrowful on account of it. He said we did not realize that he was a servant of god or dictated by his spirit or we would never treat him as we often did. . . ."[15] According to family lore, Heber blessed Elias with all the strengths of his father and none of the weaknesses of his mother. If this be true, it certainly explains the ensuing tension.

At the 1861 April conference, he once told a story of a man who was proud of his son but whose wife pulled the son from him. Then, without explanation and perhaps unconsciously, he continued the story in the first person—"I said, God my father will take that child from you[r arms] far quicker than you took him from mine, and not more than ten days afterwards it was in its grave."[16] This story seems to be a thinly disguised incident in his own family.

Several of his sons brought their father sorrow. His eldest, William, was disfellowshipped for a time in 1860 for drunkenness,[17] and in 1863 Vilate wrote to another son that she hoped he would never cause her the sorrow "that William does."[18] In 1864 Heber expressed disappointment that his son "Brigham has no interest in matters of my business and is drawn away from his studies."[19] Vilate once wrote that David was trying to "heal the wound he has made in his father's heart, and mine. . . ."[20] David was for a time inactive in the church but later served as a stake president, Isaac had problems with liquor, and Solomon took little interest in the church until he was in his mid-thirties. At the funeral of a son, Heber said on December 14, 1864, "Nineteen of my children are in the spirit world, and the parting with them has not given me as much sorrow, nor brought as many white hairs on my head, as those have done who now live."[21]

However unromantic, detached, and disappointed Heber may have been, he did his best for the physical welfare of all his dependents. During the winter of 1848–49 and for several years thereafter his families lived in the one-room homes within the fort, with other families, in tents, wagon-boxes, and other temporary shelters. (We know, for example, that Vilate used her wagon-box as a private bedroom for four years until Heber finished his large family home.[22] She obviously preferred that privacy to the crowded cabins with only blankets for partitions.) They also lived in "adobe row," some small dwellings he built on the south side of his ten-acre lot.

During the following spring the fort was generally abandoned and the Saints began to build more substantial homes. Heber commenced a large home on the lot which took nearly three years, until February, 1852, to finish. This home, facing west, years later was officially designated 142 North Main Street. It stood until the 1920s, when it was razed and the Kimball Apartments built in its place. It consisted of a white two-story frame rectangle thirty feet wide by fifty-six feet long containing sixteen plastered and painted rooms.[23] To this core were added wash-, wood-, and storehouses. Several years later Heber added a splendid two-story porch on the west end, which commanded a full view of Temple Square, most of the city, and the Valley.

On the main floor, Vilate's quarters were in the front and Sarah Peak's in the rear. A "Girls' Parlor" opened off Vilate's rooms and there was a large dining room. In the parlor was a huge piano which, although several pianos were hauled west from Winter Quarters, Heber most likely imported from St. Louis to keep his promise to his daughter Helen. In the Old West a piano was as much a symbol of permanence, stability, respectability, and dignity as it was an instrument. On the second floor in the front was Heber's private bedroom. Opposite was a spinning room. Elsewhere were the storage room and several large and small bedrooms for some of his wives and children. The parlor was enormous—18 by 40 feet. Here guests were entertained and family funerals were held.

The Kimball household was so extensive that Heber kept his own storehouse on the premises. Later in her life one of his daughters recorded a charming little story about an incident with her father in this storehouse.

> My sister Sarah was two years younger than me and one day when we were very small, father took us to his store-house where he kept supplies of shoes, drygoods and whatnot for his family. He was going to give us each a pair of shoes. Like all little girls we went in delighted with the prospect of having some pretty new shoes. Father placed us on a table or counter, and took off our old shoes. He took down from

a shelf two pairs of old ladies' shoes. I can see them now, low topped, wide soles, low heels. He put them on our feet, laced them up and tied them, then told us to walk. We were horrified. I kept a stiff upper lip but I saw that Sarah was weakening. Father gave one of his characteristic laughs, sat us up on the table again and took them off. Then he put on our feet some shoes that were anything but pretty but they came somewhere near fitting us, and we went home rejoicing.

This puzzled me for a long time. Why should my father who seemed to know everything take the time to put such shoes on the feet of two little girls when anyone could see that they would not do at all? It finally dawned upon me that had he, in the first place, given us the shoes that finally pleased us we would have been greatly disappointed. But after our first shock we went away happy and contented.[24]

Which wives lived in the big home and how they were selected has not been recorded. We do know that in the late 1860s Vilate, Sara Peak, Ellen Sanders, Ruth Reese, Christeen Golden, Laura Pitkin, and Adelia Wilcox lived there at times. The rest of his family lived in different homes "within a rifle shot (about 200 yards)" of the big home.

In 1857, Sarah Ann Whitney, Lucy Walker, Ellen Sanders, and Martha McBride lived together in one house; Mary Ellen Harris, Mary Smithies, and Elizabeth Doty lived at one time across the street from the main home; at another time Sarah Ann Whitney, Lucy Walker, Mary Houston, and Presendia Huntington lived in another home on the Kimball block; once Hulda Barnes, Harriet Sanders, and Presendia Huntington lived together. There was, apparently, considerable shifting around. Several wives lived at a distance. Lucy Walker later lived in Provo, Amanda Gheen went to Bountiful, and the Moon sisters apparently settled in Farmington.

Since Heber was the most married man in the modern Western world, his opinions of women are noteworthy. (One must keep in mind, however, that his love for his first wife, Vilate, was unqualified and that some of his harsher comments may have been deliberate rhetorical overstatement.) Although he claimed that "No man on this earth loves women better than I do," that "I hate to have the ladies angry with me, above all things," and that "they were made for angelic beings," he could be rough and unflattering about them in his sermons.[25]

Not surprisingly he stressed obedience: "I had rather have one woman that is humble than twenty that are not"; "I do not want a woman to tell me that she loves me, when she does not keep my commandments"; "It is the duty of a woman to be obedient to her husband, and unless she is, I would not give a damn for her queenly right. . . ." Women were to be led, and Heber advised the sisters to leave a man who was so weak they could lead him.[26]

He certainly must have disturbed the sisters in general and his wives in particular when he declared in reference to Brigham Young and Jedediah Grant, "I love these men, God knows I do, better than I ever loved a woman; and I would not give a damn for a man that does not love them better than they love women. A man is a miserable being if he lets a woman stand between him and his file leader; he is a fool, and I have no regard for him; he is not fit for the Priesthood." Or "I love brother Brigham Young better than I do any woman upon this earth, because my will runs into his, and his into mine. . . ." or "Why should I love a woman more than a man. They are no more to me than good men." He announced that if any of his wives were to object to his sustaining Young over them and threaten to leave, "I should reply, 'Leave, and be damned.'" He would give them "all the writings [bills of divorcement] you want; and, besides that, I will give you the means to help you away."[27]

Sometimes he publicly criticized a man who "had a woman straddle of his neck." Most men with only one wife could hardly have afforded such statements. The much-married Heber, however, could and did. He claimed he seldom quarreled with his wives, because "when a man begins to dispute them about nine times out of ten I get up and say, 'Go it,' and then go off about my business; and if ever I am foolish as to quarrel with a woman, I ought to be whipped; for you may always calculate that they will have the last word."[28]

He criticized the sisters for their idling around the Tithing House from morning until night: "What are you lounging about there for, with your dresses and petticoats, looking as though they were sadly in want of soap and repairing?"; for their quarreling, and divorces: "Some woman will marry a man one day, and call for a divorce the next." He criticized them for their "little peevish, trifling complaints" and for their tattling, lying, and mischief-making: "You never saw a woman that is continually parading the streets, but what was a tattler," "I can tell you there are not one-half of the women that are fit for wives when they are married. They have not been instructed in home manufacture, and some of them have scarcely learned to wash the dishes properly or to take care of things about the house; and the young men are just as bad."[29]

He was particularly critical of women's love of finery. It was hard to build the Kingdom of God "while you take a course to make slaves of your husbands through your love of finery." He mocked them: "Oh, dear, I want to know if we ain't going to have any more ribbons." He had to "pay every dime I can get for morocco shoes, for my women to wear to meeting." He excoriated men for being under "pettycoat government," and considered bonnets "a cursed disgrace to the Saints." The Sisters should have been content with homespun cloth as he was.[30]

Apparently he realized that he was critical. Once in full oratorical flight he stopped and asked, "Brother Brigham, am I scolding?" Young said "I don't know," and then Heber adroitly concluded, "He says he don't know; and if he don't, how is it likely that you should?" Some of the Sisters must have bristled when he said, "I will tell you one thing, and that is, all you that are ladies will not find fault [with the preaching]; but the woman that finds fault with me I can analyse her, and show you she is not a lady." On another occasion he asked, "Now, am I hard upon the sisters? No, the good woman sits here and says it is heaven to her to listen to such teachings. I do not wish to say anything to such a person; but it is these that are guilty that I am after."[31]

About domineering women he said, "When you see a woman with ragged skirts, you may know she wears the unmentionables, for she is doing the man's business, and has not time to cut off the rags that are hanging around. From this time henceforth you may know that woman wears her husband's pants."[32] Later he added, "You know that I have said that the women who goes about with the lower edges of her clothes draggled into strings and fragments are the women who rule their husbands; they are so constantly making snaps and flirts, like a whip lash."[33] His wives do not seem to have resented his sharp words. At least no surviving documents record such displeasure. Indeed some, in spite of these publicly expressed sentiments and private domestic discord, praised and admired him.

On the subject of plural marriage he made but a few characteristically blunt observations. He believed God instituted the plurality of wives "to raise up a pure posterity," that "Some of the most noble spirits are waiting with the Father to this day to come forth through the right channels and the right kind of men and women,"[34] that "The Lord designs that we shall be separate and distinct from every other people and wishes to make us His peculiar people, and to raise up for himself a pure seed . . . for this reason did he give the revelation on plurality of wives, as sacred a revelation as was ever given to any people. . . ,"[35] and finally "The principle of plurality of wives never will be done away with although some sisters have had revelations that, when this time passes away and they go through the veil, every woman will have a husband to herself," and that it will be practiced in heaven. He told the story: "In the spirit world there is an increase of males and females, there are millions of them, and if I am faithful all the time, and continue right along . . . He [Joseph Smith] will say to us, 'Come along, my boys . . . Where are your wives?' They are back yonder; they would not follow us. 'Never mind,' says Joseph, 'here are thousands, have all you want.'"[36]

In reference to the trouble some younger wives had with elder ones he said, "Now on the doctrine and practice of plurality, one woman will sometimes think that she is queen, and the others have no right to speak or to do anything without her consent. If I had a case of that kind to adjudicate, I would be very apt to say to the woman, 'Serve her faithfully, bear with her patiently, and the day will come when you will set above her, no matter where she is now.'"

In further acknowledgment of the trials of polygamy, he once comforted a girl whose plural-wife mother sometimes "felt badly" by saying, "Pshaw . . . there is not one respectable Woman in this church but what would feel bad under such circumstances, and I know there is no Woman can ever feel worse than my Wife has done, and she is just as good a Woman as ever lived, and I never blamed her for feeling bad but loved her the more."[37]

Contrary to widespread belief, polygamy was never popular among Mormons. Despite the penchant of many writers to fantasize about the romantic delights of polygamy and the desires of many men to have mistresses and concubines, few in or out of the Mormon Church have ever cared much for the real and legal responsibilities of plurality. To most it appears to have been an onerous obligation, coupled with the imperative to be fruitful. There is little evidence that men became Mormons to have more than one wife. On occasion, in fact, Heber would harangue the young men to take more wives. "I wish more of our young men would take themselves wives of the daughters of Zion," he complained, "and not wait for us old men to take them all."[38] He did not think that taking even two wives was obeying the celestial law in full. In his view a righteous man had to have several.

In this respect neither he nor Young was successful with his own sons. Of Heber's thirty-one sons who lived to maturity only three, William, Abraham, and David Patton, took plural wives;[39] of Young's seventeen sons only four practiced polygamy. Estimates of the percentage of Mormon families involved in plural marriage in Utah vary from 2 to 20 percent, but it was probably close to 15. All estimates, however, show the Mormons woefully negligent in living this commandment.[40]

To promote plurality (right after he took his young last wife), Heber even went so far as to suggest that the reason he and Young held their ages so well was because of polygamy: "I would not be afraid to promise a man who is sixty years of age, if he will take the counsel of brother Brigham and his brethren, that he will renew his age. I noticed that a man who has but one wife, and is inclined to that doctrine, soon begins to wither and dry up, while a man who goes into plurality looks fresh, young, and sprightly. Why is this? Because God loves that man, and because he honours His work and word. Some of you may not believe this; but I not only believe it—I also know it. For a man of God to be confined to one woman is small business; for it is as much as we can do now to keep up under the burdens we have to carry; and I do not know what we should do if we had only one wife apiece." [41]

This statement suggests that, in spite of the economic and domestic problems of polygamy, there were definite physical and psychological benefits. Perhaps he was implying that a man with several wives could always find companionship with at least one. Heber was a good example of this argument. After he took his last wife at age fifty-six, he begot seventeen children by her and by four other wives. Some Mormons even believed that one reason the old biblical patriarchs lived so long was because of polygamy.

Some of his wives also praised the institution. "Those who have entered into the plurality with honest hearts," said Laura Pitkin, "are sure of a great glory. Some years ago he [Heber] said to me that such women were sanctifying themselves both body and spirit and that the first and greatest blessings were for them." [42]

Mary Ellen Harris saw it as a test requisite to learning more of the great commandment of love. "Well, after looking at plural marriage under all its disadvantages and disgust I could think of," she said, "I came to the conclusion that the Lord must have a tried people. What test could be given to prove us like this? If we are Saints we must love our neighbor as our self, and truly and faithfully show this love in all the walks of life. Could I love the woman whose husband I should take for my own? Could she ever love me, and forgive me for taking such a step. These feelings weighed me down for a season." [43]

Adelia Wilcox, shortly before her death in 1896, wrote her brief memoirs, which included some observations regarding polygamy and Heber's family during the years 1856 through 1867. Part of her account is unique. She tells how, in 1856, as a twenty-eight-year-old widow with two children, she arranged for her future. While she and her non-Mormon husband were en route from Illinois to California in 1853, he was killed in Fillmore, Utah, during the Walker [Indian] War. Thereafter she lived for two years in Springfield as the second wife of a Gideon D. Wood. The first

Mrs. Wood, however, had resented her, so Adelia had her sealing, or marriage, cancelled and went to Salt Lake City.

> Now I began to think seriously upon my condition, upon this state and my future state of existence and felt that I should choose one that would not only be able to save himself, but me also. That is one who by his daily walk and habits and good counsel would make such impressions on my mind that I would want to walk the same path that he trod. . . .
>
> Now I could think of no person that could fill this responsible place better than Heber C. Kimball for I had always looked upon him as being as near perfect as man could be and live in the flesh. So I concluded to become his wife, but before doing so I wanted to know how sister Vilate Kimball felt to have more added to their large family.
>
> I did so. She seemed perfectly willing, but gave me to understand that there was a great many things to put up with in such a large family. Now this I was prepared for and made up my mind to so live that I would not be a detriment to them. So on the 9th of October 1856 Vilate went to the Endowment House with me and gave me to her husband to be his wife for time and all eternity.[44]

This candid observation clarifies much about Mormon polygamy. An unqualified, unexplained commandment of God though it was, a means of raising up a righteous seed too, it was also a way of honorably guaranteeing widows and unmarried females economic security and social position on the frontier. (This comment also provides more evidence of Vilate's support of plural marriage.)

Adelia went to live with several of Heber's wives, Sarah Ann Whitney, Lucy Walker, Ellen Sanders, and Martha McBride, "all eating at the same table, but each one having their own separate rooms." The worst they had to contend with, she said, "was having so many children together for when they were all in the house they made a good deal of confusion. This we got along with as well as we could be expected for each woman tried to cultivate her share of patience. . . . All trying to do their part in the good cause they were engaged in." They were very busy, mending, spinning, making clothes, and engaged in other such chores. Occasionally, she said, "when our Lord [Heber] could find time he would come in and visit us and instruct and teach us our duty and if he saw anything he thought was wrong in any one of us he was not slow to tell us."

Once Adelia suffered an infected hand and could do little. For weeks she was waited on and cared for by the others, Ellen Sanders in particular. Whatever jealousy there may have been was submerged.

Sometime later Adelia went to live in the "big house" on North Main Street with Vilate, Mary Ellen Harris, Christeen Golden, Ruth Reese, Sarah Peak, Mary Smithies, Laura Pitkin, and nine children. "I found them all good women," she said, "each one took their share of work and everything went in order." Laura spun, knitted, and laid out dress patterns; Ruth was a good tailor and made Heber's clothes, and Christeen did his washing and saw that his clothes were kept in order. They all shared in the general housework, doing Vilate's for her as "her health was very delicate."

During the summer of 1862 Vilate went to live with her son William at his ranch in Parley's Park and left Adelia in charge of the big house. At this time Heber's son Abraham, son of Clarissa Cutler, who had remained in Winter Quarters with her father, came to Salt Lake City. He was then a rough sixteen-year-old on his way to fortune in California. Out of curiosity he hesitatingly decided to look up the father he had never known. Tired, dirty, nearly in rags, and fearful of the Mormons, Abraham entered the Kimball yard at dinnertime. As soon as Heber learned who he was he welcomed Abraham with open arms, ordered up food, a bath, and a complete change of clothing: a lost one had returned. Such a reception ended Abraham's plans for California. He stayed. "We got to have gay times that fall," Adelia noted, "after he [Abraham] came when the boys were at home."

"Brigham and Solomon were near his age," Adelia added, and Charley would come up, and he was as much a boy as any of them. And I got to thinking sometimes they would tear the house down, they were so rough. And, [daughter] Mary E. would lock herself up in my room to get out of their way. Abe lived with us for awhile and with Ruth and Christeen and when school commenced we were all very thankful for we had a little rest from the noise and confusion that they made."[45]

The following spring, Abe, a newly baptized and ordained Elder, and his half-brother Charles went east, Charles to England on a mission and Abraham to Manti, Iowa, to bring back his half-brother Isaac, son of Emily Cutler, who had also chosen to remain in Winter Quarters with her father.[46] (Both mothers had long since died.) Abe returned with Isaac and in 1865 married Adelia's daughter Mary Eliza.

Apparently Vilate spent more than one summer with her son William; perhaps she wanted to escape the heat of the Valley floor. Ludlow records meeting her there in June, 1863, when his overland coach stopped to change horses: "I found myself," he wrote, "in a sunny, low ceiled sitting-room, where a fine-looking matron, somewhere in her well preserved fifties, sat talking to a pair of very tidy and prepossessing young women, both under twenty-five and each holding a healthy baby." [47]

As Ludlow chatted away he complimented Vilate regarding what he took to be her two daughters and grandchildren. "These babies, sir," Vilate said gravely, "are the children of my *son*, now abroad on the Lord's business—my *son*, Mr. Kimball, after whom this place is called. These young ladies are his wives, and I am the first wife of one you have often ere this heard of in the States—Heber Kimball, second President, and next to our prophet Brigham Young in the government of Utah." Such was Ludlow's first personal contact with plural marriage. He was frankly astonished that the two young wives appeared so content. He could not understand why they had not "pounced upon each other with a tigrine spring, seamed each others' faces with relentless nails, tore hair, gouged eyes, bit, maimed, killed!"

His description of Vilate is unique:

> Mrs. Heber Kimball the first, though rapidly nearing her grand climacteric, was the finest-looking woman whom I saw in Utah. In the Highlands of Scotland she might have been Helen McGregor [wife of a famous eighteenth-century chief]; in Palmyra, Zenobia; in France, Joan of Arc. . . . She was considerably above woman's middle size; her hair, slightly grizzled, was dressed neatly back beneath a plain, snow-white cap; her figure was erect, and the embodiment of strength and endurance; her eyes, which seemed a bluish gray, were fearless, and looked straightforward; her mouth was almost masculine in its firmness; her nose a finely cut aristocratic Roman. . . . her manner [was] perfectly self-poised, replete with influential and winning dignity, and expressive of a powerful will, strong for the control of her own faculties, as well as the whole nature of other people; her voice pleasant, yet commanding; her general expression that of pride without self-consciousness, and courage untainted by braggadocio. She was a woman to make you stop and look back after her in a crowded thoroughfare; she would have arrested your attention anywhere, on Broadway, the Strand, or the most thronged portion of the Parisian Boulevards." [48]

Ludlow was not surprised, when he later met Heber, that she was "the wife to whom he most deferred, and in whose wisdom he had the most implicit confidence."

NOTES

1. *Journal of Discourses*, vol. 5 (July 29, 1857), 91, vol. 5 (Aug. 30, 1857), 161, vol. 4 (Dec. 21, 1856), 145.

2. Fanny Stenhouse, *Tell It All* (Hartford, Conn.: A.D. Worthington, 1890), 385. The title varies from edition to edition.

3. The actual number of Young's wives is debatable (he had children by sixteen), but not the number of his children. As a descendant of both Kimball and Hess, the author is related to about half the Mormons of Utah.

4. Historian's Office Journal, Nov. 26, 1860, Church Archives.

5. H. C. Kimball to William Kimball, Dec. 21, 1854, *Millennial Star*, vol. 17 (Apr. 21, 1855), 252.

6. Mary Ellen Kimball Journal, Mar. 15, 1859, Church Archives.

7. William Kimball to H. C. Kimball, June 28, 1855, H. C. Kimball Papers, Church Archives.

8. Quinn, "Organizational Development and Social Origins of the Mormon Hierarchy," 248–91, and Campbell and Campbell, "Divorce among Mormon Polygamists: Extent and Explanations," 5.

9. Endowment House Sealing Records, June 17, 1856, Church Archives.

10. O. F. Whitney, *Life of Heber C. Kimball*, 426.

11. H. C. Kimball to Vilate Kimball, Feb. 12, 1849. Original in possession of Spencer W. Kimball. Used by permission.

12. Private Memorandum Book, Feb. 3, 1852, H. C. Kimball Papers, Church Archives.

13. *Journal of Discourses*, vol. 2 (Apr. 2, 1854), 153, vol. 5 (Sept. 27, 1857), 277.

14. Mary Ellen Kimball Journal, July 5, 1857, Church Archives.

15. *Ibid.*, 9.

16. *Journal of Discourses*, vol. 9 (Apr. 7, 1861), 26.

17. *Journal History of the Church*, Jan. 1, 1860.

18. Vilate Kimball to Charles Kimball, Sept. 21, 1863, H. C. Kimball Papers, Church Archives.

19. H. C. Kimball to David and Charles Kimball, Feb. 21, 1864, H. C. Kimball Papers, Church Archives.

20. Vilate Kimball to Charles Kimball, Sept. 27, 1863, H. C. Kimball Papers, Church Archives.

21. *Journal of Discourses*, vol. 10 (Nov. 29, 1864), 371.

22. Vilate Kimball's obituary, *Deseret News*, Dec. 25, 1867.

23. H. C. Kimball to Solomon Kimball, Feb. 29, 1852. Original in possession of Spencer W. Kimball. Used by permission.

24. Alice K. Smith, "Musing and Reminiscences on the Life of Heber C. Kimball," *Improvement Era* (June, 1930), 559.

25. *Journal of Discourses*, vol. 5 (Aug. 2, 1857), 136, vol. 5 (Aug. 30, 1857), 195, vol. 2 (Apr. 2, 1854), 154.

26. *Ibid.*, vol. 4 (Oct., 1856), 122, vol. 4 (Nov. 2, 1856), 165, vol. 4 (Nov. 9, 1856), 82, vol. 5 (July 12, 1857), 30.

27. *Ibid.*, vol. 4 (Dec. 4, 1856), 138, vol. 4 (Jan. 25, 1857), 277, vol. 8 (June 3, 1860), 87, vol. 5 (July 12, 1857), 28, vol. 5 (Sept. 27, 1857), 274.

28. *Ibid.*, vol. 5 (Sept. 27, 1857), 277.

29. *Ibid.*, vol. 4 (Dec. 21, 1856), 144, vol. 4 (Jan. 25, 1857), 277, vol. 5 (Sept. 27, 1857), 276, vol. 6 (Dec. 13, 1857), 126, vol. 6 (Dec. 27, 1857), 189.

30. *Ibid.*, vol. 5 (July 12, 1857), 33, vol. 5 (Aug. 2, 1857), 136, vol. 5 (Aug. 2, 1857), 137, vol. 8 (Oct. 6, 1860), 251, vol. 8 (July 1, 1860), 111.

31. *Ibid.*, vol. 8 (July 1, 1860), 111, vol. 5 (Aug. 30, 1857), 159, vol. 5 (Sept. 27, 1857), 276.

32. *Ibid.*, vol. 2 (Apr. 2, 1854), 154.

33. *Ibid.*, vol. 4 (Dec. 21, 1856), 144.

34. *Ibid.*, vol. 5 (July 26, 1857), 92.

35. *Ibid.*, vol. 11 (Apr. 4, 1866), 210.

36. *Ibid.*, vol. 4 (Feb. 1, 1857), 209.

37. Mary Haskins Parker Diary, typescript, 31–32, University of Utah, Salt Lake City.

38. *Journal of Discourses*, vol. 3 (Oct. 6, 1855), 125.

39. William married five wives and had twenty-six children. Abraham married three wives and had fourteen children by the first two. David had two wives. Three of Heber's adopted sons, Charles Hubbard, John Forsgren, and Hans C. Hansen, were also polygamists. At least two of Heber's daughters, Helen and Ann Alice Gheen, lived in polygamy, as did at least two daughters of Young.

40. Ivins, "Notes on Mormon Polygamy," 230.

41. *Journal of Discourses*, vol. 5 (Apr. 6, 1857), 26. There is a female version of this view by the semi-official "high priestess" of early Mormonism, Eliza R. Snow—a childless wife of two prophets, Joseph and Brigham, and sister to a third, Lorenzo Snow. No other woman in Mormon history, not even Joseph's first wife, Emma, ever played a role comparable to Eliza's. She wrote, "From personal knowledge I bear my testimony that Plural Celestial marriage is a pure and holy principle, not only tending to individual purity and elevation of character, but also instrumental in producing a more perfect type of manhood mentally and physically, as well as in restoring human life to its former longevity." Spencer J. Palmer, "Eliza R. Snow's Sketch of My Life: Reminiscences of One of Joseph Smith's Plural Wives," *Brigham Young University Studies*, vol. 12 (Autumn, 1971), 129–30.

42. Laura Pitkin Kimball Journal, Dec. 16, 1858, Church Archives.

43. Mary Ellen Kimball Journal, May 9, 1858, Church Archives.

44. Adelia Almira Hatton Memoirs, 17.

45. *Ibid.*, 18, 19, 20, 24.

46. As noted above, Abraham was born at Nauvoo, did not go west with his father, and was reared by his grandfather, Alpheus Cutler, after his mother died when he was an infant. Cutler never did go west, but established his own church, the Cutlerite, and settled in Manti, Iowa. It was from Manti that Abraham started

out for California in 1862. The Cutlerite church still exists in Independence, Mo., and in Minnesota, but has less than fifty adherents. This was not the first time Heber had tried to establish contact with these two distant sons. In 1855 he wrote his son William that when he returned from his mission in England, "I want you when you come to make calculation when you come to find Father Cutler, hunt up those two brothers of yours, and bring them with you if you possibly can. Write to Franklin or some of them, and find out [how] they feel about it and if you cannot get them, get some clothing for them. If you were to leave money it would be spent without their receiving the benefit." H. C. Kimball to William Kimball, May 28, 1855, H. C. Kimball Papers, Church Archives.

47. Ludlow, *the Heart of the Continent*, 307–13.
48. *Ibid.*, 310–11.

CHAPTER 21

Kimball at Home

Heber seems to have done his best as a father and husband in showing affection, if not love, to all of his extended family. Home and family life appears generally to have been as happy and healthy as the highly unusual circumstances would permit.

He was also very patriarchal, a benevolent dictator who insisted on order, discipline, obedience, neatness, cleanliness, good manners, and high morals. He was concerned that his children be taught "true principles," but he had little time for teaching himself. In 1855 he wrote to four of his wives, Ann and Amanda Gheen, Lucy Walker, and Sarah Ann Whitney. "I say to all my wives teach our children to pray and teach the truth plain and simple. . . . I have no time to teach children. I teach you and you teach them and my head teaches me. . . . Now if I listen to my head and you listen to your head and the children to thare head how long will it take to make a heaven at home." And there was protocol. Each family member was in turn assigned to superintend routine family affairs, to act as major-domo in trying to end confusion and solve minor problems.[1] Vilate super-vised the table, at which one's position seemed to matter. "Mother," an adopted daughter wrote an absent family member, "arranged all at the table in what she termed proper order . . . I was seated next to Vira and opposite David . . . but when you return I expect to be moved away around the end of Anna."[2]

Above all, the cardinal rule was that no one wife under any circum-stances was to reprove, correct, or sit in judgment on another wife. That was Heber's exclusive prerogative. Little is known on the touchy subject of disciplining plural wives. One "outsider," however, recorded an informa-tive anecdote which might be true. An Italian, Count Leonetto Cipriani, broke his 1853 overland trip to California, as did many others in those days, to take a look at the Mormons. Apparently the Count's English was not very good, for instead of meeting a member of the First Presidency, he ended up interviewing Apostle John Taylor—a former missionary to France—in French. On the subject of correcting polygamous wives Taylor is supposed to have said, "We correct them by admonition and with gentleness, and when that does not suffice we impose a silence, a punishment which we have found to be most effective with a woman."[3]

Heber loved neatness, but did not want to see his wives "tired out, lifeless, and numb." He was orderly and disliked noise, but if necessary, "a person could come and turn the stove over and do it in order and it would not disturb him."[4]

He was a stickler for cleanliness. Once at a conference in Payson in 1855 he chided the Saints, urging them to "slick up a little" and saying that their bedbugs would get him or an angel if they stayed overnight there. Two days later at a conference in Ephraim he criticized the people for having everything in a "common splather."[5] He was even more particular about personal cleanliness. "The people," he said, must learn and practice cleanliness in this life; some people think they can live all their days in filth and dirt, never even wash their bodies then die and go to heaven and be clean. But if you do not learn and practice this lesson in this life you will have to learn and practice it in the next before you will be received into the society of those who are clean and pure and holy."[6]

In 1868 he spoke to the brethren on personal cleanliness before going through the temple. They were to change their clothing completely to be clean in body and spirit, and to refrain from intercourse with their wives for several days preceding. Women were not to go to the temple for a week "after menses were upon them."[7]

Heber's emphasis on cleanliness may have been partly religious, and partly a matter of good hygiene. He and his family suffered from sore eyes, the ague, gastroenteritis, bilious fever, head colds, liver complaints, quinsey (tonsilitis), falls, and accidents. Heber fell on the ice once and broke a finger; later he was badly hurt by being thrown from a wagon. He seems to have suffered progressively from bowel and stomach disorders. By 1865 he was afflicted with rheumatic pains, wore glasses, used false teeth, and claimed to be "naturally consumptive." Probably because of Willard Richards, Heber favored Thompsonian herbal doctors. In 1860 the family physician, Dr. Hovey, prescribed four powerful emetics for him within less than two months.[8] Because of or in spite of the treatment, he survived and regained his health.

The primitive, if not barbaric, Thompsonian system was based on two principles—cleanse the body and then restore lost heat. First, the body was cleansed or purged by emetics and enemas; second, the lost heat was restored by having the patient take hot baths, eat cayenne pepper and ginger, and drink medicines made from bayberries, sumac, and red rasp-berries[9]—hardly an ideal treatment for an inflamed stomach and bowel lining. Once, probably jokingly, Heber asked why people referred to good and bad health. Health could only be good; to him "bad health" was a contradiction in terms.

In later life Heber was still physically impressive—six feet tall, weigh-ing over 200 pounds, barrel-chested (some say his chest was as thick front to back as from side to side), dark-eyed, balding, with sideburns which met under his clean-shaven cheeks and chin, and muscular, resembling the blacksmith he had been in his youth. He dressed well, probably had a flat, high-pitched voice, and wore hats whenever possible to conceal his bald-ness and prevent head colds; his photographs radiate confidence.

Heber was equally strict about propriety and corrected his family if he felt they needed it. The Sabbath was to be kept holy, for instance. His children were not allowed off the property, beyond the stone walls, and decades later one of his sons admitted, "And I hate rock walls yet!"[10] Heber was distressed one Sabbath when he discovered a wife ironing. On another day several wives got a lecture on prudence and economy when he found some good bread thrown in the swill pail and scum on the home-made beer. A child wearing his hat in the house bothered him. "If chil-dren," he said, "are allowed bad manners at home they will practice them the same abroad and besides we always judge the character of the parents by the manners of the child."[11]

Sometimes his admonitions were blunt and personal. He chided Mary Ellen Harris about letting her mind wander "Mary Ellen you are a singular woman. Although a good woman, you talk too much. You are like your mother in this respect, and she is a good woman too. . . . I say this for your good, for my feelings are tender towards you and you have many good qualities which are worthy of imitation. You are peaceable, kind hearted, industrious, and cheerful, but you must cultivate your mind that you may improve or you will get in dotage." Mary Ellen was then about forty, childless, and a tutor of many of his smaller children. On another occasion he wrote to Ann and Amanda Gheen, Lucy Walker, and Sarah Ann Whitney, "Now what I have riten fore the benifet of all, for you to lock upon when I am not with you fore when I am with you and talk it goes in one ear and out the other. . . ."[12]

After morning prayer and during the evenings he freely gave advice and counsel on spiritual and practical matters, settled problems, answered questions, heard his smaller children's lessons, or discussed current topics. The family were not great readers, early Great Basin culture being more practical than bookish. After Heber's death only thirty-one books and a few copies of the Book of Mormon were listed on the inventory of his property (and unfortunately the book titles were not given). All kinds of topics were discussed, however, from Joseph Smith's revelations to the laying of the trans-Atlantic cable, from the nature of the spirit world to the Civil War, mail and telegraphic service, the Pony Express, the prices of goods, fights, shootings, murders, buying mules, army deserters going to California, sleigh rides, the unheated Tabernacle, building a barn, the spectacular Donati's Comet of 1858, and an 1860 eclipse.

He told his family of a special cane he had, one made from a plank of the rough oak boxes in which the bodies of Joseph Smith and his brother Hyrum were transported from Carthage to Nauvoo. Brigham Young and other church leaders also had similar canes. He prized his very highly, and said that when he was done with it he would hand it on to his heirs and that the day would come "when there will be multitudes who will be healed and blessed through the instrumentality of those canes in consequence of their faith and confidence in the virtues connected with them. . . ."[13] There are at least two traditions in the Kimball family regarding the subsequent history of Heber's cane: the descendants of one son, Abraham Alonzo, claim to have it; so do the heirs of another, David Patton.[14]

Heber also told of an unusual rod he had received from Joseph Smith. En route to his first mission to England in 1837, he had dreamed "that the Prophet Joseph came to me while I was standing upon the forecastle of the ship, and said, "Brother Heber, here is a rod (putting it into my hands), with which you are to guide the ship. While you hold this rod you shall prosper, and there shall be no obstacles thrown before you but what you shall have power to overcome, and the hand of God shall be with you. . . ." This rod which Joseph gave me was about three and a half feet in length."[15]

Later Joseph did give him and Brigham Young real rods, because "they were the only ones of the original twelve who had not lifted up their hearts against the Prophet."[16] When Heber wanted to find out anything that was his right to know, "all he had to do was to kneel down with the rod in his hand, and . . . sometimes the Lord would answer his questions before he had time to ask them."[17] At least twice in Nauvoo, for example, he had used this special rod. In September, 1844, he "went home and used the rod" to find out if Willard Richards would recover from an illness and if the church would overcome its enemies. In January, 1845, he inquired of the Lord "by the rod" whether the Nauvoo temple would be finished and if his sins were forgiven. All the answers were affirmative.[18] Unlike the cane, there are no family traditions regarding this unusual rod; it has completely disappeared. Perhaps it was an aid to guidance and revelation. There is no evidence that it was a divining stick or "water witch," popular at that time.[19]

Heber never flagged in giving his family and the church practical advice. Nothing was too small for his notice. He was inclined to think that pork and fine flour were not good for the health, for instance. He admonished his family and others on everything from the use of asafetida bags to ward off illness to the saving of grain and the development of home industry. Not even fashion and tact escaped his notice and censure. One day he let loose:

> I am opposed to your nasty fashions and everything you wear for the sake of fashion. Did you ever see me with hermaphrodite pantaloons [trousers with flys] on? Our boys are weakening their backs and their kidneys by girting themselves up as they do; they are destroying the strength of their loins and taking a course to injure their posterity. . . . You may take all such dresses and new fashions, and inquire into their origin, and you will find, as a general thing, they are produced by the whores of the great cities of the world. . . . There is a new fashion that our boys have got hold of, and Spanish bits and bridles, and then with their hermaphrodite pantaloons they look ridiculous. I will speak of my own boys, for they are like the rest. . . .[20]

In a less irritated manner he once wrote a friend, "The sisters of our city are commencing to bring about a reformation in regard to dress, to carry their dresses on their shoulders, instead of their hips, and they reduce the quantity from 10 and 15 yards to 6 and 7, and dispense with girting; it makes a wonderful stir with the ladies, and is a great relief in expense to the brethren."[21] This was the "Deseret Costume" introduced in 1855, but of very brief popularity.

There are many short notices about the continual round of births, blessings, deaths, sicknesses, and marriages. One wife recorded some of Heber's casual table chitchat about the third marriage of his eldest son in 1857. From this specific marriage perhaps we can generalize about other plural marriage ceremonies. During the ritual Heber placed the hand of the third wife (Lucy Pack) into the hand of the second wife (Martha Vance), who placed it in the hand of the first wife (Mary Davenport), who finally gave Lucy to William. By so doing Heber hoped to "stop the mouths" of the first two wives so that William could "keep what he has received in peace." He also said he had taken three grafts from the three families, the Davenports, Vances, and Packs, and grafted them onto his "first young tree," William, and as with trees, only time would tell which branches would develop the best fruit.[22]

Heber seems to have been very careful to take his core group of wives out in turn. He took "two to a wedding," for example, "several" out riding, visited with "various" wives, and took "seven wives and a daughter" to a party. In 1861 Brigham Young had a party to which his formal invitation to Heber generously and diplomatically read, "Invite as many of your wives as you please." Once, at such a party, he was in a droll mood and told a woman who he knew was against polygamy that he would introduce her to his *wife*. He then presented her to "five or six ladies of various ages, one after the other, and said: 'There now, I think I'll quit now, I'm afraid you're not too strong in the faith.'"[23]

Such simple acts as being taken out to a party, wedding, dinner, or anywhere publicly were of great importance to plural wives. Their legal and social position was thereby reaffirmed and acknowledged. One wife wrote, "This may be done in many ways, sometimes by small acts of kindness at home; and again by taking you out from home and showing others that you are indeed a lawful wife and companion."[24]

Other kinds of fun were not wanting in the Kimball home. There were parties, picnics, carriage rides, family outings up the canyons, to the lake, and to Antelope Island,[25] and holidays—especially the Glorious Fourth and Christmas. One Christmas morning forty-two children and grandchildren showed up for presents.

Sometimes the boys devised fun of their own. "We had a brother," Heber's most famous offspring later wrote, "who was somewhat of a general, and he trained us boys—that is, when Father was away. He would get us behind the barn, where no one could see us; then he would put a chip on one of our shoulders and tell one of the other boys to knock it off. Then we would fight. That was part of the training he gave us, and when we asked why he did it, he said, 'It makes you tough.'"[26] The same source admitted to stealing fruit. "My father had a great garden, and it was fenced in by a six or eight foot stone wall. He told us we couldn't have any of the fruit; but we got it anyhow, and I will tell you how we got it. This same brother of ours took one of the boys and dangled him over the wall with a rope, and he loaded his shirt bosom and pockets with apples. One time, Father Tucker, the gardner, got after him with a willow and lambasted him. Brother said that would make him tough."[27]

Heber was also greatly concerned about education and regretted deeply he had not been able to do better for his older children. "I should have educated my children," he lamented in 1854, "but I have been poor and penniless. Instead of helping my children who have now come to maturity they have been required to help me obtain an honest subsistence. This would not have been the case could I have retained my possessions: but no sooner had I accumulated a little property than it was taken from me by legalized mobs, and neither me nor my brethren could obtain redress."[28]

To provide a better education for his younger progeny he first turned one of his rooms in the fort into a schoolroom and subsequently built three private elementary schoolhouses on his block in 1849, 1854, and 1860. All the children in his neighborhood were invited to attend free. But even then some of his younger children did not take advantage of what he offered. On the wild and woolly frontier, much to his disappointment, his children did not always appreciate education; they preferred going off to play.

What his sons may have lacked in formal education they partially made up for in frontier skills, however. They could use a whip, ax, or hoe to perfection, ride bareback like Indians, and handle their bowie knives and revolvers well. And by 1864 things were improving. Twenty-five of his children were then in "brother Doremus' school" and "brother Tripp's school." Heber's children were a striking contrast to the physical degeneracy and wretchedness which non-Mormons believed would follow a practice as pernicious as polygamy.

Heber was also proud of his sons' missionary service. Between 1849 and 1867 he sent eight sons on missions (five of his own—William, David, Brigham, Charles, and Isaac—and three adopted sons—Daniel Davis, Peter Hansen, and John Forsgren) to England, Denmark, and Sweden. After his death other sons, including Abraham, Jonathan Golden, Hyrum, Elias, and Andrew, also went on missions.

There are extant forty-four letters between these missionaries and their parents for the period 1854–66 which reveal some interesting facts about Heber as a father. With one exception the personal parts of the letters are disappointingly routine. The exception concerns the death of a grandchild, who had accidentally smothered in an undetected smoldering fire. Heber wrote the father, Charles:

A more kind mother, or a woman more attentive to a child never lived than Alvira [Charles's wife]. Her whole time was devoted to the interest and safety of that child that we could scarcely prevail on her to go to a party or to a theatre, to leave it for a few hours. Mother Free [Charles's mother-in-law] herself and a little girl were sitting in the

house when this was done: thus you can see the design of the destroyer to grab at a thing and destroy it like a thief in the night, that
comes when you least expect him.

He tried to share Charles's grief by adding:

Your poor Father has buried 19 lovely children, even as that was, and
5 grandchildren, which all have felt of my heart strings and caused
them to bleed; still this is a different death to what any of those died. I
have no idea that the child ever suffered one particle of pain, or knew
the cause until the spirit was separated from the body. . . . When
those children come forth in the morning of the resurrection, we shall
have much more joy in receiving them there, than we did in receiving
of them here in the flesh. . . .
    Now Charles don't mourn, don't lay it to heart, but be comforted;
be faithful on your mission; your little one is saved, therefore save
others if you can, and if you are so happy to save Charles [that is,
yourself], what great joy you will have in the Kingdom of God. . . .[29]

Heber wrote often of his great pride in his sons' work and faithfulness
and instructed them to honor their Priesthood, magnify their membership
and calling, be humble, prayerful, kind, affectionate, and merciful, keep
His commandments, and listen to His voice.[30] In 1863 he wrote eloquently:

David and Charles, hear your father, for he speaketh unto you and
to all whom it may concern; leave your families at home, and there let
them remain, nor let your spirits reach after them when your poor
bodies are in England; commit them unto the care of the Almighty
and he will preserve them with your little ones. God says, "Draw near
unto me and I will listen to your cries." Be humble, be meek, and not
one hair of your heads shall fall to the ground unnoticed. I had no
father or mother in the flesh to say this to my wife and little ones.
Remember all these things, bear them in mind, seek to learn wisdom
and get experience.
    My earnest prayer to God, in the name of his Son, is, to help my
sons to honor the holy priesthood of the Son of God, which is of more
value than all the world besides. I have seen sorrow, I have mourned, I
have lamented, when I have seen Elders return from their missions
having dishonored their calling and their Priesthood.[31]

He was particularly insistent that they should be simple and direct in
their teaching of the people: "Learn to be very simple in your teachings,"
he advised, "for the people are very ignorant they are like children. Don't
learn to be artificial preachers; live near to God, and let the Holy Ghost
tell you what to say. You know your father is sometimes complained of

because of his simplicity and plainness. . . . I said but little, but what I did say went to the hearts of the honest."[32] He directed them to "preach short sermons. Be sure that they are dictated by the spirit and power of the Holy Ghost; its like giving salt to sheep; if you give them all they want, they become cloyed, then they are not for the shepherd. Give just enough so they will be craving for more; then they will follow the shepherd and cry for more."[33]

In 1865 he voiced a sentiment of many Mormon fathers:

> My heart yearns with desire to write to you because you are ever before me, and my desires and prayers for your welfare and prosperity are unceasing. . . . Do not think, however, because I thus write that I long for you to return. No, I wish you to stay and accomplish a good mission for it is a lengthy journey to the island of Britain. You are obtaining an experience which will be of more worth to you than all you have learned at home since you were born, and if you are humble God will make you mighty to the accomplishment of his purposes in the earth, and you will attain to every desire of your hearts in righteousness.[34]

Regarding polygamy he warned, "I never was sent forth to preach to the world the plurality of wives . . . nor to have anything to do with them in any way, but to treat them with respect."[35] Let the mysteries alone," he added, "the doctrine of plurality does not belong to the world; that belongs at home, in the sheep-fold, and no where else. This is the only place to court wives, where you can get them according to the order, with the consent of him that holds the keys."[36]

He had reason to be concerned. One adopted son (Peter Hansen) not only acquired a wife and a son on his first mission to Denmark in 1852, but even considered taking a second wife after his first wife immigrated to Utah.[37] Another son wrote how plentiful women were in England. Heber cautioned all missionaries, "Deseret is the bee hive and the place to get bees," he said. "Through the agency of women more of the Elders are destroyed than any other influence." "Keep hands off, and lips off, and be sure and not kiss but where you have a right to and if any woman wants kissing let her husband kiss her if she has got one, if not, let her splice out her patience until she gets one."[38] He warned, "Don't grace yourselves in the eyes of women; don't let the women touch your arms, let them walk by themselves if they want to walk with you."[39] Once, to make a point in his rough manner, he warned the missionaries, "You will get love sick so that you will puke. Take lobelia . . . and puke it all out."[40]

Through these same sons Heber and Vilate tried to keep alive their contacts with their respective families back in New York. Whenever possible Heber had his sons look up their relatives while going to and from their missions. In 1854 William, for example, stopped over in Mendon. "I found everything just as I expected," he reported. "Fathers house and barn and the hul plase was not altered any. Elder Weavers and J. Rodgers and the school house and Tomblinsons Plase and all was just as I left them 21 years ago."[41]

Heber remained on good terms with his brother Solomon, but his sisters Melvina, Eliza, and Abigail apparently disowned him when they learned of polygamy. Vilate and her brother Roswell also remained close. Roswell was a former Presbyterian minister who, although dissatisfied with standard Christianity, could not bring himself to join the Mormons. His letters to Vilate reveal his deep and enduring love for his baby sister, his equally deep resistance to all their overtures that he join her faith, and his mortification at her "association with a people so despised as the Mormons."[42]

There were occasional visitors in the Kimball home. In 1858 Colonel Thomas L. Kane, in Utah as part of the Utah War peace mission, called on Heber. He was impressed by his host's grand piano and played it. That same year Colonel Carlos A. Weight of the Fifth U.S. Infantry, "an old school fellow and playmate," also called. The following year an old Mendon friend, Ethan Allen, stayed three days with the family. He claimed to be a descendant of the revolutionary hero by the same name.

When Heber wished to impress a visitor, he first showed him his own ten-acre estate and then walked the guest up today's Capitol Hill, just north of his property, which afforded an unexcelled view of the city and Valley. There artists and photographers came to record the Mormon Mecca, which in 1860 had a population of more than 8,200, and from there Heber could survey the growth of the headquarters of the Kingdom of God. Kane, Weight, Allen, and others would have seen a checkerboard of ten-acre blocks spreading out to the east, south, and west. The blocks were divided into eight lots of one and a quarter acres each; the houses, mainly simple one-storied adobe structures, were centered on each lot, set back twenty-feet, and positioned so that no two faced each other. This was done for uniformity, to maximize privacy, and to minimize the spreading of fires. The blocks were separated by twenty-foot-wide sidewalks and 132-foot-wide streets. Visitors would have seen parks, gardens, fields, farms, cattle, chapels, schools, and business houses of all kinds—the Crossroads of the West, an oasis between the mountains and the desert.

Walking the one and a half blocks south from the Kimball home to the principal intersection of Main and Brigham (now South Temple) streets and turning east on Brigham Street, the visitor would have passed on the left a complex of church buildings—the General Tithing Office, Bishop's Storehouse, Deseret Store, Deseret Museum, mint, and *Deseret News* building. Next was Brigham Young's estate and his main residences. The Lion House, where most of his wives lived, was so designated from a stone lion *couchant* over the entrance. Visitors usually counted the number of dormer windows (there are twenty) to try to determine the number of Young's wives in the same more or less humorous manner that twentieth-century visitors to Salt Lake City sometimes asked if the enormous Heinz 57 sign on a mountainside represented the number of his wives. Next came the Bee Hive House (crowned by a beehive, Utah's symbol of industry), the governor's office, and the Eagle Gate leading into Young's private farm. On the right was the Church Historian's Office.

Turning south on State Street, the Social Hall was to the left and the Seventies' Hall of Science on the right. On the northwest corner of State and First South streets stood the famous Salt Lake City Theatre, modeled after London's Drury Lane Theatre. Diagonally across the street was the new City Hall. Proceeding west on First South the visitor would have returned to Main Street, which was lined with small businesses—general stores, bakeries, saloons, clothing stores, pharmacies, restaurants, photographers' shops, a Masonic hall, and the territory's best hostelry, the Salt Lake House, where dignitaries stayed. One block north, on the southwest corner of Main and Brigham, stood the two-storied red sandstone Council House, the first permanent public structure in the region, which also housed the territorial library.

Across the street was Temple Square—the outdoor *sanctum sanctorum* of the Great Basin, a ten-acre block bounded by Main, Brigham, West Temple, and North Temple streets, cater-cornered from Heber's inheritance. Here were to be seen the Endowment House, a proto-temple until real temples could be built, and the first Tabernacle, which served for all general church meetings until the famous Tabernacle of today was completed in 1867. At the time of this hypothetical tour, all that would have been visible of the new Tabernacle would have been the huge 250-by-150-foot oval foundation and most of the forty-six piers to support the dome.

Finally, the visitor would have stopped to admire the mighty substructure of the great Salt Lake temple, which measured 171 by 92 feet. Begun in 1853, the temple was of a gray granite from the mouth of little Cottonwood Canyon. Built to withstand earthquakes, and to stand during the Millennium, the footings are sixteen feet wide and eight feet deep, the basement walls are eight feet thick, and the upper story walls when finished were six feet thick. Inverted arches are constructed in the foundation to distribute the enormous pressure of the great walls. Some of the stones weigh over three tons. When finished in 1893, the walls rose 107 feet and the towers were up to 210 feet high.

Forty years under construction, the temple's massiveness was and is not only uniquely and marvelously expressive of the Heroic Will of the early church and the Great Basin's Community of Obedience, it is also a nineteenth-century example of the monumental, God-directed architecture of antiquity, the high Middle Ages, and the Baroque era. The rest of Salt Lake City was (and mid-twentieth-century temples have been) scaled more to the humanistic proportions of man in this world.

NOTES

1. H. C. Kimball to Ann, Lucy, Amanda, and Sarah Ann, Dec. 31, 1855. Original in possession of Mrs. Kenneth Huffman. Used by permission. Laura Pitkin Kimball Journal, Jan. 12, 1859, Church Archives.

2. Sarah M. Kimball to Brigham Kimball, Feb. 17, 1867. Original in possession of Spencer W. Kimball. Used by permission.

3. Ernest Falbo, ed., *California and Overland Diaries of Count Leonetto Cipriani: From 1853 through 1871* (Portland, Ore.: Champoeg Press, 1962), 112.

4. Mary Ellen Kimball Journal, Feb. 15, 1857, Church Archives.

5. Public Miscellaneous Minutes, May 10 and 12, 1855, Church Archives.

6. Wilford Woodruff Journal, Dec. 16, 1866, Church Archives.

7. Historian's Office Journal, Jan. 31, 1868, Church Archives.

8. Laura Pitkin Kimball Journal, Apr. 2–May 27, 1860, Church Archives.

9. The English did not appreciate the Thompsonian method. There is evidence that Richards got into serious trouble in London. A London newspaper reported that he "was taken up for murder, that he had given a woman some cayenne and ginger and she lived two weeks after it." H. C. Kimball to "Dear Brethren," Mar. 12, 1839. Original in possession of J. Leroy Kimball. Used by permission.

10. Richards, *J. Golden Kimball*, 294.

11. Mary Ellen Kimball Journal, Oct. 24, 1858, Church Archives.

12. *Ibid.*, Aug. 22, 1858. H. C. Kimball to Ann, Lucy, Amanda, and Sarah Ann, Dec. 31, 1855. Original in possession of Mrs. Kenneth Huffman. Used by permission.

13. *Journal of Discourses*, vol. 4 (Mar. 15, 1857), 294. He went on to add, "In England when not in a situation to go, I have blessed my handkerchief and asked God to sanctify it and fill it with life and power, and sent it to the sick; and hundreds have been healed by it; in like manner I have sent my cane. . . ."

14. The respective assertions are as follows. In 1882 Abraham Alonzo recorded in his journal, "I had been quite satisfied for a number of years that I was the proper one to act for my Father from a promise made concerning a cane, which

I have in my possession, made from one of the boards of the boxes that the Prophets Joseph and Hyrum were brought from Carthage in, according to the statement made by Heber C. Kimball. . . ." (A. A. Kimball Journal, March 18, 1882, in author's possession.) In O. F. Whitney, *Life of Heber C. Kimball*, 466, we read, "This cane is now (1888) in the possession of Bishop Abram A. Kimball who testifies that healing virtues attach to it."

The cane apparently went from Abraham Alonzo to his son Abraham Alonzo, Jr., and both the son and grandson of Abraham Alonzo, Jr., have at different times assured the author that they were still in possession of it. A second claim to possession was made at a Kimball family meeting held June 14, 1945, in Salt Lake City. Three descendants of David Patton Kimball stated that the cane went from Heber to his son David Patton, then to David Patton's son Heber Chase Kimball. At this meeting Heber Chase Kimball himself addressed the gathering and said the following: "Since I was eight years old I have had in my possession the cane. I received it shortly after my baptism into the church. On the handle of the cane is engraved the name of Heber C. Kimball. It has all the virtues and power which have been referred to and it yet will be the means of blessing and healing thousands as it is recorded in the history of my Grandfather Kimball which was written by his grandson, Orson F. Whitney . . ." ("Minutes of a Meeting Honoring Heber C. Kimball and Thomas S. Williams, June 14, 1945," 6–9, copy in Utah State Historical Society, Salt Lake City.)

This is the only source the author has found regarding this cane in the David Patton Kimball family. We may never know which cane, if either, is the original. Heber may very well have had several canes or walking sticks, as they were popular in his day. These particular canes were made of oak, and some, but not the one in the A. A. Kimball family, have little windows in the head of the cane behind which are hairs from the Prophet's head.

15. O. F. Whitney, *Life of Heber C. Kimball*, 115.

16. "Sacred History," typescript, 1, Solomon F. Kimball Papers, Church Archives. It is sometimes claimed that Apostle David W. Patten never "lifted up his heart against the prophet." During July, 1837, however, he insulted Joseph, who "kicked him out of the yard." He was later forgiven. Wilford Woodruff Diary, June 25, 1857, Church Archives. I would like to thank Ronald K. Esplin for drawing this to my attention.

17. "Sacred History," typescript, 1, Solomon F. Kimball Papers, Church Archives.

18. H. C. Kimball, Journal 92, Sept. 5, 1844, Church Archives; *ibid.*, Jan. 25, 1845; letter, July 25, 1843 (incorrectly dated 1842), H. C. Kimball Papers, Church Archives.

19. It is possible that these rods may have been in some way connected with a rod possessed by Oliver Cowdery. "You have another gift, which is the gift of working with the rod: behold it has told you things: behold there is no power save God, that can cause this rod of nature, to work in yours hands . . . whatsoever you shall ask me to tell you by that means, that will I grant you, that you shall know."

Book of Commandments (Zion [Independence, Mo.]: W. W. Phelps, 1833), Section 7.

20. *Journal of Discourses*, vol. 6 (Dec. 27, 1857), 191.

21. "H. C. Kimball Discourse, March 23, 1853," H. C. Kimball Papers, Church Archives.

22. Mary Ellen Kimball Journal, Feb. 8, 1857, Church Archives.

23. Stenhouse, *Tell It All*, 384.

24. "A Sketch Pioneer History," 35, Mary Ellen Kimball Papers, Church Archives.

25. In 1857 this island was the scene of a romantic incident involving Heber's son David Patton and his bride, Caroline Williams. Caroline was the sixteen-year-old daughter of a wealthy merchant, Thomas S. Williams, who had been excommunicated in 1856 and was then preparing to return east. The father was thoroughly against the marriage and had his daughter guarded night and day. On April 13, however, she escaped, married David quickly and secretly, and they fled to Antelope Island. Williams was enraged and, blaming Heber, threatened to kill him; he was finally arrested for disturbing the peace. The newlyweds did not dare to return until Williams left for the east.

26. Richards, *J. Golden Kimball*, 18.

27. *Ibid.*, 18–19.

28. *Journal of Discourses*, vol. 3 (Mar. 19, 1854), 106.

29. H. C. Kimball to Charles Kimball, Feb. 21, 1864, H. C. Kimball Papers, Church Archives.

30. H. C. Kimball to William Kimball, June 29, 1854, *Millennial Star*, vol. 16 (Oct. 7, 1854), 634.

31. H. C. Kimball to David and Charles Kimball, July 27, 1863, *ibid.*, vol. 25 (Oct. 17, 1863), 667.

32. H. C. Kimball to David and Charles Kimball, Nov. 11, 1863, *ibid.*, vol. 26 (Feb. 6, 1864), 91.

33. H. C. Kimball to Brigham and Isaac Kimball, Dec. 7, 1866, *ibid.*, vol. 29 (Jan. 26, 1867), 59.

34. H. C. Kimball to David, Charles, and Brigham Kimball, July 17, 1865, H. C. Kimball Papers, Church Archives.

35. H. C. Kimball to David and Charles Kimball, July 27, 1863, *Millennial Star*, vol. 25 (Oct. 17, 1863), 669.

36. H. C. Kimball to David and Charles Kimball, Nov. 10, 1863, *ibid.*, vol. 26 (Feb. 6, 1864), 91.

37. Heber's displeasure over this is reflected in a remark Peter wrote to his adopted brother William, "I have never as yet been honored with a line from your honorable Father or any of his good family. . . ." Peter Kimball to William Kimball, June 20, 1854. Original in possession of Spencer W. Kimball. Used by permission.

When Peter returned he brought his wife and child and began working for Heber on Antelope Island. During Oct., 1855, he wrote Heber, "Now I am going to ask you for one thing, which is wanting in my being fully satisfied, and that is to let me have the woman which I fetched with me, for I know she is innocent and her real desire is to be with us . . . I know she will behave well towards Ann, and I think Ann would treat her well. . . ." Peter Kimball to H. C. Kimball, Oct., 1855. Original in possession of Spencer W. Kimball. Used by permission.

William also seemed to think taking a wife while he was a missionary was all right. "I hope Daniel [Davis] will come to this country," he wrote his father from England in 1855, "it will do him good and I think he will get a wife as women are so plentiful. . . ." William Kimball to H. C. Kimball, June 28, 1855. Original in possession of Spencer W. Kimball. Used by permission.

38. Historian's Office Journal, Apr. 9, 1862, Church Archives.

39. Public Miscellaneous Minutes, May 1, 1865, Church Archives.

40. General Minutes, Apr. 22, 1864, Church Archives.

41. William Kimball to H. C. Kimball, written on board the *Canada*, May 25, 1854. Original in possession of Spencer W. Kimball. Used by permission.

42. Roswell G. Murray to Vilate Kimball, Mar. 23 and Apr. 4, 1855, and William H. Kimball to his parents, Oct. 4, 1855. Originals in possession of Spencer W. Kimball. Used by permission. H. M. Whitney, *Woman's Exponent*, vol. 8 (Aug. 15, 1880), 42. Laura Murray to Vilate Kimball, June 23, 1858. Original in possession of Spencer W. Kimball. Used by permission.

CHAPTER 22

Reluctant Diplomat

The Utah War ended ten years of isolation, and the army of occupation forecast the growing number of Gentiles who would follow. When the Saints trudged back to Salt Lake City in 1858 it was some time before life resumed its normal course. The Tabernacle was closed, no public meetings were held, and the members of the First Presidency retired and were seldom seen. Heber and others routinely provided an armed escort for President Young when it was necessary for him to appear in public. Eventually, however, the people took up their usual activities where they had left off.

With the entrance of Governor Alfred Cumming into Utah, the church was put in a position where, for the rest of Heber's life and beyond, it had to learn to accommodate, if not to make compromises with, a federal regime and an increasing number of non-Mormons in the territory. Up to that time Heber's vigorous personality, total integrity, raw courage, and indomitable faith had been invaluable in spreading the Restoration, building the Kingdom, helping the church resettle several times, and steeling the Saints against all kinds of opposition. The new era called for talents which Heber did not have: tact and diplomacy. To his death he continued to strengthen the Kingdom and to fight the various economic and religious challenges and political and judicial crusades in his rugged manner—a manner which grew increasingly anachronistic and ineffective.

The new governor, administering what might be called Utah's Reconstruction, tried to be just and do his job well. He was largely successful, even though some in Washington favored a punitive program. He got along well with the people and their elected legislators, gave peace, security, and order to the community, and administered justice fairly. He had little control, however, over the soldiers—isolated troops with little to do. Heber knew exactly what to expect from the Camp Floyd area. Troublesome troops had been in the Valley before. In 1854 President Franklin Pierce had ordered Lieutenant Colonel E. J. Steptoe to lead about 300 men to Utah—175 soldiers and 130 civilian teamsters, herders, and bureaucrats. Ostensibly Steptoe was to capture the Indian murderers of Lieutenant John W. Gunnison and seven other members of the U.S. Topographical Survey, who had been slain while surveying for possible routes for the proposed Central Pacific Railroad in 1853. His sealed orders, however, were to oust Young as governor of the territory. But after an investigation Steptoe refused to replace Young, and the troops left during the summer of 1855.

A disgusted Heber later wrote to his eldest son, on a mission in England, that the troops had been playing "with some of the skitty-wits, alias whores," that there had been trouble over women, and that some "of our silly women" returned east with the army. The civilians with the army were not much better. "Holman, the States Attorney," he wrote, "when he went to Salt Creek, he in company with Coffman one of Kinney's clerks, stabled a squaw and caught the clap. They were under the doctor's care for several weeks in this city." [1]

The troops at Camp Floyd were worse. Sometimes the soldiers bought the Indian women's favors with coats, caps, pants, or money; sometimes they got the braves drunk and took their women or simply drove the men away with bayonets. In time the braves became so demoralized they started procuring for their own wives. Nor were white women considered off limits to officers. One bragged that he was "going to make the attempt" on one of Young's daughters-in-law whose husband was away.[2] Another insisted on and claimed the right to sleep with a Salt Lake City married woman.[3] In general the army did not consider plural wives as legal wives and therefore assumed them to be approachable.

The army also beat up a few Mormons, occupied Provo for a while, and even conspired to arrest Young. In general, the troops augmented, if they did not introduce, drunkenness, prostitution, and rioting. Far worse than the troops at Camp Floyd (over whom there was some military discipline), however, were the camp followers—gamblers, procurers, prostitutes, and their like—holed up at Fairfield, or Frogtown as it was sometimes called. The entire Camp Floyd period to 1861 was a time of demoralization.

Heber believed the army would create more apostates than there had been since the difficult days at Kirtland. He was, characteristically and realistically, concerned over the women and advised them to carry weapons to defend their honor. Through 1860 he excoriated the troops and some territorial officers in his sermons. They stood "ready to debauch and destroy this people," he said. The army was a "curse," it "contaminated" the Saints. The soldiers were "enemies, sharks, sawfish. . . . A more wicked set of scoundrels never lived than we have got here!" "Have we not become highly civilized," he sarcastically asked; "there never were such things known in these valleys until the army came. I never knew of such drunkenness, whoring, or murder, until then. . . . Every little while there is somebody shot."[4]

The army did not take such criticism lightly. One of their number, Kirk Anderson, started a newspaper, the *Valley Tan*. From November, 1858, through February, 1860, Anderson championed the non-Mormons in the territory, opposed polygamy, and attacked the "wrongful" domination of Utah by the Mormon Church. To "reflect back the pecularities of Mormonism," to "show the pitiable condition of the Mormon people, the disloyalty they are taught, and the tyranny that grinds them in the dust," the *Valley Tan* often quoted from Heber's outspoken public sermons.

Since Utah was technically under occupation, some of Heber's friends tried to persuade him to be less abrasive. Some of the brethren, he said, "think that I had better not say anything about the United States." Once, when cautioned to hold his tongue, he responded characteristically, "I shall when I get ready." At another time he said, "There are some people that think I am very hard . . . but I can tell you that I am not as severe as I ought to be."[5]

In a public meeting at which Heber was present, Brigham Young's son Joseph admonished the poeple not to use "low vulgar or obscene expressions," and Albert Carrington, editor of the *Deseret News*, "made a few remarks on the same strain. . . ."[6] Since Heber had long been criticized by the Gentiles for his coarseness, it is likely that he deeply resented these sentiments expressed publicly and considered them to be aimed directly at him. He did, however, change his platform manner. He gave fewer talks, and those he did give were often mild, short, bland, hortatory, full of scriptural quotations (which he had hardly ever used before), and contained little of his habitual spice and ginger.

Heber then turned to another of his favorite topics—economic development. If, for whatever reason, he could not or would not continue to criticize the Gentiles, he could at least minimize their economic power over the Saints. After 1858 he added the related theme of economic independence. For example, he endlessly cautioned the Saints not to sell grain to the army even if the army did pay high prices. The people should store it up against the future.

He urged the people not to patronize Gentile merchants, to be content with homemade clothes, to be diligent in cultivating the earth, to be either independent of imports or to do their own importing. He hated "little bonnets, for they are a cursed disgrace to the Saints"—meaning they had to be imported. If the Saints had to have certain things they should make them themselves. "Why don't you raise sheep," he asked, "and make your own dresses instead of putting on those rotten [imported] rags?"[7]

At the outbreak of the Civil War in April, 1861, the troops were withdrawn from Camp Floyd, the *Valley Tan* ceased publication, and Governor Cumming retired to his native Georgia. The Mormons were not only glad to get rid of the troops, but they gained economically, for part of what the army did not transport back to Fort Leavenworth was auctioned off,[8] enabling the Mormons to acquire four million dollars worth of materials for approximately $100,000. In a way this fulfilled Heber's prophecy that the United States would have to pay for the cost of the 1857 "move South" and for the mistreatment of the church in general.

Although Utah was far removed from the scenes of combat, the Civil War greatly affected the Mormons, for they held the key position on the overland route, the vital link in uniting the North with the West. The First Presidency faced a trilemma; support the Union, support the South, or try to remain neutral or indifferent. Had the church supported the South, they might have expected the right to keep their "peculiar" institution of polygamy and to receive full statehood quickly. Moreover, the federal government had hardly protected the church in Missouri and Illinois and had recently sent an army against it. In fact many Mormons, including Heber, considered the war just punishment for the wrongs the United States had allowed them to suffer. Most Mormons, however, were from England or New England and therefore closely tied to the North. And more important was the strong Mormon conviction that the Constitution was divinely inspired. As early as April 6, 1861, Heber had declared patriotically, "We shall never secede from the Constitution of the United States."[9] The church and the territory formally declared support for the Union.

Basic Mormon loyalty to the Union was further demonstrated by the fact that, when so many states were trying to secede from the Union, the Mormons were trying to get in. During the unsettled period of the war the church thought it would be a good opportunity to prove that Utah supported the Constitution and the Union and a propitious time to re-petition for statehood. Consequently a mass meeting of January 6, 1862, in Salt Lake City chose delegates to a constitutional convention to make formal application for statehood. The sixty-seven delegates from sixteen counties convened on January 20. By the 23rd it had drafted a constitution, nominated Young for governor, Kimball for lieutenant governor, and Dr. John M. Bernhisel (Utah's legal territorial representative and another physician among the Mormons) as representative to Congress from the proposed State of Deseret.

A general election of March 3 both ratified the nominations and elected members to the legislature. As in 1849 the people had no choice over the nominees and could only vote for or against the slate. The following June, Bernhisel presented the constitution and a memorial requesting admission to the Union and to the House of Representatives. Although Kansas, West Virginia, and Nevada became states at this time, not only was the Mormon petition not granted, but Congress took the occasion to pass the Morrill Anti-Bigamy Act of that same year—the first of a series of measures against plural marriages which penalized polygamists, disincorporated the church, and limited the amount of real estate it could hold to $50,000. Congressional displeasure reflected in this act had been brewing since the public admission of polygamy by the church in 1852. The act was more a nuisance than a threat, and no serious anti-polygamy action took place in Utah until after Heber's death, following the Edmunds Act of 1882.

As in 1849, however, the Mormons paid little attention to Washington's refusal and went right ahead with the ghost State of Deseret, which they kept alive until 1870. The creation of the unofficial State of Deseret added one more layer to Utah's government, which already had three: the church, the military, and the civil. Not much is known of Heber's activities as lieutenant governor of this fourth government. His duties probably differed little from those as First Counselor to Young, but he never again sat in the territorial legislature.

Utah's first Civil War governor and Cumming's replacement, John A. Dawson, held office less than a month, during December, 1861, before he left in disgrace for having made improper advances to a widow. Before a new governor could be appointed the church willingly responded in April, 1862, when Lincoln requested a 120-man detachment of the Nauvoo Legion (the Utah militia) to guard the mail and telegraph service along the overland road in central Wyoming ("in or about Independence Rock") for ninety days against Indian depredations.

At the time of this service the new governor, Stephen S. Harding, arrived in July. In spite of the guard duty, Harding was quick to criticize the people in general and Heber in particular. On August 3, 1862, only two weeks after his arrival, he reported back to Secretary of State William H. Seward that the people were "not loyal." As evidence he said he had sat in the Bowery "sabbath after sabbath [he had been there only two weeks!] hearing their declamations." Harding then singled out a sermon by Heber as a prima facie example of Mormon disloyalty. "Two weeks ago tomorrow I heard Heber C. Kimball, the second president proclaiming [word unclear] and defiantly, that he was a prophet of the living God, and what he declared to be true *was true*, and then went on to say that 'the Government of the United States is dead, thank God its dead.' 'It is not worth the head of a pin': that 'the worst had not yet happened, that the remnant of the Gentiles that would be destroyed by pestilence, famine, and earthquake,' to which infernal sentiment the [people] around me sent up a hearty 'amen.'" [10]

Partly as a result of Harding's accusations, the assignment to guard the overland road permanently was not given to the Mormons—a decision which greatly altered the evolution of church and Utah development. Washington placed Colonel (later General) Patrick Connor in charge of the Third California Volunteers and assigned them the task. It was expected by all that Connor would settle at Camp Floyd. But Connor, disliking and distrusting Mormons, insisted on building a permanent camp on elevated ground just three miles east of Salt Lake City, where he could easily control the city if necessary. Connor and his troops arrived in October, 1862, and established what came to be known as Fort Douglas. The presence of troops permanently housed in the Valley resulted in a new anti-Mormon newspaper and a greater influx of Gentiles, especially merchants. It was Connor's avowed purpose to dilute the influence of the church in Utah. To this end he also vigorously promoted mining, hoping to start another "rush." Although much mining was undertaken the ore was not rich enough to excite many.

Connor also established a newspaper, the *Union Vedette*, which he published from November, 1863, through November 1867. In his desire to "give an exposé of the treasonable acts of these (so called) prophets," he took his cue from the *Valley Tan* and Governor Harding, and soon resumed the attack on Heber. Connor knew a good target when he saw one and he was undoubtedly familiar with Heber's reputation as a "rip snorter" in the pulpit. Connor, however, had to wait a bit to find something to pillory Heber with, for during this period Heber seldom fulminated against the non-Mormons. Finally on July 20, 1864, Connor found something to seize upon and came on strong. A sermon by Heber in the Tabernacle, the *Vedette* announced, was the "disloyal mutterings and filthy antics of an old ape wearing a red bandanna over his senseless cranium," and it labeled "the most indelicate remarks on Polygamy unfit for publication in any respectable paper." Five days later the *Vedette*, describing the July 21 "Sabbath at the Tabernacle," reported that Heber's "whole discourse was without one pure idea, and full of the most blatant disloyalty. In fact, it was nothing but a low coarse obscene tirade of abuse against the

Government of the United States." To the end of the war the *Vedette* kept up its attack on the church, quoting Heber frequently. Once Heber said something that was for him relatively mild: "We are now living in one of the most eventful days that was ever known. The Lord is now withdrawing his spirit from the face of the earth. . . . The stars and stripes are said to be emblems of freedom and Christianity. When I read of the raids of the Union armies destroying millions of dollars worth of property and leaving women and children to starve, I say God save us from such Christianity as that." The *Vedette* picked this up and labeled it "balderdash, disgusting ribaldry, and filth."[11]

On another occasion when Heber denounced adultery, the *Vedette*, noting that he was a polygamist, complained that "the *hypocrisy* of this Mormon Leader would shame a criminal upon the gallows."[12] When Connor could find nothing current from Heber to bewail he would quote from some of Heber's vigorous 1857 sermons, from the time when Utah had been threatened by the Utah expedition.

Heber never bothered to answer the Gentile abuse. One of his few known comments regarding either the *Valley Tan* or the *Vedette* was rather mild. "General Connor," he said, "and also the *Vedette* are issuing their proclamations to the world, as though the mountains here are full of silver and gold, and that Connor and the troops are here to sustain the Gentiles in their rights. . . . Connor's design is to disentangle the people from under the bondage of the leaders of this people and to make a free people of them, as he says."[13]

With the end of the Civil War in April, 1865, relations between Fort Douglas and the church temporarily improved. As if to symbolize the new spirit of good feeling, Mormons and Gentiles jointly celebrated Lincoln's reinauguration and the Union victory at Appomattox. The two groups united again on April 15 in memorial services for the assassinated President. Stenhouse reported that even General Connor and the *Vedette* expressed a desire for the feud to end, which it did for a while, although it erupted later with "the same old tune."[14]

NOTES

    1. H. C. Kimball to William Kimball, May 20, 1855, William H. Kimball Papers, Church Archives.
    2. William Mulder and A. Russell Mortensen, *Among the Mormons: Historic Accounts by Contemporary Observers* (1958; Lincoln: University of Nebraska Press, 1974), 274.

3. Historian's Office Journal, Sept. 28, 1858, Church Archives.

4. *Journal of Discourses*, vol. 7 (Aug. 28, 1859), 234–35. It was also at this time that the Saints discovered the first ghoul in their midst. After his apprehension large piles of clothing taken from graves was discovered. Many mothers fainted at the sight of objects taken from their children's bodies. Lynch justice was harsh: the man, John Baptist, was branded, his ears were cut off, and he was exiled to Antelope Island in the Great Salt Lake. Historian's Office Journal, Aug., 1862, Church Archives.

5. *Ibid.*

6. C. L. Walker Journal, Aug. 18, 1861, Church Archives.

7. *Journal of Discourses*, vol. 8 (July 1, 1860), 111.

8. Army of Utah Records, vol. 12, July 11, 1861, National Archives, Washington, D.C. The army took back to Fort Leavenworth 165,000 pounds of clothing, 35,000 pounds of ordnance stores, 11,483 pounds of medical supplies, and 5,000 pounds of quartermaster stores.

9. *Journal of Discourses*, vol. 9 (Apr. 6, 1861), 7.

10. U.S. State Department, Territorial Papers, Utah 1853–73, M12, roll 1, National Archives.

11. *Union Vedette*, Jan. 27, 1865.

12. *Ibid.*, Feb. 11, 1865.

13. H. C. Kimball to David and Charles Kimball, Feb. 21, 1864, H. C. Kimball Papers, Church Archives.

14. Stenhouse, *The Rocky Mountain Saints*, 611–12.

CHAPTER 23

Brigham's Outspoken Preacher

As a church leader, Heber's main ecclesiastical assignment was to preach, to give advice, to exhort the Saints to good works, repentance, and obedience—to mold them into a new Chosen People. To this end he spoke often and deserved his reputation as a colorful and outspoken preacher.

Although most of the nineteen wards in Salt Lake City had some kind of building for school and public gatherings, almost all of Heber's preaching was done in the Old Tabernacle on the southwest corner of Temple Square. The tabernacle seated 2,000, the largest such hall on the frontier, but by 1853 was too small. The Bowery, seating 8,000, was then erected nearby, but could only be used in good weather. Sometimes Heber also spoke in this place. The famous later Tabernacle was not finished until 1867.

More than 140 of Heber's sermons or informal homilies were recorded. They reveal his preaching to have been an unusual mixture of orthodoxy, power, and peculiarities, some of which at first seem almost quirky.[1] In Heber's day speculative theology was practiced in the church; since then Mormon theology has been pretty much standardized. He laid it on the line, minced no words. His job was to build and strengthen the Kingdom with what talents and energy he had.

Lacking formal education, he capitalized on his natural gifts. Perhaps he believed that the Saints got enough standard sermonizing from his colleagues and that it would be better for him just to be himself and let others be artful. Generally he dispensed with subtleties, knowing very well how unsophisticated many of his hearers were. If he thought they needed the message in a forthright manner that is the way they got it. He was never maudlin or sanctimonious.

He was perfectly aware of his provocative oratorical style and made little effort to tone it down. He believed he was effective and complained when he was edited, when "Brother Carrington clips out words here and there."[2] Of his outspoken platform manner he freely admitted that "you must expect, when you see brother Heber stand before you to speak, that you will hear what is called the rough [h]etchel [a tool for breaking up flax] to this generation." He acknowledged that he was plain, definite, unpremeditated, eccentric, rough, disjointed, hard, and severe. He also realized that he was "sometimes considered vulgar by those who are themselves vulgar." By way of explanation or apology he occasionally said, "Excuse me, I never use rough words, only when I come in contact with rough things; and I use smooth words when I talk upon smooth subjects, and so on, according to the nature of the case that comes before me," or "Well, excuse me for that language."[3]

Though in many ways puritanical, Heber was a humanist, full of imagination and humor. No audience ever dozed through his sermons, for they might miss his tough, personal, or witty remarks. He was also earthy. Sometimes his language offended—but no matter. The people had to be motivated to exceptional righteousness, for they were then, at last, free from the Gentiles, free to build the Kingdom, where as the hymn declares, "none could hurt or make afraid." Later, as Gentile wickedness seeped into the Mormon Arcadia, Heber denounced it harshly, and was faulted for his rough language by those in and out of the church.

Heber's theology was similar to his preaching—firmly orthodox in an unorthodox fashion, individual, and bold. Other than constantly exhorting the people to be good and obedient, he seldom presented or developed any particular theological or doctrinal themes. Many old-time Mormons felt that prepared sermons smacked too much of sectarianism. One's preaching should be "by the spirit." Quite literally did they accept the divine pronouncement, "Take therefore no thought what ye shall say. . . ." When non-Mormons quote some of Heber's provocative statements, it is difficult for Mormon apologists to claim he was quoted out of context, for he was seldom *in* context. He usually preached extempore without a specific subject in mind. In any given "sermon" (some of which fill ten or more printed double-column pages) he would range simply and disjointedly over a variety of topics with only an occasional sign of oratory or attempt at rhetorical effect. One auditor reported his voice was often loud and high. Another observed, "He affects the Boanerges style and does not at times distain the part of Thersites [an argumentative soldier during the Trojan Wars] . . . he prefers an everyday manner of speech, which savors rather of familarity than of reverence. The people look more amused when he speaks than when others harangue them, and they laugh readily, as almost all crowds will, at the thinnest phantom of a joke. Mr. Kimball's movements contrasted strongly with those of his predecessor; they consisted of a stone-throwing gesture delivered on tiptoe, then of a descending movement. . . ."[4]

He seldom quoted scripture, but was fond of imagery. "Comparisons, analogies, metaphors, and the like came naturally and helped him to convey his messages with concreteness and vigor."[5] To stress repentance and obedience he often used his two favorite metaphors: the clay in the hands of the potter and the tool of the blacksmith—elements of trades he had worked at. Through the former, probably derived from Jeremiah, Isaiah, and Paul's Epistle to the Romans, Heber stressed the passivity of the clay and the potter's ability to mold it into a "vessel of honor." To him the Saints should be like that clay. Those who were "refractory and snappish" must, like brittle clay, be thrown back into the mill to be ground over again "until it becomes passive."[6]

A typical example of this oft-repeated metaphor is as follows:

> I do not know that I can compare it [the proper course in life] better than by the potter's business. It forms a good comparison. This is the course you must pursue, and I know of no other way that God has prepared for you to become sanctified, and moulded, and fashioned, until you become modelled to the likeness of the Son of God, by those who are placed to lead you. This is a lesson you have to learn as well as myself. . . . You have come from the mill, and you have been there grinding. For what purpose? To bring you into a passive condition. You have been gathered from the nations of the earth, from among the kindreds, tongues, and peoples of the world, to the Valley of the Great Salt Lake, to purify and sanctify yourselves, and become like the passive clay in the hands of the potter. Now suppose I subject myself enough, in the hands of the potter, to be shaped according as he was dictated by the Great Master potter that rules over all things in heaven and on earth, he would make me into a vessel of honor.
>
> There are many vessels that are destroyed after they have been moulded and shaped. Why? Because they are not contented with the shape the potter has given them, but straightaway put themselves into a shape to please themselves; therefore they are beyond understanding what God designs, and they destroy themselves by the power of their own agency, for this is given to every man and woman, to do just as they please. That is all right, and all just. Well, then, you have to go through a great many modellings and shapes, then you have to be glazed and burned; and even in the burning, some vessels crack. What makes them crack? Because they are snappish; they would not crack, if they were not snappish and wilful.[7]

Likewise the Saints should be like passive iron, which a blacksmith can forge into an "axe that will be as keen as a razor." Brittle and snappish iron had "to go back into the furnace again . . . because it was not passive."[8] He remarked, "When you find a man or woman snappish and fretful, and not willing to be subject, you may know there is a good deal of dross in that character. . . . That dross has got to come out."[9]

Through these teachings and others using such images as the violin and the violinist, the sheep and the shepherd, the limbs and the tree, the troops and their file leader, he continually stressed submission to church authority, becoming one of the main sources of rhetorical authoritarianism in Mormonism. And when metaphoric suggestions failed, he fostered submission to established authority in more direct language. He never wearied of insisting that the Saints do their duty, follow their leaders, listen to counsel—virtues he reiterated in every sermon. Heber continually held up Brigham Young as Joseph's sucessor, a prophet, leader, revelator, priest, governor, head, seer, holder of the keys to life and salvation, and dictator. "If I should tell you what the will of the Lord is," he once said, "it would be: do as my servant Brigham Young tells you to. Be content with your place. . . ."[10]

It would be erroneous to conclude that either Heber or the church tried to keep people under thoughtless subjection or desired a servile following. To Heber the road to happiness, success, blessings, and ultimate exaltation was one of virtue and obedience, submission to God, and doing right. All people should aspire for the best, for the highest. If you will all honor the place you are now in," he said, "you will be raised higher as soon as you are ready."[11]

Heber taught a very positive and humanistic view of God. To him God was "a lively, social and cheerful man." He reasoned, "I am perfectly satisfied that my Father and my God is a cheerful, pleasant, lively, and good-natured Being. Why? because I am cheerful, pleasant, lively, and good-natured when I have his spirit. . . . That arises from the perfection of His attributes; He is a jovial, lively person, and a beautiful man." A God without a sense of humor was inconceivable to Heber. In his straightforward manner he said, "The Lord looks upon us as a good father looks upon his boys who are in the field at work. . . . That is the way my Father feels, and I feel so, when I have His Spirit and that is the reason I can comprehend Him when I have his spirit. You have heard me say that I felt joyful, funny, and jocular, according to the portion of the Spirit of the Lord I enjoyed . . . and that makes me think that my Father in heaven felt so before me."[12] (No biographer, editor, compiler, copyist, or translator has ever permitted the biblical Father or Son even to smile: the New Testament

God of Love is always grave. Not so in the Book of Mormon account of Christ's New World ministry. There the Son of Man smiled not once, but twice [3 Nephi 19:25, 30]. Heber may have noticed this.)

Heber helped promulgate the unusual Mormon belief that "our Father in heaven was once as I am, if faithful I shall be as he is now." [13] This fundamental doctrine in Mormon theology was first publicly enunciated by Joseph Smith, and in spite of Heber's well-turned phrase, it lives today in the words of Lorenzo Snow: "As man is God once was; as God is man may become." [14]

Heber passed on a few other observations about Joseph Smith somewhat at variance with the usual, almost mythic, view of a serene, completely confident Prophet of God. According to Heber, Joseph's legs sometimes "trembled when speaking." Joseph would "hold men up to see whether this people would worship them, to see whether they had discernment enough to know the difference between a righteous man and a wicked one. . . ," and if the people preferred the latter, "he was perfectly willing that we should have the opportunity to prove ourselves." Heber appreciated the difficulties the young, sensitive, and kind Prophet had in communicating with the Saints and controlling them. At times Joseph felt his mind closed because there was no room "in the hearts of his people for the glorious truths." Joseph "used to say in Nauvoo that when he came before the people he felt as though he were enclosed in an iron case, his mind was closed by the influences that were thrown around him; he was curtailed in his wishes and desires to do good; there was no room for him to expand, hence he could not make use of the revelations of God as he would have done. . . ." [15]

Though authoritarian himself, Heber did not see Joseph Smith in that light. "Joseph could not so thoroughly control the people," he said, "for they were wild like bulls; but when he could not make them do what he wanted them to do, he suffered them to do what they pleased." Heber thought a bishop in Utah had more influence over his ward than Joseph had over the church in his day. [16] Joseph would sometimes test men in unusual ways, especially to see if they were obedient. Once Joseph ordered Heber to drive his team between two trees where even one horse could not go. Heber said he could not. Joseph stared at him, and said again, "Drive through." Heber jerked his reins out and popped his whip. "There," said Joseph, "that will do. I only wanted to see you try." [17]

As would be expected, to Heber there was nothing mysterious about man's relationship to the Deity: our spirits are literally God's children and we are watched over by Him or His agents. Once Heber asked rhetorically, "Did God produce us? He did, and every son and daughter of Adam upon the face of this earth; and he produced us upon the same principle that we produce one another." Whether the Father himself monitored every act and thought of the Saints was immaterial to Heber. "Some may think that the Almighty does not see their doings, but if He does not, the angels and ministering spirits do. They see you and your works and, I have no doubt but they occasionally communicate your conduct to the Father, or to the Son, or to Joseph. . . ." He, of course, did not accept the Virgin birth of orthodox Christianity. "According to the scripture," he insisted, "he [Christ] is the first begotten of his father in the flesh, and there was nothing unnatural about it." [18]

To Heber life had a clear and vital purpose: it was a time to do what had to be done and could only be done in the flesh. "If we make good use of our lives, and of our bodies, and of our talents, it will be well with us, but if we do not, we have to give an account of the deeds done in the body." This was the time to overcome passions. He chided the Saints for thinking that they were "going to step right into the presence of God when you leave this state of mortality." Our emotional instincts had to be tamed —if not here, then there—before the Last Judgment. [19]

Closely related to his understanding of the purpose of this life was Heber's eschatology, his ideas regarding the resurrection and life after death. He fully accepted the Mormon doctrine of a literal and universal resurrection (even of animals). He believed, however, that many, through sin, would be resurrected only to a second death, a form of annihilation. He reasoned ontologically that some "men will sin so that they will be damned spiritually and temporally. There will be a dissolution of the natural body and of the spirit, and they will go back into their native elements, the same as the chemist can go to work and dissolve a five-dollar gold piece. . . ." [20]

He seems to have believed that many, through the dishonoring of their God-given spirits and bodies, would not be worthy to continue this existence beyond resurrection, that their bodies and spirits would have to be annihilated and they would have to start existence all over again as "an intelligence." All that they had gained and learned as spirit children of God and as mortals would be taken from them and they would regress to whatever type of existence they had had before they became spirit children of God. [21]

He also taught that after death "we . . . have to pass by sentinels that are placed between us and our Father and God"; no one, however important, could lead another into the celestial world, "because Justice sits at the door, and will not admit a single soul until he has paid the uttermost farthing." [22]

Heber had the interesting, plain, and sensible cosmology of a man in harmony with nature. As to the origin of the earth he answered, "From its parent earths . . . the earth is alive. If it was not it could not produce." Everything upon the earth grew before it came here." In fact, Adam and Eve "actually brought from heaven every variety of fruit, of the seed of vegetables, the seed of flowers, and planted them in this earth on which we dwell." [23]

He accepted and taught the unique Mormon belief that this earth is not only our home now, but will be the location of our heaven and hell after death, after the Last Judgment, and after the earth itself has been perfected and cleansed by fire.

> When we escape from this earth, we suppose we are going to heaven: Do you suppose you are going to the earth that Adam came from? that Elohim [God the Father] came from? where Jehovah the Lord [the pre-mortal Christ] came from? No. When you have learned to become obedient to the Father and God of this earth, and obedient to the messengers He sends—when you have done all that, remember you are not going to leave this earth. You will never leave it until you become qualified, and capable, and capacitated to become a father of an earth yourselves. Not one soul of you will ever leave this earth, for if you go to hell, it is on this earth; and if you go to heaven, it is on this earth; and you will not find it anywhere else. [24]

Not only was heaven to be on this earth, but, according to Heber, very much like this earthly life: all the good things of this existence would be elevated to the ultimate degree. Even the church organization would be similar. In the next life we would "see the church organized just as it is here, and you will find all the officers down to the Deacon," and see that Joseph "calls and sends Elders to preach the Gospel to the spirits in prison." [25]

To Heber, angels were "men who stood fast through tribulations; they are prophets and apostles and patriarchs who once lived upon the earth, and bore testimony of the truth of the Gospel of the Son of God," and he apparently believed that the "Holy Ghost is a man; he is one of the sons of our father." In reference to Judas he taught a gruesome end. "Judas lost that saving principle, and they took him and killed him. It is said in the Bible that his bowels gushed out; but they actually kicked him until his bowels came out." [26]

Heber claimed, as did a few other Mormons of his day, that Christ was married—indeed that Christ was married to both Mary and Martha and that the famous wedding of Cana was in reality Christ's own wedding. [27]

In his own mind Heber was not only a follower of Christ, but a literal descendant. In his last public sermon, two months before his death, he said, "You do not know who Heber C. Kimball is, or you would do better." [28] If one can accept the possibility of Christ's marriage, then such a descent is possible.

Perhaps the most unusual theological point the witty Heber ever voiced an opinion on was on the "burning issue" of whether or not resurrected bodies would leave a hole in the earth when they were called forth. He did not believe they would. [29] Such questions amused early Mormons in the same way some twentieth-century Mormons argue with mock gravity such profundities as whether the Pearly Gates swing in or out.

Possessing a balanced sense of humor, Heber could joke of things about which most men are overly sensitive—his bald head and his lack of formal education. "All my lazy hairs were gone," he said, because on his first mission he quickly found out how unlearned he was. "I began to study the scriptures . . . and I had so little knowledge that the exercise of study began to swell my head and open my pores in so much that the hairs popped out." He said on another occasion that "my hair was not burnt off by the sun; it came out by the roots, through studying and labouring in the great Latter-day work." He may also have been jesting when, in reference to prophecy, he advised people to "prophesy, but be sure to prophesy right." In reference to his rough style and lack of education he said, "I can make grammar faster than you can swallow it; and my grammar is just as good as anybody's, if their's is not better than mine." [30]

Alternating with his serious sermons and his humor were Heber's bluntness and saltiness. Even Mormons winced sometimes at what he said. In 1857 President Young commented publicly, "He is very careless in the use of language—I will liken brother Heber's language to the conduct of some of this people. He talks just as ideas happen to come into his mind; and some of the people act just as it happens at the moment, not thinking what they do. . . . He has so long been in the habit of making his own dictionary and using his words out of it, that it would be difficult for him to change his style now." [31] In the late 1850s when he lambasted the U.S. troops stationed in Utah, some Saints cried out, "Heber! don't for God's sake! All the world will be upon us!" To which he replied, "Damn the world." [32]

Once in the Tabernacle, as Heber warmed up to criticizing the U.S. Army and federal officers, he asked Utah's delegate to Congress, John M. Bernhisel, "Are these Federal officers our masters?" By that time, however, the embarrassed Bernhisel had left the stand. Whereupon Heber "commanded in a tone of authority, 'Come in here, Bro. Bernhisel, out of that vestry. You always run when I get at it.'"[33] His style was effective withal. The Saints listened and many reformed.

As a missionary he seems to have been a plain and simple preacher. This brusqueness began to appear in Nauvoo after the assassination of Joseph Smith, and as he began to feel the weight of authority and responsibility as a church leader. After 1846, as a member of the First Presidency, he became more forceful still. By 1852 he was publicly "damning" enemies of the church and sending people "to hell cross lots." To sinners in and out of the church he thundered, "For God's sake cease this course; for your sake, for my sake, and for Christ's sake. . . ." Once in 1857 he announced, "There are poor, miserable curses in our midst . . . may God Almighty curse such men and women, and every damned thing there is upon the earth that opposes this people." To those who raised his ire he might say, "I wish I had some stones! I want to pelt your cursed heads, for you lie like hell." On one occasion he said, "If men don't stop stealing and saying that I uphold them I will kill them with my own hands, so help me God."[34]

By the mid-1850s he had become fearful of Gentile contamination and lasciviousness, and there is a direct relationship between the earthiness of his language and the amount of sin and contamination he attributed to the growth of a non-Mormon population, especially federal troops and territorial appointees. As uncompromising as the old apostle Jude, he would thunder publicly, "There are men now sitting close by this stand as wicked as hell, who associate with apostates, with whoremasters, and with whores . . . ;" and regarding the wicked: "Do I love the wicked? Yes, I love them in so much that I wish they were in hell . . . that's loving the wicked, to send them there to hell to be burnt out until they are purified."[35]

When some women left or threatened to leave Utah with the soldiers he said, "The women will be damned that will go; she shall dry up in the fountain of life . . . but they ain't any a going unless they are whores." Easterners would surely have been stunned by "If I am not a good man, I have no right in this church to a wife or wives, or to the powers to propagate my species. What, then should be done with me? Make a eunuch of me, and stop my propagation."[36]

Heber was so outspoken that many visitors to Salt Lake City made it a point to meet him, or at least to hear him preach. To reporters he was good "copy," to tourists he was an attraction as big as Brigham Young. For years he was carefully monitored by Gentiles, garnering condemnation as well as adulation.

For a decade after the inauguration of the first regular and commercial stagecoach service from the Missouri River to San Francisco in 1859 and the coming of the railroad in 1869, Salt Lake City became a popular and welcome stopover. By that time patrons of the Russell, Majors & Waddell, Ben Holladay, and Wells, Fargo & Company stages were usually exhausted after ten or more days and nights of rough coach travel, indifferent food, and fear of *banditti* and Indians. Among those non-Mormon visitors who both heard and recorded Heber were four newspapermen, two military men, two professional humorists, several adventurers and travelers, an artist, and a governor and his lady. Some who criticized Heber were rather snide and brief, suggesting that neither they nor their readers could or should take him seriously; after all he was a Mormon of little formal education and many wives. Furthermore, Victorians of Heber's day—a day when prudery became absurd, when almost all words referring to the covered parts of the body, to specifically male or female animals, to garments such as trousers, breeches, shirt, corset, or to the biblical ass and cockatrice, were avoided, when Lady Gough decreed in her *Etiquette* (1863) that "the perfect hostess will see to it that the works of male and female authors will be properly separated on her bookshelves. Their proximity, unless they happen to be married, should not be tolerated"—could abide no public references, however oblique, to female anatomy or to procreation. Heber, although very conservative and puritanical in many respects, was totally unconcerned about such conventions. He saw nothing wrong in discussing what was natural, legal, and engaged in by his own God. But to proper easterners, some of Heber's language was unforgivable.

One of the earliest recorded negative views was filed by a special correspondent of the *New York Herald*. Captain Jesse A. Gove, a member of the Utah expedition of 1857–58, was indignant when Heber was so "vulgar" as to say the following:

> In our city there are a great many poor women. I am aware of that, and they will be eternally poor, for they waste everything they can get hold of, and they are nasty and filthy, for I see them dragging their dresses behind them; and though they are so poor that they cannot get up in the morning and wash their faces and hands before breakfast, yet they have got about eighteen or twenty inches of their dresses dragging in the mud. Now you look, when you go out of this meeting, and see if you do not see several of them. . . .
>
> I was speaking to a lady, the other day, about long dresses, and, said she, "That's the fashion Queen Victoria established"; says I, "What the hell has Queen Victoria to do over here?". . . .
>
> I remarked to Dr. Lorenzo, a few days ago, when it was tremendous

muddy, and a woman was walking through the mud with her dress whopping over, and then stretching out, and then whopping over on the other side, you follow that woman home, and you find she has muddied her feet clear up to—her legs.[37]

In 1863 Fitz Hugh Ludlow, a young and sophisticated member of New York City's literati traveling overland to California, broke his journey at Salt Lake City to inspect the Mormons. Ludlow was impressed enough with Heber to devote to him in his book *In the Heart of the Continent* more than eighteen pages, most of which was favorable. (Although in an appendix Ludlow destroyed his objectivity by telling, or retelling, one of the wildest anti-Mormon tales of corruption and revenge in print.) But Ludlow reported that Heber misquoted scripture to suit his purposes and talked a long time without saying anything. And like other proper people, he disapproved of some of Heber's topics of conversation, which "by the common consent of civilized communities in this age, are wholly withdrawn from the currency of talk, [but which] were his most favorite and habitual topics of conversation. . . . Heber's favorite audience is one largely consisting of 'the beloved sisters,' and to this end he expatiates by the hour after a fashion; which would crimson the cheeks of an assembly of Camilles, not utterly lost to the memories of pure home childhood."[38]

In 1865 Heber was scrutinized by two editors and an adventurer. Samuel Bowles, editor of the *Springfield* (Massachusetts) *Republican*, and a few friends went west that summer to get better acquainted with the post–Civil War country. They stayed in Salt Lake City for eight days. After meeting Young, Bowles concluded, "Of his companions, Heber C. Kimball is perhaps the most notorious from his vulgar and coarse speech. He ranks high among the 'prophets' here and is as unctuous in his manner as Macassar hair oil, and as pious in phrase as good old Thomas a Kempis."[39]

Bowles's companion, Albert D. Richardson, editor of the *New York Tribune*, dismissed Heber as "a large man, with an oily sensual face, and a bald head, which he protects by wearing his hat on nearly all occasions . . . [he is] one-third Aminidam Sleek, one-third John C. Calhoun (in disloyalty, not ability), and one-third circus clown."[40]

That same year James Knox Polk Miller, a young, rather self-righteous eastern adventurer, went west, with $3,500 in cash and aspirations to fame and fortune. For a season he tried merchandising in Salt Lake City. On one bleak, snowy April Sabbath he went to a general conference of the church just to hear Heber talk. "In person," Miller noted—rather incorrectly it seems—"he is of the Abe Lincoln order, tall, gaunt and boney; his manner of speaking is a sort of vulgar talking, rambling discourse in the course of which he often starts in a sentence at a terrible yell and delivers the last three or four words in a voice so low that it is unaudible at a distance of 20 feet. He is decidedly uneducated, and I presume, owing to the realization of the fact, he confines himself mostly to remarks, or rather to attacks, not particularly characterized by either moderation or decency."

But most upsetting to Miller, as it had been to the good Captain Gove, was Heber's reference to female anatomy. According to Miller he said, "I went a courting in those days. I wanted to court my wife in proper style so I bought her a dress before I married her. It took 5 yards in those day. A man could tell what he got in those days. Now you can't tell how much is under there (motions)."[41] Apparently it was the "motions" that offended most.

One of the earliest positive opinions about Heber came from a Jewish artist. Solomon Nuñes Carvalho came west as an artist-photographer with Frémont's expedition in 1854. Because of illness he left the expedition and spent some time in Salt Lake City. He met Heber and recorded perspicaciously that he was a "noble looking man over six feet and well proportioned, he speaks fluently, his language is inornate, and indicates an original mind without cultivation."[42]

In 1858, at the conclusion of the Utah War, Colonel Thomas L. Kane, who had first visited the Mormons at Winter Quarters in 1846, was among them again. He and Heber had always liked each other, and Kane was not stinting in his praise. "Mr. Kimball," he declared, is "a man of singular generosity and purity of character."[43] At the same time, Utah's new governor, Alfred Cumming, described Heber as "a fierce, brave, unflinching, unchangeable man . . . a fine man." He discovered that the members of the First Presidency "were three exceedingly fine, intellectual men," and admitted he had been deceived in what he had heard of them.[44]

In 1859 Horace Greeley, founder and editor of the *New York Tribune*, made his famous overland journey to San Francisco, which included a week's stopover in Salt Lake City. While there he heard sermons in the Tabernacle. He did not like them, observing that they were "intensely and exclusively Mormon," and much more Judaic than Christian. He must have been delighted, however, to have heard Heber in top form, and he never forgot a typical Kimballism, "I do pray for my enemies: I pray that they may all go to hell."

On the afternoon of July 13 Greeley met President Young "in the sec-

ond-story parlor of the largest of his houses, "where he was also introduced to Heber and D. H. Wells. Afterwards he wrote that the members of
the First Presidency were "plain men, evidently born and reared to a life of
labor, and looking as little like crafty hypocrites or swindlers as any body
of men I ever met," and that most Mormons he had met were "pure-
minded, well-meaning people." [45]

In 1861 Sir Richard Burton, the famous orientalist, spent three weeks
in Salt Lake City, and though he minutely recorded almost all he saw and
heard, he wrote nothing titillating about Heber. "It is only fair to both
sides," he did record, "to state that Mr. Kimball is accused by Gentiles of
calling his young wives from the pulpit, 'little heifers,' of entering into
physiological details belonging to the Dorcas [Welfare?] Society, or the
clinical lectureroom, rather than the house of worship, and of transgress-
ing the bounds of all decorum when reproving the sex for its *penchants*
and *ridicules*." He then added, "At the same time I never heard, nor heard
of, any such indelicacy, during my stay at Gt. S. L. City. The Saints abjured
all knowledge of the 'fact,' and—in this case . . . so gross a scandal should
not be adopted from Gentile mouths." [46]

The young Samuel Clemens, who had not yet become Mark Twain,
spent two days in Salt Lake City in 1861. His brother Orion had been appointed secretary to the territorial governor of Nevada, and Sam was to be
his assistant. Ten years later he wrote of some of his experiences in *Roughing It*. To him Heber was "a shrewd Connecticut Yankee," a saint of "high
degree," and a "mighty man of commerce." Regarding polygamy, Sam allowed as how he was willing to enter it

> until saw the Mormon women. Then I was touched. My heart was
> wiser than my head. It warmed toward those poor, ungainly and pa-
> thetically 'homely' creatures, and as I tried to hide the generous mois-
> ture in my eyes I said, 'No—the man that marries one of them has
> done an act of Christian charity which entitles him to the kindly ap-
> plause of mankind, not their harsh censure—and the man [Heber?]
> that marries sixty of them has done a deed of open-handed generosity
> so sublime that the nations should stand uncovered in his presence
> and worship in silence. [47]

Three years later another humorist was among the Saints. Charles
Farrar Browne, better known as Artemus Ward, an eastern newspaper re-
porter turned lecturer, spent part of the fall of 1864 in Salt Lake City. Prior
to this visit he had published an imaginary and unflattering *Visit to Brigham Young*, which concluded with his well-known words, "I girded up my
Lines and fled the Seen. I packt up my duds and Left Salt Lake, which is a

2nd Soddum & Germorrer, inhabitid by as theavin & unprincipled set of retches as ever drew Breth in any spot on the Globe."[48] In Salt Lake City some Gentiles fully expected that he would end up wearing a wooden overcoat or having his throat nicely slit from ear to ear. Instead, Ward stayed over for two weeks with no unpleasant incident.

On the basis of that visit Ward developed an extremely popular lecture on the Mormons, tickets to which read "Admit The Bearer And One Wife, Yours Trooly, A. Ward."[49] This lecture, which probably seemed hilarious to contemporaries but seems only ridiculous today, included the following parody about Heber and polygamy.

> Mr. [Heber] Kimball is the first vice-president of the Mormon church—and would—consequently—succeed to the full presidency on Brigham Young's death.
>
> Brother Kimball is a gay and festive cuss of some seventy summers —or some-eres thereabout. He has one thousand head of cattle and a hundred head of wives. He says they are awful eaters.
>
> Mr. Kimball had a son—a lovely young man—who was married to ten interesting wives. But one day—while he was absent from home —these ten wives went out walking with a handsome young man— which so enraged Mr. Kimball's son—which made Mr. Kimball's son so jealous—that he shot himself with a horse pistuel.
>
> The doctor who attended him—a very scientific man—informed me that the bullet entered the inner parallelogram of his diaphragmatic thorax, superinducing membranous hemorrhage in the outer cuticle of the basiliconthamaturgist. It killed him. I should have thought it would.
>
> I hope his sad end will be a warning to all young wives who go out walking with handsome young men. Mr. Kimball's son is now no more. He sleeps beneath the cypress—the myrtle—and the willow. This music is a dirge by the eminent pianist for Mr. Kimball's son. He died by request.
>
> I request to say that efforts were made to make a Mormon of me while I was in Utah.
>
> It was a leap year when I was there—and seventeen young widows —the wives of a deceased Mormon—offered me their hearts and hands. I called on them one day—and taking their soft white hands in mine—which made eighteen hands altogether—I found them in tears.
>
> And I said—"Why is this thus? What is the reason of this thusness?" They hove a sigh—seventeen sighs of different size—They said— "Oh—soon thou wilt be gonested away!"
>
> I told them that when I got ready to leave a place I wentested. They said—"Doth not like us?"

I said—"I doth—I doth!"

I also said—"I hope your intentions are honorable—as I am a lone child—my parents being far-far away."

They then said—"Wilt not marry us?"

I said—"Oh—no—it cannot was."

Again they asked me to marry them—and again I declined. When they cried—

"Oh—cruel man! This is too much—oh! too much!"

I told them that it was on account of the muchness that I declined.[50]

Ludlow, the above-mentioned New York City bohemian who had criticized Heber's language, also recorded some positive observations.[51] One day in June 1863, Ludlow was visiting the Salt Lake Theatre and was introduced to several prominent men of the territory. "Out of all present," he observed, "I recognized one man as the ruling spirit the moment I set my eyes on him, and it required but small discrimination of character to do so. He more fully met my preconceived ideal than any of the Saints I saw on that or any other time. He might have stood for a full-length statue of 'The Mormon.'"

Ludlow continued, "He was a man apparently somewhat over sixty, but showing none of the infirmity of years. He was erect, portly, full-chested, broad-shouldered, powerfully made, about six feet high, and weighed two hundred pounds. . . . Everything about him spoke of rude animal vigor. His face was very striking; a compound of keen wit, finesse, insight into character. . . . His bright eyes were small and twinkling; his well proportioned nose regular, but coarse . . . his chin was double and shiny, from the twin effect of good living and close-shaving."

Ludlow summed up this character sketch by writing, "His *toute ensemble* spoke a man who, to the utmost, relished and possessed the seventh heaven of bodily bliss; unalloyed by the slightest complication with poetic fantasies, undisturbed by the least intrusion of metaphysical obstacles or problems . . . the man who had climbed to the second place in the nation of one hundred thousand people, was one of the most energetic apostles of the Latter-day faith, and shared Brigham Young's most intimate friendship, must have possessed very strong qualities whereby to accomplish these things. . . ."

Then followed a full description of Heber's dress:

His dress is not a sectarian uniform, nor is it absolutely eccentric; still it is curious. One would not like to dress in such fashion anywhere out of Salt Lake City, nor even there, unless he were an apostle. The costume consists (beginning as is proper from the base), imprimis, of a pair of plain but well blackened and polished cowskin shoes, with simple galloon strings running through two holes each in flaps and upper; next, a pair of pantaloons, fashioned out of the identical buff and apparently cotton fabric, which twenty-five years ago was worn in the nursery by the author's contemporaries, under the agreeably Shemitic-sounding name of nankeen (and which he may say, fascinated by its clean look, no less than its cool and pleasant memory, he has often sought for in the shops of adult experience); thirdly, of a vest identical in material with the pantaloons; next, of an alpaca coat, whose pattern, though ecclesiastical, the ungodly call "shadbelly," but which, to unconverted ears, will be familiar as a "cutaway" or "clawhammer jacket." . . . The aperture of the nankeen vest is cut to a medium depth, and discloses a faultless frill of delicately hand-stitched linen, white as a snowflake fresh caught on the apostolic bosom. A narrow black stock, of silk, loosely holds the turn-down collar about a throbbing, manly throat; while, last of all exterior embellishments, a sugar-loaf hat, of the finest yellow leghorn, puts the top finish on my statue of Heber Kimball.

Like many others, Ludlow made it a point to hear Heber in the pulpit and devoted four pages of small type to what he heard. He was, quite frankly, disappointed—"It was not indecent." All he heard from the celebrated haranguer were some "disloyal" remarks about the U.S. troops stationed in Utah. "I confess," he claimed, "that I felt my curiosity disappointed while my good taste and ethical sense were relieved, for I had braced my self to stand any amount of deviation from the line usually followed by preachers."[52]

In balance, Heber comes off well. Perhaps the key to these contradictory views lies in the sensitive observations of a woman—Elizabeth Cumming, wife of Governor Cumming. After an extended period in Utah, she concluded, "In H. Kimball's reported speeches, he is coarse, vulgar, denunciatory. In conversation he is plain, sensible, straight forward and gentlemanly—full of humor, sometimes witty but nothing coarse or disagreeable as I saw him."[53]

Heber also seemed to have some special talent, perhaps a spiritual gift, for prophecy, and he eventually gained the reputation among Mormons as a prophet. He did not profess to be one, but he came to think he might be, because, as he said, "people all the time are telling me that I am." Brigham Young, a pre-eminently practical man, admitted on several occasions, "I am not a visionary man, neither am I given much to prophesying. When I want any of that done I call on brother Heber—he is my Prophet, he loves to prophesy, and I love to hear him."[54]

Heber's gift was not to reveal the mind and will of God to His people, for that was the exclusive prerogative of the chief "Prophet, Seer, and Revelator," that is, the President of the Church—Brigham Young. But Mormon theology holds that all members of the First Presidency and the Quorum of the Twelve Apostles are "Prophets, Seers, and Revelators," so Heber had the right to his gift in expressing inspired promises, warnings, and predictions, running from minor, offhand remarks to utterances of major import. Mormon historians have suggested that he prophesied more than any other Mormon leader save Joseph Smith. Certainly he touched the minds and souls of Mormon followers during the first thirty-eight years of their history as few others have done.

Here are samples taken from various sources of such statements which came to pass. One of the first on record is a prediction to Parley Pratt that he would go on a mission to Canada and that his invalid wife would bear him a son. On Heber's first mission to England in 1837 he told his companion Willard Richards, "I baptized your wife today"; Richards later married this woman. In England in 1840 he told a Sister not to marry a certain young man she was engaged to, as he would apostatize and leave the church; she was to wait, for her future husband had not at the time joined the church.

Prior to the exodus from Nauvoo he promised the people that in five years they would be better off than they were then. He also said they would have twenty-dollar gold pieces. Just before quitting Winter Quarters he predicted that two infant sons who remained behind with their mothers would eventually come to Utah. In 1853, at the laying of the first cornerstone of the Salt Lake temple, he said the power of evil would rage and the Saints would suffer persecution when the "walls reached the square."

He continually warned the people to store up grain against hard times. He said the army would not enter Utah in 1857, that they would not have to burn their homes or cut down their orchards, but would eventually prosper and live in peace. After the army came in 1858 he proclaimed in 1859 that it would leave the next year. In 1857 he predicted that it would be but a few years before the states would be divided. The North, the South, and California were to be separate. In Provo in 1863 he took dinner with a man who had six sons and told him his seventh should also be a son. He told a rich man, William Godsby, "William, you are a man of affluence and wealth, but you are desserting the truth, and if you do not repent and turn to the Lord, you will see the day that you will beg for your flour."

During one of the trying economic times of John Taylor, who later became president of the church, Heber boldly prophesied that Taylor would yet live in the largest and best house in Salt Lake City.

Some of his prophecies were insignificant, offhand utterances. Once he gave a man a half-dollar and told him to keep it and he would never want for money. At another time his hat blew off on Main Street and as he gave chase, one of a group with whom he had been speaking laughed at him. "Never mind," he told that person, "your hat will blow off some day, but your head will be in it."

Shortly before Heber's death he had a long conversation with Amanda H. Wilcox, who went straight home afterward and recorded that he had told her that most of the buildings on Main Street would be replaced with others three to six stories high, and had specified that a six-story building would be built on the southeast corner of Main and South Temple, that on the northeast corner of the same intersection a building would rise that would "be a credit and honor to the inhabitants of this whole intermountain region," and that on the southwest corner a "large fireproof building will be erected with an addition to it on the west." He added that because of polygamy "our brethren would be imprisoned until the penitentiary shall be full." (The truthfulness of this account has been questioned. For some of Heber's prophetic misses, see chapter 18, note 19.)

NOTES

1. Mormons have seldom worried about being considered "peculiar." They simply refer to 1 Peter 2:9, "But ye are a chosen generation, a royal priesthood, a holy nation, a peculiar people." Some Mormons seem to pride themselves on being peculiar. In my youth I was fortunate enough to hear a little old lady once declare, "Yes, we are peculiar, but please, let us not be too damn peculiar." The uniqueness of Mormonism has given the faith few natural allies.

2. *Journal of Discourses*, vol. 5 (Aug. 2, 1857), 99–100, an indication that Heber's printed sermons have been edited.

3. *Ibid.*, vol. 6 (Nov. 8, 1857), 34. While Heber may have been unusually free in his language, he was not the only churchman to be so. The General Council Minutes of his day reveal a great deal of rough language.

4. Richard F. Burton, *The City of the Saints*, ed. Fawn M. Brodie (New York: Alfred A. Knopf, 1963), 289.

5. Davis Bitton, "Heber C. Kimball's Authoritarian Imagery," paper read at Conference on the Language of the Mormons, Provo, Utah, 1974.

6. *Journal of Discourses*, vol. 1 (Oct. 9, 1852), 161.

7. *Ibid.*

8. *Ibid.*, vol. 5 (Aug. 2, 1857), 131.

9. *Ibid.*

10. John Pulsipher Scrapbook, Apr. 2, 1854, Church Archives.

11. *Ibid.*

12. *Ibid.*, vol. 5 (Aug. 23, 1857), 180, vol. 4 (Feb. 8, 1857), 222.

13. Public Minutes, Aug. 8, 1864, Church Archives.

14. In the famous King Follett funeral sermon of Apr. 7, 1844 in Nauvoo, Joseph Smith said, "God himself was once as we are now, and is an exalted man, and sits enthroned in yonder heavens" (Roberts, ed., *History of the Church*, vol. 6, 305). This may have been the first public mention, but there is evidence that the belief was held privately earlier. In 1839 Lorenzo Snow is supposed to have had this insight regarding man's relation to the Deity. He related it to Brigham Young, who thought it was true but told Snow to "lay it on the shelf" and in due time it would be taught publicly by Joseph Smith. Thomas C. Romney, *The Life of Lorenzo Snow: Fifth President of the Church* . . . (Salt Lake City: Nicholas G. Morgan, Sr., 1955), 46–47.

15. *Journal of Discourses*, vol. 2 (Sept. 17, 1854), 220, vol. 3 (Oct. 6, 1855), 124, vol. 10 (June 27, 1863), 233.

16. *Ibid.*, vol. 4 (May 31, 1857), 330.

17. John Zimmerman Brown, *Autobiography of Pioneer John Brown* (Salt Lake City: Stevens & Wallis, 1941), 76.

18. *Journal of Discourses*, vol. 6 (Nov. 29, 1857), 101, vol. 3 (Mar. 2, 1856), 228, vol. 8 (Sept. 2, 1860), 211.

19. *Ibid.*, vol. 5 (July 11, 1852), 34, vol. 3 (Apr. 18, 1852), 22.

20. *Ibid.*, vol. 5 (July 26, 1857), 95, vol. 5 (Sept. 27, 1857), 271.

21. No one has ever defined the Mormon use of the term "an intelligence," but it seems to be close to "character," "personality," or an eternal *something* with the capacity to learn. The expression derives from Section 93 of the Doctrine and Covenants, the most philosophical of Joseph's revelations: "Man was also in the beginning with God. Intelligence, or the light of truth, was not created or made, neither indeed can be."

22. *Journal of Discourses*, vol. 1 (Nov. 4, 1852), 356.

23. *Ibid.*, vol. 10 (June 27, 1863), 235. Cf. Genesis 2:5.

24. *Loc. cit.*

25. *Ibid.*, vol. 4 (June 29, 1856), 4.

26. *Ibid.*, vol. 10 (Feb. 6, 1862), 102, vol. 6 (Dec. 13, 1857), 125–26, vol. 5 (Aug. 23, 1857), 179.

27. Mary Ellen Kimball Journal, 54, Church Archives.

28. The author has in his possession a letter from J. Golden Kimball, a son of Heber, stating that Heber believed he was descended from Christ.

29. Stenhouse, *The Rocky Mountain Saints*, 560.

30. *Journal of Discourses*, vol. 4 (Sept. 28, 1856), 197, vol. 5 (July 12, 1857), 31, vol. 5 (Apr. 6, 1857), 23, vol. 4 (June 21, 1857), 366.

31. *Ibid.*, vol. 6 (Nov. 8, 1857), 34.

32. *Ibid.*, vol. 5 (Aug. 23, 1851), 181.

33. *Valley Tan*, Sept. 14, 1859.

34. *Journal of Discourses*, vol. 4 (Sept. 28, 1856), 109, vol. 5 (July 12, 1857), 32; John Pulsipher Scrapbook, Aug. 13, 1854, Church Archives; *Journal of Discourses*, vol. 5 (Aug. 23, 1857), 178.

35. *Ibid.*, vol. 4 (Dec. 21, 1856), 140, vol. 4 (Feb. 8, 1857), 223.

36. *Ibid.*, vol. 5 (Aug. 2, 1857), 132, vol. 5 (July 12, 1857), 29.

37. As reprinted in Otis G. Hammond, ed., *The Utah Expedition, 1857–1858: Letters of Captain Jesse A. Gove . . . Special Correspondent of the New York Herald* (Concord: New Hampshire Historical Society, 1928), 209.

38. Ludlow, *The Heart of the Continent*, 342.

39. Samuel Bowles, *Across the Continent* (Springfield, Mass.: Samuel Bowles, 1866), 87.

40. Hirshson, *The Lion of the Lord*, 267. "Aminidam Sleek" does not appear to be a known pseudonym or a fictional character. Someone, perhaps Richardson himself, seems to have been imitating the neologistic habit of Dickens by joining Aminidam (Aminidab of the Old Testament?) with Sleek (from slick, city slicker?).

41. Andrew F. Rolle, ed., *The Road to Virginia City: The Diary of James Knox Polk Miller* (Norman: University of Oklahoma Press, 1960), 53, 55, 56.

42. Solomon Nuñes Carvalho, *Incidents of Travel and Adventure in the Far West* (1854; reprinted New York: Jewish Publishing Society of America, 1954), 244.

43. Thomas L. Kane, *The Mormons: A Discourse Delivered before the Historical Society of Pennsylvania, March 26, 1850*, 2nd ed. (Philadelphia: King and Baird, 1850), 871.

44. Historian's Office Journal, Apr. 15, 1858, Church Archives.

45. Horace Greeley, *New York Daily Tribune*, Aug. 20, 1859, as cited in Mulder and Mortensen, *Among the Mormons*, 327.

46. Burton, *The City of the Saints*, 290.

47. Mark Twain, *Roughing It* (Hartford, Conn.: American Publishing, 1872), 117–18. Bowles is quoted in the *Vedette* of Dec. 4, 1865, as having observed, "The second president and favorite prophet of the church, Heber C. Kimball, who in church and theatre, keeps the cold from his bare head and the divine afflatus in, by throwing a red bandanna handkerchief over it, is even less fortunate in the beauty of his wives. . . ."

48. Artemus Ward, *The Complete Works of Artemus Ward* (New York: G. W. Dillingham, 1887), 63. Ward, the "dean of American humorists," was only superficially funny, relying too much on unnatural dialect and typographical oddities. Twain, on the other hand, was deeply and seriously humorous. Had Ward not died at the early age of thirty-three he might have developed his humor more fully.

49. Ward's ticket was a burlesque, but there were similar announcements in Utah which were real. "TICKETS: $5.00 per couple, and $1.00 for each Additional Lady." *Deseret News*, July 10, 1867.

50. Ward, *Complete Works*, 282–84.

51. Ludlow, *The Heart of the Continent*, 342.

52. *Ibid.*, 509. While General William B. Hazen was in Utah in 1866 to determine whether a larger military force was needed in the territory to protect the people from the Indians, he concluded that the Saints were "probably the most law abiding people on the continent" and that Heber was an "able and indefatigable" man. *Daily Union Vedette*, Apr. 8, 1867.

53. Elizabeth Wells Randall Cumming to her sister Sarah, Great Salt Lake City, June 17, 1858, as cited in Mulder and Mortensen, *Among the Mormons*, 310.

54. *Journal of Discourses*, vol. 1 (Apr. 6, 1853), 133, vol. 5 (Apr. 30, 1857), 167.

CHAPTER 24

The Last Years

During Heber's last four years the church and Utah continued to grow and develop, but his greatest contributions to Kingdom-building were behind him. This period in his life is very sketchily documented. It appears that he was often ill, that he traveled and spoke less, that he spent much time with Vilate in her parlor by a maplewood fire, "occasionally looking at . . . Shadows" (silhouettes) of his absent children, and was saddened by certain events beyond his control.[1]

We may assume that he was involved with such important developments as the reorganization of the Sandwich Islands (Hawaii) mission, the organization of the Netherlands mission, the organization of the four new stakes which were established within a year of his death, bringing the total to eight, the completion of the great Tabernacle, the revitalization of the Sunday School and the Relief Society, and the calling of hundreds of missionaries. He also remained in charge of the Endowment House.

Thousands were brought to Utah by great church ox-team trains and the Perpetual Emigration Fund Company, and the Kingdom was expanded by thirty new colonies on Utah's borders and in Idaho and Nevada. Economic self-sufficiency, always one of Heber's deep concerns, moved forward. Within a year of his death the Zion's Cooperative Mercantile Institution (ZCMI) was in operation.

By 1865 Heber had devoted seventeen years in Utah building the Kingdom until it was so strong that it could withstand all efforts to topple it. He had participated fully in meeting two great challenges to the Kingdom in Utah: nature and the military. The Mormons had not only tamed part of the desert and withstood the U.S. Army, but had blunted most other attacks emanating from Washington.

Heber was also to be involved until his death (although few specifics about his activities have been preserved) in the third great crisis facing the church in Utah during his lifetime—a crisis so severe that by 1869 Congress seriously considered completely dismembering Utah by giving parts of it to adjoining territories. Between 1861 and 1868 Utah Territory had already been whittled down to one third its original size. When organized in 1850 it had extended from the California line on the west to the Colorado Rockies on the east with north and south borders much as they are today. In 1861, 1862, and 1866 Nevada Territory was created and enlarged, and in 1868 the northeast section of Utah was given to Wyoming, making that territory a rectangle and giving Utah its distinctive shape.

Meanwhile the good feelings between the Mormons and the Gentiles immediately following the Civil War deteriorated. The unexplained murders of two Gentiles in 1866 precipitated the new crisis. The first was in April, when S. Newton Brassfield, a Nevada freighter who had induced a plural wife to leave her absent husband and marry him, was murdered. Brassfield's assassin was never apprehended, but many chose to believe the Mormons as a group were responsible. The following October Dr. J. King Robinson was beaten to death by an unknown assailant. The motive for this crime was never determined, but many believed Mormons had killed him because he had tried to take from the city an important piece of municipal property, the Warm Springs. Rumors spread alleging Mormon intimidation, and all the old tensions between Mormons and Gentiles reasserted themselves. The political and economic crusade against the church continued, this time backed by a new element, other religious denominations. "It was as though," Andrew Neff has noted, "the thread of controversy had been picked up where it had been dropped when the Saints abandoned the field in Nauvoo."[2]

During the mid-1860s two new antipolygamy bills were introduced into Congress. The Wade bill of 1866, aimed at the destruction of local self-government, and the Cragin bill of 1867 were harsher still. Although neither was enacted into law, they caused much trouble for the church, working against the domestic tranquillity of Heber and many others and giving Utah Gentiles ammunition to use against the church. Of the legislation to eliminate the "twin relic of barbarism" Heber said, "Plurality is a law which God established for his elect before the world was formed, for a continuation of seeds forever. It would be as easy for the United States to build a tower to remove the sun as to remove polygamy, or the Church and Kingdom of God."[3]

In mid-1865 General Connor started anew his negative comments on the Mormon scene. The *Vedette* began relatively mildly. In June, according to the *Vedette* (the sermon is otherwise unrecorded), Heber told the "sisters how they ought to form hymeneal unions to advantageously fulfill their chief aim in life, to wit—'breed the biggest children.' That they should 'sour' on their custom of smallest women marrying husky husbands. . . ." Connor's paper called this a harangue "of unusually heavy style."

The following September, when Heber was in Tooele, he apparently preached one of his old-style sermons. According to the *Vedette* (again in an otherwise unrecorded and unverified sermon) Heber asserted, "The Gentiles are our enemies; they are damned forever; they are thieves and murderers, and if they don't like what I say they can go *to hell, damn them!*" Connor, understandably, considered this treason. Whatever good feelings he may have had toward the church faded.

In November the *Vedette* gave full play to Albert D. Richardson's intensely critical view of the Mormons which he published in the *New York Tribune* and which featured a full Kimball sermon (a likewise unrecorded and unverified one of September 27, 1865). In December the *Vedette* also featured Samuel Bowles's criticism of the Mormons and Heber, which Bowles printed in the *Springfield* (Massachusetts) *Republican*. Connor's animus toward Heber became such that when he could find nothing current to criticize him for, he again ransacked some of Heber's strong sermons of 1857. Heber's reference to polygamy in heaven was ridiculed as "Heaven a Harem"; his innocuous remark that, when he had on occasion blessed his handkerchief, cane, or cloak and sent them to the sick and the sick had recovered, was seized upon and blown up to "blasphemous arrogance," "infamous pretension," a "most odious doctrine," and an act of "criminal design."

At the time of the Brassfield murder Connor printed a scurrilous rumor that while Heber was officiating in the Endowment House he was so smitten by a young lady he was supposed to seal in marriage to another man that he dismissed the groom and married her himself.

Not all the troubles of Heber's last years were caused by his family and the Gentiles. The Black Hawk Indian War broke out in 1865 and raged until 1868, taking the lives of between 100 and 150 whites and Indians and the abandonment of twenty-five settlements in central and southern Utah. Also greatly affecting Heber's happiness were some acts by several churchmen which he construed to be an attempt to ease him out of the First Presidency and his position as successor to President Young. This situation, which may have existed only in his own mind, seems to have represented, for Heber, a final trial of his Job-like faith. In the cause of his faith he had suffered much and long and had every right to expect that his last years would be ones of consummation and harvest. For some reason he felt this was denied him. He lived long enough to endure what he considered to be a maneuvering to reduce his influence, and he realized a sense of inadequacy. After more than thirty years of total devotion and dedication to the Restoration he felt himself bypassed, a champion of an outdated manner of Kingdom-building. Heber and the rough, impetuous Galilean Peter were somewhat alike. Both had been essential in the beginning of the movements to which they devoted their lives, but both lived to be overshadowed by better-educated Pauline types. It was not for Heber to stand before Agrippa or to preach on Mars' Hill.

What offended Heber may have been simply carelessness or thoughtlessness. It is also possible, given the realities of the all-out crusade against the Mormons, especially the anti-polygamous bills, that some church leaders actually were trying to neutralize Heber's abrasiveness by bringing into his place someone more diplomatic and adept at negotiating with Gentiles and by arranging for Heber not to succeed Brigham Young as President of the church.

The 1850s have been called by Mormon historian Charles Peterson an era of Mormon nationalism, characterized by militant rhetoric and a strain of uncompromising independence, an attitude well exemplified by Heber. By the 1860s, however, it became clear that this stance was counterproductive, and most church leaders became more practical and conciliatory toward Washington and the Gentiles. In any event, as is often the case, what a person thinks to be true is as painful as if it were true.

With all of his humor and saltiness, Heber was an unusually sensitive man—it was part of his sincere nature. He was almost always kind, even-tempered, and humble, and ordinarily did not respond publicly to slights. Years earlier in Nauvoo he had been refused credit for some merchandise and "went home and cried like a child."[4] At another time, after his second British mission, he "felt he was treated rather cooly and went home and wept."[5] Once, in 1846, when Parley Pratt and John Taylor asked the Quorum of the Twelve not to let Heber speak publicly "for he was so simple," and treated him as if "he was not a man of sense," Heber kept his peace.[6] But sometimes he could not keep his hurt feelings to himself.

By the mid-1850s he was becoming defensive and cantankerous—defensive because of his lack of education and sophistication, cantankerous because of age, illness, and disappointment. He had been at his best as a missionary and Pioneer. As the Kingdom grew and matured he must have realized that he was becoming increasingly anachronistic and incapable of making the significant contributions he had made in its early days.

In 1854 he announced in the territorial legislature, "I want to speak and not be here like a Dumb Dog. I am ignorant of many technicalities, but when you come to the truth I know that as well as Professor [Albert]

Carrington, Professor [Orson] Pratt, Professor [George A.] Smith, or Professor [Wilford] Woodruff."[7] This statement has been used to suggest that he took political life seriously; but it is possible to read more into it. Carrington, Pratt, Smith, and Woodruff were all better educated than Heber and his unnecessary use of the title "Professor" before each of their names seems sarcastic, reflecting his suspicion that they looked down on his lack of education.

Admittedly this is only supposition, but there is further supportive evidence. Although, as already noted, Fanny Stenhouse was not an unbiased commentator on the Mormon scene, there is no particular reason to discount totally her views on Heber vis-à-vis the educated. She claimed that, although "naturally Heber was a kind-hearted man," he sometimes poked fun at people who pretended to be educated. According to her account Heber once said, "Here are some edicated men jest under my nose. They come here and they think they know more than I do, and then they git the big head, and it swells and swells until it gits like the old woman's squash —you go to touch it and it goes ker-smash; and when you look for the man, why he aint thar. They're jest like so many pots in a furnace—yer know I've been a potter in my time—almighty thin and almighty big and when they're sot up the heat makes 'em smoke a little, and then they collapse and tumble in, and they aint no whar."[8]

On one occasion in 1856, when Heber was in the Deseret (tithing) Store, he concluded that A. P. Rockwood had not properly noticed or greeted him. Heber was offended and reportedly said, "As I pass you by I cannot even get your eye. You do not speak to me. You are as dry as an old Cabbage leaf wilted up. You have not the spirit of God and you have tried to ride me for years and if you do not wake up and do your duty I will ride you and that too with Sharp spurs."[9]

In 1860 Heber publicly said, "You need not try to step in between me and my President, for you cannot do it without hurting yourselves. . . . My name is Faithful—my name is Integrity!"[10] This is a surprisingly defensive statement from one who had been a member of the First Presidency since 1847. Also in 1860 Heber confided in Wilford Woodruff that "Many . . . [who] occupy high positions in the Church . . . feel as though the whole Church depends upon them and such think as to Brother Heber, He is of no account, he has been a good man in his day, but his usefulness is about over, he is like an old horse that has lost his teeth and it is time to turn him out to grass. . . ." He went on to add that he had to "carry around many people by the ass of their Breeches that want to trample upon me, but I shall live to see the ass of their Breeches come off and they will go down while I shall rise."[11]

During 1864 Brigham Young ordained three of his sons, John Willard, Joseph Angell, and Brigham, Jr., as Apostles, giving some credence to the supposition that Young wished a son, not Heber, to succeed him. Later that year, in August, Young conferred upon Brigham, Jr., "all the power I hold as one of my counselors." [12] This seemed further to suggest that Brigham, Jr., was becoming the heir apparent to the Presidency. Reinforcing this supposition was the opinion of the Utah correspondent of the *New York Times*, who reported (immediately following Heber's death):

> The Young dynasty, however, has been strengthening itself of late years, in such a way as to indicate very plainly that it did not mean to permit the supreme power to pass out of its own ranks. . . .
>
> As regards his [Brigham Young's] own successor his designation would be unquestionable and final, and as regards his purpose of confining the succession within his own family there was a good deal known *before the death of Kimball* [italics added]. Until very recently it was believed his eldest son was meant for the leadership when it became vacant, but, for some reason unknown outside of the wall that incloses his headquarters, this individual is understood to have been set aside in favor of another member of the dynasty, Brigham Young, Jr., who is pronounced to be possessed of the peculiar talents required in the head of the Mormon Church and State.

Heber was not told of these 1864 ordinations for four months and was terribly offended when he did learn of them. [13] He told a son that "the power of the Priesthood" placed on the head of John W. Young "would not stick" and that Apostle "George Q. Cannon was among those who were trying to get between him and President Young. . . ." [14] Whatever Brigham Young meant by these acts of 1864, the shadow of dynastic pretensions which they cast mortally offended his First Counselor, his most loyal of all followers, and his friend of more than thirty years. Research to date has failed to turn up any comment by Brigham Young regarding the matters which so perplexed and hurt his longtime friend and counselor. He apparently made no effort to explain or excuse himself to Heber.

Again, in September, 1864, the *Deseret News*, whose editor was the same Albert Carrington who had already (in 1861) indirectly criticized Heber's language, printed an editorial rebuking members of the community who "resorted to swearing and obscenity in language." It is doubtful that this was directed at Heber, but the *Vedette* of September 28 gleefully insisted that it was, and labeled it an official rebuke of Heber by his own people. In anguish Heber appealed to his God. "In the evening of January 12, 1865," he confided in a private memorandum book, "I was told by the Lord that I should not be removed from my place as first counselor to President Young, and those who had oppressed me when it was in their power to do me good, shall be removed from their places. That Daniel H. Wells, Albert Carrington, Jos. A. Young and others were among that number." [15]

In 1866 Brigham Young again bypassed his First Counselor. He ordained Joseph F. Smith (one of Heber's foster sons) an Apostle and set him apart as a counselor in the First Presidency. Heber was not consulted, present at the ordination, or officially told of it until some time later. [16] Although he never was supplanted as First Counselor, Heber must have felt insecure in his position in the Kingdom. "Those were days of sorrow for father," a son wrote, "and he became so heart broken towards the last that he prayed to the Lord to shorten his days." [17] Whatever the reality of Heber's fears and suspicions, he remained loyal to the last. There is no recorded work of his in criticism of Brigham; Heber chose to place the blame for his sorrow on others.

The greatest sorrow of his life, however, was the death the following year of Vilate, his companion of forty-five years. Vilate had led an incredibly difficult life and her sufferings undermined her health. In 1864 one son tactlessly wrote her, "Yours and father's photographs came safe. Father looks well, but I never saw any change as you have. You look poor, careworn, and nearly gray." [18] Toward the end she failed rapidly. When she died at age sixty-one on October 22, 1867, it was recorded that "she had been out of her mind for many months." [19] Her death took away much of Heber's zest for life.

In April, five months after Vilate's death, he preached his last recorded sermon in Bountiful. As he looked out over his co-religionists his hurts began to show. He became unusually, unnaturally somber. He seemed defensive and exceptionally critical. Never before had he begun a sermon by saying, "I have not the least disposition to talk to you if you do not wish me to, and if you say you do not want me, I will say good morning and go home." He continued, "It is difficult for many here even to hold my name sacred; and when I have heard of what some men here would do, I have asked myself what manner of men they were. . . . Do you doubt that I am one of the Lord's anointed. . . ? Some of you would like me to present the truth clothed in a fine dress and with hoops rather than that I should present it stark naked; but I speak this for your good. . . . The office of an apostle is to tell the truth, to tell what he knows."

He advised the people to behave themselves, to read the Bible and the Book of Mormon. He accused them of sitting in judgment on their neighbors. He urged a reformation in Bountiful, for some of its residents were not honest, would not pray unless seen by others, and "if some of you were going to my mill here, and should find a chain, you would look around to see if any person saw you, and if not, you would hide the chain at once. . . . There are many here today who, unless they repent, will never see my face again after my eyes are closed in death."

He paused, then in a strange afterthought announced, "I am inclined to think that pig meat is not good, and that fine flour is not good, and the finer the flour we eat the shorter will be our lives. It would be better for us to eat coarse bread, such as the Graham bread." Another pause, then he gave what he may have felt was, and was indeed, a final benediction. "I now feel to say peace be with you, peace rest upon you, and I say my peace shall rest upon you. Amen."[20] With that Heber slowly and heavily took his seat.

Six weeks later, eight months from the day Vilate died, Heber was dead. In late May, 1868, he had traveled to Provo to visit a wife, Lucy Walker, who lived there.[21] Arriving after dark, and forgetting that he had instructed one of his sons to deepen a ditch near his home, he drove his horse into the excavation. The animal's lunging threw him violently to the earth, where he lay for some time before being found. After A. F. McDonald, a local Saint, found him, he suggested sending for Brigham Young, who was then in Provo, to administer to him. Heber declined, saying, "I command *you* to administer to me and anoint me with oil in the name of the Lord; do not be in the least afraid; you hold the same Priesthood and authority from God as President Young or myself, and God hears and answers the prayers of His humblest servants and people."[22] In the "household of faith" it is considered a lack of faith to prefer one good man's administrations over another's; Heber was making this point.

He quickly revived, did not appear to be seriously injured, and was soon well enough to return to Salt Lake City, where for a while he seemed to recover, attending services and speaking in the Tabernacle on June 7.[23] But on June 11 he suffered a paralytic stroke and began to fail rapidly. Facing for the first time the immanence of death, Heber called to his bedside Lucy Walker, who had married Joseph Smith about a year before his martyrdom. Heber told her he had appreciated her example as a wife and mother of nine of his children, that none had excelled her in home life, and thanked her for every kind word and act. Then, concerned about how well he had treated a wife of Joseph's and about the fact that he would soon be seeing Joseph, he weakly squeezed her hand and asked plaintively, "What can you tell Joseph when you meet him? Cannot you say that I have been kind to you as it was possible to be under the circumstances?"[24] (Early Mormons seem to have been as concerned about meeting Joseph Smith after death as about meeting their Maker.) Heber may have called other widows of Joseph to him, for of the nine whom Heber had married, five—Lucy, Presendia Huntington, Martha McBride, Sarah Ann Whitney, and Mary Houston—were still alive and married to him in 1868. The other four had separated from him for various reasons. No records exist, however, of any parting words to anyone else. Perhaps he did not have the time, for after June 12 he was able to utter only an occasional sentence.

By June 21 Heber was in great pain. He requested President Young and members of the Quorum of the Twelve to administer to him, and that much relieved him. That evening he rallied, opened his eyes, and for some time was conscious and appeared to recognize those who stood around him. The next day, Monday, in his hot upstairs bedroom surrounded by family and church authorities, and with Brigham Young sitting on the edge of the bed fanning him with his right hand, Heber C. Kimball lapsed into unconsciousness, and gradually passed away without a contortion of countenance or the slightest movement of limb. It appears likely that Heber died of a subdural hematoma. When he was thrown to the still-frozen earth by the lunging horse, the blow to the head had jarred the brain violently, tearing blood vessels and producing blood clotting and paralysis. Medically, only a surgical operation to open the skull could have saved his life, and such operations were not performed in his day.[25]

As Heber died, those present were aware of the absence of gloom and despair. One called it a "scene of victory and triumph." Another found his death calm and peaceful, and reflected on the joyous time when Heber would be reunited in the spirit world with David Patten, Willard Richards, Jedediah Grant, Parley Pratt, and "the thousands of others who have gone before, and like them have been faithful." Brigham Young was thinking that he did not feel one particle of the spirit of death and, because of all Heber had done in life, that his "death was far better to him than the day of his birth."[26] Such sentiments are typical of the Mormon thanatopsis. To the "righteous" death is positive, a step up, a return. The personality remains intact, reunions are real, families remain together, and a rejoining of body and spirit in the resurrection is awaited.

The day of the funeral, Wednesday, June 24, was observed throughout Utah Territory as an official day of mourning. Though the rain fell, the new Tabernacle, draped in black, was packed with more than 8,000 bereaved Saints, the largest funeral ever held in the territory. Twelve men bore the coffin from the Kimball home to the Tabernacle, accompanied by many of the First Presidency and Quorum and a band playing the unusually poignant "Dead March" from Handel's oratorio *Saul.*

The cortege proceeded south on North Main Street, west on North

Temple Street, south on West Temple Street to the west gate of Temple Square, and finally entered the Tabernacle from the north. The closed coffin, covered with silver-trimmed black velvet, was deposited upon a draped bier surrounded with seven elegant vases of roses and other flowers. President Young called the meeting to order and the choir sang a new hymn written for the occasion by Eliza R. Snow:

> Be cheer'd O Zion—cease to weep:
>   Heber we deeply loved:
> He is not dead—he does not sleep—
>   He lives with those above
>
> His flesh was weary: let it rest
>   Entombed in mother Earth,
> Till Jesus comes—when all the bless'd
>   To life will be brought forth.
>
> Let wives and children humbly kiss
>   The deep afflicting rod:
> A Father to the fatherless,
>   God is the widow's God.

Apostle George Q. Cannon offered the opening prayer.

John Taylor, George A. Smith, and Daniel H. Wells eulogized Heber's life, devotion to the church, and missionary work. President Young ended his remarks by saying:

> I will relate to you my feelings concerning the departure of Bro. Kimball. He was a man of as much integrity I presume as any man who ever lived on the earth. I have been personally acquainted with him forty-three years and I can testify that he has been a man of truth, a man of benevolence, a man that was to be trusted. Now he has gone and left us. . . .
>
> For this family to mourn is perhaps natural; but they have not really the first cause to do so. How would you feel if you had a husband or a father that would lead you from the truth? I would to God that we would all follow him in his example in our faithfulness, and be as faithful as he was in his life. To his wives, his children, his friends, his brethren and sisters, to this family whom God has selected from the human family to be his sons and daughters, I say let us follow his example. He has gone to rest. We can say of him all that can be said of any good man. The Lord selected him and he has been faithful and this has made him a great man. . . . We pay our last respects unto Brother Kimball.[27]

Afterward the band played the "Doxology" and the choir sang "O My Father," a favorite Mormon funeral hymn. Bishop Edwin D. Woolley offered the benediction, and a procession, with the band playing the "Belgian Dead March," accompanied the coffin to the family cemetery on Heber's property, where he was buried next to Vilate.[28] He was survived by at least twenty-one wives and forty-one children, most of whom lived in or near Salt Lake City.

Some eastern newspapers paid Heber high tribute. On June 25 the *Omaha Daily Herald* noted that "since Mr. Kimball had been one of the principal and leading men of the Mormon faith, nearly since its organization, an extended notice may not be without interest to the general reader," and then printed a biographical sketch. It observed that Heber "was probably the most popular man in the community with Jews, Gentiles and Mormons" and that "his death is probably the greatest affliction to the people of Utah since the death of their first Prophet, Joseph Smith."

On the same day the *New York Times* commented, "The Mormons, by the death of Heber Kimball, have lost their most prominent man next to Brigham Young. He illustrated in himself all the more striking peculiarities of the Mormon leaders—their energy and astuteness, their self-sacrifice and selfishness [selflessness?], their devotion to the Church and their power over its devotees . . . in every way he was fitted, and fitted himself, for his destined position as Young's successor."

As the *New York Times* suggests, Heber's life did demonstrate fully the weaknesses and strengths, if not of the faith, then of the flock. His life illustrates an authoritarianism, paternalism, lack of sophistication and professionalism, and the subordinate role of meditation and contemplation seen often in Mormon life. But he was a larger-than-life Mormon with a deep personal testimony of and commitment to the Restoration, an example of self-sacrificing devotion to building the Kingdom and promulgating the message. He was the archetypical missionary and polygamist. He represented integrity, faithfulness, simplicity, fearlessness, and dynamism at its best. Without strong pioneering leaders like Heber, a despised faith and people would not have been able to make the Mormon Kingdom flower in the wilderness.

NOTES

1. H. C. Kimball to David, Charles, and Brigham Kimball, Nov. 20, 1864, H. C. Kimball Papers, Church Archives.

2. Andrew Love Neff, *History of Utah: 1847–1869*, ed. Leland Hargrave Creer (Salt Lake City: Deseret News Press, 1940), 865.

3. H. C. Kimball to David, Charles, and Brigham Kimball, Jan. 28, 1866, H. C. Kimball Papers, Church Archives.

4. Historian's Office Journal, Jan. 2, 1860, Church Archives.

5. Wilford Woodruff Journal, Feb. 23, 1859, Church Archives.

6. Brigham Young Papers, Council Minutes, Nov. 16, 1846, Church Archives.

7. Historian's Office Journal, Dec. 20, 1854, Church Archives.

8. Stenhouse, *Tell It All*, 388.

9. Wilford Woodruff Journal, Oct. 3, 1856, Church Archives.

10. *Journal of Discourses*, vol. 8 (June 3, 1860), 276.

11. Wilford Woodruff, Historian's Private Journal, Mar. 14, 1860, Church Archives.

12. Manuscript History of Brigham Young, Apr. 24, 1864. Church Archives.

13. Stenhouse, *The Rocky Mountain Saints*, 663.

14. Solomon F. Kimball, "Sacred History," typescript, 2, Church Archives.

15. Private Memorandum Book, Jan. 12, 1865, H. C. Kimball Papers, Church Archives.

16. Joseph Fielding Smith, *Life of Joseph F. Smith* (Salt Lake City: Deseret News Press, 1938), 227.

17. Solomon F. Kimball, "Sacred History," typescript, 2, Church Archives.

18. David Kimball to Vilate Kimball, June 15, 1864. Original in possession of Spencer W. Kimball. Used by permission.

19. Historian's Office Journal, Oct. 22, 1867, Church Archives. I wish to thank Maureen U. Beecher for drawing this to my attention. There is a family story about Vilate's death which refers to evil spirits, a typical explanation at that time for mental disorders:

"When she first fell sick, on going into her room to administer to her, he [Heber] saw, standing at the head of her bed, an evil spirit, a female. Kneeling down he prayed, and then rebuked the apparition in the name of Jesus. It disappeared, but soon returned with a host of fallen beings.

"He then called in several other Elders, and unitedly they rebuked the evil spirits, when they departed, and he saw them no more at that time.

"Thus, he struggled on, hoping and praying to the end that she might be spared. Sometimes, in his yearning for the continuance of their companionship here a while longer, it seemed as though he would prevail with the Lord. But the last hope of this at length faded, the end came and he bowed in resignation to the inevitable." O. F. Whitney, *Life of Heber C. Kimball*, 472–73.

20. *Journal of Discourses*, vol. 12 (Apr. 29, 1868), 188–89.

21. A search in the Utah County Courthouse has failed to reveal exactly where the house stood. There is some evidence, however, for placing it near the northeast corner of the intersection of University Avenue and First North Street.

Officially Heber was in Provo to organize the School of the Prophets, sort of an adult education program.

22. O. F. Whitney, *Life of Heber C. Kimball*, 448.

23. There was a brief mention of this sermon in the *Deseret News* of June 10, 1868. "President H. C. Kimball spoke at some length on the power and order of the Priesthood, instructing the congregation upon various things connected therewith. He pointed out the blessings flowing from obedience to the authority which the Lord has conferred upon His servants on the earth; and the evil results which follow disobedience and rebellion; for the Lord governs and rules in all worlds, and we cannot, if we would, get to any place where His power is not." This sounds like the old Heber preaching. Evidently he had recovered from whatever was bothering him in Bountiful, or perhaps he felt death near and wanted once more to reiterate his standard message of obedience.

24. "Statement of Mrs. L. W. Kimball," n.d., typescript, p. 7, Lucy Walker Kimball Papers, Church Archives.

25. Following a stroke in 1979, Heber's grandson Spencer W. Kimball, the eighty-four-year-old President of the Mormon Church, subsequently underwent surgery twice to drain a subdural hematoma.

26. *Deseret News*, June 24, 1868.

27. *Ibid.*

28. In this graveyard thirty-two Kimballs, thirteen Whitneys, and eleven friends were eventually buried: a total of fifty-six. Of Heber's forty-three wives, seven were buried here: Vilate, Sarah Peak, Laura Pitkin, Sarah Ann Whitney, Ann Gheen, Theresa Morley, and Ellen Sanders. Two Indian women, Kate and Mobie Vance, were also interred here. Since that time many individuals have been re-buried elsewhere.

Epilogue

After Heber's death his family broke up and scattered. "None of his sons had trades," his first biographer wrote. "Realizing that city life was no longer their lot, they resolved to separate . . . but few remaining in the city of their birth, and, at the expiration of fifteen years, many had become almost strangers to each other." [1] A son recalled, "When I was fifteen years old, our father passed away, and we were left, as many children are left, to wander and fight our battles as best we could." [2]

William remained at his ranch at Parley's Park, south and east of Salt Lake City; Abraham was in southern Utah; Solomon went to Arizona; and eleven sons, including Jonathan Golden, Elias, Isaac, and David Patton, went to the Bear Lake country on the Utah-Idaho border; others went to California. Among the few who remained in Salt Lake City, Heber Parley occupied the big house on North Main Street. Heber C. Kimball's younger children remained with their mothers.

It would appear that most of Heber's thirteen inheriting wives remained in Salt Lake City, living in the big house and others throughout the city. Various Salt Lake City directories list them into the early years of the twentieth century.

In 1887 the Kimball family began to reunite. One of their number, Solomon, returning to Salt Lake City from Arizona in 1886, was dismayed with the lack of family unity and the "disgraceful" condition of the family cemetery, where his father and fifty-five other members of the family were interred. Solomon called a family meeting at the old cemetery on the Kimball block and several decisions were made: to organize a Family Association, to do genealogy work, to fence and landscape the cemetery and erect thereon a suitable monument, and to appoint a Committee on Reunion to plan a family gathering in Salt Lake City for June 14, 1887, the eighty-sixth anniversary of Heber's birth.

About 300 attended that reunion, including nineteen sons, six daugh-

ters, and several widows. Buoyed up with their success, the family organized, appointed a five-man Committee on Publication, which set aside
several thousand dollars of undivided estate property for the cemetery
project, and engaged a grandson, Orson F. Whitney, a son of Helen, to
prepare Heber's biography, which was published the following year. This
family organization still has annual reunions, at which strawberry short-
cake, "grandfather's favorite dessert," is invariably served.

NOTES

1. O. F. Whitney, *Life of Heber C. Kimball*, xi–xii.
2. Richards, *J. Golden Kimball*, 275.

APPENDIXES

APPENDIX A. THE WIVES AND CHILDREN OF
HEBER C. KIMBALL

The standard source regarding the number and names of Kimball's wives and children is Orson F. Whitney, *The Life of Heber C. Kimball* (Salt Lake City: The Kimball Family, 1888), pp. 430–36. Whitney, a grandson of Heber, made his compilation when many of Heber's wives and children were still alive and it therefore should be accurate and complete. He lists forty-five wives and sixty-five children. He does seem to have made two mistakes: he listed Sarah Buckwalter and Sarah Schuler as two individuals, which they were not, and he counted Martha McBride and Martha Knight as two, which they were not. Sarah's first husband was John Buckwalter. Her full name should be Sarah Schuler Buckwalter Kimball. Martha's first husband was Vinson Knight and her second was Joseph Smith. Her full name should be Martha McBride Knight Smith Kimball. Kimball, therefore, had or was sealed to forty-three wives, not forty-five. It should also be remembered that many of these "wives" were not connubial; they were "wards" whom Heber agreed to support and protect. He had children by seventeen of his wives.

Kimball married between 1822 and 1857 and sired children (including two sets of twins) between 1823 and 1868. He had forty-five sons (sixteen named Heber) and twenty daughters. He married five sets of sisters. (Some Mormons hoped sororal polygamy would lead to greater domestic harmony.) Fourteen of his wives had been married previously. At the time of marriage, nine of his wives were in their teens, seventeen in their twenties, five in their thirties, nine in their forties, and three in their fifties. Sixteen wives separated from him during his lifetime for various reasons, but none of his widows remarried after his death. Forty-one children and at least twenty-one wives survived him. His wives were generally long-lived—thirty lived to be over sixty, fifteen over seventy, seven over eighty, and one lived to be ninety-two. The last survivor among his children, Rosalia, died in 1950. This listing is as complete and accurate as a study of temple, endowment house, patriarchal blessing, family genealogical, and cemetery records—as well as obituaries, memoirs, journals, autobiographies, and biographies—can make it. Since many variant dates, places, and spellings are found in the sources, however, the vital statistics of Heber's family may never be known with complete accuracy.

1. Hulda BARNES, born Oct. 1, 1806, New Ashford, Berkshire County, Massachusetts, parents unknown, died Sept. 2, 1898, Holden, Utah. Married and sealed to HCK Feb. 3, 1846. No children. Apparently came to Utah in 1853.

2. Abigail BUCHANAN, born Jan. 9, 1802, Waltham, Middlesex County, Massachusetts, parents and date and place of death unknown. Married and sealed to HCK Feb. 7, 1846. No children.

3. Charlotte CHASE, born May 11, 1825, Bristol, Addison County, Vermont, daughter of Ezra and Tirzah Wells Chase, died Dec. 15, 1904, Lewisville, Idaho. Married HCK Oct. 10, 1844, sealed to HCK Feb. 7, 1846. No children by HCK. Separated from HCK in 1849, married Thaddeus C. Hix (or Hicks) in California, Dec. 13, 1850, by whom she had six children. After his death in 1868 married William W. Dixson of Harrisville, Utah, in 1869, whom she divorced in 1876 and then married Dr. Tyrus Hurd of Ogden, Utah.

4. Clarissa CUTLER, born Dec. 23, 1824, Silver Creek, Chautauqua County, New York, daughter of Alpheus and Lois Lathrop Cutler, died 1852 in Kansas Territory, on the Grasshopper River near present-day Thompsonville, Jefferson County, Kansas. Married HCK Feb. 29, 1845, sealed to HCK Feb. 2, 1846. One child by HCK: Abraham Alonzo Kimball, Apr. 16, 1846–Sept. 25, 1889. Separated from HCK in 1848, married Calvin Fletcher in 1849 and had one daughter, Mary Alzina Fletcher, born Mar. 12, 1850, Silver Creek, Mills County, Iowa, died Feb. 14, 1859, Manti, Iowa. Abraham entered polygamy taking three wives, Mary Eliza Hatton Wilcox, Lucy Adell Brown, and Laura Moody. He had fourteen children by the first two. (The author is a descendant of this wife.)

5. Emily Trask CUTLER, born Feb. 23, 1828, Hanover, Chautauqua County, New York, daughter of Alpheus and Lois Lathrop Cutler, died 1852 in Kansas Territory, on the Grasshopper River near present-day Thompsonville, Jefferson County, Kansas. Married HCK during Dec., 1845, sealed to HCK Feb. 2, 1846. One child by HCK: Isaac Kimball, Oct. 13, 1846–June 24, 1914. Separated from HCK in 1848, married Franklin Pratt in 1849, and had one daughter, Emily Miranda Pratt, born Mar. 15, 1852, on the Grasshopper River in present-day Jefferson County, Kansas.

6. Elizabeth DOTY (Cravath, Murray, Brown), born Apr. 29, 1808, Fairfield, Herkimer County, New York, daughter of Ira and Betsy Murray Doty, died Jan. 21, 1889, Kamas, Utah. Married HCK for time only Apr. 11, 1856. No children by HCK. She bore her first husband, Austin Cravath, four children. He died in 1844 and she was sealed to him for eternity the same day she married HCK for time. In 1846 she married William Murray. In 1848, after his death, she married Alfred Brown and bore him one son, who died the same year. She is usually referred to as Elizabeth Cravath in the sources.

7. Mary DULL (Duell), born Nov. 23, 1807, Quinard Township, Montgomery County, Pennsylvania, daughter of Christian and Elizabeth Dull (Duell), date and place of death unknown. Sealed to HCK May 21, 1848. No children.

8. Mary FIELDING (Smith), born July 21, 1801, Honidon, Bedfordshire, England, daughter of John and Rachel Ibbotson Fielding, died Sept. 21, 1852, Salt

Lake City. Married HCK Sept. 14, 1844, sealed in the Nauvoo temple for time to HCK Jan. 15, 1846. No children by HCK. Married her first husband, Hyrum Smith, brother of Joseph Smith, Dec. 24, 1837, and bore two children. Also mothered the four surviving children of the six Hyrum had by his first wife. Hyrum was assassinated with his brother June 27, 1844, at Carthage, Illinois. Her son Joseph F. Smith became the sixth President of the Mormon Church; her grandson Joseph Fielding Smith became the tenth. HCK preached her funeral sermon, *Journal of Discourses*, vol. 8, (Sept. 23, 1852), 246–47.

9. Amanda Trimble GHEEN, born Jan. 18, 1830, East Whiteland, Chester County, Pennsylvania, daughter of William Atkins and Esther Ann Pierce Gheen, died Nov. 4, 1904, Salt Lake City. Married HCK during Dec., 1845, sealed to HCK Feb. 2, 1846. Children by HCK: William Gheen, Mar. 3, 1851–Mar. 24, 1924; Albert Heber, Sept. 13, 1854–Mar. 2, 1944; Jeremiah Heber, Aug. 15, 1857–May 25, 1887; and Moroni Heber, May 23, 1861–May 23, 1887.

10. Ann Alice GHEEN, born Dec. 20, 1827, West Whiteland, Chester County, Pennsylvania, daughter of William Atkins and Esther Ann Pierce Gheen, died Oct. 12, 1879, Salt Lake City. Married HCK Sept. 10, 1844, sealed to HCK Jan. 7, 1846. Children by HCK: Samuel Heber, Dec. 9, 1851–Apr. 18, 1943; Daniel Heber, Feb. 8, 1856–Apr. 26, 1936; Andrew (a twin), Sept. 6, 1858–Aug. 31, 1924; Alice Ann (a twin), Sept. 6, 1858–Dec. 19, 1946; and Sarah Gheen, May 31, 1861–Feb. 8, 1913. The daughter Alice Ann Kimball divorced her first husband, David Patten Rich, in 1882. She later became the fifth wife of Joseph F. Smith, President of the Mormon Church, on Dec. 6, 1883, and bore him four children. Her twin brother, Andrew, is the father of Spencer W. Kimball, twelfth President of the Church of Jesus Christ of Latter-day Saints.

11. Christeen GOLDEN, born Sept. 20, 1822, Mercer County, New Jersey, daughter of Jonathan and Mary Golden, died Jan. 30, 1896, Utah. Married and sealed to HCK Feb. 3, 1846. Children by HCK: Cornelia Christeen, June 7, 1850–Dec. 23, 1853; Jonathan Golden, June 9, 1853–Sept. 2, 1938; Elias Smith, May 30, 1857–June 13, 1934; and Mary Margaret, Apr. 30, 1861–Sept. 28, 1937. Jonathan Golden is the best known of all of HCK's children; he later became senior president of the First Council of Seventy. Elias became the first Mormon chaplain in the U.S. Army; his wife, Luella Whitney, was the last of HCK's daughters-in-law to die.

12. Sophronia Melinda HARMON, born Apr. 5, 1824, Conneaut, Erie County, Pennsylvania, daughter of Jess Perse and Anna Barnes Harmon, died Jan. 26, 1847, Winter Quarters. Married and sealed to HCK Feb. 3, 1846. No children.

13. Mary Ellen HARRIS, born Oct. 5, 1818, Charleston, Montgomery County, New York, daughter of Mathias and Sarah Harris Able, died Oct. 28, 1902, Salt Lake City. Married HCK Oct. 1, 1844, sealed to HCK Jan. 26, 1846. One child by HCK: Peter Kimball, Dec. 19, 1855–Sept. 27, 1860. She is sometimes called Mary

Ellen Able. Apparently her father was named Harris. Mathias Able may have been her stepfather.

14. Elizabeth HEREFORD, born July, 1789, Asenor, Herefordshire, England, parents and date and place of death unknown. Sealed to HCK Feb. 7, 1846. No children by HCK. Apparently separated from HCK in 1850.

15. Mary HOUSTON, born Sept. 11, 1818, Jackson, Syark County, Ohio, daughter of James and Mary Ettlemann Houston, died Dec. 24, 1896, Salt Lake City. Sealed for time to HCK Feb. 3, 1846. No children by HCK. Also sealed for eternity to Joseph Smith Feb. 3, 1846.

16. Presendia Lathrop HUNTINGTON (Buell, Smith), born Sept. 7, 1810, Watertown, Jefferson County, New York, daughter of William and Zina Baker Huntington, died Feb. 1, 1892, Salt Lake City. Married and sealed for time to HCK Feb. 4, 1846. Children by HCK: Presendia Celestia, Jan. 9, 1849–May 9, 1850 (drowned); and Joseph Smith, Dec. 22, 1851–Mar. 29, 1836. She married Norman Buell about 1827 and bore him seven children. He left the church in 1839 and she married Joseph Smith Dec. 11, 1841, and was sealed to him for eternity the same day she married HCK for time. She was a sister of Brigham Young's wife, Zina Huntington, and served as a midwife in the Kimball family.

17. Sarah LAWRENCE (Smith), born May 13, 1826, Pickering Township, Ontario County, Canada, daughter of Edward and Margaret Lawrence, died in California, date unknown. Married HCK Oct. 12, 1844, sealed to HCK for time Jan. 26, 1846. No children by HCK. She married Joseph Smith c. May 11, 1843. She apparently did not go west until 1850. Of the sixteen women who left HCK, she is the only one known to have sought a formal divorce, which was granted June 18, 1851. She then moved to California. HCK may have become acquainted with her when she did sewing for his family.

18. Martha MCBRIDE (Knight, Smith), born Mar. 17, 1805, Chester, Washington County, New York, daughter of Daniel and Abigail Mead McBride, died Nov. 20, 1891, Ogden, Utah. Married HCK Oct. 12, 1844, sealed for time to HCK Jan. 26, 1846. She bore HCK one son who died in infancy. She married Vinson Knight July 26, 1826, and bore him six children. Knight became the presiding bishop of the church until he died July 21, 1842, in Nauvoo. Later that year she married Joseph Smith.

19. Margaret MCMINN, born Apr. 7, 1829, Philadelphia, Pennsylvania, daughter of Robert and Mary Dull McMinn, date and place of death unknown. She may have married HCK Feb., 1846. Nothing further is known about her except that during the summer of 1844 HCK roomed with a "Sister McMinn and daughter" in Philadelphia and "took a ride with Sister McMinn's daughter."

20. Dorothy MOON, born Feb. 9, 1804, Eccleston, Lancashire, England, daughter of Matthias and Alice Plumb Moon, died in Utah probably in the 1870s.

Married and sealed to HCK Mar. 14, 1856, Salt Lake City. No children by HCK. One of HCK's five Utah wives. Also one of HCK's English converts, immigrating to Nauvoo in the 1840s.

21. Hannah MOON, born May 29, 1802, Eccleston, Lancashire, England, daughter of Matthias and Alice Plumb Moon, died Dec. 4, 1877, buried in Farmington, Utah. Married and sealed to HCK Mar. 14, 1856, Salt Lake City. No children by HCK. Sister of Dorothy Moon. One of HCK's five Utah wives. Also one of HCK's English converts, immigrating to Nauvoo in the 1840s.

22. Theresa Arathusa MORLEY, born July 18, 1826, Kirtland, Geauga County, Ohio, daughter of Isaac and Lucy Gunn Morley, died Oct. 7, 1855, Salt Lake City. Married and sealed to HCK Feb. 3, 1846. No children.

23. Vilate MURRAY, born June 1, 1806, Florida, Montgomery County, New York, daughter of Roswell and Susannah Fitch Murray, died Oct. 22, 1867, Salt Lake City. Married HCK Nov. 22, 1822, sealed to HCK Jan. 7, 1846. Children by HCK: Judith Marvin, July 29, 1823–May 20, 1824; William Henry, Apr. 10, 1826–Dec. 29, 1907; Helen Mar, Aug. 22, 1828–Nov. 15, 1896; Roswell Heber, June 10, 1831–June 15, 1831; Heber Parley, Jan. 1, 1835–Feb. 8, 1885; David Patton, Aug. 23, 1839–Mar. 28, 1883; Charles Spaulding, June 2, 1843–July, 1897; Brigham Willard, Jan. 29, 1845–July 23, 1867; Solomon Farnham, Feb. 2, 1847–Feb. 7, 1920; and Murray Gould, Jan. 20, 1850–June 29, 1852. Vilate was Heber's first wife. William, one of only three sons of Kimball to enter polygamy, had five wives and twenty-six children. William's wives were Mary Marion Davenport, Melissa Burton Coray, Martha Jane Vance, Lucy Amelia Pack, and Naomi Eliza Redden. David Patton married Caroline M. Williams and later Juliette Merrill. Helen Mar was one of the two daughters of Kimball to enter polygamy. She was first the wife of Joseph Smith and later of Horace K. Whitney. Horace also married Lucy Amelia Bloxum and Mary Cravath. Through her writings, Helen became one of the outstanding female defenders of plurality. Heber Parley had a daughter, Winifred, who first married a Mr. Shaughnessy (and later Richard Hudnut of cosmetics fame). Her daughter, Winifred Shaughnessy, took the stage name of Natacha Rambova and was the second wife of Rudolph Valentino. One of Helen's sons committed suicide in 1886, the only known case in the Kimball family.

24. Sarah PEAK (Noon), born May 3, 1811, Old Staunton, Strafordshire, England, parents unknown, died Dec. 3, 1873, Salt Lake City. Married HCK during 1842, sealed to HCK Jan. 15, 1846. Children by HCK: Adelbert, 1842/43–1843; Henry, c. 1844–died before 1868; Sarah Helen, July 1, 1845–Dec. 1, 1860; and Heber, 1849–50. She first married William S. Noon in England and had two daughters, Harriet Frances (born Dec. 5, 1830) and Elizabeth (born Apr. 19, 1831). Noon deserted her in Nauvoo and returned to England. She was HCK's first plural wife and he assumed responsibility for her two daughters. In a letter dated

Aug. 1, 1854, she reveals how concerned she was over what her family in England thought about her polygamous marriage. Edward Martin Correspondence, Church Archives.

25. Ruth L. PIERCE (Cazier), born Feb. 11, 1818, Oswegotchie, St. Lawrence County, New York, daughter of Rev. Isaac and Elizabeth Taylor Pierce, date and place of death unknown except that it was after 1861. Married and sealed to HCK Feb. 3, 1846. No children by HCK. She first married Monroe Cazier Apr. 29, 1838, and bore him six children. After his death she married HCK, but separated from him early. There is some evidence that she came to Utah in 1852. On Aug. 14, 1861, she married John Harrington.

26. Abigail PITKIN, born July 17, 1797, Hartford, Windsor County, New York, daughter of Paul and Abigail Lathrop Pitkin, died May 15, 1847, Winter Quarters. Married and sealed to HCK Jan. 7, 1846. No children by HCK. She was one of the two spinsters with whom HCK hoped to enter polygamy in an effort to spare Vilate's feelings. Abigail was a friend of Vilate.

27. Laura PITKIN, born Sept. 10, 1790, Summers, Tollane County, Connecticut, daughter of Paul and Abigail Lathrop Pitkin, died Nov. 16, 1866, Salt Lake City. Married and sealed to HCK Feb. 3, 1846. No children by HCK. She was a friend of Vilate and one of the two spinsters with whom HCK hoped to enter polygamy in an effort to spare Vilate's feelings. She often served as a midwife in the Kimball family.

28. Ruth Amelia REESE, born May 10, 1817, Beaver, Crawford County, Pennsylvania, daughter of John and Susannah Owen Reese, died Nov. 26, 1902, Salt Lake City. Married and sealed to HCK Feb. 3, 1846. Children by HCK: Susanna R., July 10, 1851, died same day; Jacob Reese, Apr. 15, 1853–May 30, 1875; and Enoch Heber, Sept. 29, 1855–Aug. 20, 1877.

29. Ellen SANDERS (née Aagaat Ysteinsdatter Bakka), born Apr. 11, 1823, Atraa, Telemark, Norway, daughter of Ystein Sondresen and Aase Olsdatter Rommerasen Bakka, died Nov. 22, 1871, Salt Lake City. Married HCK Nov. 5, 1844, sealed to HCK Jan. 7, 1846. Children by HCK: Samuel Chase, Feb. 13, 1848–July, 1848; Joseph Smith (twin), June 2, 1850–Nov. 29, 1864; Augusta (twin), June 2, 1850–Oct. 5, 1861; Rosalia, Nov. 25, 1853–Feb. 22, 1950; and Jedediah Heber, Mar. 10, 1855–June 24, 1927. She was one of the three women of the 1847 first Pioneer company. Her twins were the first set in the Kimball family. Rosalia was the last of HCK's sixty-five children to die.

30. Harriet SANDERS (née Helga Ysteinsdatter Bakka), born Dec. 7, 1824, Atraa, Telemark, Norway, daughter of Ystein Sondresen and Aase Olsdatter Rommerasen Bakka, died Sept. 5, 1896, Meadowville, Rich County, Utah. Married and sealed to HCK Jan. 26, 1846. Children by HCK: Harriet, May 8, 1852, died same day; Hyrum Heber, July 6, 1855–June 4, 1943; and Eugene, Jan. 15, 1863–Aug.

14, 1932. She was a sister of Ellen and at one time worked in the HCK home to help Vilate with her four small sons.

31. Sarah SCHULER (Buckwalter), born May 15, 1801, Chester County, Pennsylvania, daughter of William and Sarah Crull Schuler, died Jan 25, 1879, Salt Lake City. Married HCK for time Feb. 7, 1846. No children by HCK. She married her first husband, John Buckwalter, Feb. 21, 1828, and bore him eight children. He died Mar. 1, 1841. She did not come west until 1852 and never lived with HCK.

32. Sarah SCOTT, born Oct. 25, 1817, Belfast, Ireland, daughter of Jacob and Sarah Warnock Scott, date and place of death unknown. Married and sealed for time to HCK Feb. 3, 1846. No children by HCK. Also sealed for eternity to Joseph Smith Feb. 3, 1846.

33. Sylvia Porter SESSIONS (Lyon), born July 31, 1818, Newry, Oxford County, Maine, daughter of David and Patty Bartlett Sessions, died Apr. 13, 1882, Bountiful, Utah. Married for time to HCK Jan. 26, 1846. No children by HCK. She married her first husband, Dr. Winsor Palmer Lyon, in 1838 and bore him six children, most of whom died in infancy. While her first husband was living and with his permission, she married Joseph Smith for eternity Jan. 26, 1846, and married HCK for time. She separated from HCK in 1847 and married Ezekiel Clark Jan. 1, 1850. She bore him one child in Iowa City, Iowa. She apparently returned to Kimball in 1854.

34. Mary Ann SHEFFLIN, born Oct. 31, 1815, Speedwell, New Jersey, daughter of Hugh and Margaret Brown Shefflin, died Sept. 26, 1869, Salt Lake City. Married and sealed to HCK Feb. 4, 1846. She bore HCK one child, Mary Ann, dates unknown. She separated from HCK about 1850 and later married Alfred Walton, Nov. 1, 1855, Salt Lake City. The separation must have been amicable for she was buried in the Kimball family cemetery. In reference to this matter Heber wrote a son on Dec. 21, 1854: "Mary Ann Kimball has taken upon her her original name, Mary Ann Shefflin, as she could not endure any longer without having a man to herself, there were no tears on the subject; but the matter took its natural course. This is quite a relief to your father." (Historian's Office Letterpress copybooks, vol. 1, pp. 45–57.)

35. Mary SMITHIES, born Oct. 7, 1837, Barshal Eves, Lancashire, England, daughter of James and Nancy Ann Knowles Smithies, died June 8, 1880, Salt Lake City. Married and sealed to HCK Jan. 25, 1857, Salt Lake City. Children by HCK: Mary Melvina, Aug. 29, 1858–May 8, 1933; James Heber, Apr. 9, 1860–June 2, 1866; Wilford Alfonzo, Oct. 6, 1863–Nov. 15, 1928; Lorenzo Heber, Feb. 6, 1866–July 2, 1929; and Abbie Sarah, Jan. 15, 1868–Feb. 23, 1943. She was the first child born to Mormon parents in England. Heber blessed her as an infant and promised her she would be a mother in Zion. She was his last wife. Lorenzo Heber was HCK's last son and Abbie Sarah his last child.

36. Sarah STILES, born Mar. 5, 1893, Suffield, Hartford County, Connecticut, daughter of Daniel O. and Sarah Buckland Stiles, died about 1899, place unknown. Married and sealed for time to HCK Feb. 3, 1846. No children by HCK. She may have been sealed for eternity to Joseph Smith Jan. 26, 1846. She may also have later married Alanson Barney.

37. Rebecca SWAIN (Williams), born Aug. 3, 1798, Loyalsack, Lycoming County, Pennsylvania, daughter of Isaac and Elizabeth Hall Swain, died Sept. 25, 1861, Cache Valley, Utah. Married and sealed for time to HCK Feb. 7, 1846. No children by HCK. She married her first husband, Frederick Granger Williams, one-time counselor to Joseph Smith, Dec. 25, 1815, and bore him four children. He died Oct. 25, 1842. She was sealed to him for eternity Feb. 7, 1846.

38. Frances Jessie SWAN, born June 20, 1822, Edinburgh, Scotland, daughter of Douglas and Margaret Craig Swan, date and place of death unknown. Married HCK Sept. 30, 1844, sealed to HCK Feb., 1846. One child by HCK: Margaret Jane, Apr. 9, 1846–Aug. 10, 1846. In 1851 she separated from HCK and went to California, where she married a Mr. Clark.

39. Lucy WALKER (Smith), born Apr. 30, 1826, Peacham, Caledonia County, Vermont, daughter of John and Lydia Holmes Walker, died Oct. 1, 1910, Salt Lake City. Married HCK Feb. 8, 1845, sealed for time to HCK Jan. 15, 1846. Children by HCK: Rachel Sylvia, Jan. 28, 1846–Dec. 22, 1847; John Heber, Dec. 12, 1850–Nov. 28, 1918; Willard Heber, Jan. 25, 1853–Dec. 5, 1854; Lydia Holmes, Jan. 18, 1856–Apr. 15, 1928; Ann Spaulding, Mar. 18, 1857–Nov. 27, 1932; Eliza, May 14, 1859–May 18, 1906; Washington Heber, Oct. 22, 1862–after 1863; Joshua Heber, Oct. 22, 1862, died in infancy; and Franklin Heber, Aug. 28, 1864–65. She married her first husband, Joseph Smith, May 1, 1843, and was later sealed to him for eternity.

40. Ruth WELLINGTON, born Mar. 11, 1809, Waltham, Middlesex County, Massachusetts, parents, date, and place of death unknown. Married and sealed to HCK Feb. 7, 1846. No children. She may have been married to HCK in Philadelphia July 23, 1844.

41. Sarah Ann WHITNEY (Smith), born Mar. 22, 1825, Kirtland, Ohio, daughter of Newell Kimball and Elizabeth Ann Smith Whitney, died Sept. 4, 1873, Salt Lake City. Married HCK Mar. 17, 1845, sealed for time to HCK Jan. 12, 1846. Children by HCK: David, Mar. 8, 1846–Aug. 18, 1847; David Orson, Aug. 26, 1848–Apr. 16, 1849; David Heber, Feb. 26, 1850–after 1868; Newel Whitney, May 19, 1852–after 1868; Horace Heber, Sept. 3, 1855–after 1868; Sarah Maria, 1858–Aug., 1902; and Joshua Heber, Feb. 23, 1861–Apr. 6, 1925. She married Joseph Smith July 27, 1842. Most records give only the date Sarah Ann was *sealed* to HCK in the Nauvoo temple, raising the question of the legitimacy of their first child, David. One sensational account of this marriage is H. Michael Marquardt, *The Strange Marriages of Sarah Ann Whitney to Joseph Smith the*

Mormon Prophet, Joseph C. Kingsbury and Heber C. Kimball (Salt Lake City: Modern Microfilm, 1973). What Marquardt failed to find, however, was the record of the March 17, 1845, *marriage* of Heber to Sarah in the Newel K. Whitney 1841–45 Account Book & Diary, Special Collections, Brigham Young University, Provo, Utah. (Newel was father to Sarah Ann). By the time the Nauvoo temple was finished sufficiently for marriage ceremonies Heber had married at least thirteen other wives, and all his marriages were subsequently solemnized (some for time, some for eternity) in the temple during January and February, 1846. The situation with Sarah Ann was by no means unusual. There are other suggestions of a March marriage in Heber's journal on Feb. 6, March 27, April 15, April 19, and May 22, 1845.

42. Adelia Almira WILCOX (Hatton, Brown), born Mar. 29, 1828, Bloomfield, New York, daughter of Eber and Catherine Noramore Wilcox, died Oct. 19, 1896, Kanosh, Utah. Married and sealed to HCK Oct. 9, 1856, Salt Lake City. No children by HCK. She married her first husband, William Hawthorne Hatton, May 15, 1844, and bore him three children. One daughter, Mary Eliza Hatton, married Abraham Alonzo Kimball, one of HCK's sons. After Hatton was killed by Indians Sept. 13, 1853, at Fillmore, Utah, Adelia became a plural wife of Gideon Durphy Wood on May 25, 1854. There was friction with the first Mrs. Wood, so Adelia got her sealing or marriage cancelled Oct. 5, 1856, and went to Salt Lake City, where she eventually married HCK. She was one of the five Utah wives.

43. Nancy Maria WINCHESTER, born Aug. 19, 1828, Black Rock, Erie County, Pennsylvania, daughter of Stephen and Nancy Case Winchester, died Mar. 17, 1876, place unknown. Married HCK Oct. 10, 1844, sealed for time to HCK Feb. 3, 1846. No children by HCK. Also sealed for eternity to Joseph Smith Feb. 3, 1846. She separated from HCK in 1865 and married Amos George Arnold Oct. 12, 1865. She bore him one child.

It is possible that Heber was sealed to other women. More than one woman requested that this be done. In addition to the above-mentioned account of Adelia Wilcox, there is evidence that a Jane Benson had made a similar application. Nevertheless, she married James Bonsall. Kimball "told him to take good care of her for him." (Historian's Office Journal, May 21, 1856, Church Archives).

Kimball may have had still other wives sealed to him posthumously. While this practice has long since been discontinued, it did exist for a period after 1844. According to the Endowment House Sealing Records, on June 15, 1874, Sarah Boothman, on Oct. 12, 1876, Diadama Hare, and on Oct. 19, 1876, Rebecca Ann Scott were sealed to Heber. In 1882 Heber's son Abraham Alonzo sealed Elizabeth Parkinson to Heber (A. A. Kimball Journal, 234, in author's possession).

Michael Quinn of Brigham Young University has found evidence of still another possible wife of HCK. In an entry in *Endowment House Record, 1851–53*, #65, under date of June 8, 1851, James Goff was sealed to a woman named Lydia,

APPENDIX B. THE ESTATE

For all of Heber Kimball's prudence, and despite his threat to leave all his property to the church, he died intestate. He was survived by thirteen inheriting wives, forty-one inheriting children, at least eight other wives who had not formally separated from him, and an undetermined number of adopted and foster children. Ten of his inheriting wives had children; the other three were entirely dependent on him. The eight other wives appear to have been living with relatives and friends elsewhere, mainly in Utah. (The following information comes from Heber's estate papers in the Utah State Archives and the Utah Historical Society.)

The gross value of his estate was figured at $100,580 (or the equivalent of more than $2,000,000 in 1980), less debts of $15,255, leaving a net of $85,324, or approximately $1,600 per heir.

The estate procedures were very complicated and were not finally completed until 1876. In fact some undistributed property was discovered in 1887, and there was a question about one city lot which came up as late as 1938.

A general inventory of his estate at his death follows:

Personal property	$20,150
in main home	
in homes of other wives	
at Grantsville ranch	
Real estate	72,750
Salt Lake City lots, houses, gristmill,	
carding mill	
San Pete Valley farm and ranch	
Provo house, lot, meadow	
Davis County farm and flour mill	
Richfield farm	
Cache Valley farm	
Grantsville herd ground and house	
Livestock	$5,955
Grantsville	
Salt Lake City	
Accounts receivable	1,725
	$100,580

The first act of the court was to order an inventory of his property. This extremely detailed document reveals much about the life and economics of his family. The listing of personal property in his main home, for example, includes several copies of the Book of Mormon, thirty-one other assorted books, furniture, carpeting, pens, needles, stamps, lamps, belts, bolts, hinges, tools, brooms, lobelia, tea, coffee, and a spitoon, for a total value of $5,052.

The personal property used by his thirteen inheriting wives was retained by them in 1868 and accounted as part of their inheritance.

The distribution of Kimball's property to wives in 1868 and 1875 and to children in 1876 was as follows:

	1868 (retained personal property)	1875	1876	Total
1. Lucy Walker	456	5,850		
2. John H.				
3. Lidia H.			1,355	7,134
4. Ann S.				
5. Eliza				
6. Washington				
7. Ann Gheen	333	5,900		
8. Samuel H.				
9. Andrew			1,172	7,405
10. Daniel H.				
11. Alice A.				
12. Sarah				
13. Sarah Ann Whitney	394	5,300		
14. David H.				
15. Newel W.			1,440	7,134
16. Horace H.				
17. Sarah M.				
18. Joshua W.				
19. Amanda Gheen	355	5,775		
20. William C.				
21. Albert H.			315	6,445
22. Jeremiah H.				
23. Moroni H.				
24. Mary Smithies	297	4,400		
25. Malvina				

26. Wilford			1,697	6,396
27. Lorenzo				
28. Abbie				
29. CHRISTEEN GOLDEN	806	2,825		
30. Jonathan G.				
31. Elias S.			661	4,292
32. Mary M.				
33. HARRIET SANDERS	310	2,925		
34. Hiram H.				
35. Eugene			484	3,720
36. RUTH REESE	364	3,000		
37. Jacob R.				
38. Enoch H.			264	3,628
39. PRESENDIA HUNTINGTON	448	825		
40. Joseph			32	1,305
(plus home occupied by his mother)				
41. ELLEN SANDERS	264	1,925		1,189
42. Jedediah H.				
43. MARY HOUSTON	121	200	(plus home)	321
44. SARAH PEAK	309	200		509
45. MARY ELLEN HARRIS	147	200		347
46. Heber P. Kimball (Vilate)*		2,090		2,090
47. Helen M. Whitney (Vilate)		1,500	470	1,970
48. David P. Kimball (Vilate)		1,500	225	1,725
49. William H. Kimball (Vilate)		1,500	178	1,678
50. Rosalia Edwards (Ellen Sanders)		900	127	1,027
51. Abraham A. Kimball (Clarissa Cutler)		550	395	945
52. Solomon F. Kimball (Vilate)		700	232	932
53. Isaac A. Kimball (Emily Cutler)		600	190	790
54. Charles S. Kimball (Vilate)		300	237	537
55. Daniel Davis (adopted)		500		500

*Children 46 through 54 were of age. The names of their mothers are given in parentheses. Daniel Davis was the sole adopted child to inherit. It is clear from Davis' diary that he was very close to Heber and was treated like a member of the family.

At the final distribution in 1876 the gross breakdown was:

Total value of the estate	$100,580
Less estate debts	15,255
Distributed to wives	50,352
Distributed to children	12,194
Living expenses 1868–75	22,799
Balance	00

From these figures it appears that his ten inheriting wives and their thirty-two minor children were treated equally, similarly the three childless wives. Apparently family responsibility and the amount of property previously received from Kimball determined the distribution to his ten married children.

Heber C. Kimball's posterity includes scores of missionaries, bishops, stake and mission presidents, and individuals as varied as great-granddaughter Natacha Rambova (née Winifred Shaughnessy), the second wife of Rudolph Valentino; a son, Jonathan Golden Kimball, who held a high church position and is regarded as the Mormon Will Rogers; a daughter, Alice, who became a plural wife of Joseph F. Smith, the sixth President of the church (1901–18) and Heber's foster son; and a grandson, Spencer W. Kimball, who became the twelfth President of the Church of Jesus Christ of Latter-day Saints in 1973.

APPENDIX C. HEBER C. KIMBALL DOCUMENTS

A Typical Page from H. C. Kimball's Journal, June 4, 1837, Kirtland, Ohio.

   This is a portion of the first page of his first extant journal and describes his call to England. (Courtesy Historical Department, Church of Jesus Christ of Latter-Day Saints.)

A Page from H. C. Kimball's First Extant Letter to Vilate, June 27, 1837, New York City. (H. C. Kimball Papers, Church Archives.)

This letter was written the day before he sailed for England.

New York June 27 1837

My Dear Wife

Having this opetunity to comunicating a few words to you I improve it, on
tuesday the thirteenth I toock the parting hand with you in whom I Love So dear,
we got to buffalow the next morning we stade till most night wating for brother
talor [Taylor] he did not come we twock a line boat and went on our journy got to
rochester Elder Hide twock packet boat so as to guit to new york at the time
pointed brother richards and my self Stade in Rochester 16 hours I se[e] Miss
Mack gloplin [?] and Sent word to [word unclear] She was thare few days before
they was all well, I rote a leter and put in the ofice at lobby not nowing that I
should see annyone in Rochester, they sed that they should gow thare in about a
weack, from thare we went to utica, thare we twock the Rale Rode to Albany then
I went to Richford with brother Richards to see his friends we got thare in the
morning; and left the next morning; we left thare and go to New York the 21. In
the Afternoon at [word missing] oclock and found our brethren all thare, some of
the inglish brethren, the brethren ware hiring thare bord, I hireed mine one day it
cost one dollar a day we thought best to hire a room; and bord our selves we obtained a small room of Eliger fordham in a store house he let us have it for six cents
a weack, so that we could have our own hird hous, so that the law would protect
us, we take our blackets and sleep on the flower I have not slep in a bed but fore
nights sens I left home, I was taking with a relax when I got to Albany and held me
three or fore days; and run me down qute weack, it was in changing my food I had
[word missing] four warm meals since I left Kirtland and dont Expect to till we
quit to Europe=the first day that we got to keeping hous thare was a prest come
and pitched [preached] fowl abus [abuse ?] I went with brother fordham to see a
widdow that was believing and thare was a baptist prest come to see me and we
converssed to gether about tow or three hours it was the means convinsing one
that set by for he denide the word so we warn them of the truth, thare is three
wimmen that are waiting to Recieve the truth one of them wants to gow to Zion,
and may [the] lord heft [help] him to gow

An Example of H. C. Kimball's Eloquence, from a letter to his brother Solomon,
January 2, 1857. (H. C. Kimball Papers, Church Archives.)

I am happy my family are happy. They do not murmer nor complain, but
praise and thank the Lord our God for his goodness to us that we are away here in
the tops of the mountains a thousand miles from the Christian nations, and I
thank God for this, and that and everything that God Almighty has seen fit in the
last days to bring about.

You may think strange of my making these remarks, it is these very Christians
that have driven me from Ohio, & Missouri & Illinois and from the Iowa Territory, and robbed me of my goods and of my homes, and habitations, and perse-

cuted me in old Mendon, and every other place where I have ever been. These are the kind of Christians that I rejoice before God that I am delivered from them. They are the ones that killed Joseph Smith, and Hyrum, and David Patten, and hundreds of others, and these Christian armies were led by Methodist and Baptist Priests, and Presbyterian Priests, and my house that I built and lived in and lands are still standing there in Kirtland, Ohio. I have one of the best houses in the city of Nauvoo standing there now that belongs to me with several other places: my habitation that I erected in Mo. I have lands there, my houses were burned with my goods within them. In Nauvoo when I left there, I left my looking glasses hanging up, my bureaus my bedsteads, tables, stand, stoves and almost everything else and I [was] driven out in the month of Feb., to take my shelter in the wilderness with defenseless women and children.

This done by a Christian people. Is that nation satisfied with their hellish designs upon us, no! no! There are men right in our midst every day declaring that if they can't have the privilege of seducing our daughters they will bring the U.S. troops on us. I can say in the name of Israel's God that that Christian nation that has served me and my brethren and driven us from State to State, and from town to town, and from synagogue to synagogue, and from Territory to Territory, and from the Territory into the tops of the mountains in to an inland country 1,000 miles from everybody, that this same thing that they have heaped upon me and upon my brethren, I say in the name of Israel's God, and by that virtue that God Almighty has placed in me, that Christian nation in which you dwell shall receive the same back on to their heads, which they have heaped on to us, and it shall be doubled on to them, for the nation of the U.S. have shed innocent blood, and shed the blood of prophets and the rest of that nation has consented to it, and he that consents to an evil on his fellow is the same as the administrator, and that is according to the law of the land, and this has all been done by those that you consider to be an enlightened Christian nation, for to exceed the light that existed in the days of Jesus and the Apostles, for you call this an enlightened age and full of new invention, true as to that, but have turned their ears to Fables, and are running after Baal, and lifted up in the pride of their hearts, and heaped to themselves teachers having itching ears, for the paltry sum of a little gold or silver, and when they can get a little more gold or silver in a Railroad station of or a Canal, they will leave their sanctum sanctorums for the paltry sum of a little———gold that will soon corrode and vanish away. Jesus says, lay up your treasures in heaven where moth nor rust can't corrupt and thieves break through and steal.

BIBLIOGRAPHIC NOTE

This work is based on all the pertinent primary and secondary sources I could locate over a period of nine years' research. All the major sources—all of Kimball's personal papers and speeches and the hundreds of other Kimball family papers in church and non-church collections, other church, county, state, national, Masonic, British, and private archival materials, newspapers, magazines, journals (including all Mormon publications printed during Kimball's lifetime), theses, dissertations, pamphlets, monographs, histories, travel accounts, newsletters, and other Mormon and non-Mormon materials have been cited in the notes. Many official and little used church minute books and office journals were also consulted. Especially valuable is R. B. Thompson, ed., *Journal of Heber C. Kimball* (Nauvoo, Ill.: Robinson and Smith, 1840) and *President Heber C. Kimball's Journal . . .* (Salt Lake City: Juvenile Instructor Office, 1882), and a five-part "Synopsis of the History of Heber C. Kimball," *Deseret News*, Mar. 31–Apr. 28, 1858.

Most of the recent research by professional historians of the Mormon History Association which has been presented at their past fifteen annual meetings and published in such journals as the *Journal of Mormon History, Brigham Young University Studies, Dialogue, Sunstone, The Ensign*, and the *Utah Historical Quarterly*, and in many monographs has been studied and cited in the notes. All pertinent non-Mormon and "anti-Mormon" works have also been used and cited.

The main printed secondary sources on Kimball are Orson F. Whitney's *Life of Heber C. Kimball*, 2nd ed. (Salt Lake City: Stevens & Wallace, 1945), first published in 1888; the Kimball Family *Newsletter*, 1945–present; biographical sketches in Andrew Jenson, *Latter-Day Saint Biographical Encyclopaedia. . . ,* 4 vols. (Salt Lake City: Andrew Jenson History Co., 1901–36); Frank Esshom, *Pioneers and Prominent Men of Utah* (Salt Lake City: Utah Pioneers Book Publishing Co., 1913); Preston Nibley, *Stalwarts of Mormonism* (Salt Lake City: Deseret Book, 1954); Edward W. Tullidge, *Life of Brigham Young . . .* (New York: Tullidge and Crandall, 1876); Lawrence R. Flake, *Mighty Men of Zion* (Salt Lake City: Karl D. Butler, 1974); Matthias F. Cowley, *Prophets and Patriarchs* (Chattanooga, Tenn.: Ben E. Rich, 1902); and Kate Carter, ed., *Heber C. Kimball: His Wives and Children* (Salt Lake City: Daughters of Utah Pioneers, 1967). Many articles on Kimball appeared in older Mormon publications such as the *Improvement Era*, the *Utah Genealogical and Historical Magazine*, and the *Contributor*.

Davis Bitton read a paper, "Heber C. Kimball's Authoritarian Imagery," before the 1974 Conference on the Language of the Mormons, and James F. O'Connor even wrote a 1978 thesis at Brigham Young University on "An Analysis of the Speaking Style of Heber C. Kimball." There is also an amateur readers' theater musical, "Heber C!"

INDEX

Robinson, Ebenezer, 60
Robinson, J. King, 290
Rochester, New York, 14, 15, 215
Rochester, 78
Rochester Daily Advertiser, 15
Rockwell, Orrin Porter, 143, 154, 198
Rockwell, Merrit, 143
Rockwood, A. P., 293
Rocky Mountains, 4, 122, 146, 156, 167, 168
Ross, William, 69n
Ross, Mrs. William, 64, 103
Roubidoux smithy, 181
Russell, Isaac, 41, 52

Sackett's Harbor, New York, 38
St. Albans, Vermont, 38
St. George Temple, 199, 201
St. Louis, Missouri, 55, 59, 104, 106, 137, 138, 142n, 146, 160, 190, 233
Salem, Massachusetts, 108
Salt Lake City, Utah, 15, 144, 187–299 *passim*
Salt Lake Tabernacle Choir, 202
Salt Lake Temple, 199, 255–56
Salt Lake Theatre, 202, 255
Sanders, Ellen. *See* Kimball's wives
Sanders, Harriet. *See* Kimball's wives
San Diego, California, 191, 197
San Francisco, California, 276, 279
Sangamon Journal, 103
Sanitation on western trails, 132
Santa Fe, New Mexico, 192
School of the Prophets, 300n
Schools in Utah, 202–3
Schuler, Sarah. *See* Kimball's wives
Scotland, 70, 73, 314
Scott, Rebecca Ann, 315
Scott, Sarah. *See* Kimball's wives
Scott, Ursula, 4
Scotts Bluff, Nebraska, 159, 161
Second Endowment/Anointing, 92n, 105
Separatists. *See* Puritans
Sessions, Patty Bartlett, 132
Sessions, Sylvia Porter. *See* Kimball's wives
Seward, William H., 264

Shakers, 87
Shakespeare, 71
Shaughnessy, Winifred, 311, 320
Shefflin, Mary Ann. *See* Kimball's wives
Sheldon, Vermont, 4, 5, 6, 6n, 7n, 37, 38
Sheridan, 44
Sheridan, Richard, 111n
Sierra Nevada, 197
Slavery, 55–56, 148, 149n, 192, 193, 197, 212
Social Hall, 202, 207
Smith, Alice K., 242n
Smith, Elijah, 27
Smith, Emma, 59, 98–99, 183n
Smith, George A., 62, 69, 70, 71, 104, 113, 180, 293, 298
Smith, Hyrum, 82, 83, 113, 122, 141, 204n, 217n, 248, 309, 315, 327
Smith, Jerusha, 182
Smith, John, 173
Smith, Joseph: 41, 46, 51, 53, 56, 71, 76, 113–23 *passim*, 125n, 143, 178, 204n, 217n, 218n, 243n, 248, 271, 274, 327; character, xi, xvn; meets Young, 3; meets Kimball, 3; in New York, 14–17 *passim*; in Kirtland, Ohio, 27, 29, 33–41 *passim*; and Zion's Camp, 27, 29, 33–41 *passim*; revelations, 3–4, 33–34; and Kirtland Safety Society, 40; in Missouri, 58–61; in Nauvoo, 64–69 *passim*, 81–109 *passim*; and Masonry, 83–85, 91n; and temple ordinances, 85–86, 105; and polygamy, 86, 87, 95, 97, 98–99, 237, 311; runs for the presidency, 106; and the *Nauvoo Expositor*, 107; death, 108, 111n; widows of, 122, 125n, 183n, 296–97, 307, 308, 310, 313, 314; Kimball's views of, 272–73
Smith, Joseph, III, 183n
Smith, Joseph F., 295, 309, 320
Smith, Joseph Fielding, 309
Smith, Samuel, 15, 19
Smith, William, 35, 60
Snow, Eliza R., 243n, 298

A Note on the Author

Stanley B. Kimball is a great-great-grandson of Heber C. Kimball. He spent his early childhood in Utah. In 1959 he received his Ph.D. from Columbia University and is currently professor of history at Southern Illinois University at Edwardsville, where he has taught for twenty-one years.

Professor Kimball has written four books of Mormon history, four books of East European history, and over sixty articles on these subjects; belongs to every major professional society in both fields; and currently serves as historian of the Mormon Pioneer Trail Foundation. He served as a guide for the *National Geographic* study of the Mormon Trail. For his work on the Mormon Trail, the Department of the Interior in 1974 awarded him the Outdoor Recreation Achievement Award. He and his wife Violet have four children.

MORMON TRAIL
1846–47

Missouri

River

R O C K Y

Continental

Divide

Oregon

Oregon

River

South
Pass

Trail

Ft. Bridger

Salt Lake
City

Green

River

M
O
N
Z
S.

Colorado

see inset below

Scottsbluff
Chimney Rock
Ancient Ruins
Ft.   Bluff
Laramie North

South

Loup

R.

Platte

Oregon

Winter
Quarters

River

Staging
Ground

Council
Bluffs

Mount
Pisgah

Garden
Grove

Grand R.
Locust Cr.
Liberty

Missouri

Trail

Independence

Mississippi

Des Moines

R.

Sug
Cree
Stag
Grou

Charit
R.
Salt

Ri

Oregon

Great
Salt
Lake

Echo
Cave
Canyon

Weber

Salt Lake
City

Bear R.

Trail

Cache

The
Needles

Emigration Canyon
"This Is The Place"
Monument

Mormon
Ferry

Green

Fork

River

Blacks

Fort Bridger

South
Pass

Sweetwater

Oregon

Pacific
Springs

R.

Continental

Divide

Devil's
Gate

Independence
Rock

Trail

North Platte

Mormon
Ferry

River

Deer
Cr.
Horseshoe
Cr.

Laramie

Heber
Springs

R.

Fort
Laramie

0   50   100

miles

Bier